# Lappé Calls *Wasted Wealth* "An Extremely Valuable Contribution"

"I learned a great deal from reading it and believe that your book will be an extremely valuable contribution. . . . I am delighted . . . that someone is working on the question that has so dominated my thinking—the notion of scarcity. . . . [In the writing of *Rediscovering America's Values]* your insights have been helpful."

—Frances Moore Lappé, author of *Diet for a Small Planet, Rediscovering America's Values,* and other books, and founder of Food First: The Institute for Food and Development Policy

## A Wealth of Information, Long Overdue Solutions

"The breadth of information you bring to bear to make your main points is very impressive. Drawing together so much information and focusing it the way you do is bound to be enlightening to your readers. . . . We have to first understand what is going wrong before we can organize to effectively change it. And you *do* provide an analysis and set of solutions. What more could one ask for in a book?"

—Thomas Michael Power, Ph.D., Professor and Chairman, Department of Economics, University of Montana

## An Impressive Analysis of Waste

"I am most impressed with the case you make about wastage in the economy overall—not only the obviously wasteful arms industry. Given the predicament that the country now finds itself in . . . a book detailing the pervasive waste in U.S. society [is] of more than ordinary interest. . . . Everything you have to say about wealth and control of the social order is valid."

—Herbert I. Schiller, Ph.D., University of California–San Diego

# THE WORLD'S WASTED WEALTH

# THE WORLD'S WASTED WEALTH

*The Political Economy of Waste*

J. W. Smith

**NEW WORLDS PRESS**
**kalispell, montana**

Book editing, design, and production services provided by
PageWorks, E. 4555 Ohio Match Ave., Post Falls, ID 83854.
Cover photograph by Quicksilver Photography, Coeur d'Alene, Idaho.

93 92 91 90 89 5 4 3 2

Printed on acid-free paper

**Library of Congress Cataloging-in-Publication Data**

Smith, J. W., 1930–
The World's Wasted Wealth: the political economy of waste / J. W.
Smith.
Includes bibliographical references.
ISBN 0-9624423-0-5 (lib. bdg., alk. paper). — ISBN 0-9624423-1-3
  (alk. paper).
1. Waste (economic)  I. Title.
HC79.W3S47       1989
338.9—dc20       89-13535
                 CIP

*To Ada*

*... when we take into account both the resources used up by the military as well as the economic product forgone, then we must appreciate the social cost of the military economy, 1946–1988, as amounting to about twice the 'reproducible assets' of U.S. national wealth.*
—Seymour Melman, *Profits Without Production*


*In military spending and other segments of the economy, we waste over 50 percent of our wealth. Eliminate that waste and we could either be twice as rich or have twice the free time.*
—J. W. Smith

# Contents

# Preface

We are twice as rich as we think we are. After thirty years of research and study, I have come to the conclusion that our economic system of production and distribution is based on the distribution of wasted productive capacity through unnecessary labor, not efficiency, as one would expect or believe. In fact, over 50 percent of our industrial capacity has nothing to do with producing for consumer needs.

The waste of the arms race, as described in *Profits Without Production,* by Columbia University Professor of Industrial Engineering (Emeritus) Seymour Melman, is both tragic and unnecessary. The U.S. alone has wasted on arms production and forgone production of consumer goods enough to replace twice every home, every business, every factory, and every railroad—excluding household goods, every manufactured thing in the United States.

This treatise anticipates the abandonment of the arms race. This is an opportune moment to restructure. We can simultaneously reduce the workweek and eliminate poverty not only in the United States but throughout much of the world. Instead of building machines of destruction, we need only build machines of production for the world's dispossessed.

Waste, poverty, and welfare can be eliminated while improving your quality of life. When you buy a copy of this book, if you wish, your name or the name of your group or organization will go on a list to be sent to your state and national representatives along with a copy of the book. If you want the concepts in this book given serious consideration, this is your opportunity to say so; we will deliver your letter to your representatives along with their copies of the book. The power of new ideas can be measured by the amount of grassroots support they inspire. If this book inspires you, spread the word—call or write your friends and have them tell their friends. The ability of the writer and the publisher to tell the world about a new book is limited; word of mouth is infinite in its capacity for change.

In addition, send any instances of wasted capital, labor, or resources you identify to the publisher, with complete documentation where available. It will be sent to me and considered for possible inclusion in an appendix to a revised edition. Any errors you detect, or comments, negative or positive, you have about the book are also appreciated. Write with your name and address to New Worlds Press at the address on the copyright page.

This is not the work of an academician or an ivory-tower intellectual. I've spent my life in the Pacific Northwest: breaking horses for a living, riding the rodeo circuit for ten years, farming and ranching, and railroading throughout Montana, Idaho, and Washington.

# Foreword

The *World's Wasted Wealth* is an intriguing examination of the horrendous amount of mad, unnecessary work in the world today. J. W. Smith demonstrates that an economic elite organizes production and distribution to funnel maximum profits to themselves. The great majority of people in the industrialized nations have a job, but a significant number of these jobs are actually only a territory carved out of the economy, producing nothing, but guiding a share of society's production to themselves—a psychological necessity if they are to justify their claim to this share.

This book is written with academic footnotes, but in a style that any reader can understand. It is a useful tool in helping people understand how the economic system operates in an era of supernationalism that affects their daily lives in ways they don't even realize. Smith develops enough issues that the book would make a great text for an economics issues course with a lot of classroom debate as students take the issues raised and analyze them from various angles. He examines a wide range of complex issues and makes them understandable: agriculture, communications, finance, health care, insurance, land tenure, law, poverty, transportation, and war.

Smith skillfully shows how the power structure manipulates the economy to continually drain off more and more wealth into the hands of the very rich, and to the government for huge military spending. He also describes changes to both the capitalist and communist systems that will be demanded by the people once they see the tremendous waste in both economic systems.

—Dr. Robert Waltmire, Professor of Economics (emeritus), Central Michigan University

# Acknowledgements

This treatise, like all knowledge and accomplishments, is the result of many people's thoughts and efforts. My special thanks go to the thousands of authors and reporters who each had a special window on the world and knew that what they viewed was of importance. Their work was the hard part—synthesizing their clear views of reality into the economic and political landscape was comparatively easy.

Attempting to describe these writers' views to my peers and fellow workers clarified and eventually formed a synthesis of all their thoughts which became this book. Without the patient listening of these friends, this book would never have materialized. Don Palmer with his sincere concern for his fellow human stands out among these friends. Jim Murray, Montana State Director of the AFL-CIO, provided sincere support. Tom Shaughnessy and Dewey Baker provided much encouragement in the concluding phase. And Fred Rice, manager of Freddy's Feed and Read in Missoula, encouraged me to write this book as well.

Of those directly supporting my effort with their talents special thanks goes to Michael Kriesberg; he had the patience to teach me the basics of writing. The encouragement of Frances Moore Lappé, co-founder of The Institute for Food and Development Policy and author of *Diet For a Small Planet,* is especially appreciated. Her faith and advice on the first rough drafts were critical to my confidence and the structure of this book. Equally important was the original recognition and support by John Photiades, Ph.D., Professor of Economics at the University of Montana, who among other things suggested the book's subtitle. With his insights and sincerity in understanding the world I am sure John could see more in these words than I could. Bill Elison, social science librarian at the University of Montana's Mansfield Library, was especially helpful in finding key sources. Professor Scott Walker, University of Idaho economics professor (emeritus) and an economist at the Federal Trade Commission for eighteen years, provided helpful insights, and editor Barbara Tucker helped clarify my thoughts during the writing process.

Professor Thomas Power, Ph.D., Chairman of the University of Montana's Economics Department, and economics professor (emeritus) Dr. Robert Waltmire of Central Michigan University, graciously agreed to proofread the final draft for factual and logic errors. Their advice and sincere approval is greatly appreciated; any errors that remain are my own. Herbert I. Schiller, Ph.D., professor of communications at the University of California and well-known writer on modern communications, gave of his valuable time and welcome advice. The advice of author Michael Parenti, Ph.D., on making this much shorter was followed. The writing guidance and writing skills of English professor Laurelee A. Ahlman, Ph.D., were crucial in the final structure of this book.

This project could not have succeeded without the help of computer specialists Queintin W. (Bill) Archie, Jay McCadden, and Jodi Rose of Montana Microsystems, Kalispell, Montana. They bridged the gap between my understanding and the complexities of computers and computer software. Microsystems' formation of New Worlds Press to promote and distribute this book is testimony to their faith in this book and to their friendship.

Likewise, Barbara Greene Chamberlain of PageWorks, Post Falls, Idaho, was all-important in editing and producing this book. Her talents are exceptional. Equally important was her affordable bid for book production, as compared to the high costs quoted by publishing companies. It was her recognition of authors' needs for this service at a reasonable price, and thus the formation of her company, that permitted this book to be published.

Last, and most important, I wish to dedicate this book to my children, Betty, Ada, Patti, and Cynthia, and grandchildren Sam and Will. It is hoped that this work will contribute to their understanding.

# Book One

# Introduction

Though most societies were no doubt efficient for the times in which they were formed, powerful nations disintegrated when too large a share of their labor was diverted to unnecessary tasks. The great pyramids of Egypt are the outstanding example: building these monuments to their pharaohs required an enormous share of social labor. Others, such as our ancestral aristocratic societies, expended their labors needlessly in supporting a militaristic elite bent on plundering its neighbors. Each of these societies became locked into a customary system of production and distribution. We too are, by custom, locked into a wasteful expenditure of labor.

Not long after I began working for the railroad, I realized that half of the 1.3 million railroad workers were unnecessary. This meant that 50 percent of our wages was only an honorable form of welfare. Even this was underestimated; today, hauling twice the freight, only 270,000 employees remain and still the railroad's labor force is shrinking rapidly. The railroad managers say that they can—and soon will—operate with 100,000 workers, or 4 percent of the labor per ton-mile required thirty-three years ago.[1]

With such a dramatic reduction in labor costs, why have freight charges steadily increased? Obviously other sectors of the railroad industry, or related areas of the economy, have been absorbing these savings. Economist Ralph Borsodi, in his 1927 book *The Distribution Age*, noted the phenomenon of rising prices even as labor use declined:

> It is not unreasonable for us to expect that the invention of better machines for performing every mechanical step in distribution, and the greater sub-division of the labor of those engaged in distribution, should reduce distribution costs year by year. Progress should lower distribution costs just as progress lowers production costs. Bigger freight cars and locomotives ought to lower transportation costs, but they do not seem to do so. Speedy delivery cars and powerful five-ton auto trucks ought to lower drayage costs, but they do not seem to do so. Larger grain elevators; more efficient cold storage warehouses; better terminal facilities; a better currency and a better banking system; typewriters, adding machines, book-keeping machines, cash registers—automatic machines for even such trifling operations as stamping and sealing envelopes—all ought to lower the cost of distribution. But they do not seem to do so.[2]

For thirty years I studied other authorities who described the same waste and inefficiency in insurance, law, farming, communications, medicine, the arms industries, and other sectors of the economy. The people employed within these industries were working industriously at jobs where well over 50 percent of their labor was expended unnecessarily. Yet these people were not malingering. They were performing what they believed to be productive and socially necessary tasks. I began to conceive of this distribution of social production through unnecessary labor as the consequence of a now-integrated system that had evolved slowly over time; I labeled it a *waste distribution system*.

Studying further, I realized that these people are individually and collectively defending their rights to their share of society's wealth. Their defense is based on natural alliances and loyalties generated by working together in a craft, business, or profession. The image of doing necessary and socially beneficial labor safeguards economic territories. To recognize that the work could be done with 50 to 80 percent less labor is to invite the elimination of one's job. Just as spice caravans crossing the territory of a desert sheik were forced to pay tribute, so the entire economy appeared to be divided into economic territories where each craft, business, or profession demands a toll from all who pass its way. There did not appear to be any relationship between true production and income. Again, just as with Arab sheiks, income depends upon how well those involved are able to defend their title to a particular territory and demand tribute. The labor and resources wasted in this nonproductive interception of what others have produced begs for a more accurate description—*waste distribution territories* seemed appropriate.

Studying what economists, historians, and philosophers had to say about this phenomenon, I discovered many kindred spirits. Benjamin Franklin proposed two hundred years ago that if everyone worked productively, the workday need only be five hours long.[3] That most observant of social critics, Thorstein Veblen, writing shortly after World War I, described "the apparatus and procedure for capturing and dividing the annual dividend as unduly costly . . . [it] foots up to something like one-half the work done."[4] In 1923 British philosopher Bertrand Russell estimated the necessary labor each day at four hours.[5] In 1931 Lewis Mumford, the noted American authority on cities and culture, went even further:

> Careful engineers have figured that the entire amount of work of the existing community could be carried on with less than twenty hours work per week for every existing worker: with complete rationalization all along the line, and with the elimination of duplication and parasitisms, probably less than twenty hours would suffice to produce a far greater quantity of goods than is produced at present.[6]

Stuart Chase was a corporate accountant, government consultant, and prolific author on the subject of industrial inefficiency. With engineering specialists and the entire staff of the United States Bureau of Labor for factual and statistical support, Chase concluded in his 1925 book *The Tragedy of Waste* that, at the minimum, the unnecessary labor expended was 50 percent.[7] He then spent nine more years gathering data for a new book, *The Economy of Abundance*. There he cites authoritative sources estimating the waste of human and material resources. The American Society of Mechanical Engineers, whose job it is to know just what can be done with industrial technology, pointed out that if an engineer-dictator over industry could be appointed and given complete control over raw materials, machinery and trained labor, he would flood, bury and smother the people under an avalanche of goods and services such as no Utopian dreamer in his busiest slumbers ever imagined.[8]

Seymour Melman, Columbia University Professor of Industrial Engineering (Emeritus), made a career studying waste in the American economy. His startling conclusion was that we have wasted enough on arms alone in the last forty years to completely rebuild every manufactured item in the U.S twice. His work provides the foundation for the concluding chapter of Book Two.

This treatise explores what Franklin, Veblen, Mumford, Russell, Chase, Melman and others have pointed out during the last two hundred years. The major difference is that today's technologies are far more efficient, and the systemwide waste more extensive and more deeply entrenched.

At present, the status quo is protected by branding any challenging ideas as "communist," "socialist," or "un-American." This reaction is a conditioned reflex for most Americans, who are trained to view people advocating such ideas as enemies. For perspective one should realize that when first proposed there was nothing more communist than Social Security. This right was only given to the dispossessed during the crisis of the 1930s when the threat of world revolution was high. No one today considers Social Security anything other than a right; Americans would scoff at the suggestion that it is "communist," "socialist," or "un-American." The same would be true if ever the last of our rights were claimed. All would insist on and defend these new-won rights.

We are so accustomed to the current structure of rights that we do not realize the gains that are possible by changing our laws and customs in step with the increased efficiencies of technology. Of course, those who have gained excessive rights through intercepting the production from the increased efficiencies of technology and society (see Book Three) loudly proclaim that any change in the structure of rights would harm everyone. This, of course, is only for their protection and, as this book outlines, it is not as efficient as claimed; the cost to the rest of society and eventually to all society is enormous.

This is a treatise on waste and how it can be eliminated within the current constitutional structure by reclaiming rights already enshrined in that base of our law. It is unlikely that our society would adopt such measures as have been recommended except under crisis or threat of another example. However, other societies may and it is their privilege to do so. It is also possible that depleting resources may leave no other logical choice even for us. If Americans ever realize their labor could be halved and their free time doubled with no loss of living standards (so long as technology and resources permit it this would be their right), they may insist on reclaiming these rights.

As for communism, the Soviets are having their own problems, which are also traceable to blindly following faulty ideology. Witness Soviet professor Nikolai Shmelyov describing the necessity of change:

> We really were in a pre-crisis state . . . if the economy does not embark on a thorough-going and drastic reform, we shall only be able to delay the crisis. It will be a fairly short time . . . before it hits us. There is no alternative because we have tried everything else. Even the opponents of the restructuring drive cannot suggest anything other than lifeless torpor.[9]

The Soviets have concluded that true free enterprise is a valid philosophy. (As Book Three will explain, monopoly capitalism is not true free enterprise.) Just as they recognize it is imperative they restructure, we too must adjust or risk losing our position as the world's economic leader. If we turn our wasted productive capacity to eliminating poverty in the United States and the world, the Soviets can never be a threat. This treatise will demonstrate that the advantage is all ours.

## Key Rights Retained by Property

Rights were declared for all men (not women, slaves, or Indians) after the American and French Revolutions. Through these revolutions, we gained freedom of choice, speech, religion, the vote, and so forth. These newly enfranchised justifiably felt great pride in those rights enshrined in the Bill of Rights and our Constitution. However, those great gains obscured the reality that the masses did not receive full economic rights. Key privileges were retained by those who owned land and capital (albeit in subdued form and more were permitted into the privileged class). The "divine right" of kings and the quasi-divine right of aristocracy had simply been transferred to, and embodied in, the private ownership of social wealth. The rights of men without property were still severely limited.

To ascertain that the most important rights are those conferred by ownership of land, or the tools (capital) with which to work the products from the land, we can study dispossessed societies. Those pushed off their productive land and forced into the desert effectively have no rights. It makes no difference how many are legislated for them, they will die of hunger or thirst. They may be able to vote, assemble, speak freely, and worship as they choose, but they have lost the right to live. That there is wealth for some and poverty for others is traceable to a person's income from property rights or job rights—all of which are tied to rights in land or capital.*

The gradual reclaiming of rights for all people has its roots in the aristocracy's historic claim to all rights. Their notorious disdain for work permitted others the prerogatives of developing industries. These industrialists became as wealthy as their lords, but they did not have political rights. The French Revolution, after which the Declaration of the Rights of Man was written, started over a dispute between the aristocracy and king over taxes. When the poor could be taxed no more, the king proceeded to tax the nobility. When they refused to submit, the battle began. The newly enriched bourgeoisie (industrialists, bankers, and mercantilists) saw their chance and mobilized the peasants under the banner of fighting for rights.[10]

The National Assembly was convened to end this conflict and the primary subject was rights for the bourgeoisie. In agreeing to these reasonable requests, the powerful *unwittingly declared rights for all men.* One sober delegate, Mr. Malouet, realized the consequences of their action. He warned, "[A] declaration of rights might someday be turned against the domination of the bourgeoisie."[11]

---

* It may appear that some services require little land or capital. But every service requires a location and, as will be addressed in Book Three, chapter one, commercial centers are the most productive pieces of land. The required education and tools are social capital.

He could only have meant that if the masses ever claimed those rights, the wealthy would be in trouble.

The American Constitution and Bill of Rights were great gains for the common person. It is this basic law that prevents the loss of these hard-won rights. However, the structure of the U.S. government was designed into the Constitution by the wealthy to protect their power. This was shown convincingly by Charles A. Beard in his influential book, *An Economic Interpretation of the Constitution of the United States*. Beard points out that the Constitution was designed to defend against the "attacks of leveling democracy." Although some of the original protection of property has been removed by universal suffrage, the key safeguards are still in place:

> We cannot help marveling at their skill. Their leading idea was to break up the attacking forces at the starting point: the source of political authority for the several branches of the government. This disintegration of positive action at the source was further facilitated by the differentiation in the terms given to the respective departments of the government. And the crowning counterweight to "an interested and over-bearing majority," as Madison phrased it, was secured in the peculiar position assigned to the judiciary, and the use of the sanctity and mystery of the law as a foil to democratic attacks.[12]

As Aric Press pointed out in a 1987 article in *Newsweek,* 150 years would pass before those rights would be realized by those without property:

> As a practical matter most constitutional *rights* date back no more than half a century. For much of our history, each state decided for itself the limits it would place on free speech or racial equality. It was only in the 1920s that federal judges began transforming the Constitution into genuinely supreme law. *It took more than half a century of courtroom battles to win the rights that most Americans take for granted.*[13] (emphasis in original)

Building upon those basic constitutional rights, Social Security, unemployment insurance, long-term home and farm loans, Medicare, Medicaid, equal rights for minorities, etc., were all obtained (albeit incompletely) during these last fifty years. It was the claiming of these *economic rights* that Malouet knew would give the powerful so much trouble. These gains were only won through the threat of massive civil disobedience such as the Great Depression and the equal rights marches of the 1960s. This supports Beard's thesis that the judiciary was designed to "prevent the leveling of democracy." The court system does not enforce these rights until public pressure builds towards serious social unrest.

The owners of wealth recognize that these courts have the last word on their protection. As of 1980, "one-fifth of the entire federal judiciary" had taken corporate-sponsored courses in the "laissez-faire doctrines of Milton Friedman, focusing on the necessity to leave corporations untouched by regulation and minimally touched by law."[14] This is the ongoing effort to protect the prerogatives of the wealthy.* The system has worked well to maintain the imbalances built into it at the beginning. However, just as the above named rights were claimed by the powerful through the current constitutional structure, to reclaim these rights it

---

* This was not a conspiracy. It was the automatic functioning of survival instincts.

is only necessary for the lawmakers to pass the laws and the Supreme Court to uphold the validity of that law.

Americans do have most of their rights. But it is the excessive rights of wealth and the lack of rights to productive work or retention of wealth produced by one's labor which create economic imbalances, poverty, and injustice. These rights of property were very proper when mobilizing and concentrating capital, but are improper once a society is capitalized. Once capitalized, a society produces enormous wealth and under those old rules of mobilization and concentration there is nowhere to go with this capital internally and it must be exported. This appears good at first glance but, under the rules of monopoly capital, title to this capital and the wealth it produces is relinquished only reluctantly. In the effort to retain ownership much must be wasted in trade wars, hot wars, and waste within the economy.

The waste described herein is due to these excessive rights of property and the ongoing efforts to claim the wealth produced. This first book addresses the way in which this has locked labor into a pattern of distribution and how they instinctively expand their work to claim a greater share of social production. Book Two addresses this wasted labor (60 percent) along with wasted industrial capital (50 percent) and resources (40 percent); while the waste created by wars is left uncalculated, the waste of the Cold War and that created by the arms race is discussed. Book Three describes the excessive rights of property which lock society into the old pattern and create this enormous waste. This last book also describes how these property rights are continually being increased while labor's rights relative to that productive potential have been decreased.

The only reason this is not visible in economic statistics is that the *potential* productivity of capital is increasing so fast that it does not show up in lost living standards unless and until an economic crisis occurs. Nor does this potential wealth show up in concentrated wealth at the levels one would think. It is being pulled back by this inexorable expansion of unnecessary labor: these waste distribution territories. This process can be reversed within the framework of constitutional law. It is only necessary to return to labor more rights to the enormous production of capital through eliminating this unnecessary labor and becoming fully productive. Eliminating unnecessary labor, of course, is what efficient capital is attempting to do. However, it is impossible under their rules. Under those rules labor would be totally dispossessed; with our newly won rights labor claims its share through expansion of unnecessary labor.

This looks contradictory at first, but it is in the professions that the greatest expansion of this unnecessary labor has taken place. Labor is reclaiming their share through tying their careers to these rights of property. Every insurance agency, law firm, and stock brokerage has combined the rights of property with unnecessary labor. They are working long, hard hours under enormous pressure but are producing little. Just add up the waste outlined in this treatise and it will be evident that on the average what they waste is greater than what they produce. They do, however, effectively distribute the wealth; they are waste distribution territories. With productive labor mixed in with nonproductive labor within the same job this is hard to see and this treatise attempts to highlight the waste and make it visible to all who care to look.

# The Evolution of Waste Distribution Territories

Each gain in industrial efficiency normally has three effects: production rises; those who own this technology become wealthy; and the unneeded workers—made redundant by the gains in efficiency—lose not only their jobs but their moral claim to a share of production. Though average living standards rise, they do not equal the potential efficiency gains. It is this lack of sharing of productive work—and thus the sharing of products and services—that leads to the evolution of waste distribution territories.

As industrial technology continues its elimination of workers, the territory of industrial labor steadily shrinks—witness the promised reduction of railroad employees from 1.3 million to 100,000 while freight tonnage doubles. Through efficiency of technology, the industrial labor force is rapidly decreasing. The share of production once claimed by this labor is then claimed by the owners of capital (those excessive rights of property). The nonproductive labor within the professions and other segments of the economy then relentlessly expands to reclaim a share of that production. Both individually and as a group these people defend their claims to being productive and filling a social need. Even when partly or wholly false, these claims must be made and defended as, without that legitimacy, the fundamental social rule—"no work, no pay"—would deny these people their share of social production. These waste distribution territories thus evolve and expand, absorbing labor idled by technology. It is the collective need to survive that pushes this process along. Ambitious and idealistic people searching for their survival niche within the economy either move into a territory (job or business) vacated by another or carve out their own. It is only from within such an economic territory that one can claim a share of what society produces.

The purpose of these occupations is to provide products or services. But providing goods and services becomes secondary to the claims of these expanding segments of the economy. This is visible in the traditional law of supply and demand: the greater the need, the higher the price. The supply is restricted through monopolization. The high prices that the functionally impaired must pay for essential health aids stand as damning testimony. For example, with modern technology, a hearing aid should cost under five dollars to manufacture, yet the cost to the hearing-impaired is five hundred dollars or more. (A small radio, which is much larger and more complicated, retails for five to ten dollars.)* The fictitious labor which claims that difference is a waste distribution territory structured in (and protected by) law. The excessive distribution cost of these *competitive monopolies* (see chapter three of this book and Book Three) is observable in all segments of the economy.

In our modern industrial economy, production is not the problem—it is distribution. This can be shown by the price spread between producer and consumer for almost any product. The above example of a hearing aid, which costs under five dollars to produce, yet sells for fifty to one hundred times that cost, is higher than most but not atypical. For durable consumer goods, a markup of 300 percent

---

* The innovation of specific tone control makes the hearing aid amplifier more technical, but that is a recent innovation and, true to form, those hearing aids cost three times as much. This will be addressed in depth in Book Three, chapter two.

over production costs is common. A monopoly in those durable goods is evident when one notes that, at a markup of about 50 percent, perishable unprocessed food has the lowest distribution costs.

Though certain individuals are enormously productive, collectively the higher the pay the higher the percentage of unnecessary labor. This book will outline occupations where 60 to 80 percent of the labor is wasted—except as a distribution mechanism, this unnecessary labor has nothing to do with our standard of living. These professions are legally structured so society cannot purchase those products or services outside their enormously labor-intensive—thus expensive—competitively monopolized distribution system.[*]

## These People Do Work

The people described herein are not idle. Most work conscientiously, are proud of their image as upstanding citizens, and are often unaware that much of their labor is unnecessary or that society is being overcharged (measured in labor time, not dollars) for that product or service.[**] Society accepts them as deserving, hardworking people, and customs are hard to challenge. How does one question an entire segment of the economy where people are busy, view themselves as highly useful, have a customary role in social production, wield political power, and have rights protected by law? We readily see that others' labor may be unnecessary or believe they may be overpaid. Yet when our own work is the subject, our clear perception becomes clouded. We instantly sense that not only is our claim to personal productivity in question, but also our claim to a share of what is produced. Our economic territory (our survival) is threatened. We are caught up in a web that has evolved over time in step with the gains in technological efficiency—dispossessed industrial labor has been replaced by unnecessary work in other segments of the economy.

Most readers will recognize this pattern of wasted labor within their own community or within segments of the national economy that I have not mentioned. All who wish are invited to send their observations to me in care of this publisher. Please describe the waste carefully and give authoritative sources for references if possible. Those deemed recognizable by the reader and those well referenced may be put into the appendix of a later edition along with the acknowledgment of who provided me with the information.

Wholesale elimination of this redundant labor, without sharing the remaining work, would cost all unneeded workers their moral claim to income. Those left working and fully productive would soon notice that those not working would have no money with which to buy those efficiently produced products. As these workers would be producing all society's products and services, a share of their wages and capital's profits would have to go to charity so those newly released from employment could buy the necessities of life. This is what we have now in the distribution of basic needs through the tax-supported welfare community.

---

[*] There are low to intermediate paid professions that are 100 percent productive (e.g., barbers, beauticians, musicians, waitresses).

[**] They, in turn, are being overcharged through others' unnecessary labor. It may roughly balance, but it is an incredible waste of labor and resources.

Most people believe that the present distribution system is efficient because they see their own and others' high standard of living. What is unseen—and therefore unknown—is the amount of unrealized gains lost through unnecessary labor and wasted capital and resources. This is the great secret: modern manufactured products, although cheap, could be far cheaper. The potential of industrial technology is much greater than even our most self-congratulatory praises suggest. If Americans realized they could maintain their current living standards while working over 50 percent less, they would, within the current constitutional framework, collectively reclaim the rest of their rights—the right to labor productively with social wealth (land and industrial technology)—and would be able to obtain and retain a fair share of social production.*

The measure of unnecessary labor employed within these waste distribution territories is the measure of the efficiency of technology lost to society. Though the loss of resources and useful products is high, the greatest loss is free time. Neither loss is measured by current economic theories. They assume that anyone employed is supplying necessary labor. This is not true. Unnecessary labor, along with wasted capital and wasted resources, are perhaps the dominant features of our economic landscape:

> In the postwar period economic energies, instead of lying dormant, have increasingly been channeled into a variety of wasteful, parasitic, and generally unproductive uses. This has been an enormously complex process that is still very imperfectly understood (in fact, mainstream economics does not even recognize its existence).[15]

This treatise directly addresses this process. Each chapter looks at the validity of efficiency claims of different segments of the economy and roughly calculates the wasted labor. Though unjustly earned, most income from this unnecessary labor is properly spent for food, fiber, shelter, and recreation. Thus, except for agriculture and the defense industry, most savings described will not be of money but of labor time.

To eliminate this waste, the last of our rights must be reclaimed and the 60 percent or more of wasted labor converted to free time. In this process, there need be no loss of food, fiber, shelter, or recreation. Within a context of shared work and mutual responsibilities, true freedom and equal rights can become a reality for all.

With equal sharing of productive jobs, only necessary labor would be expended. This would result in a higher standard of living, and a much higher "quality-of-life index" with two days per week spent working productively and five days per week free to spend on oneself. Or society could decide to work three days per week for a 50-percent increase in living standards. More important than increasing our already high living standards is the opportunity to use this wasted industrial capital and labor to capitalize the Third World. With those tools, billions of needy people could break the grip of dependence and poverty.

Karl Marx thought that all social surplus would be appropriated by the owners

---

\* The rights gained from the American and French Revolutions were substantial but did not include the above named rights. The Constitution, like the Bible, is subject to interpretation. If the majority actively push for rights, the Supreme Court can easily find precedent in our basic law based on the principles of justice and equal rights.

of wealth, who in turn would have this wealth appropriated from them through revolution. Society did not develop as he foresaw. These waste distribution territories reclaimed enough of that appropriated wealth to maintain a functioning balance in the distribution of production.

Marx did correctly observe how labor was appropriated but his solution (returning to the communal principles of pastoral societies) was in error. Modern societies will function most efficiently when everybody has equal rights to land and capital under the principles of *true free enterprise*.

# 1

# Insurance

---

Each year, the private insurance industry collects and holds in trust about $200 billion in premiums.[1] Collecting and distributing this enormous flow of cash requires a work force of two million. However, that $200 billion collected from society is not the total cost of insurance. Successful claimants often pay one-third, plus expenses, to their attorneys. Thus they are still out well over one-third of their loss. All such costs of litigating insurance settlements, including court costs paid by taxes, are properly considered an insurance expense.

Because insurance facts are notoriously elusive, no full accounting of costs is available. Economist Andrew Tobias, in his book *The Invisible Bankers,* roughly calculates that the insurance companies return, in the form of claims paid, an average of about 50 percent of the total annual premiums. In short, the insurance companies returned only half the money they had agreed to hold in trust and from that 50 percent the legal costs must yet be deducted.[2]

Contrast the cost of collecting and redistributing this inefficiently managed *private insurance trust fund* with the *Social Security trust fund.* In 1984 Social Security distributed $175.4 billion, or 98.98 percent, of the $177.2 billion collected and held in trust. This *social insurance* required only $1.8 billion, or 1.02 percent, for administrative costs and required a work force of only 74,500, or 3.73 percent of private insurance's army of two million.[3] In those few short sentences the unnecessary labor in the insurance industry is fully exposed. Through this wasted labor the necessities and amenities of life produced by society are distributed; it is a *waste distribution territory.* Counting legal costs, these waste distribution territories consume close to 60 percent of the money held in trust, while social insurance spends only 1.02 percent. In both cases, this fund is the public's money held for safekeeping to be distributed when the need arises.

Health, home, auto, and most other insurance would cost more than Social Security to administer, but not fifty-five times more. If we allowed a generous four times greater, the cost would be 4.08 percent of the $200 billion in premiums paid, or $8.16 billion, for a saving of $191.84 billion. The difference between the estimate of 60 percent (to administer the present private insurance system) and the liberal estimate of 4.08 percent (to administer social insurance) points out a potential 90-percent reduction in insurance administration costs. The unnecessary expense under private insurance is waste distribution that is jealously protected by those whose livelihood is earned through this unneeded labor.

## Health Insurance

The path to cheaper health insurance has already been blazed by organized labor. The share of the premium (public money held in trust) returned on group health insurance is 87 percent, while that returned on individual health policies is only 50 percent.[4] Thus, under group insurance, about 75 percent of the costs of administration are eliminated (from 50 percent of premiums to 13 percent). It is still three times greater than necessary, and the legal costs have not yet been considered.

Any insurance system only collects premiums, manages the fund, and disburses payments to claimants according to preordained formulas. These constitute social funds and belong to those insured. The collection mechanism to convert to social insurance is already in place—the *efficient* Social Security withholding system. Only a slight restructuring would be necessary to extend coverage to those on unemployment and welfare.

It matters little if these needed funds come out of increased insurance taxes or county, state, and federal treasuries, as the needs of these people are now met by taxes distributed as welfare.* Chapter six will show that if all people were guaranteed a share of the work they would be able to pay their share of the insurance premiums.

## Home Insurance

As few people can afford uncompensated loss due to fire, wind, flooding or other disasters, home insurance is a necessity. Returning only 42 percent of premiums, this is also overpriced.[5] Most people now pay home insurance along with their monthly mortgage payments. The bank or mortgage company transfers this money to the private insurance companies. Changing to a home social insurance fund would require that the loan institution transfer these funds to a publicly mandated insurance authority instead. Those whose homes are paid for would have the option of joining. The cost of administering this insurance would drop from the current 42 percent of premiums to 4.08 percent. The redundant sales, advertising, billing and money managers—wasting our money—will disappear. The difference in overhead costs (4.08 percent to 42 percent) outlines about 90 percent of the private insurance charges as unnecessary. These excessive costs appropriate the money held in trust by those falsely (even if unknowingly) claiming to be doing necessary work. If social insurance is adopted, money savings should not accrue to the insured. It should properly translate into sharing of jobs and each one working less—those reclaimed rights of labor.

---

* Physicians for a National Health Care is promoting such a health insurance based on the highly successful one in Canada. (Judi M. Garfinkel, "Doctors Push Plan for Comprehensive Care," *Guardian*, 8 February 1989, p. 7; Marjorie Hope and James Young, "Even Doctors Are Prescribing a Real National Health Scheme," *In These Times*, 8–14 February 1989, p. 17.)

# Auto Insurance

Fuel prices already include federal and state taxes to support the transportation infrastructure. Most states require liability insurance, and all lenders require collision and comprehensive insurance. What would be simpler than increasing the gasoline tax to cover insurance? All drivers and cars would be covered for liability, collision, and comprehensive. Current administrative costs of 38 percent (plus legal costs) would drop to a rational 4.08 percent; the waste distribution territory disappears.[6]

Besides the substantial savings, there would be greater equity. A retired couple driving five thousand miles per year now pays almost the same premium as a salesperson driving fifty thousand miles. Under social insurance, the one who drives ten times more pays ten times more. Since most states already share driving offense records, any increased cost due to special-risk drivers could be dealt with at the time of renewing a car or driver's license. Those people now driving without insurance because their premiums are too high would pay for their irresponsibility. The social parasitism of the uninsured motorist would be eliminated.

# No-Fault Insurance

Most accidents are just that—accidents. They are the normal consequence of using a dangerous mode of transportation and further savings would be realized by eliminating the current fault system of auto insurance. Those accidents which are the result of gross negligence or criminal behavior are already addressed by law (such as driver's license suspension and civil and criminal penalties).

Twenty-four states now have variations of no-fault auto insurance. But fierce opposition by the insurance industry (and the legal profession) has rendered most of these laws ineffective.[7] Under the adversary system of fault insurance, 55 percent of those seriously injured receive no compensation. The average for those who lose $25,000 or more is $76,341; and yet a U.S. Department of Transportation study showed they receive only an "average of $3,742, or 5 percent of their loss." By contrast, in Michigan under no-fault insurance 260 claims for "catastrophic" medical costs (more than $25,000) were compensated an average of $108,000 per loss. Of these, 32 percent were single-vehicle accidents, where there was no other driver to sue. Fifteen percent of the latter were motorcycle accidents, which are almost always catastrophic and are—under the current insurance arrangement—almost always uncompensated.[8]

Besides larger settlements to the injured under no-fault, payments are prompter. In Massachusetts (which is only a "modified" no-fault state), a survey by professor Alan Widiss showed that no-fault provided the first medical payment to 50 percent of accident victims within 7 days, 80 percent within 30 days, and 97.9 percent within 180 days. Under fault insurance, the U.S. Department of Transportation reported that only 40.5 percent of claims were settled within 90 days, and only 57.6 percent within 180 days. These figures are overly charitable toward fault insurance policies. They pay quickly and generously on minor claims but only reluctantly and below value on major ones. The average time elapsed in paying claims over $2,500 under fault insurance is 540 days.[9]

In Massachusetts, the use of attorneys dropped from 80 percent of the cases under fault insurance to less than 15 percent under no-fault. This resulted in a reduction of court cases of from 42 to 66 percent. (There was a similar drop in the Michigan study.) Professor Widiss further showed that 80 percent of those settling claims under no-fault were "fairly satisfied" to "very satisfied" with their compensation.[10] As well they should be: no-fault increased the value of claims paid in Michigan by 58 percent, not including the savings in legal fees.[11]

Fault-finding coverage, with lower payments ($20,000 liability) and slower payments, costs almost twice as much as no-fault, which paid up to $53,000 in wage losses and unlimited medical.[12] An analysis of the above studies shows that the industry's claim (referred to earlier) that they use 38 percent of the premiums to administer auto insurance is flagrantly understated; this is well under the probable true cost of 60 percent. The lower costs, prompter payments, and increased satisfactions described above are with private insurance coverage. Combining no-fault with social insurance would create even greater savings.

## Life Insurance

Occasionally an exposé fully outlines a waste distribution territory. *The Life Insurance Game,* by Ronald Kessler, and *How Life Insurance Companies Rob You,* by Walter S. Kenton, Jr., are two such insiders' accounts.

Describing his early years, Kenton insists he was an idealist who genuinely desired to help people. As a life insurance salesman he sincerely felt that he was achieving these goals.[13] Kessler recognized the same thing in himself. He insists that, "The overwhelming majority of the more than one million employees and agents are hard-working, honest individuals."[14] Tobias agrees; "The insurance industry is filled with good people who believe in their work and their companies, but who may never have challenged the assumptions underlying their efforts."[15]

These assumptions were challenged by the Federal Trade Commission using a method called "the Linton Yield":

> Of the premium dollar, only 15 cents goes to death benefits. Overhead gets 30 cents, and the remaining 55 cents, over half of every dollar paid in premiums, goes into the savings component. The average return paid to the consumer on this savings component, or cash value, was about 1.3 percent.[16]

The savings component is no different from money deposited in a savings account and for accounting purposes it must be separated from the death benefit trust fund. The Linton Yield does this. The 15 percent that goes for death benefits and 30 percent for overhead adds up to 45 percent of the original premium. As only one-third of this is returned, this exposes the administration costs as a whopping 66 percent of the death benefit trust fund.

That 1.3 percent return on savings (our money) was only one-quarter the amount (5.25 percent) offered by banks on passbook savings accounts at that time.[17] Thus the life insurance companies appropriate about 75 percent of the interest on savings properly belonging to the insured. Allowing for an annual inflation rate of 4 percent, the insured's savings would shrink 2.7 percent per year. Most of this appropriated money is not saved; it is wasted through unnecessary labor:

You don't call the agent. The agent comes to you. Typically, he makes ten telephone calls before he gets an appointment. Only one in two appointments leads to a sale . . . The agent may drive out to your house two or three times. The last trip will be to deliver the policy in person. He may take you to lunch or help you with your personal financial problems. He sells a lot of snake oil. If the bankers went through the same selling process to obtain an account, the nation's banks would go bankrupt. Agents who sell a lot of policies may be rewarded with a trip to Hawaii—on top of commissions that range from 25 percent to as much as 130 percent of the first year's premium. . . . on top of these commissions, the managers of the companies get commissions called "overrides."[18]

Under a comprehensive social insurance program that covered all essential needs there would be little need for life insurance; it and a host of other specialized, overlapping insurances could be discarded.

Some loans are insured for early death; all loans should be. Family homes or businesses then would not be lost due to an untimely death. Such debt-clearing life insurance is an example of social insurance—there are no measurable collection or distribution costs. The current practice of overcharging for this service, and using the surplus to increase profits, can be easily eliminated by law.

Those who still feel they need life insurance to protect a family's living standards could be insured under social insurance without undue cost. They need only apply and fill out a medical questionnaire that documents their medical history. This history would determine the proper premium to pay, and the records are readily referred to at the claimant's death. If the original application was fraudulent, the proper risk would be easily calculated, compensation lowered, and a penalty assigned for the original misrepresentation.

## Personal Responsibility

Life involves risks, and, unless there is malice or gross negligence, minor personal injury or property loss should not be compensated. Socially funded insurance should not cover every bump, bruise, nicked fender, or cracked window. It should cover only substantial loss or injury—the kind that affects one's standard of living. Frivolous claims would be given short shrift. This would eliminate the well-known insurance industry policy of overpaying quickly and generously on minor claims while delaying, litigating, and finally underpaying on major ones. Self-insuring for all minor losses would lower insurance costs by eliminating not only the overpayment, but the time wasted on these nuisance claims by insurance adjusters and clerks.

It should also be possible to eliminate the well-known phenomenon of mortgages rubbing against insurance policies and causing fires. By not writing insurance at full value, the insured would bear part of a loss. This potential savings to society was shown in Butte, Montana, which received national attention during a local recession. Under the current rules of insurance, the local businesses were literally going up in smoke. Faced with the same dilemma, some Bronx landlords were solving their problem the same way. Federal conspiracy charges were brought against landlords, insurance adjusters, insurance brokers, and hired torches concerning fifty fires from 1976 to 1979.[19] Since reduced property values were no secret, the decreased value should have been the maximum permitted compensable value. Had the insured known they would not be compensated for values that were not there, those fires would not have occurred. Society would have received a double saving—lower insurance premiums and not having to replace those torched buildings.

## Some Practice Self-Insurance

Three hundred towns and government units and a group of thirty-seven Colorado cities formed insurance pools and were able to negotiate more favorable rates. Because of astronomical jumps in premiums, other cities and counties may be forced to do likewise: Princeton, Minnesota, a 370-percent increase; Dallas, Texas, a hike of 1,128 percent; Fremont, California, a 1,200-percent increase with doubled deductible; and Hartford, Connecticut—the nation's insurance capital—a 400-percent rise. Though the average increase nationwide is 150 percent, throughout most of the Rocky Mountain states there is "no liability insurance to be had at any price."[20] Under pressure, local governments are following the lead of railroads and the federal government. They are depositing their insurance money in a common fund instead of with a caretaker (private insurer) who will return only 50 percent and often only when sued.[21]

## Other Socially Necessary Insurance

Health, auto, home, and life insurance described above account for about three-quarters of all policies in this country.[22] Under private insurance, other socially necessary insurances have equally excessive administrative costs: flight insurance, 90 percent (though passengers are already automatically insured by the air carrier); car rental insurance, 80 percent; industrial life insurance, 80 percent; cancer insurance, 59 percent; burglary and theft, 62 percent; and so forth.[23]

Under the umbrella of the self-insurance pools of local and state governments, social insurance could be established for health, homes, and autos. Once those are established, groups that need specialty insurance could lobby for their inclusion. With current administrative costs for private insurance exceeding 50 percent, the savings are obvious. Once aware, people would demand the increased benefits of social insurance. Everybody would be included. The thirty-five million Americans currently without medical insurance would be fully covered with no increase over present insurance costs. As human needs are more simply and effectively met, the waste distribution territory vanishes.

## Worker's Compensation Is Not Social Insurance

Generally viewed as government insurance, worker's compensation is not being advocated here. Handled by private insurance companies, this is not social insurance. Rather than protect workers, it was designed to release businesses from responsibility for job-related illnesses, accidents, or deaths. Under this private insurance, workers give up their right to sue their employers and must accept reimbursement through worker's compensation.

Since industry has retained political control of the funds, this has turned into a chamber of horrors for the injured. They are offered little or nothing and, faced with mounting medical bills and living expenses, are desperate. Worker's compensation—just like the private insurance it is—plays upon that desperation in order to arrive at a settlement below what claimants are entitled to by law. They are thus obliged to hire a lawyer who will get one-third for cases that should never have been contested and that can't be lost. Montana's Worker's Compensation Fund claims manager Peter Strizich inadvertently pointed this out, saying that, "When we get an impairment rating [from a physician] there are no ifs, ands or buts, we have to pay it."[24] Strizich fails to explain why the state doesn't promptly pay the amount stipulated by law. Workers would then not have to hire lawyers to get what is their due. Instead of investigation and prompt compensation, as stipulated by law, the burden of proof rests on the injured and unemployed worker. There are so many technical obstacles and delays that only 10 percent of the millions of injured and disabled workers receive any benefits and these few receive only one-half of what they are entitled to by law.[25] In another study, the U.S. Department of Labor concluded that only one out of twenty workers disabled from occupational disease (silicosis, asbestosis, etc.) manages to collect from such funds.[26]

## Product Liability and Malpractice Insurance

The thousands of women who were injured by the notorious Dalkon Shield, and thus unable to have children, were unaware of the cause of their problem—the manufacturer, A. H. Robbins, did know. Lawyers defending the first few cases had to advertise so that potential claimants would be alerted and step forward. Whereas most injuries from defective products are uncompensated, this case resulted in a $485-million decision against Robbins. Though very large by past standards, this award hardly compensated thousands of women for losing the capacity to have their own children.

Over one-half of that award ($268 million) went to lawyers. The Product Liability Alliance claims that virtually every study shows that more money ends up going to court costs than to claimants.[27] A congressional study concurred, finding that only one-third went to the injured and two-thirds to lawyers.[28]

Due to the excessive managerial costs, the share of insurance premiums paid to victims of defective products or medical and legal malpractice is even less—9 percent for the former and 18 percent for the latter. Thus administrative costs consume 91 and 82 percent of the respective premiums.[29] Using our estimate of 4.08 percent for social insurance, 95 percent of these costs are unnecessary. Insurance companies and lawyers can hardly claim to be productive while appropriating over 80 percent of the funds set aside for the disabled.

Each person has a statistically calculable chance of becoming one of the unfortunate injured. Insurance is a fund established to share this risk. However, there is little left over to share by the time it passes through the hands of those appointed to protect and distribute this fund. The burden for a disaster usually falls upon hapless individuals instead of being spread broadly among the population, as insurance properly should be. Money not spent on safety and compensation shows up on corporate balance sheets as profit. On society's balance sheet it shows up as unreimbursed injuries, sickness, and death.

Social insurance, combined with the Consumer Protection Agency, would eliminate the need for most product liability lawyers. Redesigned as social insurance, worker's compensation, product liability, and malpractice insurance would all be able to deliver prompt and just restitution. These centralized records would pinpoint the dangerous products, occupations, and industries and lead to the enforcement of better safety practices. If social insurance had been charting the Dalkon Shield it would have been withdrawn long before it caused sterility in thousands of women; Thalidomide could have been quickly identified as a mutation-causing chemical and never allowed to deform thousands of babies;[30] the now notorious asbestos industry would never have caused so many cancer deaths; and the poorly engineered Ford Pinto could have been identified and withdrawn early. In the meantime, the smaller number of injured would have been promptly and properly compensated. Empowered by public authority, this agency could easily keep track of accidents and injuries traceable to dangerous working conditions and faulty consumer products. They could move quickly and decisively, withdrawing products from the marketplace and simultaneously establishing grounds for immediate and full compensation.

In the same way, the current toothless medical and legal review boards could be transformed into serious disciplinary authorities. The key is establishing public control. Members of professional review boards are notoriously reluctant to chastise their colleagues; thus the almost total absence of disciplinary action taken against incompetent doctors and lawyers. One study of this problem estimated there were 30,000 bad or impaired doctors in the U.S. in 1985. Of these only 255 had their licenses revoked and most were for fraud, not incompetence.[31] Another study by the U.S. Department of Health, Education, and Welfare (now the Department of Health and Human Services) "calculates that 7 percent of all patients suffer compensable injuries while hospitalized."[32] Yet nineteen out of twenty victims of malpractice receive no compensation, and malpractice insurance costs continue to rise out of sight.[33]

Former Chief Justice of the Supreme Court Warren Burger recognized this problem in law. He claimed 50 percent of practicing lawyers are incompetent and severely harm the rights of those they are supposedly defending.[34] The public continues to pay the price of unnecessary financial and emotional damage due to the professionals' instinctive territorial protection and misplaced fraternal solidarity.

## A Surprise Gift for Everybody

A disaster in one city or state might bankrupt insurance companies that are too small to spread the risks involved. With a comprehensive system and regular deductions from all income earners, everybody would be protected. Money coming into and leaving the fund could be adjusted to guarantee both equity and equilibrium. Then that local disaster would be just a ripple on the calm surface of the deep pool of social insurance.

The forty-eight hundred insurance companies that operate in the U.S. have amassed over seven hundred billion dollars of our money, which they invest at a handsome profit. Of course, they claim to hold these funds "in reserve" in order to pay future claims.[35] Their fortunes grow at our expense. Under social insurance, there would be no need for the seven-hundred-billion-dollar reserve fund. This is the people's money, and should be returned. This is enough to buy an eight-thousand-dollar car for each of the eighty-seven million families in the country—while simultaneously delivering cheaper, more reliable insurance. This money is invested now and could not be moved suddenly without serious financial dislocations, but the potential savings is clear. The premium share that ends up in investments is not wasted, but an expensive army of insurance salespeople is hardly an efficient way to mobilize and accumulate capital. Those capital investments properly belong to those from whom they were appropriated through overcharge.

## Liberating the Insurance Industry's Army of Employees

In 1982 the insurance industry employed 750,000 clerks, 560,000 sales agents and brokers, 225,000 managers and administrators, 180,000 claims personnel, and 167,000 miscellaneous workers—nearly 1.9 million workers in all.[36] By 1987 there were 2 million. This is the normal expansion of labor within businesses and professions that are absorbing the share of social production that historically was allotted to industrial labor. The increased efficiencies of technology continue to eliminate jobs, and, far from all being replaced by productive employment in service jobs, a large share is expansion of unnecessary labor in other segments of the economy.

Those 180,000 claims agents are already holding their own, and surely one clerk with a computer can handle more claims than 1.75 agents can adjust. The collection of premiums should be automatically deducted from wages or loan payments. Allowing 120,000 clerks to handle social insurance (after all, Social Security has a total of only 74,500 workers), the total workers needed would be no more than 300,000. That is slightly more than there are managers in private insurance.

Many other workers would be released from unnecessary jobs: those who cut timber, haul lumber, and build insurance offices; dig and smelt the ore for and fabricate, service, and repair their cars; drill for, refine, and deliver the wasted fuel; and build, install, and service typewriters, computers, phones, carpets, furniture, and electrical fixtures. Add a share of the motels, hotels, and cafes which service this army and another 400,000 support workers would be freed. The total workers released for productive labor by replacing private insurance with social insurance would be at least 2.1 million.

## An Example Proves Our Point

It is instructive to examine three provinces in Canada which have social insurance:

> British Columbia, Saskatchewan, and Manitoba, offer citizens this alternative. These programs . . . have had the effect of not only reducing costs 20 percent or more over private companies, but . . . have also returned more to the people on their insurance claims than private companies normally do. In addition, state-run insurance has helped reduce local taxes by using premium "profits" to help build schools and hospitals.[37]

The above examples of premiums reduced 20 percent or more, higher compensation, and money left over to build schools and hospitals demonstrates the 55 to 60 percent savings possible under social insurance.

## Their Title Is by Bluff

The captains of the insurance industry do not have the moral authority that entitles them to a share of social income, such as is customarily equated with ownership of land and industry. Nor do they perform productive labor to entitle them to that income. The capitalized values of insurance companies are fictitious; they represent nothing more than the appropriated income (the labor) of the insured. If society were accustomed to efficient social insurance, that which is normal insurance today would be recognized for the confidence game it is and abandoned.

A part of the insurance premium (the public's money) has been used to protect this industry with mountains of misinformation. It is all an elaborate attempt to create the image of a necessary service, and entitle them to their unearned income. In this ongoing battle to prevent the establishment of efficient social insurance, the insurance industry has more lobbyists in Washington, D.C., and every state legislature than any other interest group. Their crowning achievement occurred in 1979 with the passage of a law, submitted by Senator Wendall H. Ford, a former insurance salesman and governor of Kentucky. This law forbade the national government from investigating insurance companies![38] This effectively protects the secrets of the latter's appropriation of labor. They have good reason for secrecy. It is not only the refuge of the dishonest and incompetent but the refuge of those who would fool the public and themselves into believing their nonproductive labor is essential.

In 1988 this ongoing battle was highly visible in California. Citizens' groups spent two million dollars to promote a proposition to reduce the unjust charges for insurance. When polls showed the proposition would pass, the insurance companies spent forty-one million of the insureds' dollars to promote no-fault insurance which would leave their profits intact and transfer the loss to the legal community. Recognizing this threat to their territory, lawyers spent twenty million to preserve this expensive method of redistributing wealth through the courts.[39] That proposition passed and is being challenged in court at this time. But this common sense approach is spreading like wildfire to other states. Insurance companies have set aside another seventy-one million of the public's dollars as the initial war chest to prevent that spread. It is safe to bet they will spend far more if the people should be so brash as to try to reclaim their rights.

Without equal rights to productive jobs, there is a direct contradiction between efficiency and protecting one's job. The excessive rights of those who own this unneeded industry are mirrored in a lack of rights for those who must unknowingly perform unnecessary work or those dispossessed into poverty. With a mandate from the people, such as was given by the electorate of California, Congress and state legislatures would soon enact into law a system of economical social insurance. Once the public reclaimed their rights, those lobbyists would also be freed for honest work.

The goals of the owners of this fictional capital and the workers they employ are the same—to legitimize their claim to a share of social production. Neither they nor those being shortchanged are normally aware of this fact. The perceived necessity of insurance companies is only a measure of the ability of powerful people to control the laws and persuade others of the necessity of their services. Identical deceptions will surface in other areas of business, for they are characteristic of all waste distribution territories.

# 2

# Law

---

The better the society, the less law there will be. In heaven there will be no law. . . . In hell there will be nothing but law, and due process will be meticulously observed.[1]

— Grant Gilmore, *Age of American Law*

Law is considered complex, mysterious, and incomprehensible. An observant Yale University law professor, Fred Rodell, has penetrated the web of myths which protects these "defenders of our rights." He began his book, *Woe Unto You Lawyers,* by comparing law to religions of past ages:

In tribal times, there were the medicine men. In the Middle Ages, there were priests. Today there are the lawyers. For every age, a group of bright boys, learned in their trade and jealous of their learning, who blend technical competence with plain and fancy hocus-pocus to make themselves masters of their fellow men. For every age, a pseudo-intellectual autocracy, guarding the tricks of its trade from the uninitiated, and running, after its own pattern, the civilization of its day.[2]

Jerold S. Auerbach, the renowned legal scholar, makes the same comparison:

Law is our national religion; lawyers constitute our priesthood; the courtroom our cathedral, where contemporary passion plays are enacted. . . . Five hundred years from now, when historians sift through twentieth-century artifacts, they doubtless will have as little comprehension of American legal piety as most Americans now display toward medieval religious zeal.[3]

Rodell continues:

It is the lawyers who run our civilization for us—our governments, our business, our private lives. . . . We cannot buy a home or rent an apartment, we cannot get married or try to get divorced, we cannot die and leave our property to our children without calling on the lawyers to guide us. To guide us, incidentally, through a maze of confusing gestures and formalities that lawyers have created. . . . The legal trade, in short, is nothing but a high-class racket.[4]

Using age-old methods of secrecy and mysticism, the legal profession has managed to place itself between the public and many normal functions of society. In the evolution of law, lawyers continually expanded time and labor to increase the tribute they collected from the public for the common transactions of everyday life. Their living depends on the rest of society accepting their claim to being useful. They must themselves believe and defend those claims or lose their moral right to compensation. Though viewed by both themselves and the public as necessary and productive, lawyers' work is mostly finding ways through the unnecessary maze of legal procedures developed by their predecessors. They are made indispensable because of the structure of law and thus many of their fees are only welfare in an honorable manner. Honorable only because, as in all waste distribution territories, there is much sincere work done but nothing produced. Rodell again:

> The lawyers—or at least 99 44/100 per cent of them—are not even aware that they are indulging in a racket, and would be shocked at the very mention of the idea. Once bitten by the legal bug, they lose all sense of perspective about what they are doing and how they are doing it. Like the medicine men of tribal times and the priests of the Middle Ages they actually believe in their own nonsense.[5]

Law students may be more idealistic than the average. When they later practice law, most undoubtedly believe they are protecting peoples' rights. Yet so much of their work is unnecessary, absorbs such a large share of social production, and impacts society so destructively it is hard to maintain the notion that we are dealing with good guys in a bad system. Their need to protect both conscience and income prohibits their becoming conscious of their own redundancy.

## Divorce

The potential elimination of a large number of lawyers can be viewed in our divorce courts. Most divorce lawyers, being conscientious, think of themselves as counselors holding the hands of their distressed clients as they go through an emotionally wrenching time of their lives. This practice would be commendable were it not for the long drawn-out court battles (five years is not unusual for this remnant of "trial by combat"). The resultant lowering of family assets can hardly be viewed as protecting these people. The process can be made as simple as borrowing money from a bank. There a person simply records all pertinent information on an application, and the bank officers study the facts and make their decision. If this process is all that is required of such conservative institutions as banks, why couldn't divorces be handled in a similar manner? There are surely common threads to most divorces.

Both parties could be required to record all facts on a form. This information must be accurate and complete, subject to penalty for willful deceit. A judge could look over both forms, ask questions, and make a decision. Either party who questions the fairness of the decision would be free to appeal. There would be no loss of present rights or protections. Of course, the emotional trauma in the divorce process is high, and it may appear insensitive to deal just with facts. However, with an agreement reached in a fraction of the time, the parties can go about rebuilding their lives.

Washington state handles their divorces this way and in California, 40 percent of the divorces are handled without an attorney.[6] If these states do not require expensive, time-consuming legal counsel, why is it needed elsewhere? An economic territory for intercepting social production is now visible and the pattern is easy to follow in other fields of law.

## Probate: A Pure Waste Distribution Territory

The probate system, conceived generations ago as a device for protecting heirs, has now become their greatest enemy. Almost universally corrupt, it is essentially a form of private taxation levied by the legal profession upon the rest of the population.[7]

Leo Kornfield, former editor of *Trusts and Estates* magazine, says estate work is cut and dried; "Most of the work is done by the lawyer's secretary, problems are solved gratis by the clerks of the probate court, and very little of the lawyer's own time is consumed."[8] The *Wall Street Journal* noted, "Attempts to reform probate aren't new but rarely do they succeed because few lawyers and fewer judges want to disturb the gravy train dispensing them such huge favors."[9] Former Senator Robert F. Kennedy, himself a lawyer, aptly described probate as "a political tollbooth exacting tribute from widows and orphans."[10]

The time and labor now required to complete a probate has expanded to anywhere from two to five years, with cases on record up to thirty-six years. This gives lawyers time to slowly and legally prey on these estates. The more dishonest pick some clean, and many lucrative estates are reduced by 10 to 40 percent. This is so customary that few lawyers realize the wrong involved. Instead, like all who receive their income from a waste distribution territory, they view it as a right and fair value for their specialized talents. That they unconsciously recognize the overcharge is shown when an executive's $1.9-million estate was probated for $97,000, while a fellow lawyer's $1.7-million estate cost only $2,798.[11]

Any estate transfer requires the owner's signature. Upon death, a judge replaces the deceased as the signatory of final transfer. Those employed carrying out the wills of the deceased kept expanding their labor and time until now, after hundreds of years, it is almost all unnecessary labor. Their thievery became so gross that Norman F. Dacey, a conscientious estate planner, began to advise his clients how to put their property into an *inter vivos* (during their lifetime) trust. This avoided the probate system completely. The moment the trustee's death certificate is filed, the trustor owns that property.[12]

Quick to recognize the threat to their lucrative scam, lawyers took Dacey to court. Prevented from giving good advice, Dacey wrote *How to Avoid Probate*. Here he describes the most pure waste distribution territory I have observed. Where the wasted labor in most occupations are 30 to 70 percent, the labor wasted in probate is at least 95 percent. The proof lies in how easily it can be bypassed. A person need only make out his or her own *inter vivos* trust and pay a filing fee. When the death certificate is filed, the property immediately belongs to the heirs to spend or enjoy as they please with no delays or further costs. In the courts on the lawyers' own turf there have been many attempts to strike down Dacey's ideas—all have failed.

## Standard Forms for Most Legal Needs

Most legal transactions are procedures requiring only the filling out of ready-made forms. How else could it be? If dealings between people were not customary, there would be chaos. This simplicity is blocked by our present legal system which makes simple transactions complicated and tedious, thus *expanding labor and time* to justify large compensations.

Rosemary Furman, legal secretary and court reporter, estimated that, if the public were given access to these standardized forms, about 70 percent of the legal work could be eliminated. With this access, and a little guidance from the clerks of court, literate adults could easily handle uncontested divorces, name changes, debt collections, tax matters, bankruptcies, real estate transactions, adoptions, patents, wills, trusts, and many other legal matters. Furman charged twenty-five to fifty dollars for these services while lawyers received three hundred to five hundred dollars. This only outlines the overcharge. Whenever citizens handle their own transactions, there are no costs beyond filing fees. "Everything I do," said Furman, "is the responsibility of the clerk of court."[13]

Recognizing the threat to its territory, the Florida Bar Association filed an injunction to stop her. Knowing her position to be moral, Furman continued her practice. She was arrested, convicted, and sentenced to 120 days in jail and assessed court costs. The U.S. Supreme Court refused to hear the case but the public uproar over this obvious injustice grew so loud that Governor Robert Graham granted clemency.[14]

Furman's customers filed a class action suit claiming that closing down her services denies them access to the legal system. The legal profession may wish it had ignored Rosemary Furman. Many people are now alerted to the unjust attack on a moral and honest person. If they were to press such cases in criminal or even civil court, indignant jurors might decide against the system and revolutionize the practice of law.[15]

## The Language of Law

Any law that means something definite and tangible in relation to human affairs can be written so that its meaning is plain for all to read. . . . law deals almost exclusively with the ordinary facts and occurrences of everyday business and government and living. But it deals with them in a jargon which completely baffles and befoozles the ordinary literate man . . . it is possible to talk about legal principles and legal reasoning in everyday non-legal language. The point is that, so discussed, the principles and the reasoning and the whole solemn business of the law come to look downright silly.[16]

The inscrutability of the law expands time and labor for lawyers. It provides them with the same protection the massive disinformation campaign does for the insurance industry:

Legal language, wherever it happens to be used, is a hodgepodge of outlandish words and phrases because those words and phrases are what the principles of The Law are made of. The principles of The Law are made of those outlandish words and phrases because they are not really reasons for decisions but obscure and thoroughly unconvincing rationalizations of decisions—and if they were written in ordinary English, everybody could see how silly, how irrelevant and inconclusive, they are. If everybody could see how silly legal principles are, The Law would lose its dignity and then its power—and so would the lawyers. So legal language, by obstructing instead of assisting in the communication of ideas, is very useful—to the lawyers. It enables them to keep on saying nothing with an air of great importance—and getting away with it.[17]

Lawyers intercept their share of social production by keeping secret the simplicity of everyday common agreements. Once language is simplified and the public has access to legal forms, the practice of law via obscurantism and hocus-pocus will disappear.

## Conflict Resolution Law

We ought to be healers of conflict. Should lawyers not be healers? Healers not warriors? Healers not procurers? Healers not hired guns?[18]

— Chief Justice Warren Burger

New Zealand has coded the no-fault philosophy covered in the last chapter into other areas of law:

New Zealand abolished the right to sue. There you can't go to court *even if you want to*. . . . The Accident Compensation Corporation oversees the claims process. Injured people file claims whether their injury happened at home, at work or at play, and compensation is provided fully and fairly. . . . If tried in the U.S., it would shake the foundations of the legal profession if not the entire legal system.[19]

There need to be many qualifications, such as self-insurance for minor injuries and the right to sue for intentional assaults, but the outline of a just injury and casualty law is there. The legal monopoly designed to protect lawyers, not the public, can be broken.

To bypass the unnecessary lawyers, any civil dispute unresolvable by the disputants alone should, by law, be put before a trained mediator before it goes to court (except in cases where there is the potential for physical harm, in which case the court should step in with its protective authority). This mediator *must have no monetary interest in the extension of this conflict*. For this reason, he or she must be paid by the state. The mediator's first responsibility is to take, under oath, all pertinent facts and record them on a standard form. After obtaining all facts, the mediator would then mediate the dispute. To ensure impartiality on his or her part, the mediator must record all suggestions and agreements. All people are subject to bias and a complete and open record serves to keep that potential to a minimum.

If no agreement can be reached, the disputants need only appear in front of a judge who has studied the facts already recorded. To clarify the recorded facts, the judge would ask each party any necessary questions. Once satisfied that the dispute is understood, the judge can make a decision.When a decision is made, the judge must inform both parties of their right to appeal and, if any previously unknown facts should come to light, to appear again within a prescribed time.

Instead of lawyers confronting each other on an adversarial basis, the *judge would be responsible for protection of all parties*. Of course, judges are not un-biased, and the present solemn secrecy and impenetrability of the legal codes allows that bias wide leeway. The judge must explain in writing the logic of the decision and its legal basis, including the math showing an equitable division of property and income in divorce settlements.

If either party feels he or she has been denied justice, the adversarial court system would still be available. Those appealing must be sure of the right of their position. If the decision was just, and the reasoning for the decision given in plain language, any appeal would be foolhardy. Under such an open court system, the first judge would have to be equally careful, as any injustice would be visible and overturned. This would be by right, not by the might of a richer client or better lawyer. There would be a great gain in rights and none would be lost.

The removal of secrecy in law serves a much more important function—the education of society. People easily recognize injustice and this accounts for the low repute of the present legal system. With each decision fully explained, the law would no longer be mysterious. Disputants, knowing the parameters of a fair settlement, would solve more of their conflicts themselves. The clarity and certainty of fair court decisions would eliminate the roulette wheel of the present unjust system. Justice would no longer be a game of chance or a question of who has the better lawyer. The solemn and inscrutable custom of adversarial law would be replaced by understanding, communication, and cooperation. Once accustomed to this, people will view it as normal, and this remnant of trial by combat, the current adversarial system, will take its place in history books alongside the Inquisition and other equally pernicious "judicial" proceedings.

Lawyers expanding and extending legal conflicts are looking for survival income. This requires playing by the rules of the game. Once into the game, it is only natural that they expand their territory by contracting as many battles as they can at as high a charge as their talents will command. The potential for expansion and extension of conflict is virtually limitless. "Once an adversarial system is in place, it supports competitive aggression to the exclusion of reciprocity and empathy. . . . It accentuates hostility, not trust. Selfishness supplants generosity."[20]

To avoid these undesirable responses, suppose a lawyer were to say, "I am going to establish a mediation service and will only give advice on settling disputes fairly and conserve as much of the disputants' equity as possible. If they are then unable to agree and still wish to fight, they must go elsewhere." That lawyer would immediately become a leper among his or her peers. Instead of the companionship, support, guidance, and friendship which all workers normally receive from their fellows, such a person would be viewed and treated as a traitor to the profession. Few psyches could stand that isolation. A true mediation service within the present legal structure is unavailable.

There are, of course, already many mediation services staffed with sincere, conscientious people but their options are limited. The biggest problem is they are not permitted to give legal advice and the law does not channel disputes in their direction. The legal monopoly effectively keeps most disputes within the clutches of lawyers.[*]

---

[*] As only one of many state efforts to protect the public from lawyers, "a bill to make mediation mandatory for settling domestic matters" has been introduced in the Montana legislature. The threat to the legal system assured that it did not pass; Janice Downey, "Proposed Bill Would Alter Traditional Role of Court in Divorces," *The Missoulian,* 28 February 1987.

Mediation will not become customary until conflicts are channeled to mediators by law. Under those rules, until the effort at resolving the dispute by mediation has completed its course, lawyers' roles should be restricted to giving advice. Lawyers could and should rectify the few cases of injustice that would invariably occur but only after the mediation process was complete.

Severe depletion of financial resources, bankruptcy, and alienation of children are some of the major losses to society under adversarial divorce laws. The time spent in battle may consume years of a person's life. The emotional trauma is always devastating, at times leading to suicide. A share of that trauma is because a few lawyers must earn their living from unnecessary labor.

Conversely, a study by the University of Maryland's Institute for Child Study showed 88 percent of mediated divorces resulted in joint custody agreements. There were none in court-adjudicated cases. The same study showed agreement on responsibilities and rights in 96 percent of mediated cases.[21] These same people could hardly have the same confidence and feeling of responsibility when a decision is dictated by a court.

Mediation gives a positive structure for the children of divorce. This allows the parents to keep maximum control over their lives and the raising of their children. This self-determination allows the participants to retain dignity and the ability to better determine the course of their lives. They may use their own strength, authority, and intelligence rather than accept the dictates of an uninterested and possibly biased judge who likely knows little or nothing of the individual needs of that family. As the parties are responsible for their own decisions, mediation is cooperative rather than adversarial. It resolves rather than creates problems, releasing energy for future development instead of squandering it in destructive battles. Under adversarial conflict extension law everybody may lose, especially the children. Under conflict resolution law, they may well all win.

## The Corporate Lawyer

The bar is a hierarchy of privilege, with 90 percent of our lawyers serving 10 percent of our people.[22]

— President Jimmy Carter

Corporations, of course, are among the 10 percent which have been well served. Corporate disputes are a lawyer's dream. The paperwork alone for most litigations requires teams of lawyers working for years. Being quite practical, corporate leaders have tried a new twist. By mutual agreement, they remove themselves from the jurisdiction of the court, and each side's lawyers present their case in a mini-trial. A neutral party advises both sides on how a real court might rule on the case. Right after the trial the executives meet *without their lawyers* to negotiate a settlement. They are free to continue the battle in court but usually the mini-trial settles the dispute. Corporate participants appear to favor them because they are confidential and quick one-day settlements are common. The legal costs are dramatically reduced, and by 1983, there had been over one hundred such mini-trials in the U.S.[23] Others call them summary trials:

Seven families in a Michigan town discovered contaminated drinking water in their wells. They promptly sued a company that used the suspected chemical in a nearby manufacturing plant. . . . Normally such a trial would run a grueling nine months. This one will last only three days. . . . lawyers for the plaintiffs and the defendant recount testimony and describe evidence. No witnesses will testify. When both sides are finished, the jury will issue a verdict. But it won't be binding. The jury's findings will, however, guide both sides toward an agreement in the *mandatory* negotiations that immediately follow.[24] (emphasis added)

These may be called mini-trials or summary trials but they are little more than the mediation conferences I have suggested be mandated for all civil disputes. The facts are brought out and evaluated and a compromise reached. Disputes are solved reasonably and cheaply.

## Criminal Law

As historically governments have denied people their rights, there should be no reduction in access to criminal defense lawyers. However, crime rises and falls in step with the economy. It is largely because of inequality and poverty and this is addressed in chapter six. Once equality, opportunity, and security are the right of all society, censure of friends and family will be the best crime deterrent. The reduced need for criminal lawyers would parallel the drop in crime.

## Conclusion

With 6 percent of the world's people, America has 66 percent of its lawyers.[25] They have doubled in the past ten years and tripled in the past twenty. With their increase far outstripping that of the population, it should be no surprise that lawyers do their best to create work. Lester Thurow, an economist at Massachusetts Institute of Technology, lamented, "We can't even export them because the rest of the world is too smart to accept them and the adversarial system that they would carry with them." Law schools continue to "crank them out" and in another ten years, this nation will have 930,000 lawyers—a 38-percent increase.[26] That the legal waste distribution territory will continue to expand to their benefit and not the public's is assured.

Americans paid forty billion dollars to these lawyers in 1984.[27] If we conservatively calculated the income in the law industry at 50 percent above the national average, that would be 1.33 million employed.* An analysis of the above would lead to the conclusion that not over 30 percent of that number of mediators, advisors, lawyers, judges, and clerks are needed. This would release 920,000 of our ablest citizens for productive employment. The quality of life would rise dramatically as we recovered, from those pledged to protect us, the rights now denied us.

---

* This is conservative, as there are 630,000 lawyers and judges recorded, which would leave 700,000 clerks and other support personnel; *Statistical Abstract of the U.S.*, 1984, p. 419.

# 3

# Transportation

Waste is built into the overlapping territories of the transportation industries. For example, immense sums are eaten up by the auto industry in order to make available a dazzling display of automobiles that are 99 percent mechanically (though not interchangeably) identical. Through different styles, each manufacturer tries to make every car appear different, and there are now so many models even car buffs are unable to identify them all.

In 1961, before such a proliferation of models, Franklin M. Fisher, Zvi Grilliches, and Carl Kaysen conducted a study to determine what an automobile should cost. They concluded that in the 1950s, a rationally designed automobile, efficiently produced and distributed, would have cost about one-third the then-current price. They estimated the wasted labor as accounting for fully 2.5 percent of the Gross National Product (GNP).[1]

## Who Collects the Tribute?

In 1974, eight hundred of the auto industry's best engineers met to study whether the stratified charge engine could meet the new federal emissions standards. They concluded that it could do so without expensive catalytic converters or other pollution control devices.[2] The stratified charge engine was nothing new. It was used in diesel engines in 1911, patented for gas engines in England in 1922, patented by the Soviet Union in 1958, and patented by others in the early 1960s. However, by 1973, Japan's Honda Motor Company had bought and cross-patented about 230 patents to claim exclusive rights to this valuable engine.[3]

The American auto industry was trapped. Although its engineers had long ago solved the emissions problem, the industry had chosen to ignore their solution, and did not own the patents to this critical technology. Detroit decided to bypass Honda's patents with expensive catalytic converters and other pollution control devices. This raised the price per car several hundred dollars, while increasing gas consumption.

If we assume the added price for catalytic converters was a modest three hundred dollars; the extra gas consumed, during the life of the car, five hundred dollars; and the time value of this money needlessly spent, another four hundred dollars; the total unnecessary cost to the public would be twelve hundred dollars per car sold. Allowing a modest twenty million such engines built per year throughout the world, the annual waste due to monopolizing the stratified engine technology would be $24 billion, or $408 billion over the seventeen-year life of the patent.* Allowing ten million cars and light trucks produced each year in the United States, the loss to Americans would be $12 billion per year, or $204 billion during that patent's life. The same pattern of waste characterizes every patented innovation or invention (better brakes, transmissions, or carburetors) that is denied utilization by competitors.

Now look at this carefully. That money does not go into someone's pocket—it is wasted. The resources and labor which went into those unnecessary catalytic converters and other pollution control devices, the extra fuel used, and the time value of the extra money consumed the $24 billion. Even the automobile companies did not profit—witness their struggle to survive when their illogical defense of market territory failed. However, the money paid for this unnecessary labor was properly used to provide a living for those workers. This is our distribution by wasted labor.

## With Access to Technology, Both Inventors and Consumers Win

To assess how well inventors and society would fare if technology were available to everybody, let us generously assume that one thousand recent inventors contributed directly to the stratified charge engine and deserve both credit and compensation.** Allowing for a modest twenty million such engines built worldwide each year, it would require an inventor's tax of only five dollars per engine to give these most useful citizens $1.7 billion, or an average of $1.7 million apiece, over the seventeen-year life of the patent.

Developing this innovation required much more labor, investment, and risk than inventing it. An additional fifty dollars per engine over that seventeen-year period would provide $17 billion for the development patent. The world would save $389.3 billion of the $408 billion once wasted.

Those compensations are for only a small addition to the knowledge of the internal combustion engine, which itself was built upon a mountain of social knowledge accumulated over thousands of years. Thus that $1.7 billion for the inventors, and $17 billion for the developers, would represent adequate compensation. It is safe to say that, under the present patent structure, most who had the original ideas received nothing. Corporate monopolies ended up owning this and other technologies and it was their *competitive monopolization* (see below) which created the large overcharges for society.

---

\* Under present law it is unlikely the patent will even then be free for use by everybody. After all, this invention had already been around for over seventy-five years.

\*\* The wasted labor in transportation cannot be fully explained without going into the patent structure that protects the automobile monopolies. That is addressed in Book Three, chapter two.

## The Radial Tire

Let's take, as a starting point, the introduction of the radial tire in the 1960s. It was superior to any bias-ply and was a mature development point for tires. As the radial tire was far superior to any other, there was no justifiable reason for producing others. This superior tire saved 10 percent on fuel, was safer, and sold for eighty dollars, while the top-of-the-line bias-ply tire retailed then for about forty dollars and wholesaled to state, county and city governments for thirteen dollars.[4]

Tires are produced by several companies, each of which produces many models and grades. All are coded in such a way that most people have no idea what they are buying. The confusion is multiplied when distribution companies purchase these tires and sell them under yet a different brand name. This unnecessary complexity interferes with simple value judgments, creating a dependency on price and sales rhetoric. This is *monopoly by designed confusion*. It sustains a system of duplicated manufacturing and distribution facilities which are economically wasteful. As *competitive monopolies*, they are viable only because of the overcharge.

Had this technology been available to all, the inventors could have been adequately compensated at 20 cents a tire and the developers at $1.80 for a total of $2 per tire. Allowing two hundred million tires worldwide, there would be $40 million per year for the inventors and $360 million for the developers, or $6.8 billion for both over the patent's normal life span.

Instead of the above simplicity with one basic superior tire, each dealer had to have a duplicated inventory of many brands and grades that created higher storage, accounting, and delivery charges. In place of these many confusing styles, codes, and competing dealers, a community warehouse could be stocked with only the necessary styles and sizes of the new high quality, *developmentally mature* radial tires. In carload lots, this warehouse could receive tires at a discount far exceeding the $2 royalties for inventors and development patents. With such a rapid turnover through one distribution center, the markup to the consumer need have been no more than 10 percent over the thirteen-dollar wholesale price, or a total purchase price of fifteen dollars. Thus the mounted price of a first-line radial tire, at that time, did not have to be more than twenty dollars. This would have been 50 percent of the price charged for bias-ply, and 25 percent of the introductory price of radial tires.

## Developmentally Mature:
## Efficiency through Interchangeable Parts

The major criterion for developmentally mature social capital is the cost of replacing industrial tools. The duplicated and ever-changing capital infrastructure for automobile production creates large costs. As outlined in the study by Fisher, Grilliches, and Kaysen, retooling for style changes alone causes 25 percent of the price of automobiles. Railroads avoid this particular form of waste through standardized track gauge, running gears, motive power, rolling stock, and other equipment; their machinery is interchangeable almost anywhere in the U.S., Canada, and Mexico.

The efficiencies of standardization, with only a few factories tooled to mass produce a product, have long been recognized. For example, bolts and burrs once were threaded in local machine shops and were not interchangeable. To avoid this waste, the Society of Automotive Engineers established standard sizes and threads. Bolts and burrs were now standard, interchangeable, and cheap. The cost of repairing machinery dropped drastically as mechanics, freed from having to make their own one at a time, simply bought inexpensive bolts and burrs from a supplier who mass produced them by the millions.

This standardization, however, did not go far enough. The prices of spare parts are so astronomical relative to their manufacturing cost it defies understanding. People go to wrecking yards and invariably marvel at the millions of parts lying about, none of which fit their particular cars. And anyone who has bought repairs has had the shattering experience of paying dollars for these nonstandardized items which cost only pennies to manufacture. Certainly there are none of the efficiencies of competition we hear so much about. This is a monopolized market held captive by designed obsolescence and noninterchangeability of parts. These parts too could be standardized.

Examples of the excessive costs of nonstandard parts are legion. A friend sought to purchase a shaft and gear to repair the transmission on an eight horse-power garden tractor. The price was $70. Searching around, he was able to buy the entire transmission new for $95. Another friend went to purchase a gear for a variable-speed Ford tractor transmission. The list price on this 2.5 by 5 inch gear was $1,007. He calculated that the parts of just that transmission, individually bought, would exceed the price of a new tractor. Much of the excessive cost is from maintaining extensive and expensive inventories which turn over slowly. A dealer must now stock ten, fifty, or even one hundred models of spare parts, all for different makes of cars and different models of the same brand. Most of these parts could be standardized and interchangeable.

Once standardized, and if manufacturers had equal access to patented technology (see Book Three, chapter two), every car could be equipped with the best engine, transmission, differential, carburetor, brakes, water pump, and suspension system that engineers could design. This does not mean manufacturers would be restricted to one mechanical design for these automobile components. It means that each component would have standardized housings and fittings to make them fully interchangeable. Those who formerly were unable to use a patented, superior technology could now do so. Competition would force each manufacturer to use the best. If engine housings, transmissions, and differentials were designed to be interchangeable, the enormous investment in noninterchangeable products would be replaced by unrestricted competition guaranteeing products which are superior. Inferior or overpriced parts now sold to captive customers couldn't be sold if another manufacturer's product would bolt right in its place. Instead of tens or even hundreds of designs, each with a factory complex to produce it, there would be only a few designs of high quality.

Eliminate this duplication, operate the reduced number of manufacturing and distribution facilities with fully productive labor, and costs will drop precipitously. Those high inventories, phone calls, and express charges will be largely replaced by a calculable weekly or monthly bulk replenishment of parts. The average distributor's inventory investment could drop to possibly 10 percent of present costs. Society has the right to insist on such savings; it is a matter of knowing they are possible and insisting on standardization.

Standardization could be expanded to include everything except the body of an automobile. Here the manufacturers can put their talents to work making each model unique. There would be no limit to the body styles that could be placed upon standardized chassis, running gears, and power trains. Thus customers could order any engine or power train they wished. They would know that every component had stood the test of time and that each car was the best that present engineering could produce. The emotional satisfaction associated with cars would still be available, along with others that are not. The increased free time, shared by all labor, could be spent with friends and family, or in other enjoyable activities.

## Distribution of Automobiles

The study referred to earlier concluded that there were almost two intermediaries (salespeople and their support infrastructure) for every worker building automobiles. As with other products the public is unfamiliar with, these salespeople were necessary in the development stage of the automobile. However, the automobile became developmentally mature and has been accepted by the consumer since at least 1940. There would be little real difference between taking a trip with a like-new 1940 automobile and one built in 1988. With an automobile now a necessity, there is nothing to sell—when people want one, they will buy it. It is a *prepackaged* product. Nothing of consequence is done to it from the time it leaves the factory until it is driven off the sales room floor. It is illuminating to consider why we cannot order a car just as easily as we order products from Sears and Roebuck catalog. Would not that car be just as ready to use if, at one-third the price, it were produced with standardized parts; ordered directly from the manufacturer; and picked up at a central distribution point? Custom, protection of territory and competitive monopolization have kept all those intermediaries in place long after there was any need for a sales force to market new automobiles. They could easily be bypassed.[*]

## Model Changes

As mentioned above, yearly model changes require shutting down the factories for retooling and account for 25 percent of a car's final price. New models should no longer be produced in order to meet the frivolous, but obligatory, annual schedule. Rather, all model changes would ideally coincide with periodic improvements in technology. Those who feel it necessary to reinforce their identity through car styles could still have their cars customized at less cost than all car buyers are forced to pay for yearly style changes.

## Fuel Savings

The old standard—under 20 miles per gallon family car—has given way to the

---

[*] There would still be a need for used car salespeople.

1987 leader in fuel economy, the Chevrolet Sprint. It is rated at 54 miles per gallon. Seymour Melman, Professor of Industrial Engineering at Columbia University, argues that with "new technology, requiring answers to a series of solvable engineering problems, this fuel efficiency could be raised to 82 to 113 miles per gallon."[5]

## Savings from Reduced Speed

Savings on both fuel and wear and tear could be realized through reduced speed. When the federally imposed speed limit of fifty-five miles per hour was in effect, the death rate from 1966 to 1986 fell by better than 50 percent (from 5.72 to 2.47 per one hundred million miles).[6] In 1987, the speed limit increased to sixty-five miles per hour on interstate highways. Fatalities immediately jumped 50 percent on those roads while still falling another 10 percent on the secondary routes where the speed had not been increased.[7] With governors on all cars to limit their speed to fifty-five miles per hour, it would be considerably more difficult to express aggression from behind the wheel. Many high speed wrecks, and the social costs associated with them, would be eliminated. Reasonable speed would reduce the pressure on the power train, running gears, and suspension systems; reduce the stress on the body; and extend a car's useful life.[*]

An automobile engineered for maximum longevity, built with a rustproof body, standardized parts and governors, and a public educated about conservation, could triple the car's current life. This was shown when Albert Klein of Pasadena, California, drove his 1963 Volkswagen Bug one million miles and it was still in good shape.[8] The mechanical parts of a car are easily replaceable even without the above recommended standardizations. It is rusting or other body damage— too expensive to repair—that determines a car's life. This life could be doubled or tripled using a recent technological breakthrough whereby a silicon steel coating makes steel virtually rustproof. Given a choice, most of us would doubtless opt for simple, cheap transportation, produced with the latest technology, standardized parts, rational model changes, and direct distribution.

The study referred to earlier, that of Fisher, Grilliches, and Kaysen, determined the unnecessary labor in building and distributing a car at 66 percent. There have been many laborsaving innovations since that study: robot-operated factories and assembly lines, rustproof steel bodies, longer-lasting engines. However, these calculations will be just on the 66 percent savings shown possible by that twenty-five-year-old study.

Americans spend $230 billion per year on automobiles.[9] Two-thirds of that— the value of that 66 percent savings—is $151.8 billion. Allowing $30,000 as the typical wage of an auto worker (which is almost double the national average of $17,500), we see the labor of five million workers in the automobile industry is wasted. That wasted $153 billion is 3.8 percent of the present $4-trillion economy. This is an increase from the 2.5 percent waste documented twenty-five years ago in the study we have been citing. Thus the share of the GNP provided by automobiles has increased faster than the national average. This correlates with

---

* This is not a recommendation for a particular policy, but rather a treatise on waste and how it can be eliminated.

our thesis that waste distribution territories expand to absorb the gains in efficiency of technology. This is further supported by a survey of over 225 marketing, planning, and engineering executives making a study for car makers and parts suppliers. They concluded that a car in 1995 would cost $13,800 (in 1985 dollars), as opposed to $11,600 in 1986.[10] Those unnecessary costs continue to rise as waste distribution territories expand their claims on the nation's wealth.

## Railroads

As explained in the introduction, from 1951 to 1984 the railroad labor force shrank from 1.3 million to 270,000, and eventually there will be only 100,000 workers hauling twice the freight. Thus each unit of freight will require only 4 percent of the labor required thirty-three years ago.[*] Originally, these railroad workers were fully productive and undercompensated, and they had to fight for badly needed work rules. Since that time, modern diesels have replaced the old, labor-intensive steam engines. The flagmen, who once protected the front and rear of the trains and threw the switches, have been replaced by automatic block signals and electric power switches. Watching for hot bearings and dragging equipment is now taken care of by electronic detectors which transmit a radio message when, and pinpoint where, there is trouble. For the most part, computers have taken the place of the traditional dispatchers, clerks, and telegraph operators. The former steel and tie gangs, which once required hundreds of workers per crew, have been replaced by a few operators using modern equipment. With this ever-increasing technological efficiency, once sensible work rules are no longer valid. Restructuring and the eventual reduction to 100,000 workers will again leave the railroads with a fully productive workforce.

As shown by the rising freight rates, most of the savings produced by eliminating railroad labor will not be passed on to society. The gains of technology, once claimed by outdated work rules, will then be absorbed by a corporate monopoly. As a true monopoly, railroads have historically been "cash cows" for monopoly capital. Over 50 percent of the funds obtained from the government and private investors to build these roads were diverted to the promoters' bank accounts. They then needlessly burdened these railroads with loans, diverted much of this capital elsewhere, and left the debt to be paid for by higher than necessary freight and passenger fares.[11]

Any supposed efficiency of competition for a public utility (water, electricity, telephones, water, sewers, garbage, and railroads) is sheer fiction. Railroads do have competition from trucks. But with today's railroad efficiency, it is monopoly pricing that permits trucks to compete on long hauls.

One piggyback freight train replaces 150 truck drivers, while consuming only about one-third the fuel. "A train averages 192 ton-miles to the gallon of fuel, while a truck gets only 58 ton-miles to the gallon . . . [and] to move one hundred thousand tons of freight from New York to San Francisco, you must pay for 43,416 man-days by highway [and only] 3,320 man-days by rail."[12] One hundred thousand railroad workers can haul roughly one-half the freight while 1.5 million truckers haul the other half.

---

* Rail labor dropped thirty-six thousand while this book was being written.

# Cross-Hauling

To the above unnecessary costs must be added those of cross-hauling. During World War I, the Fuel Administration saved 160 million car-miles by planning deliveries to consumers from the closest source via the shortest route. (England saved 700 million ton-miles.) After the war, shipping returned to normal, and again trains hauling Ohio coal to Illinois met other trains hauling coal from Illinois to Ohio.[13]

With computers and larger corporate buying units, it appears the cross-hauling problem should be reduced. Yet trains today meet other trains loaded with the same products, and empty railroad cars meet other matching empties. Logging trucks can be observed meeting each other and some enclosed trucks surely have similar cargoes crossing paths to distant markets.

A trucker confirmed this for me and explained the problem is brand names for identical products. It is possible to deliver a load of fertilizer to within sight of another fertilizer plant processing an identical product with a different brand name. He can then load up this identical fertilizer and deliver it back to where he came from. His example dealt with ammonium sulfate, but this must be true of most brand name bulk products. Meeting on the nation's highways might be acceptable for loads of face cream and clothes, but it is hardly justified for coal, fertilizer, lumber, and other identical bulk products. The same unplanned economy which operated wastefully with small trading units before World War I continues with large economic units today.

# Air Freight

The early days of railroads battling for markets with duplicated services is being replayed with a vengeance by the new air express companies. At least eight companies and the Postal Service now offer next-day delivery anywhere in the U.S.[14] But having nine separate pick-up services, nine separate sorting centers, and nine individual delivery services is economic insanity. This would be like having each home served by, and having to pay for, nine electric, water, phone, and garbage companies.

Frederick Smith, the originator of Federal Express, conceived the idea of guaranteed next-day priority mail delivery. He proposed using passenger jets which already covered the entire country.[15] Mail from the entire U.S. would be delivered to one central station by scheduled flights. There it would be sorted and delivered by other scheduled flights to its proper destination where it would be distributed by the waiting couriers.

With restructured patent laws (to be addressed in depth in Book Three, chapter two) an innovator such as Frederick Smith could present his or her idea to the already established Postal Service. There it should be analyzed and tested by computer. (This same study would be undertaken by every new express company.) If it proved efficient, the Postal Service need only build its central sorting station, sign the airplane contracts, hire the needed help, start the service, and pay a royalty to the innovator.

Establishing an office in every community and advertising is the major investment for this new service. Since post offices already have offices and the public knows they are there, their start-up costs would be only a small percentage of what any one of the eight competing carriers would have to bear. Frederick Smith could be well paid from royalties on his innovation, and the savings to the nation—from eliminating eight duplicated services—would be substantial.

Given the Postal Service's much lower investment, and the elimination of duplicated labor and capital, the costs for such an express service would be decidedly lower. It is only the lower volume of express mail handled by the post offices that forces them to charge as much or more than private express companies. All major postal changes require the approval of, and financing by, politicians, whose protection of business interests is well-known. Thus the postal service is not free to take quick advantage of such opportunities. This almost certainly political control is evident since the Postal Service is the *only* express carrier *not* using Smith's cost-reducing innovation.

Claims of postal inefficiency are rhetoric to hide the *secret* that such a service under a public authority would be more efficient than under competing private carriers.* Another market is thus rendered safe as competitive monopolization creates a new waste distribution territory.

## Passenger Airlines

A modern airport has row upon row of ticket counters and loading ramps assigned to different airlines. All will be busy before, and quite idle between, flights. The rules that apply to air express apply to airlines—ticket counters are their duplicated collection service.

Passenger routes were originally assigned, which prevented wasteful, competitive duplication. Thus the waste is not as great as in air freight. But in 1986 the regulation of airlines was eliminated. The battle for market territory is on and the praises of competition are loudly sung as fares drop dramatically. Airlines are going broke right and left (150 in the past eight years).[16] Mergers and buy-outs increase as the stronger companies gain control of more routes. Eventually there will be a few large airlines left and monopoly prices will inevitably return. Once a few airlines have monopolized the business, Americans might take a second look at what competition has wrought:

> Instead of being flown from A to B, as was the case before deregulation, passengers are now flown from A to C, where they change planes for B. The trip from Grand Forks, N.D., to Seattle, Wash., requires a flight east to Northwest's hub in Minneapolis. And the only way to fly from Cheyenne, Wyo., to Casper is by way of Denver—more than double the air miles from point to point. Under the hub system, the distance between two points is rarely a simple straight line.[17]

## Waste through Social Policy

A century and a half ago, it took the average person thirty minutes to walk to work. At the dawn of the automobile age, homes were established further away, and getting to work still required the same thirty minutes.[18] Today, with modern roads and high speed cars, it is not unusual to drive thirty miles between home

---

* Under a postal authority it is still free enterprise, as most postal business is by contract.

and work. When almost everyone goes to, and comes from, work at the same hour, this causes traffic congestion (often paralysis) in and near cities, and the pace again slows to walking speed. It is not uncommon to spend hours per day commuting to and from work.

This society could have been far less wasteful if it had continued to construct a rational mass transit system and built its homes within easy access of it. The statistics speak for themselves. One loaded bus will replace 35 cars each round trip. If that bus makes ten fully loaded trips per day, it replaces 350 cars. One loaded passenger train will replace 1,000 cars. A single lane of a freeway will move fewer than five thousand people per hour while a railroad track can move over fifty thousand.[19]

That there is little mass transit in the U.S. is no accident. In 1932, General Motors and other corporations formed a holding company, the United Cities Motor Transit, whose sole purpose was to buy up public transit systems and scrap them. By 1955 over one hundred public electric trolley systems had been eliminated in this way, which reduced the cities' mass transit by 88 percent. These corporations conspired to establish this wasteful social policy in order to tie the needs of the public to their own industries. General Motors, Standard Oil, Firestone, and Greyhound were found guilty of criminal conspiracy and violation of federal antitrust laws. GM was assessed five thousand dollars for the transgression.[20]

If society had chosen the more efficient mass transit, transportation would have required fewer resources. However, the social infrastructure is in place for commuting by auto. As the average car is used only 5.6 percent of the time for vacations and pleasure, over 90 percent of an automobile's use is for essential needs such as work, shopping, and hauling children to school.[21] The reduction of the workweek, documented as possible throughout this treatise, would reduce jobs and thus the rush-hour traffic. Traffic jams caused by commuting to work would disappear, and the designed efficiency of the automobile could at last reduce commuting time. It is possible that a society with each worker working two days per week would be more efficient with individual automobiles than with mass transit.*

## Conclusion

We have determined the wasted labor in the production, distribution, and maintenance of automobiles to be 5 million workers.

The long distance trucking industry employed 1.7 million in 1984.[22] Since then mixed-freight trains have been replaced by seventy-five-car piggyback trains (two trailers per railcar). Each train eliminates 150 long-haul truck drivers. Now these piggyback trains are being replaced by double-deck container trains that haul twice the prepackaged freight. I will conservatively allow a 30-percent potential labor reduction in the trucking industry, or 510,000 unnecessary truckers.

The airlines employ 568,000; using the same conservative estimate of 30 per-

---

* There would be equal savings in the extractive industries—oil, steel, copper, aluminum, glass, etc. Any rise in automobile use due to additional leisure time would represent an *increase* in living standards, and our guideline throughout is *current* living standards.

cent yields a surplus of 170,000 workers.[23] Analysis of the railroads identifies 178,000 workers who could be eliminated. A conservative 20 percent of the unnecessary primary jobs, or 171,000, will be allowed for the support workers potentially eliminated in the railroad, airline, and trucking industries, The total labor in transportation that would be released with a rationally planned transportation system is therefore about 5.86 million.

# 4

# Agriculture

One of our most sacred illusions is that U.S. agriculture is above all reproach. Not only are we the "breadbasket of the world," but Third World people are somehow incapable of emulating our productive farming methods. If there is one thing we are sure about, it is that without our food and generosity, much of the rest of the world would starve.

Yet 40 percent of the underdeveloped world which was once plagued by severe food shortages—China, Guinea-Bissau, Cuba, and other nations—now produces and distributes the twenty-three to twenty-four hundred calories per day required to sustain an adult. India has finally achieved self-sufficiency, but it is too early to tell if this will be maintained. Angola, Mozambique, and Nicaragua also achieved self-sufficiency—that is, until their economic infrastructures were sabotaged by anti-government rebels organized, trained, and armed by developed world forces.[1] These countries newly self-sufficient in food have far less cultivatable land per person than most of the countries still suffering from chronic food shortages. China, for example, has only .13 hectares per person; North Vietnam, .10; and North Korea, .07. Despite having more arable land per person, their neighbors are unable to feed themselves—Pakistan has .40 hectares per person; India, .30; Bangladesh, .16; and Indonesia, .15.[2]

The best known example of a country that is continually faced with hunger is Bangladesh, where "two-thirds of the population suffer from protein and vitamin deficiencies." Yet it is on a fertile plain blessed with plenty of water and "grows enough in grain alone to provide everyone in the country with at least 2,600 calories a day."[3] Add the vegetables and fruit grown in this rich soil, and it is obvious that nature has provided this country with the ability to feed more than the present population.

The picture becomes clearer when we study Africa and South America. The United Nations Food and Agriculture Organization estimates that only 60 percent of the world's arable land is farmed. In Africa and South America, the two hungriest continents, the figure is 20 percent, and their grain yields are only one-half that of the industrialized countries. Brazil, for example, is burdened with an enormous hunger problem, but even without cutting down any more jungle, it has 2.3 cultivable acres per person. The picture comes into focus when we learn that in South and Central America, one-half of the acres farmed—invariably the best land—grow crops for feeding cattle or for export.[4] Latin Americans, despite rampant hunger, use only a small percent of their land's agricultural potential for their own consumption, and Africa is comparable.

The remaining hungry nations in the world, mostly in southeast Asia, have such large populations that the land's capacity to feed their people entails a much smaller margin of safety. Yet they, too, could produce an adequate supply of food if they controlled their land. China, probably the shining example of rational land reform, adequately feeds over one billion people. When the population was less than half that, and the land was monopolized, there were massive famines.

Fifteen of the poorest countries in the world raise and export more agricultural products than they keep for their own use.[5] Some of the export crops and the percentage of farmland this takes away from local consumption are: Guadalupe: sugar, cocoa, and bananas, 66 percent; Martinique: bananas, coffee, cocoa, and sugar, 70 percent; Barbados: sugar cane, 77 percent. Guatemala's cotton for export is planted in blocks of fifty thousand acres.[6]

These are all familiar American consumer items, and a large share of these impoverished countries' exports come here. In 1973 the U.S. imported 7 percent of its beef, much of it from the Dominican Republic and Central America. Costa Rica alone exported sixty million pounds to the U.S in 1975. That country's per capita beef consumption dropped from forty-nine pounds per year in 1950 to thirty-three pounds in 1971. If Costa Ricans had consumed this increased production, their per capita consumption would have been three times as high—ninety-eight pounds.[7]

It becomes mind-boggling to discover that, while we import all this beef, two-thirds of the grain we export goes to feed livestock. It becomes ridiculous when one learns it requires forty cents' worth of imported oil to produce and transport every dollar's worth of agricultural exports.[8]

At the time of this writing, U.S. food imports are exceeding exports.[9] Economists teach us there must be balanced trade, and, from the perspective of maintaining the status quo, this may be true. But the status quo reflects the unequal distribution of political and economic power in the world. The "geography of world hunger" is specifically the consequence of entire populations having lost control of their land, and thus their destiny.

The world does not need our surplus grain. The impoverished need the right to control their own land and to be responsible for growing their own food.[*] Given that right, they will not generally be hungry. Monopolization of land diverts the production of social wealth to those already affluent, because only they have money to purchase and consume this production. The result is a small, well cared for elite and a large, dispossessed, and hungry majority.

## Is It Overpopulation or Who Controls the Land?

The often heard comment (one I once accepted as fact) that "there are too many people in the world, and overpopulation is the cause of hunger," can be compared to the same myth expounded in sixteenth-century England and revived continuously since.

---

[*] Industrial capital processing products from the land is an integral part of land (Book Three, chapter two).

Through repeated acts of enclosure the peasants were pushed off the land so that the gentry could make money raising wool for the new and highly productive power looms. They could not do this if the peasants were to retain their historic *entitlement* to a share of production from the land.* Massive starvation was the inevitable result of this expropriation.

There were serious discussions in learned circles about overpopulation as the cause of this poverty. This was the accepted reason because a social and intellectual elite were doing the rationalizing. It was they who controlled the educational institutions which studied the problem. Naturally the final conclusions (at least those published) absolved the wealthy of any responsibility for the plight of the poor. The absurdity of suggesting that England was then overpopulated is clear when we realize that "the total population of England in the sixteenth century was less than in any one of several present-day English cities."[10]

The hunger in underdeveloped countries today is equally tragic and absurd. Their European colonizers understood well that ownership of land gave the owner control over what society produced. The most powerful simply redistributed the valuable land titles to themselves, eradicating millennia-old traditions of common use. Since custom is a form of ownership, the shared use of land could not be permitted. If ever reestablished, this ancient practice would reduce the rights of these new owners. For this reason, much of the land went unused or underused until the new owners could do so profitably. This is the pattern of land use that characterizes most Third World countries today, and it is this that generates hunger in the world.

Those conquered people are kept in a state of relative impoverishment. Permitting them any substantial share of social wealth would negate the historic reason for conquest—namely plunder. The ongoing role of Third World countries is to be the supplier of cheap and plentiful raw materials and agricultural products to the developed world. Nature's wealth was, and is, being controlled to fulfill the needs of the world's affluent people. The U.S. is one of the prime beneficiaries of this well-established system. Our great universities search diligently for "the answer" to the problem of poverty and hunger. They invariably find it in "lack of motivation, inadequate or no education," or some other self-serving excuse. They look at everything except the cause—the powerful own the world's social wealth. As a major beneficiary, we have much to gain by perpetuating the myths of overpopulation, cultural and racial inferiority, and so forth. The real causes must be kept from ourselves, as how else can this systematic damaging of others be squared with what we are taught about democracy, rights, freedom, and justice?

If people were given rights to their own land, every country in the world could—as in the past—feed itself. This accessibility would have to be permanent and consistent. Any alienation of their rights to the land or underselling of local

---

* Along with the myth of overpopulation, we are told that large agricultural units are more productive than smaller ones. That this is not true was proven by a World Bank study. This showed that in Argentina and Brazil the smallest farms produced eight times more per hectare than the largest estates; in Colombia, a convincing fourteen times more; and in India, a modest but measurable 40 percent more. The reason for the poor showing of larger holdings can be seen in Colombia's typical pattern of absentee ownership. There the largest estates comprise 70 percent of the land and only 6 percent of that acreage is farmed.

agricultural production with cheap imports would disrupt food production and ensure that hunger continued. Then, of course, many would point to these non-productive people and say, "They don't understand; they'll never change." But it is we who do not understand. With undisturbed access to their own land, no people in the world would need our food. Then there would be no reason to plant the one-quarter of our crops that are for export.[11] Most of the work expended for this $36 billion worth of exports is unneeded—here too is a waste distribution territory.[*]

## Unnecessary Production for Home Consumption

Frances Moore Lappé, who was pursuing her education in community organizing, was frustrated by the realization that she was not learning anything that would affect the underlying reasons for poverty and hunger. She quit. She then undertook to educate herself by mastering basic source material ignored in academic circles. She insists that all the necessary information is available to prove clearly that every country in the world could feed itself. Lappé became a leading authority on food and nutrition and *Diet for a Small Planet* was her first effort to share this knowledge with a hungry world. Since then she has energetically lectured in countries all over the world. One dramatic consequence is that Mexico and Norway have tried to plan their food programs around her teachings.[12]

Lappé learned that: (1) The human body can manufacture all the amino acids that are the building blocks of protein, except eight. These are called the essential amino acids. (2) These nutrients are found in grains and vegetables but not all eight in any one. (3) If any essential amino acid is missing or short in a person's diet, that sets the limit on the body's ability to build protein. And (4) it is only necessary to eat a meal of vegetables and grain that include all eight in adequate amounts, and the body will build its own protein. For fulfilling the need for human protein, an amino acid is an amino acid whether it is in meat or vegetables.[13]

Our preferred source of protein is beef. Knowing this, Lappé studied the efficiency of beef production. She was astounded to learn that a cattle feeder must feed his steers sixteen pounds of perfectly edible human food in the form of grain to produce one pound of beef. She recognized this was "a protein factory in reverse."[14] Cattle are ruminants, and their stomachs efficiently convert roughage (grass) into edible meat. Being inefficient converters of grain to meat, cattle must consume enormous amounts of this human food. The overwhelming share of this grain is converted into fat, bone, intestines, and manure.[15]

Delving into this waste of grain, Lappé's research showed that the proper combination of leafy vegetables produces, on the average, fifteen times more protein per acre than grain-fed beef, while peas, beans, and other legumes produce ten times more, and grain, five times.[16] The grain fed to livestock is subtracting from, not adding to, the already short supply of human protein. To eliminate hunger, the poor of the Third World (and First World) should obtain their amino acids to

---

[*]  These exported crops are mostly grains, which are the cheapest to raise and account for two out of every five acres of our agricultural land.

produce protein from the proper proportion of vegetables and grain, with a small amount of meat for flavor.

There are claims that prime beef is superior in taste, but the United States Department of Agriculture (USDA) tests show that young beef fed grain for a short time has no discernible taste difference from prime feedlot beef.[17]

It has only been since World War II that farmers have fattened prime beef. Tests on Montana beef fed on high quality roughage, lower amounts of grain, and no chemicals, and marketed before one year of age, showed 42 milligrams of cholesterol against the conventional 73 milligrams.[18] If we returned to those old standards, the quality of the beef would be higher (measured by leanness, not by marbling) and the quantity available only slightly reduced. Just eliminating the last two weeks of cattle feeding ("finishing") would have saved consumers eight cents per pound at 1974 prices.[19] Feeding grain to cattle for an extended period of time also began after World War II. Today feedlots furnish 90 percent of the cattle slaughtered.[20] This practice, along with the great expansion of exports, explains how the surplus feed grain generated by modern farming technology was in part and temporarily consumed.

If people throughout the world could be taught how to obtain cheap protein, and had access to their land, there would be no need for hunger in any country. Global production exceeds three thousand calories of food per day for each person, while the daily need is only twenty-three to twenty-four hundred calories. Counting the grain required to produce the meat they eat, the consumption by the well-to-do of eight thousand to ten thousand calories per day is a major cause of world hunger.[21]

There needs to be a change in public education on food to correspond with the training to be responsible for one's own health. It will be argued in the next chapter that sensible nutrition should be thoroughly taught to everyone in school. The gain in health from reducing meat consumption is well established, but more education is needed on the principles of cheap and adequate protein as presented by Lappé. With this knowledge, most people would be able to make intelligent choices and thus regain control of this critical area of individual and social well-being. Society's health and the quality of life would rise accordingly. The cost would be lower, not higher as the purveyors of misinformation would have us believe.*

Because animal fat is the primary reason for cholesterol buildup, heart attacks, and other cardiovascular diseases, many people are already reducing their meat consumption and lowering their food costs. Heart attacks decreased 26 percent from 1970 to 1983, and total cardiovascular diseases were down 40 percent as of 1987.[22] If the availability of cheap and nutritious sources of protein were promoted—just as beef has been for fifty years—there would be a mass defection from what Lappé calls the "Great American steak religion." Under the above principles, the cost of the average American meal would go down as the nutritional value went up. Many would opt for a good Oriental style meal, balanced to include the essential amino acids to build protein. This is "just what the doctor ordered"—reduce meat and fat intake and increase the consumption of grains,

---

* Processing food consumes capital and labor while lowering the nutritional value. The price per unit of nutrition can only be more expensive, not cheaper.

fruit, and vegetables. The variety of foods is far greater with a vegetable- and grain-rich diet than with a meat-based one, and meat need not be eliminated, only reduced. After all, there are only a few cuts of meat available, whereas an estimated 350,000 vegetables can be developed for food.[23]

## It Was Done with the Best of Intentions

In the design of all this waste in agriculture, there was no conspiracy or intention to harm other people. When this country was being settled, it was the dream of every settler to own his own land. Here was all this "virgin country" and few people. (The U.S. is still relatively underpopulated and, if Lappé's concepts were used, about 15 percent of the nation's farmland would feed the American people.) Farmers cleared the land and improved farming methods while scientists genetically increased agriculture's productive potential. To survive economically the farmers had to sell this surplus production, and politicians designed ways to market this unneeded food. Much ended up as "fed beef" consumed by Americans. Much was exported to dispossessed people who no longer controlled their own land, and thus could not feed themselves. We loaned their governments money to buy this food and this further enforced upon them the extraction and export of their natural resources to pay back this debt. This is a rerun of how earlier metropolitan centers substituted "trading for raiding" as a means of obtaining resources from other countries (see Book Two)[24]

Not only is much of the production of U.S. agriculture for export unnecessary, but it results in great harm to the very people we profess to be helping. In 1974 we exported over 60 million tons of grain, of which only 3.3 million tons were aid, and most of that did not reach the starving.[25] For example, during the past six years 84 percent of our agricultural exports to Latin America was given to the local governments to sell to the people. This undersold local producers, destroyed their markets, and reduced their production. What we believe to be aid is actually destroying those countries' local economies.[26] This trade is for *our* benefit, not *theirs,* and it—along with other methods of "plunder by trade"—is a direct cause of the hunger of the world's dispossessed people.

A large share of the world's food problem is because we must sell, rather than that they must buy. This places a heavy burden on those already impoverished countries. The cost to our own economy is also high. The U.S. is losing 1 percent of its topsoil per year due to intensive farming practices. The value of this fertility loss is estimated at twenty dollars per acre per year. At that rate, America's soil fertility will be exhausted in one hundred years.[27] Thirty-two million acres are irrigated by groundwater, and in over half, the water table is falling over six inches per year. The giant Oglala aquifer irrigates almost half of these acres, and in north Texas, it is already almost exhausted. It is predicted that two-thirds of U.S. groundwater supplies will be depleted by the year 2020.[28] The elimination of both unnecessary farm production and the manufacturing capacity to produce that unneeded economic activity would result in the saving of valuable natural resources. It would also reduce the pollution created by these activities.

# Conclusion

The unneeded exports for the year 1983 amounted to $36 billion. The share of U.S. agriculture inefficiently and unnecessarily spent on fattening beef was about $10 billion.[29] That is a total of $46 billion worth of labor that need not have been expended if this society maximized its health, living standards, and free time. Instead of this waste, we ought to be able to make productive use of our social wealth, even while respecting others' right to theirs.

Dividing this $46 billion by an average wage of $20,000 (the American average is $17,500 and surely farm labor is well below the average) conservatively shows that 2.3 million farmers and their support workers would be free to share truly productive employment. That 2.3 million is, of course, more people than there are farmers. That extra labor is utilized in farming's extensive use of high-technology machinery, the labor to furnish the required supplies, and the labor that moves the produce to markets.

This chapter appears to bear out the farmers' image of being more productive than other workers. Eliminating the 35 percent of their production that is damaging other economies and America's health would still leave farming twice as efficient as any sector of the economy we have studied so far. However, agriculture is resource intensive. Where most segments of the economy waste largely labor, agriculture squanders a lot of capital and resources. These resources are critical to future generations, as well as to impoverished people throughout the world today.

# 5

# The Health Care Industry

With much justification, America's medical community claims to provide the best medical service in the world. Yet we have nine million children who lack routine medical care, eighteen million children have never visited a dentist, and thirty-five million uninsured people receive little or no health care. In the richest country in the world tens of millions have medical problems that go untreated. Despite this lack of proper medical care for 15 percent of its citizens, and a 40-percent reduction in time spent in hospitals, health care costs in 1985 rose to 10.8 percent of America's $4-trillion GNP.[1] In Great Britain, with free medical care for everybody, the cost for that year was only 5.1 percent of their much smaller GNP, or 54 percent cheaper than our privatized medical care.[2]

Mentioning socialized medicine triggers an instinctive defense from doctors. There are claims it is inefficient, provides poor care, and robs physicians of their independence and initiative. Yet a poll in 1984 showed that 87 percent of British citizens were satisfied with their health care, while 70 percent of Americans were *dissatisfied* with theirs.[3] Nonetheless, we continually hear about inferior British medical care. The medical community is practicing the same control of public perception as the insurance industry. These well-cared for and largely satisfied British citizens spend 54 percent less of their GNP than dissatisfied Americans, outlining another waste distribution territory.

That these territories are expanding, well-protected, and secure is shown by the 1987 report from the Department of Health and Human Services. Medical care rose from 10.8 percent of the GNP in 1985 to 10.9 percent in 1986 and to 11.1 percent in 1987, and is anticipated to take 15 percent by the year 2000. The study concluded that "changing patterns of use, rather than an aging population, will account for a large portion of the nation's health care costs . . . 'The magical new products medicine has produced have a cost to society.'"[4]

In no way do I claim the waste this exposes is the result of intent. These territories expand relentlessly in all segments of the economy. Businesses must operate at their maximum to maximize profits and people must maximize their labor time to earn a good living. The expansion of business and labor ensures that moral claim to more of what society has to offer. Psychiatrists Richard Bandler and John Grinder explain the process well in one statement in their book *Frogs Into Princes*. One of their fellow psychiatrists treated patients in a state clinic and averaged six visits per client, with few returning for more treatment. "In his private practice he is apt to see a client twelve or fifteen times . . . and it never dawned on him what caused that. . . . The more effective you are the less money you make. Because your clients get what they want and leave and don't pay you anymore."[5] The health industry mirrors this psychiatrist's practice. They are good conscientious people and unaware that it is the structure of the health industry that creates much unnecessary work.

Perhaps doctors appear unfairly portrayed, as there is an enormous infrastructure behind them that does most of the labor and creates most of the charges. However, they are the ones who are in direct contact with the patients and it is their organizations which dictate the direction of American health care.

## Examples of Waste that Expose the Pattern

In 1988 hospital bed occupancy averaged only 60 percent.[6] Private hospitals, like any businesses, must cover expenses and make a profit and they are trying interesting innovations to capture customers. A CBS news investigation of programs for youths with drug, alcohol, or mental problems discovered a system greedy for patients and willing to prey on parents' worst fears. Catchy ads announce, "There is nothing in this world that holds greater promise than a young life." On screen then appears "a good boy gone bad," accompanied by a hard sales pitch, with the hospitals claiming that they have the expertise to guide such otherwise lost youths back to the proper path.[7]

In this investigation, parents called hospitals advertising children's mental health care and outlined symptoms easily identified as those of a normally rebellious teenager. With one exception, they were told it sounded like the syndrome of alcohol or drug abuse. The hospitals could be excused for their statements if care had been taken to confirm these over-the-phone diagnoses. Instead, with no further checking into the endless possibilities of upsetting but normal behavior, their advice was to lock the child away for treatment.

The child used for this test fortunately did not have to endure the shattering emotional experience of institutionalization, but what about those who had no need for such care and were nonetheless entrapped? Overanxious parents could easily be the only problem. Once they responded to that ad, their child might be enmeshed in a system designed more for intercepting a share of society's production than for treating alcohol-dependent or chemical-dependent patients.

The horror of the scenario is compounded by these hospitals' inability to prove the efficiency of their recovery programs. Those left untreated seem to recover as quickly as those treated.[8] The personal cost to an individual trapped in one of these greedy territories can be enormous. A teenager, facing the traumatic experiences of all teens, is now faced with the image-shattering ordeal of institutionalization. This is a prescription for disaster. Self-confidence is essential to every person's mental health and I can think of few experiences more likely to shake anyone's confidence than being institutionalized.

An episode of the *Sally Jesse Raphael Show* featured young women who, at fourteen years of age, were unjustly institutionalized.[9] With remarkable insight, these young ladies figured out the fraud and outwitted the system. A member of the Minnesota Mental Health Association and patient advocate was instrumental in freeing one of these girls. He pointed out that when hospital occupancy declined they expanded into child care and "hospitals and psychiatrists were preying upon parents and children." Seventy-five hundred children per year were institutionalized in that state and "typically only those who had insurance were hospitalized and the cures and discharges came miraculously when the insurance ran out."

One mother on this show described how her outstanding son had been wrongly institutionalized and destroyed while another whose stepson caused continual havoc within the family avoided the worst of the system. This second family spent fifty thousand dollars with health professionals before learning about the self-help support group called "Tough Love." This commonsense group, similar to Alcoholics Anonymous, proved to be the answer. This boy had learned to gain attention by wreaking emotional havoc upon everybody and all he needed was firm control. Tough Love's suggestion of treating him firmly with "We love you but these are the rules" was the answer. Such simple and cheap answers could hardly pay the way for the mental health industry. The motivation is profits rather than caring for emotional needs:

> The average cost of a single episode of hospitalization in a private psychiatric hospital in Houston is $40,000. [But] equivalent care given through his center, which does not require hospitalization, costs an average of $3,200, less than one-tenth of the cost of hospital care. . . . Many children and adolescents with minor psychiatric problems are needlessly hospitalized when they could be treated more quickly, more inexpensively and at least as effectively outside the hospital . . . Indeed, hospitalization can be harmful . . . In the past five years *there has been a four-fold increase in the number of children and adolescents admitted to private, profit-making psychiatric hospitals,* even though there is no evidence that hospital care is superior to outside care.[10] (emphasis added)

As the law changed, troubled teenagers became big business. Large corporate chains like Charter Medical Corporation, the Hospital Corporation of America, the Comprehensive Care Corporation, and National Medical Enterprises are expanding their facilities into new states as quickly as local laws allow. "Private psychiatric beds for teenagers is the fastest growing segment of the hospital industry," says Dr. Jerry M. Winter, president of the American Academy of Child Care and Adolescent Psychiatry. In 1980 there were only 184 free-standing psychiatric hospitals, according to the National Institute of Mental Health; in 1988 there were 450.[11]

Unnecessary professional care is an example of trust in assigned authority. As we learned in insurance and law, and will see again in other segments of the economy, this claim to complexity and need for their technical knowledge is a trademark of all professions. Specialized knowledge is only a small part of their services; the rest is made necessary by keeping it mysterious. Like the witch doctors and medicine men of old, these modern-day medicine men ply their trade. As Fred Rodell recognized of the legal profession, "They blend technical competence with plain and fancy hocus-pocus to make them masters of their fellow man." Greater use of hospitals provides more labor for doctors and the medical support structure. Those unnecessary services validate their claim to a larger share of what others produce; providing essential human services seems to have become secondary. The unnecessary burden put upon society and the damage inflicted upon unfortunate people are blanked out of the consciousness of those who benefit financially.

*Newsweek* editor Gregg Easterbrook began the research for his treatise "The Revolution in Medicine" with the conventional belief that modern technology caused this great expense. Looking behind the scenes, he detected more mundane reasons for these costs:

> Though only a cynic would contend that the typical physician thinks, "Guess I'll run up a few needless tests to pad my bill," every doctor knows at some subconscious level that additional procedures are financially beneficial—and human nature dictates that what is in the back of the mind can be as influential as what is in front. . . . The incentives were to keep people in the hospital, to perform more tests and procedures, to increase costs. . . . [These] X-rays and bloodpanels [are] high-markup products that are hospital cash cows. . . . customary fee [became] a phrase that can mean almost anything a doctor wanted it to mean. The more the health-care system ran up the bill, the more it would profit. . . . "It was nirvana. Everybody charged what they wanted."[12]

## Routine Operations

> It was an ominous sign that [operation] procedures most beneficial for the surgeons themselves seemed to grow at the fastest rate. Through the 1970s, for example, the frequency of heart operations for men tripled; the coronary bypass came into widespread use. Researchers now question whether the bypass is really worth it for many recipients—life is prolonged for just one in 10. But bypass operations are unquestionably worth it for surgeons, whose fees average $5,000 for a few hours' work. . . . [The necessity is further questioned when] fee-for-service surgeons, for example, are twice as likely to perform a coronary bypass as HMO [Health Maintenance Organizations] surgeons.[13]

In a 1985 investigation, the Senate's Special Committee on Aging charged that unnecessary operations for hernias, hemorrhoids, gallstones, enlarged prostates, heart disease and other conditions were cutting short the lives of thousands of Americans and wasting billions of dollars. Significantly, these operations increased 130 percent after Medicare was enacted. The American College of Surgeons and the American Surgical Association concluded that 4.5 million operations per year—30 percent of the total—are unnecessary, and an additional 50 percent perhaps beneficial but not essential to save or extend life. Assuming only *half* the expected mortality rate, that would cause about 30,000 needless deaths a year.[14] One example would be stripping the carotid artery that supplies blood to the brain; this has a moderately high risk of death and has been judged "one-third unnecessary and one-third questionable."[15]

Another study done by John and Sonja McKinlay of Boston University found that localities with fewer doctors had lower mortality rates. More significant is that during hospital strikes in the U.S., Canada, Great Britain, and Israel, the death rates went down. (In the Israeli and New York strikes, the hospitalization rate dropped 85 percent.) "It was as if the population were in better health when medical care was limited to emergencies."[16]

A doctor in Los Angeles studying hysterectomies unearthed the following unsettling statistics: in 88 percent of the cases, the need to operate was not established; in 48.2 percent, the only indication was a "backache"; in 5.4 percent, "there were no symptoms at all"; and in fully 60 percent the operations were not justified. In spite of the severe health problems caused by depriving the body of essential hormones, "they take it out and examine afterwards."[17]

That 50 percent of these operations are unnecessary is demonstrated by comparing the U.S. system with British medical practice. Not working under the *cut-for-a-fee* system, surgeons there operate only one-half as often as their American counterparts. I know of no evidence that suggests the British would be better off with twice the number of operations. Instead, the free medical care would suggest that their doctors are only operating when necessary.

Except that their medicine is "socialized," British medical practice is comparable to ours. Like us, they practice curative rather than preventive medicine. If they were to evolve to a truly socially responsible medical policy of preventive medicine, they would lower their costs much further even as they live more wholesome, disease-free lives.

## Births

In 1984, over 20 percent of the births in the U.S. were Caesarean, twice the rate of ten years earlier; by 1988 they were almost 25 percent. Caesarean births generate much higher fees and require twice the length of hospitalization. They are also hazardous and an open invitation to further medical complications.[18] Experts on animal husbandry would know they were dealing with a disaster long before problem births reached 10 percent and only a small percent of these would require Caesarean deliveries.* Nor did these operations improve infant mortality rates. In 1971, the U.S. ranked fourteenth from the top while Holland ranked third. Most births in Holland occur at home with the help of midwives, and hospitals are used only if problems are foreseen.[19] This much lower mortality rate with home delivery exposes the unnecessarily dangerous and expensive U.S. practice of handling most births as surgical procedures in hospitals.

## Defensive Medicine

In 1983, due to the high cost of malpractice insurance, 6 percent of the obstetricians quit and 25 percent had abandoned this practice by 1989. Many of the almost 25 percent of all births that are by Caesarean section are performed by doctors trying to avoid being sued. In short, many times those assaults on mothers are because lawyers are winning multi-million-dollar childbirth malpractice suits.[20] Other defense strategies are X rays, exploratory surgery, and blood tests.[21] These defensive practices have been estimated as accounting for 25 percent of America's health bill.[22]

## Drugs

A Senate subcommittee hearing in 1977 concluded that 30,000 people died each year from adverse reactions to prescribed drugs, while other studies sug-

---

* The medical community is now being advised not to use Caesarean section except in emergencies, even when the mother has had a previous Caesarean section.

gested 100,000.[23] Expecting to disprove such damning indictments, the Pharmacists Association and the American Medical Association (AMA) conducted their own investigation. They were astonished when their own study showed that "Medications in hospitals alone killed from 60,000 to 140,000 Americans per year, and make 3.5 million others more or less seriously ill."[24]

A study by the National Institutes of Health found that 60 percent of all medication and 80 to 90 percent of all antibiotics used were unnecessary and "the federal government in 1980 estimated that only one Valium prescription in thirty was really medically necessary." A British study showed that "More than half of all adults and almost a third of all children take medication every day. Yet 90% of the time people get well (or can get well) without therapeutic intervention."[25]

This unwholesome dependence on drugs quite regularly damages individuals or particular groups of people. The notorious sedative thalidomide caused 16,000 infant deaths and led to another 8,000 children being born without arms or legs.[26] And the anti-arthritic pill Oraflex killed 124 before it was pulled off the market.[27]

Even more tragic are the possibly 300,000 who developed tardive dyskinesia from drugs prescribed to treat various mental illnesses. These people suffered severe nerve damage, creating uncontrollable muscle spasms, jerky movements, tongue-biting, and difficulty in walking and virtually every human activity as all require control of the nervous system.[28]

Another drug, diethylstilbestrol (DES), was extensively prescribed from 1945 to 1970 for pregnant women to prevent miscarriages. The unwanted side effects include daughters who are unable to conceive and who are susceptible to a whole range of cancers (ovarian, cervical, vaginal, etc.); sterile sons with genital and urinary defects; and increased cancers, blood clots, and strokes in the women treated.[29]

Even more damaging is Depo-Provera. It was designed as a long-lasting birth control injection; although it was never approved in this country for that purpose, through a loophole in the law it continues to be marketed. It causes "permanent sterility, irregular bleeding, decreased libido, depression, high blood pressure, excessive weight gain or loss, breast tenderness, vaginal infections, hair loss, stomach pains, blurred vision, joint pain, facial hair, acne, cramps, diarrhea, skin rash, tiredness, and swelling of the limbs."[30]

Besides the thousands of chemical drugs on the market that cause these unwanted reactions, there are three thousand different antibiotics with thirty thousand derivatives. Yet experienced clinicians judge that from two to four dozen basic drugs would suffice for 98 to 99 percent of drug-treatable illnesses.[31] Indiscriminate use of these antibiotics has produced many drug-resistant bacteria. These tough germs now cause one hundred thousand deaths per year, and they are still increasing. Significantly, the death rate from one of these resistant diseases—bacteremia—is now up to pre-antibiotic levels.[32] Most such problems are avoided by countries like Czechoslovakia and China, which use only ten to fifteen antibiotics for all their health needs, saving the potent ones for emergencies.[33]

> Investigators today liken our natural flora to a protective carpet that is an integral part of our anatomy. Remove the carpet, and you strip away one of the critical layers of our body's defense system, leaving us dramatically more vulnerable to infection.[34]

Inside one's body (and outside) there is an ecological balance of microorganisms that is the key to good health. These "normal bacteria provide a natural host defense mechanism against infection, [and] only occasionally, in well-understood diseases when the balance is upset, is medical intervention helpful."[35] Many times it is antibiotics which create this imbalance. Given hygienic living conditions and nutrition, good health is the normal condition of man and animal. Interfering unnecessarily with the human organism is most likely damaging.

## Medical Technology and Patents

One million older Americans have cataract surgery each year at a cost of four billion dollars, of which two billion is considered overcharge. One-third of these operations are unnecessary, and Medicare is being charged anywhere from $310 to $700 for an interocular lens valued at $50. To sell these overpriced products, salespeople were offering doctors kickbacks through bank accounts in Barbados.[36] So "The Great Pacemaker Scandal" is not an isolated event.

In 1980 a pacemaker salesman offered Dr. Richard Blum of Colorado Springs five hundred dollars each time he removed a competing company's unit from his patients and installed one this salesman was promoting. Blum promptly threw him out and notified Medicare. This led to a congressional investigation, which uncovered "The Great Pacemaker Scandal." An army of four hundred salespeople was involved. Some were making more than $1 million per year by offering bribes, kickbacks, and junkets to Europe or the Caribbean. For this purpose, a yacht and a fleet of airplanes and helicopters were kept ready.[37] These doctors' fees were as high as $2,500 for a simple operation for which specialists said $500 was more realistic. Medicare was charged $3,425 for the pacemakers, while Europeans paid one-third as much. (Even that is too high. How does one justify $1,100 for what amounts to an electronic watch when its predecessor, the more complicated electronic wristwatch, sells for $3 to $15?) Untrained doctors, with limited knowledge of pacemakers, heart operations, or even the heart itself, were attempting to install these devices without ever having witnessed the operation before. At times, the salesperson had to show the doctor how to operate.[38]

Compounding the charge that the operation was three to five times too expensive were studies that showed 30 to 75 percent were unnecessary. Some of these unneeded pacemakers caused serious aftereffects. Shirley Morehead of Tucson, Arizona, went through six operations and spent sixty thousand dollars before her last doctor informed her that her heart was perfectly healthy. Morehead was only one of over two hundred thousand Americans who, by 1983, had unneeded pacemakers installed.[39]

Being paid for overpriced and unneeded pacemakers and operations is only a particularly dramatic way of intercepting social production, but it bears looking at carefully.* Four hundred salespeople, thousands of doctors, and countless other people must have known about this particular scam. Yet until Richard Blum blew the whistle, no one breathed a word. Some have suggested the motivation was simply greed. That is involved but none of this is that different from what is

---

* How the patent system is designed to monopolize technology is addressed in depth in Book Three, chapter two, and will not be covered here. However, monopolization of patents is the guiding principle behind these examples of overpriced medical technology.

*normal* in every waste distribution territory. It was just a little more dishonest, because both the financial and physical damages were directly traceable to doctors' unnecessary operations and overcharges. Though most unnecessary work that is done is not as visible as this dramatic example, every nonproductive claim upon social production involves measurable damage to society. We are roughly estimating that loss in wasted labor, capital, and resources. The loss in quality of life is unmeasurable.

## The Greater the Need, the Higher the Charge

Few have challenged or even recognized the unfair tax upon the unfortunate created by vastly overpriced products and services. There is a consistent pattern; the greater the need, the greater the overcharge. Though the need of the handicapped is great, they are quite powerless to defend themselves. The first efforts to develop mechanical aids for these unfortunate people were undoubtedly undertaken with noble intentions. Typically no profit was involved and much labor and time was donated as generous people tried to help the unfortunate. However, those who knew the value of these aids claimed patent rights and the handicapped now must pay them forever. Witness the hearing aids mentioned in the introduction. Each is only a tiny amplifier, yet it costs ten to twenty times as much as a radio, which is hundreds of times larger and much more complicated.

There is a similar overcharge for other badly needed aids for disadvantaged people. For example, the reading glasses I am wearing: they work beautifully and only cost five dollars at a "fit yourself" self-service counter. A pair obtained through an eye specialist for over two hundred dollars were useless. That particular misfit was no doubt an exception—the overcharge wasn't.

The same overcharges are present with patented drugs which are critical to patient treatment. Witness the prescription drug MPTP. With the first clue that it might be of benefit in treating Parkinson's disease, the price skyrocketed from eleven dollars a gram to ninety-five hundred dollars.[40] This scene was replayed when AZT (azidithymidine) showed promise in controlling the AIDS virus. The cost to these desperate people, trying to save their lives, shot up to ten thousand dollars per year. This high price is not for developing this drug. "The discovery was made at the National Cancer Institute lab in Detroit and all original research was done at U.S. government expense."[41]

The tens of thousands of patented drugs and antibiotics on the market are "molecular manipulations" of already available and inexpensive medications. These drugs are astoundingly cheap to manufacture. It is the patents that preserve them as private property and entitle the owners (not the discoverers) to charge all the market will bear.[42] They are promoted to doctors and the public at high costs. The problem is identical to our exports (see Book One, chapter four, and Book Two, chapter one). It is imperative that a product be sold even though it may be of little use to the buyer, so doctors are inundated with promotional material to the tune of thousands of dollars per doctor.[43]

Trade names are a special territory within the larger drug business. These brand name drugs normally sell for much more than an identical generic drug. Druggists, noting the large price spread, started pocketing the difference.[44] If one segment of the economy doesn't overcharge, it seems inevitable that another will take up the slack.

The prices noted for mechanical, electrical, and chemical medical services are above the true value of the labor involved in developing, manufacturing, and distributing these essential products. A mechanical, electrical, or chemical engineer could quickly expose these high-priced items as simple, inexpensive technology. Those competing pacemakers, interocular lenses, hearing aids, and other devices to aid a defective body would be far cheaper and of higher quality if they were distributed through a public authority responsible for the needs of the nation's handicapped. The inventors, who now receive little, could be paid by a formula reflecting the benefits to society. High pressure sales and waste would be replaced by a calm, sensible process of invention, engineering, education, and cheaper distribution. There should be no need to make fortunes on others' misfortunes.

## Title to Medical Techniques

Peer pressure, prestige, and the need to draw customers ensure that hospitals will purchase expensive medical machines. There seems to be an "insatiable desire to one-up each other on technology, and fascination with gadgetry in competition with other health providers."[45] They then must generate revenue to cover those costs.

In addition to patents for these medical machines and drugs, ownership of techniques is gaining much attention. Corporations are being formed to patent embryo transfers, gene splicing, and other advanced medical procedures. Any doctor or hospital wishing to use this new knowledge will have to obtain a special license and pay a royalty.[46] This added tax, though common to medical equipment, drugs, etc., has not, up to this time, been an added cost for an operation. If ownership of operations had been established years ago, every bill for almost any operation would have royalties tacked on to pay whoever owned those patented procedures. Every future improvement in an operational procedure will be patented. Just like the stratified charge engine described earlier, the monopoly on these processes will never run out. The high profit from owning technology (patents) is being duplicated by claiming title to techniques.

## Piecework

Business has long recognized the efficiency of paying for production by piecework. The more units a worker completes within a specified time, the higher his or her pay, with no increase in unit cost to the employer. However, the boss invariably either controls the piecework price or negotiates with the laborer on it.

Medicine is lucrative for owners and practitioners precisely because patients have nothing whatever to say about cost. That decision is made entirely by those being paid. Any boss knows that if those he paid had the last word on how much they received, his business would quickly go bankrupt. This is the well-publicized financial condition of Medicare, Medicaid, and most people who have had extensive medical treatment.

# Waste from Insurance Rules

Standard hospitalization insurance does not pay for out-patient care. A study by the Rand Corporation found that 40 percent of hospital admissions were inappropriate because they involved simple procedures which could have been handled just as well in a doctor's office.[47] These same policies usually require X rays and other tests before they pay on claims. This is often an unnecessary, time-consuming, and wasteful practice that is part of the 25 percent of health care costs attributed to defensive medicine.

# The High Cost of Peer Loyalty

Physicians seem to be willing to pay an absurdly high price for the notion of professional loyalty.... Doctors rarely report peers to state license boards, and not because they don't know who to report.... Everybody in the hospital, and I mean everybody, knows who the bad doctors are years before their names show up in the paper.... In Pennsylvania more than 25 percent of malpractice payments were accounted for by 1 percent of practicing physicians. A good bet is that this 1 percent comprises a guided tour of the state's bad doctors.... [These] doctors get to fob their mistakes off onto a pool of funds underwritten by the majority, and they keep right on practicing.[48]

Incompetent doctors are responsible for most malpractice claims. If it were social policy, it would be a simple process to discover who they are, have them properly trained, and restrict them to procedures in which they are competent or revoke their licenses.

# The High Cost of Dying

Twenty-eight percent of America's medical bills are incurred during the last year of life:[49]

Until our era the vast majority of Americans died at home. Today 80 percent die in hospitals.... An estimated 10,000 Americans are being sustained in what doctors call "persistent vegetative state." Maintaining life in an ICU [intensive care unit] costs a minimum of $100,000 dollars annually. That's roughly 1 billion dollars per year to keep heartbeats present in the forever comatose.... [When the respirator was developed,] use was to be temporary; the idea that someone would be hooked up and left there was not in the plan.... it simply became the next standard step, as the terminally ill deteriorated, to pass them up the line to ICU.[50]

In the survival time of terminally ill patients, there is no statistical difference between home care and hospital care.[51] Companionship and care of relatives, the comfort of a familiar environment, the security of religion, and narcotics to relieve pain could equal or exceed hospital care during a patient's last days.

Almost universally these patients have made it clear that they would prefer a quiet, dignified death. Yet to extend life a few more days, terminal patients are kept on life support systems, spending more than a person can normally expect to save in a lifetime. Our heroic efforts are a function of current ideology and social structure. In Holland, where voluntary euthanasia is a practical option for the terminally ill, one out of six chooses it rather than face a tortured, painful death.[52]

Is this not strange? In this country it is not normal to support a terminally ill patient's right to a dignified death and a doctor would be considered negligent if he or she failed to make every effort to keep the person alive a few more days—even if it costs tens or hundreds of thousands of dollars. At the same time, there is no adequately functioning mechanism for calling this same doctor to account when unnecessary exploratory surgery, invasive treatment, or drug prescription causes death in a healthy individual who could otherwise have lived for many more years.

## Corporations Take Over

Harold Luft, a health economist at the University of California, notes that, "Classic economic competition would leave you to believe that the more competition the lower the cost. In fact, what we found was the more competition the higher the cost."[53] Just as described in chapter three and again addressed in Book Three, chapter two, there are *competitive monopolies* functioning in corporate medicine that increase, rather than decrease, labor and costs.

With the collection mechanism in place and intercepting 11.1 percent of the nation's GNP, it is no surprise that corporations take notice. After all, they are designed to organize the production of products and services. They are even better designed to guide the distribution of any social surplus to corporate owners, managers, and employees. In 1950

> individuals paid 65 percent of health costs; government paid 22 percent; private insurance, at 9 percent, was barely a factor . . . [By] 1985, federal state and local funds underwrote more than 40 percent of medical costs. Private insurance pays slightly more than 30 percent; individuals pay slightly less than 30 percent out of their own pockets. . . . wherever government guarantees tread, corporations are sure to follow. In the wake of Medicare the for-profit chains would form.[54]

Corporate takeovers of medical complexes, hospitals, nursing homes, hospital supply and food companies, and pharmaceutical companies are all a step in the direction of rationalizing the nation's disorganized health care system. A few large corporations manufacturing expensive technical equipment and producing drugs eliminates much organizational waste and theoretically provides cheaper patient care per hour than a fragmented system.

However, there is a fundamental flaw—the corporate owners of the facilities, tools, and services must maximize their use and price to maximize their profits. There is a direct conflict between the pursuit of health and the pursuit of wealth.[55] If they have their way, the pharmaceuticals, surgical procedures, and hospital corporations they own or control will be used at a level well beyond true need.

Corporations with interlocking directors representing all the facets of health care and wielding immense political power are in a prime position to intercept an ever larger share of the nation's production. It is done under the umbrella of providing an essential service. When an unsuspecting patient makes an office call he or she can become stuck in a spider web designed to feed corporate coffers. The cheaper patient care per hour can turn (and is turning) into a battle for society's financial life. The ad campaign of one of the large hospital corporations, Humana Inc., explains the process:

> The corporation, it would seem, is seeking more revenue from one of its underutilized operating rooms by playing, as ads have always played, on the weaknesses and insecurities of frail humanity. But this time it's not a cosmetic or a mouthwash that's being hawked—it's invasive surgery that, even under conditions of necessity, should not be lightly undertaken. But corporate practice calls for each branch of the "operation" (the appropriate word here) to earn its share of profits. Staff surgeons must cut; hospital beds must be filled. Besides, who can really hold a corporation responsible for what an individual freely chooses to do? The surgery will in every way be voluntary.[56]

Corporate divisions must be kept busy, regardless of whether the services they provide are needed. In 1985 advertisements doubled when the nation's hospital bed occupancy dropped to 64 percent. Some ads even boasted of first class accommodations and gourmet chefs.[57] But there are more direct methods of assuring maximum use of corporate hospital space:

> The understanding was that the doctor would refer his patients to the company hospital and make use of the company's facilities for medical tests, X-rays, and so on. . . . But two years later the physician was confronted with a punitive raise in rent. He had been made to understand that the corporate executives had not been pleased with the small number of patients he had admitted to the hospital—a physician's badge of honor in any other circumstances—or with the small volume of tests he had ordered. He was now encouraged to leave the glamorous office in the corporation building and hang his shingle elsewhere.[58]

This quotation describes the instinctive development and protection common to all waste distribution territories. Few doctors would fight such a system—especially when they receive a share of the profit from prescriptions and operations. Corporate doctors and other employees become an integral part of a system designed more to intercept money than to be productive. Not surprisingly, a government study concluded that "Only one hospitalization in eight was medically indicated."[59] In the corporate patronage system, anyone who does not fit the mold is soon weeded out. Conservative medication and preventive medicine are not even considerations.

Corporate political power is especially dangerous. If the government can be induced to continue financing those who cannot pay for their own health insurance, there will be a guaranteed stream of money, much like that which feeds the notorious military-industrial complex. It is a familiar pattern—milking the public treasury.

Passing laws favoring one's own company is the simplest way to intercept social production. Then one need only run wide open and maximize income. So long as political control can be maintained, this is a mortgage on the nation's wealth and taxes are the guarantee of payment. Such a policy benefits corporations like Hospital Corporation of America. They own 230 hospitals, manage another 196, and receive 44 percent of their revenue from Medicare and Medicaid.[60] Janitors, bookkeepers, nurses—all people employed within this industry—are as much a part of the protected territory as the doctors, corporate owners, and executives. No matter how small the wage, their living depends upon defending against the least suggestion that the system is not fully productive.

In corporate medicine, the thirty-five million Americans who are now outside the protection of private or public insurance can be ignored. It is normal procedure to turn away those who are not insured or who cannot give assurance that they are able to pay. Normally, the critically ill are stabilized before being transferred to a public hospital. Yet some of those who are denied admittance do not survive the transfer and in two such documented instances the patients drove themselves to another hospital before dying.[61]

## Iatrogenic Illness

According to the U.S. Department of Health and Human Services, 7 percent of all patients hospitalized in the U.S. are further sickened because of that hospitalization.[62] Ivan Illich offers evidence that as many as 20 percent of all who enter a university hospital contract an iatrogenic (doctor-caused) illness. He insists research hospitals are "relatively more pathogenic, or, in blunt language, more sickening . . . with an accident rate like that on his record a military officer would quickly be relieved of his command; a restaurant or a night club would be closed down by the police."[63] With lowered resistance, sick people are vulnerable to infections, so those contracted during a hospital stay should not all be counted. However, unnecessary operations, illness contracted during unnecessary hospitalization, and serious side effects of excessive or unneeded drugs must be counted.

One surprising iatrogenic illness is viral hepatitis, contracted from transfusions with infected blood. The risks from this routine practice are high.[*] The 190,000 infected annually suffer permanent damage and many die. Since the use of donor blood for surgical patients is mostly unnecessary, this tragedy is avoidable. Laser technology that will cauterize the cut is here now and there are doctors who, recycling the patient's blood, operate routinely and never use donor blood.[64]

When first introduced, blood transfusions saved countless lives. But the technology is here to eliminate a large share of that procedure. Another economic territory of distribution through unnecessary labor has established itself within the medical community. "These blood banks can be intensely competitive, luring donors with ad campaigns and vying for lucrative hospital contracts."[65]

## Alienated and Lonesome

General practitioners say that 75% of all patients have no organic lesion and come to the doctor looking *for comfort at least as much as treatment.* These sick people have no clinically definable disease, even though their troubles are real and can lead to organic lesions. Doctors call them "functionally ill" or "psychosomatic," and more often than not are willing to treat their symptoms with expensive and poisonous medications. That is where the fraud comes in. In effect, these truly ill *people who have no definable disease are most often people who can't cope any more and come to ask for help and exemption from duty.* In another age they

---

[*] A new test has just been devised to discover this virus in donor blood, so this iatrogenic illness should significantly decrease.

would doubtless have gone to confession, made a pilgrimage, or immersed themselves in prayer. . . . And the doctor, in most cases, will play the game and treat as
a chemically treatable illness what is basically merely the incapacity of the
patient to bear the situation he or she has to face. . . . [Such an illness is more accurately understood as] the inevitable response of a healthy individual to a situation that is not.[66] (emphasis in original)

Society should be structured to support these alienated, lonely people. Part of
the answer lies in each person's gaining the right to productive employment,
earning both self-respect and a fair share of what society produces. The increased
free time available through the elimination of wasted labor would permit the
restructuring of society and better integrate these people. Properly structured,
this could do away with much of their need for a medical crutch.

## Preventive Hygiene

Good hygiene has more to do with health than does high-tech medicine.
Through good hygiene, cholera and typhoid practically disappeared before the
organisms that caused them were isolated. Scarlet fever, diphtheria, and whoop-
ing cough declined 90 percent before vaccinations and antibiotics were introduced. After the introduction of these modern medicines, the frequency of these
diseases continued to decline at the same pace. Tuberculosis declined 75 percent
before the first sanatorium was built. This same pattern holds for scarlet fever,
typhus, smallpox, diarrhea, and dysentery. For these diseases, the introduction
of modern medicine is virtually invisible on statistical charts.[67]

As opposed to technical cures, purifying water, installing sewers, removing
slums, exterminating rats, eating good food, using toilet paper and soap, washing
hands, and sterilizing medical tools and supplies all contributed to better health
through good hygiene. "The piping in of drinking water and literacy" alone are
calculated to be responsible for 85.5 percent of the differences in life expectancies
of different societies. Corporations have learned that for every dollar spent on
educating their workers on preventive health care (diet, on-site health clubs, exercise sessions, etc.) $2.32 is saved on insurance claims.[68] The medical com-
munity has been taking credit for what is properly credited to society for
providing a more wholesome environment, better food, and potable water. Investing money in a more hygienic environment and nutritious food will provide more
handsome returns to society than most investments in medicine. The problem is
the financial incentives are all skewed towards overmedication:

> Surgeons average about $1,000 per hour. An internist who spends an hour coun-
> seling a patient to alter his lifestyle in order to avoid future surgery will be lucky if
> he can bill $50. Medicare pays around $1,400 for a 45-minute cataract extraction
> and about $22 for 45 minutes of physical examination and diagnosis. "Scopes"
> pushed inside joints or organs pay more than "scans," viewing the inner body
> without breaching it. Anytime a doctor sticks something into someone, he receives
> a bonus. . . . "In medicine doing the right thing often doesn't pay very well."[69]

## Prevention, Not Cure

Migrating populations duplicating the health of their countries of origin demonstrate that degenerative diseases have social and political causes. "Cardiovascular diseases, hypertension, and, in particular, hypercholesterol are very rare in so-called primitive people, no matter what their ages. They afflict the aging in our [developed] civilizations alone."[70] An analysis of mortality tables shows that 68 percent of all deaths in the U.S. are from degenerative diseases and cancer.[71] Heart disease fell 26 percent from 1970 to 1983 and strokes 48 percent, mostly the result of improved lifestyles.[72] By 1987, cardiovascular disease had declined 40 percent.[73] That reduction, recognized by the medical community to be the result of improved lifestyles, shows that if our society were restructured to preventive medicine, citizens are ready and willing to do their part. Yet, despite their inability to prevent or cure most debilitating sicknesses, it is chemical and surgical medicine that is now social policy.

Even as the American people achieve such dramatic health improvements through prevention, the cost of medical care for cardiovascular disease continues to rise rapidly—$72.1 billion in 1985, and $85.2 billion in 1986. Those waste distribution territories are in place and expanding according to rules governed by the need of the medical community for income, not the health needs of the people.

What most doctors now call "prevention" consists of finding "the disease" as quickly as possible, so they can work their surgical and chemical cures. In contrast, prevention involves a social commitment to wholesome living conditions: eliminating air and water pollution; eating unadulterated, natural foods; and exercising regularly. People are concerned about pollution but do nothing about it because there is no easy way to take meaningful action. Industries that profit by dumping poisons into the air and water still have the controlling voice. Adulterated and denatured foods are similarly protected by a powerful constituency. If society is to lower the risk of environmentally caused diseases, they must organize for political control.

## Positive Structures to Build On

Health Maintenance Organizations (HMOs) are a step in the right direction, but their doctors are still trained in curative, not preventive, medicine. They serve about 11 percent of the population and are saving about 25 percent on health care costs.[74] This rational approach to reducing health care expenditures draws bitter opposition from those providing expensive and unnecessary medical services.

The dental profession has been in the forefront of preventive medicine:

> The National Institute of Dental Research found that dental cavities have declined by 36 percent among children ages 5 to 17, and that 49.9 percent of these children had no tooth decay at all. . . . It is declining 35 to 36 percent every seven years.[75]

> Any child today should be able to live a lifetime with his or her natural teeth intact. . . . treatment needs of kids are now minuscule and the bulk of treatment needs lie with the 45- to 75-year-olds.[76]

Dentists are one of the bright spots within the professions. But "the effect is showing by a decline in their business. . . . Some dental professionals point to a *busyness problem and the need to fill dental chairs*" and have branched out into more exotic areas of orthodontics (emphasis added).[77] As the efficiency of their labor increases, they too are turning to unnecessary labor for survival.

## The Most Effective Medicine Is Cheap and Simple

"Nine-tenths of all effective medical knowledge consists of simple, inexpensive treatment that is within the capability of any motivated lay person who can read directions."[78] People should be taught to be responsible for their own health and to use simple medical techniques. For problems they do not understand, there should be screening clinics to separate the 10 percent of the patients who need a specialist from those who can either doctor themselves or be treated then and there. The use of expensive, high-tech medicine for illnesses with simple cures is custom and hocus-pocus. The mystery must be eliminated. Medical technology should, of course, be maintained and improved for the 10 percent who truly need it, but for the rest the less medicine the better:

> In nine cases out of ten, there is no point in having a medical professional diagnose and treat a common illness. The symptoms are clear, the remedies well-known and very cheap, and if they promote healing, these medical professionals are not necessary for healing. Also, in China it only takes three weeks to train a "barefoot doctor," who while continuing to work as a factory or farm laborer, will know how to treat common afflictions, dispense medications (for which he or she is perfectly able to recognize the counterindications and incompatibilities), and recognize the cases that require a specialist; and all this with an accuracy that arouses the admiration of western doctors who have been on the spot. . . . According to the director of the World Health Organization, the diagnosis and treatment of skin diseases can be learned in a week by anyone with a college degree.[79]

Cooperative social policies are much more effective than corporate policy for eliminating diseases. Preventive medicine is effective in China, where leprosy has been reduced 80 percent, even while the fifteen million cases worldwide are increasing.[80] To the credit of China's social policies, venereal disease is also almost extinct.[81]

## Conclusion

Most of the overcharges described are nourished by the social structure of medicine, not human greed or incompetence. If the prevailing mystification of rather simple health problems could be dispelled, the community would be on an equal footing with those who control the secrets of medical care. Doctors' moral claim to much of their income would be exposed as seriously deficient, and society could be restructured to eliminate the waste and damage of excessive medication. The public and screening clinics could handle most health problems and doctors could then concentrate their time and expertise on the 10 percent of medical problems that are complex and require their care.

If these changes were carried out, the public's health would improve rapidly, the cost of medicine would drop precipitously, and many employed within the medical profession would be freed for productive work. The secretive, private system of medicine needs to be changed to one based on people taught to take primary responsibility for their health. Those with special needs (10 percent) would be directed to specialists. The chemical-based, curative approach would be replaced by an emphasis on disease prevention, which would be rooted in a broad social commitment to a clean environment, nutritious food, and regular exercise. The apathetic could not avoid the benefits: the food would be more nutritious; the environment kept clean; healthy habits would become customary; and under peer pressure most would conform. Though business would be free to produce as they chose, their efforts would be towards the same goals as society as there is where the market would be.

The 54-percent greater cost of American health care, compared to Great Britain's roughly comparable system, measures unnecessary operations, unneeded medicines, iatrogenic diseases, and overcharges. It does not measure the potential gains from preventive medicine, improved lifestyles, and a clean environment. For those, I will conservatively allow a further 35 percent potential savings. This leaves plenty of slack for the scores of technical, ideological, and defensive objections that are sure to be raised to these proposals. To be credible, those objections will have to address the 68 percent of deaths from degenerative diseases that even the medical profession admits are preventable.

This basic restructuring of American medical practice would bring the potential savings to about 70 percent of the $400 billion our nation now spends annually on what we are accustomed to calling health care. Saving $280 billion would leave $120 billion for legitimate care of those with real needs. Using an average wage of $20,000 per year, the potential savings of labor in the medical community, including the many support workers, would be fourteen million workers.

This is a large figure, to be sure, but we should not forget how these waste distribution territories expand. Medical care in America has no tradition of community control. This territory has been wide open to expansion of the superior rights of the profession. With a different set of rights, the right to work productively, doctors could evaluate differently. They might ask, could this patient have been healthy through improved lifestyle? Could he or she have diagnosed and treated himself or herself if the information had been easily available? Could a screening center have handled this problem? If they would ask themselves those questions, motivated, alert, *preventive* doctors would have no problem agreeing with the wasted labor outlined above.

# 6

# Poverty and Rights:
# The Struggle to Survive

By this time, we should be familiar with the sincerity with which people will protect the economic territory that provides them their livelihood. Besides the necessity of a job for survival, people need to feel they are good and useful to society. Few ever admit, even to themselves, that their hard work may not be fully productive. This same emotional shield requires most people to say with equal sincerity that those on welfare are "lazy, ignorant, and nonfunctional."

Those above the poverty level vigorously insist they are honest and productive and fulfill a social need. It is important to their emotional well-being that they believe this. They dare not admit that their segment of the economy may have 30 to 70 percent more workers than necessary and that the dispossessed should have a relatively equal share of jobs and income. This would expose their own redundancy and, under current social rules, undermine their moral claim to their share. They would have to find another territory within the economy or drop into poverty themselves.

## Someone Else Owns Their Piece of Earth

Few poor people own land upon which to stand, sit, lie down, raise their family, or be buried. Most must pay tribute to a landowner for every social activity. This was graphically revealed on a *60 Minutes* documentary. Here a demoralized family of six was living in a roach-infested, decrepit, single room renting for two thousand dollars per month. Their food and clothing budget came from yet another welfare fund. These people could live well on one-quarter the total paid by New York's Department of Welfare, yet the federal rules for temporary housing under which this rent money was distributed did not permit it to be used for permanent, quality housing or other needs. These rules created the opportunity for this slumlord to charge what can only be described as extortion. In New York City alone, there are four thousand similarly trapped families (including ten thousand children) on welfare.[1]

This deteriorated room would have a value in materials and labor, less depreciation, of under four thousand dollars. The rent to properly compensate this value at 10 percent per year would not exceed forty dollars per month plus utilities and taxes—roughly one hundred dollars. The remaining nineteen hundred dollars per month represents tribute from monopoly control of living space. This landlord controls the living space which properly belongs to the shattered welfare recipients. We allow no income for ownership of land. Every person is *morally,* and ought to be *legally,* entitled to his or her space on earth. After all, no one built that earth. Thus there can be no claim for labor expended. It is only monopolization of land that permits one person to charge another for living space. (Though the reader may sincerely challenge this statement, I suggest he or she wait until this subject is addressed in Book Three, chapter one.)

## Someone Else Also Has Their Job

As can be seen in protected, well-paid union employment, a job is a recognized territorial niche within the economy. Because someone else has appropriated their job rights, the poor have either inadequate jobs or none at all. They lack organized protection, influential family or social connections, and/or political strength. Every well-paying job is claimed by someone else and without the legitimacy of ownership or employment they cannot claim their share of social wealth.

The poor want to work but are prevented from doing so because job opportunities are monopolized. When even low-paying jobs are advertised, typically hundreds or even thousands apply. Denied this most basic of rights, the right to work, they end up desperate. Witness the case of the jobless worker who advertised in 1975 to sell one of his kidneys for five thousand dollars. The Kidney Foundation reported one hundred needy people making such offers. Today, there would be a ready sale at the established market price exceeding thirteen thousand dollars—seven times the price of gold.[2]

## Those Who Give Up

A local sixty-two-year-old civil engineer, after a pressing search, was unable to obtain even a job washing dishes. With no money, facing eviction, and too proud to go on welfare, he placed a television set on the hood of his car in a closed garage, started the engine, and quietly departed this world. He was buried through my church.

Listening to a lecturer whose profession was counseling grieving families I posed a question. What percentage of suicides are good, productive, proud people, who just no longer have the income to survive, can find no work, refuse to accept charity, and simply give up? His answer was, "Quite high." A close reading of the obituary page will reveal many of these proud people. They are neither ignorant nor lazy; they just have no rights to employment of any kind.

When jobs disappear due to corporate decisions or gains in technological efficiency many are unable to find alternative employment. The lack of self-respect that only having a job and taking care of one's responsibilities can restore will destroy what were once good decent people. A study by Dr. Brenner of Johns Hopkins University concluded that for "each one-percent increase in unemployment there will be 37,000 additional deaths." Those traceable to a direct cause included "920 more suicides; 650 more homicides; and 500 additional deaths from cirrhosis of the liver. There would also be an increase of 4,000 in mental hospitals and 3,300 in prisons."[3] In the recession of 1974–75 there was a "2.3-percent increase in the nation's mortality rate"—45,900 people.[4]

## Building Proud and Functional People

While farming for several years, I learned much about farm tax loopholes. They were so big, they more than made it possible for me to recover the tax paid on my railroad income. To this windfall were added thousands of dollars per year in crop supports, land development payments, and generous compensation for not raising any crop in the first place. Other farmers, oilmen, corporations, and landlords, are quite familiar with this phenomenon of making good money and paying no taxes, while receiving substantial government support. (In 1987, total government agricultural payments amounted to almost one-half of all net farm income.) This is business, corporate, and farm welfare. The money comes from the same source as welfare for the poor—taxes. But the recipients of government support for their businesses receive it as a right, and—in this form—it preserves their dignity.

The media constantly remind us that farmers are important to our society, and Congress loyally votes more money for them while trumpeting the great social benefits. This useful, functional image is a cornerstone of our ideology. The recipients of this type of welfare are left with their identity and self-respect not only intact but strengthened. They stand tall and are proud of their image as useful people. Unaware that much of their labor is wasted, they live under the illusion that they are fully productive. They are emotionally and spiritually protected—actually, nurtured and trained—just as children are raised by good parents who want to ensure that they will grow up to be functional and well-balanced adults.

The "welfare class" is permitted no such illusion. In spite of the rhetoric reaffirming opportunity and plentiful jobs, these are seldom available to the poor. Yet through the same media comes another cornerstone of our ideology—the horror stories of welfare queens and able-bodied men living high off the labor and taxes of others. Congress faithfully listens to this testimony and votes money for temporary support and for retraining the unemployed for jobs that aren't there. First denied opportunity, they are then trained to dependency. They are only allowed to receive welfare in this *dishonorable* manner. It is this kind of support, given as welfare and charity, which destroys their self-image and shatters their belief in themselves. This is a system guaranteed to damage these people psychologically and to make them nonfunctional.

On national news, young students in a Harlem school were being interviewed about their career hopes. Not yet understanding poverty's invisible bars, they enthusiastically announced they wanted to be doctors, astronauts, and lawyers. The reporter, knowing well what these children had to look forward to, noted, "These hopes and dreams will hold until they face the real world."

Millionaire Eugene Lang sensed the problem when he gave a graduation speech to a sixth grade class in one of New York's inner city schools comprised of sixty-one black and Hispanic slum children. He offered to place five hundred dollars per year per student in a trust fund for six years. Upon each student's graduation, this would pay her or his college tuition. Whereas a large share of slum schoolchildren never graduate (only 75 percent do nationwide), 90 percent of these students graduated and went on to college. Lang's experiment was considered so successful that thirteen other philanthropists are following his lead.[5]

Another perceptive individual was a black pilot also featured on national news.[6] For years he had searched out black high school dropouts and made them this offer: "If you go to school and get good grades, I'll teach you to fly." Eighty percent of his students went on to college and of these once discouraged youths, 237 are now fliers and comprise 15 percent of the nation's Afro-American pilots—all this from one person who knew the importance of identity for everyone. His success suggests what might be accomplished if giving these youths opportunity were really our social policy.

A concluding example would be a Women's Economic Development Corporation speaker who in 1984 asked a group of businessmen to finance new businesses for women on all economic levels, including some on welfare. Some of the listeners promptly walked out of the meeting. Of fifteen hundred businesses that this program started, only fifty had closed as of 1988. That is a pretty good record considering that 90 percent of small businesses fail. Some who succeeded in dance studios, cleaning businesses, day care centers, animal training, labeling and mailing services, and clothes design were formerly welfare mothers. Some of their businesses reached six figures and at least one (producing a salsa sauce) became a multi-million-dollar success. Given equal access to financial capital, these women proved they were productive people.[7]

Young people are idealistic and, given a decent chance, most will be good, productive citizens. We owe it to all children not to destroy them emotionally and spiritually, as has been done to the present welfare class.

## Welfare Costs

Once alerted to look for waste in distribution, we find dozens of established territories within the welfare economy: food stamps; school lunch programs; Aid to Families with Dependent Children; nutrition for the elderly; maternal and child health services; women, infants, and children supplemental food program; supplemental security income; pensions for needy veterans; general assistance; earned income tax credits; low-income housing; low-rent public housing; interest reduction payments; rural rental housing loans; employment and training services; summer youth employment; Job Corps; senior community employment; work incentive programs; social services; energy assistance; low-income energy assistance; Pell grants; Head Start; college work-study; supplemental education; opportunity grants; vocational rehabilitation; child nutrition; child welfare; Indian Health Services; community health centers; and state temporary disability insurance.[8] There are many subdivisions and duplications of these programs at the federal, state, county, and city levels. Not only are these services duplicated, but each agency duplicates work—processing applications, investigating eligibility, disbursing payments, etc.

Though the above programs are listed as social welfare, an analysis of each would conclude that most are essential to the person and to society and are really rights. If the dispossessed are ever to gain their full rights the language must be restructured to conform to that reality. Witness the following math. The language of social welfare and welfare leaves the impression these people are receiving something to which they are not entitled. This is hardly true. Through lack of property and job rights, these people are receiving much less than what they should.

In 1984, U.S. social welfare (there is that image-setting word) expenditures covering Social Security, Medicaid, Medicare, and the above programs came to $592.6 billion (that awesome figure they are supposedly unjustly receiving), of which about $392 billion is considered a right (such as Social Security, earned by a lifetime of work, or education, which prepares a person for work).[9] Social scientist Charles Murray, of the Manhattan Institute for Policy Research, characterizes the remaining $200 billion as welfare or charity.[10] Murray is here taking the negative reaction to the word "welfare" to its maximum. Instead of welfare, most of this $200 billion does not reach those in poverty; it too is considered a right by those above poverty who intercept these funds.

This can be demonstrated by simple math. If the 33.7 million Americans in poverty in 1984 actually received the $200 billion Murray terms as welfare, this, plus the $80 billion they now earn in the labor market, would be $280 billion, averaging over $8,000 per person or $32,000 per family of four in poverty.[11] If these sums reached the poor, they would be considered middle class citizens and there would be no poverty—large sums are going somewhere else.

Murray himself admits that only $109 billion of this $200 billion is actually distributed as welfare. This leaves $91 billion wasted in distribution. An average wage of just over $18,000 per year would back up Charles Murray's claim that there are five million professionals employed in administering these funds and would account for the $91-billion welfare distribution costs.[12] Much, if not most, of the remaining $109 billion distributed as welfare still does not reach those in poverty. Much is distributed to people who are above the poverty level for such purposes as student food stamps, school lunch programs, summer youth employment, work incentive programs, vocational rehabilitation, community health centers, subsidized housing, etc. Most who receive this support do not view it as welfare but as a "right"—just as the oilmen, businesspeople, and farmers view theirs. These middle class citizens protect their self-image by classifying their substantial government support as due them for being productive citizens. This leaves the poor alone with the shame of welfare, even though they receive only a pittance.

With average per-capita earnings of $2,500, those in poverty would need only an additional $80 billion to double individual income to $5,000, or $20,000 per family of four. This is twice the current poverty level. Thus a modest 40 percent of present welfare expenditures—if it only reached them proportionate to need— would put America's 33.7 million who are officially counted as poor well above poverty.

## A Negative Tax Can Replace the Welfare Bureaucracy

That $91 billion—or 44.5 percent of what Murray terms welfare—expended in distribution is wasted can be confirmed with a little mental exercise. I will use conservative economist Milton Friedman's plan of a negative tax to replace the multiple welfare bureaucracies.[13] Such a reverse tax would distribute tax money to the poor and make up the difference between low earnings and a predetermined income level above poverty. However, that tax would be far less than that now expended to finance the current inefficient welfare system. The five million professionals now processing and investigating welfare claims and distributing payments immediately become redundant. This would save the $91 billion they consume of the current welfare distribution costs. That potential savings represents the free time that could be shared by all as the quality-of-life index goes up consequent to eliminating waste distribution territories and sharing productive work.

The thought of using a negative tax to pay someone for doing nothing goes against our cultural training. But consider the support for industry, business, and farmers—that is just a negative tax by a different name. Many billion-dollar corporations have received government subsidies (a negative tax) exceeding the taxes they paid. For example, General Electric earned $2.66 billion in 1981, paid no income tax and received a $90-million rebate (negative tax) from the government.[14] Between 1982 and 1985 AT&T received a negative tax of $635.5 million, Dupont $179 million, Boeing $121 million, General Dynamics $90.9 million, Pepsico $89.3 million, General Mills $78.7 million, Transamerica Corporation $73.2 million, Texaco $68 million, International Paper $59.8 million, Greyhound $53.7 million, and IC Industries $53.7 million.[15] And farmers almost universally receive more money from the government than they pay in taxes. For the already affluent, the principle of a negative tax is well established. Consider also the waste distribution territories exposed in this book—large numbers of people are working, and many are well paid even though a large percentage of their labor produces nothing.

## Equal Rights Will Eliminate Paying for Nonproductive Work

Left unmodified, Friedman's concept of a negative tax would restructure U.S. society and make it similar to Great Britain's, where a large segment of the population has no hope of ever getting a job. There the government furnishes survival maintenance, known as "the dole," which is resented by both the poor and well-to-do. The income is not earned and the moral right is missing. Along with the ideological rhetoric of freedom, opportunity, and individual achievement, it is designed to provide for people's minimum needs and prevent the poor from claiming their right to a just share of nature's abundance. A negative tax must be combined with rights to productive employment. If not, it would only perpetuate welfare status for those who cannot establish a territory within the economy.

Everybody should obtain his or her share of social production through work. This can be done either by increasing economic activity—thereby creating jobs for everybody—or by sharing present jobs. Economists consider the former to be the proper route to full employment. But when much of present employment is supporting a waste distribution infrastructure this is illogical. Modern industrial technology is so productive that when a society is fully capitalized and its infrastructure developed, employing everybody forty hours per week productively is impossible. Equality can only be realized by eliminating these waste distribution territories, drastically reducing the workweek, and sharing and being fully paid for productive jobs—all would then participate in both production and consumption. For able-bodied people, this would eliminate the need for either welfare or a negative income tax.

## Sharing Rights to Productive Labor

By right, the first jobs for which they are qualified should go to the functionally impaired (answering services for the blind, accounting and secretarial work for those in wheelchairs, janitorial work for the learning disabled, etc.). Surely there are jobs for all these people, whose self-esteem would be greatly improved if only they could achieve self-sufficiency. The severely impaired should have the opportunity, but not the obligation, to work. It is safe to say that most would choose to work. It is those who have been faced with dependency who can best appreciate the need for the pride, equality, and independence achievable through productive labor.

Others would have the right to a job much as they do now—through talent, education, tests, interviews, contacts, seniority, etc. The major change would be a dramatic cut in the workweek, which would permit realization of that right. Who would object to a greatly reduced workweek with no loss of income?

## With Rights Go Responsibilities

With a respectable living assured through a negative income tax and the right to a job, there remains the obligation to work. Only through work do citizens rightfully earn their share of production. With computers it would be quite simple to match productive jobs to the available labor force. If there are not enough available jobs, the average workweek must be reduced. If there are increased labor needs, the workweek need only be lengthened to compensate. With workers' increased free time, there would always be a readily available labor force for miscellaneous jobs. There would need to be social support for moving to areas of labor surplus jobs from areas where jobs are scarce. To do less would be asking these people to bear the burden for the rest of society's job security.

While wages and prices are being rebalanced to compensate for the elimination of unnecessary jobs, a negative tax should be used to support those with reduced income. In order to qualify for negative tax, workers should have to accept offered employment. Professionals, overqualified workers, and specialists should maintain rights to job openings in their fields.

A negative tax should be based on the previous year's insufficient income, which was caused by lack of opportunity to exercise the right to a job. This income would go far toward restoring finances shattered by the previous unemployment and, of course, could be borrowed against to survive while unemployed. Just like farm, oil, and other business welfare recipients, these people would view this as a right and have an increased incentive to work. This will protect that most valuable of all resources, the people themselves.

## Retirement

The requirement to accept employment in order to be eligible for negative tax payments need only be eliminated for those reaching retirement age. Each would then be free either to continue work or to draw his or her negative tax. The increased leisure time could be used to produce more for the needy elderly or a higher living standard for all. It would be possible to work two days per week and retire at sixty-five. If society chose to work five days per week, the retirement age could be lowered to fifty years of age while doubling the present inadequate monthly average of under five hundred dollars in Social Security income (1987). The combinations of work, vacation, and retirement are many. For example, for their share of about 104 working days, some workers may like to work four days a week for six months and be off for the next six. Others might prefer to work two months and be off two while still others might like working in two-week shifts. All workers would benefit from the shortened workweek without any lowering of living standards. They can all look forward to a secure and early retirement.

## Welfare Disappears

With true insurance, the elimination of legal hocus-pocus, cheap transportation, a public taught responsibility for its own health, and with rights to a productive job, much waste will be eliminated. This will result in a reduction in living costs—which translates into higher living standards. If all have rights to a productive job and the able-bodied share the responsibility to work, negative tax payments should then be an infrequent occurrence in a person's life. There would be no welfare. There need be only those injured, unemployable, or retired who draw negative tax support, and this would be their right.

## Measuring the Number of Unemployed

That the true level of unemployment is double the official figure is accepted by many economists.[16] The reason for the discrepancy is that only those signed up for unemployment insurance, and recorded as actively seeking work, are counted. Such statistics conveniently overlook too many people: Native Americans on reservations, where unemployment reaches as high as 70 percent; black youths, whose unemployment hovers above 50 percent; workers who no longer sign up; the discouraged who quit looking for work; and those with part-time work being counted as employed, even if it is as little as one hour per week. They are all part of the true level of unemployment.[17]

There are the two to three million so-called "street people" in America whose confidence has been destroyed. They do not even have a change of clothes or a place to clean up to ask for a job. Without an address, they will not be hired.[18] Though most people consider them hopeless, on TV interviews they say this is not the life they want. One-third are families with children.[19] We can safely assume they are not there by choice. With the proper support to rebuild their shattered confidence, most could be retrained and employed.

Counting the functionally impaired and the desperate street people, the actual count of unemployed could be increased by possibly another five or six million. However, we will not count these. They will be left to cover the estimated two million workers who would be between jobs in a full-employment economy, and to offset any other objections detractors of this thesis will make. Nor will we count the unemployed teenagers who would like to work. (In 1983 this was roughly 51 percent of Afro-Americans, 30 percent of Hispanics, and 21 percent of white teenagers between sixteen and nineteen years old.[20]) As with a reduced workweek there would be available time for both school and work, the numbers of working teenagers could be greatly increased even while improving both their educational opportunities and job skills (see Book Three, chapter four). All these will not be calculated in the potential reduction of the workweek.

Among the five million welfare workers described by Charles Murray are those with necessary jobs. Almost exclusively those are furnishing services to the functionally impaired (quadriplegics, severely retarded, and otherwise totally incapacitated). However, the *unessential* workers require a support structure to build and maintain the offices, cars, etc. Under a restructuring of rights, the necessary welfare jobs and the uncounted support jobs should roughly balance. Thus five million could be released for productive work.

To this should be added the 11.4 million unpaid homemakers who would enjoy the freedom, challenge, contact with their peers, and the new identity that a paying job entails. A look at the other choice—being full-time housekeepers while their husbands or wives are free most of the week—would assure that conclusion. If the proper workweek were two days, each could accept the responsibilities of the home for two days and they could share them for three.

Assuming equal pay, the home of a single breadwinner is now at a severe disadvantage compared to one in which both are employed. To avoid this the rights and responsibilities of a job could be held jointly. One spouse could use the rights of both and work twice the national average while the other stayed home. This would maintain equality and rights to a fair share of social production for each family.

Under the above conditions, the unemployment level should be close to zero. Economists will immediately warn about the high cost of labor under those conditions, but this would not be a problem. With computers matching workers with jobs, and almost everybody having more free time, no employer should have to look far for needed workers. With everybody working less than one-half the week, competition would be fierce for extra work. This would not be out of desperation but out of a desire to work for the many products or satisfactions a modern economy can provide.

Industrial technology is now so efficient, the waste distribution territories to intercept the goods produced so extensive, and the social loss so enormous, that the great majority would gain by elimination of this system of waste distribution. Welfare is a devastating blow to anyone's self-esteem. A good self-image and pride are essential for any individual to function—to destroy these is to destroy the person. We feel we are virtuous when giving charity, but nothing could be further from the truth. Raising our image in our own eyes and others' by charitable deeds only robs the disadvantaged of their necessary self-respect. These people only need access to social wealth through a guaranteed right to their share of productive employment. They would then no longer need others' charity. They would have pride, and they would be productive. The previous givers of charity could then work much less. This is recognized by no less than America's foremost industrialist Henry Ford. His philosophy was unequivocal:

Blindfold me and lead me down there into the street and let me lay my hands by chance on the most shiftless and worthless fellow in the crowd and I'll bring him in here, give him a job with a wage that offers him some hope for the future, some prospect of living a decent, comfortable and self-respecting life certainly, and I'll guarantee that I'll make a man out of him.[21]

An honest accounting would show the unemployed on welfare as contributing just as much to social production (but wasting much less) as labor expended within the waste distribution territories of these professions—both zero. Unnecessary insurance salespeople, unnecessary lawyers and workers who produce unnecessary drugs, unnecessary operations, and unnecessary chemicals are more wasteful to society than idle people. Make a living taking in each other's wash (or, to quote economist Lester Thurow, "giving each other heart transplants") is a contradiction. Indeed it is apparent in today's falling living standards for labor.

Response to the occasional personal disaster deserving sympathy and support is not charity; this is cooperative support. Most receive this daily from family and friends and any of us may need that support from the community at some time in our lives. But no one should require charity because he or she lacks access to living space or productive employment. That denial only perpetuates a system of wasted resources and demoralized people. A sensible and fair balance of freedom, rights, and responsibilities would make social justice—with a good living standard for all—a reality.

In the prophetic words of William Blake, the great English poet:

> Pity could be no more
> If we did not make somebody poor;
> And Mercy no more could be,
> If all were as happy as we.

# 7

## Conclusion

Seven more segments of the economy were originally planned to be included in Book One. However, the pattern is well established and including them would be overwhelming. Each is briefly described below and for the serious reader key sources are cited.

### Energy

In the electric power industries, almost 24 percent of the population is served by consumer-owned electric utilities (13.4 percent are publicly owned, 10.2 percent are rural cooperatives). The rest are privately owned companies which charge 42.5 percent more for electricity than those publicly owned (7.17 cents per kilowatt-hour as opposed to 5.03 cents). As private utilities serve higher density population centers and should have lower costs, the spread is even greater than these statistics show. There are even greater savings yet. Publicly owned utilities provide enough income for the communities to build swimming pools, stadiums, and parks.[1] Other energy companies (oil, coal) have no public agency to compare with—their records are secret—but an honest study would undoubtedly show the same overcharges.

### Crime

Crime and its prevention are wasted social energies. Though it would take a long time to rebuild those damaged psyches, the implementation of the concepts in this treatise will eliminate many of crime's basic causes. These people should all be productively employed, including those in prisons. After all, every day's work they do is one day someone else can relax.

While researching for her book *Kind and Unusual Punishment*, Jessica Mitford learned that strict disciplinarian prison wardens calculated that 80 to 90 percent of those imprisoned did not belong there. The waste distribution territory aspect can be seen in the current promotions for private prisons. Along with others with secure property and job rights, these influential people will decide who should be imprisoned and why. The majority imprisoned will be those who through circumstances have not attained equal rights. There are many aspects of rights and circumstances (luck), ranging from parental care to parental abuse, and care, neglect, or abuse from the community, that contribute to the problem. In Book Three I will address the economic rights that these dispossessed do not have. If the dispossessed were ever to reclaim those rights, there would be much less crime.

The wages and profits of those operating the justice/prison system will be earned through the incarceration of those unable to cope with the injustice they can instinctively see but cannot understand. Even now our prison population has doubled in the past ten years. We have more imprisoned per capita than any developed country except South Africa. The percentage incarcerated is still increasing and billions of dollars are earmarked for new prisons.[2] By 1989 1 in every 240 Americans will be in prison.

## Chemicals and Nuclear Radiation

Every exposé on these segments of the economy tells the same story. Corporations are dedicated to finding cheap chemical replacements for food or production—chemicals considered cheap only because the corporate balance sheet conveniently leaves out the cost to society of a destroyed environment and damaged health. Other corporations are then formed to clean up this pollution. In the future, these same corporations could end up owning the remaining pure water and living space. People would then be employed polluting the countryside, others cleaning it up, and still others vending the luxuries of what clean air and water remains to those who can afford to pay.

The one-hundred-billion-dollar nuclear weapons program is a good example. They polluted so much of the countryside and groundwater that it is expected to require much more to clean it up than to build those bombs. Many areas are so polluted (with both chemical and nuclear waste) that they can never be reclaimed and will become "national sacrifice zones." Some experts have calculated that, at the current level of radiation pollution, nine thousand Americans per year are dying from cancer induced by radiation poisoning.[3] Due to the long-lasting nature of some radiation, that cost will be borne for hundreds or even hundreds of thousands of years. Book Two, chapters four, five, and six, demonstrates that these weapons were never needed.

In studying the pollution problem, *Newsweek* reporter Gregg Easterbrook noted that, "More than 80 percent of [the $100 billion] Superfund spending [legislated for cleaning up air, land, and water] has gone to consultants and their kinsmen, who have a pecuniary interest in dragging the process out: to keep the meter running."[4] The waste distribution territory principle of claiming to be doing productive labor while producing little is in full force.

Where most of the waste we have covered up to this point has been labor, Book Two addresses the 50 percent of U.S. industry that is also wasted. This unnecessary industry has no connection to our needs for food, fiber, shelter, or recreation. Instead it reduces our quality of life. Industrial pollution could be reduced 50 percent by eliminating this unnecessary production. Some could be turned towards cleaning up the pollution of a waste distribution society, but this industry was never needed and the easiest and cheapest method of clean-up is to not produce those chemical and nuclear wastes in the first place.

# Nursing Home Care

Mary Adelaide Mendelson in her classic *Tender Loving Greed* explains that, in a properly structured group home, 50 percent of those in nursing homes are perfectly capable of taking care of themselves. They are trapped because society is not structured for them to be independent. Much of this unnecessary labor has been allowed for in the preceding chapter, but the specific methods of intercepting others' wealth through unnecessary labor in the nursing home industry are well explained by Mendelson.

# Funerals

That society is being overcharged here is no secret. Jessica Mitford's *The American Way of Death* and others explain the process well.[5]

# Business Administration

Seymour Melman has calculated that well over 50 percent of the administrators of corporate America are unnecessary. They are there to intercept production, not to produce.[6] Book Two shows that 50 percent of our industrial capacity has nothing to do with caring for consumer needs. The unneeded administrators in private business are thus closer to 75 percent.

# Government Waste

This is the pet complaint of many. However, most is not government waste; it is private industry milking the public treasury. This was well outlined by William Greider in *The Education of David Stockman and Other Americans*. Stockman parroted the familiar line of government waste, yet noted that almost everyone he knew was working for the government and "protected from the dynamic risk-taking of the private economy":

> Stockman and other conservatives meant not only the layers and layers of federal bureaucrats and liberal politicians who sustained open-ended growth of the central government but also the less visible infrastructure of private interests that fed off of it and prospered—the law firms and lobbyists and trade associations in rows of shining office buildings along K Street in Washington; the consulting firms and contractors; the constituencies of special interests, from schoolteachers to construction workers to failing businesses and multinational giants, all of whom came to Washington for money and legal protection against the perils of free competition.[7]

After deducting for all this bureaucratic waste, Stockman calculates:

> That leaves seventeen cents for everything else that Washington does. The FBI and national parks, the county agents and the Foreign Service and the Weather Bureau—all the traditional operations of government—consumed only nine cents of each dollar. The remaining eight cents provided all of the grants to state and local governments, for aiding handicapped children or building highways.[8]

The private interests Stockman identified are using their money and influence to structure into law extra rights for themselves. These increased rights permit the interception of a part of the nation's wealth without doing productive labor. They show up as reduced net income (loss of rights) for those whose labors produced that intercepted wealth.

I will not count the wasted labor, capital, and resources in the above seven segments of the economy. There are also many other segments not addressed. The reader is encouraged to send to this publisher any such waste observed, along with the documentation, and if it can be referenced from authoritative sources, it may be included in an appendix to later editions. For example, what about the insanity of spending billions on advertising cigarettes, whiskey, and beer? Our agriculture is then employed in raising crops for these health-damaging habits and the government pays more hundreds of millions of dollars to these farmers in crop support. Then more millions are employed trying to stem the damage caused by these habits. There are many more areas of wasted labor.

## The Mathematics of Waste

In totaling up the segments of the economy we have addressed, a totally productive work force would reduce employment in insurance by 2.1 million; law, 920,000; transportation, 5.86 million; health, 14 million; agriculture, 2.3 million; and welfare, 5 million.* This totals 30.18 million unnecessary jobs.

There are 108.5 million workers employed in the U.S. (1986). Subtracting the 30.18 million unnecessary jobs we have calculated up to this point leaves 78.32 million jobs. Of these, 19.5 million are part-time workers employed an average of three days per week. That is equivalent to 12 million full-time jobs. Subtracting those phantom 7.5 million jobs (19.5 million part-time workers less the 12 million full-time equivalent jobs) leaves 70.82 million "real" full-time jobs available.[9]

The official unemployment rate for 1985 was 7.3 percent, or 8.5 million. With the true number of unemployed double that, there are 17 million.[10] (Professor Bertram Gross, using roughly similar criteria, calculates it at 20 million.[11]) The unnecessary workers, the 17 million unemployed workers, and 11.4 million unemployed homemakers totals 58.58 million people who could be idle if the rest worked a fully productive five-day week.

The 108.5 million workers now employed, the 17 million unemployed, plus the 11.4 million homemakers not now working outside the home, yield a potential workforce of 136.9 million for the 70.82 million full- time jobs available (359.1 million workdays per week). If all shared this work, we need work only an average of 2.62 days per week—with no loss of food, fiber, shelter, or recreation—and there is much more waste to count.

---

* If Murray's figure proves too high, just allow the above seven segments of the economy not included and those in Book Three.

# Book Two

# Introduction

$T$he employment of unnecessary labor exposed in Book One requires additional structures, tools, and transportation; possibly 10 percent of U.S. capital is wasted in the support of unnecessary labor. Book Two addresses segments of the economy that waste not only our labor but capital and resources desperately needed by the world's dispossessed people.

> Up to and during the course of the fifteenth century the towns were the sole centers of commerce and industry to such an extent that none of it was allowed to escape into the open country. . . . The struggle against rural trading and against rural handicrafts lasted at least seven or eight hundred years. . . . The severity of these measures increased with the growth of "democratic government". . . . All through the fourteenth century regular armed expeditions were sent out against all the villages in the neighborhood and looms and fulling-vats were broken or carried away.[1]

> — Karl Polyani quoting Henri Pirenne's *Economic and Social History* and Eli F. Hecksher's *Mercantilism*

Note Pirenne's and Hecksher's recognition that the "severity of these measures increased with the growth of democratic governments." Although in those early years the power brokers knew they were destroying others' tools (capital) in the ongoing battle for economic territory, few of today's powerful are aware of the waste and destruction created by the continuation of this struggle for markets. Instead, they feel that it is they who are responsible for the world's improving standard of living and that they are defending not only their rights but everybody's rights.

This illusion is possible because in this battle for the monopolization of social wealth, and the reclamation of that wealth, industrial capital is so productive that even as capital, resources, and labor are indiscriminately consumed, the living standard of our country continues to improve. And societies are so accustomed to long struggles for improved living standards that to think it could be done much faster seems irrational.

Since the advent of modern capital, societies have never fully utilized their productive capacity because trade wars, hot wars, and cold wars have wasted production and destroyed capital. The losses from trade wars and hot wars will be addressed but not measured. The losses from the Cold War will be measured; since World War II, that alone has wasted enough industrial capital, resources, and labor to have capitalized the entire world to a respectable standard of living.

# 1

## Trading Can Be Raiding

### Colonial Trade Wars

The leading mercantile cities [of Europe] resorted to armed force in order to destroy rival economic power in other cities and to establish a completer economic monopoly. These conflicts were more costly, destructive, and ultimately even more futile than those between the merchant classes and the feudal orders. Cities like Florence, which wantonly attacked other prosperous communities like Lucca and Siena, undermined both their productivity and their own relative freedom from such atrocious attacks. When capitalism spread overseas, its agents treated the natives they encountered in the same savage fashion that it treated their own nearer rivals.[1]

The destruction of another society's capital to protect markets substituted "trading for raiding."[2] Instead of appropriating another's wealth through violence, societies learned to accomplish this through unequal trades. It was the weaker, less developed countries that lost out in these exchanges, and it is the military power of the more developed countries that maintains this unequal relationship.

As raiding gave way to trading—always dominated by armed strength—political control of commerce came to depend on such methods as treaties, tariffs, and staple laws, which effectively channeled business through trading companies controlled by the powerful. These early methods of monopolizing trade restricted not only the rights of other societies but those within a society. In order to police these unequal treaties, the military, which provided the power to dictate the terms, was never far in the background. Colonialism—the systematic plundering of Africa, Latin America, and Asia—was simply raiding weaker societies on a mass scale.[3]

In spite of efforts to protect themselves, the world's weaker societies were no match for imperial intrigues. Their wealth was continuously drained by unequal trades. This could be done by purchasing below or selling above the true value of a commodity. The purchase of products a society does not need, or which it can produce for itself—if permitted the requisite technology and capital—is a sale 100 percent overvalued. Even several hundred percent, as that society is then denied the benefits of the multiplier factor that would be gained if this money moved through the economy creating more commerce.

If a society spends one hundred dollars for manufacturing within its own country, the money paid for that production continues through the economy as each recipient spends it for his or her needs. That one hundred dollars' worth of primary production can add as much as five hundred to two thousand dollars to the Gross National Product (GNP) of that country. If it is spent in another country, circulation of that money is within the exporting country. This is the reason an industrialized exporting country is wealthy and an undeveloped importing country is poor.

A shortsighted developed society could lose out through careless import/export policies as well. Over a period of two hundred years, Spain plundered shiploads of gold and silver from her Latin American colonies. While the Spanish were concentrating their labors on appropriating other societies' wealth, they ignored the production of consumer products for the upper classes and imported them instead. In 1593, an advisor explained this to King Philip II:

> The Cortes of Valladolid in the year 1586 petitioned Your Majesty not to allow the further importation into the kingdom of candles, glassware, jewelry, knives and similar articles; these things useless to human life come from abroad to be exchanged for gold, as though Spaniards were Indians . . . the general remote cause of our want of money is the great excess of this Kingdom in consuming the commodities of foreign countries, which prove to us discommodities, in hindering us of so much treasure, which otherwise would be brought in, in lieu of those toys.[4]

Britain and France supplied these "toys," and Spain's wealth ended up in British and French vaults.[*] Although Spain was immensely wealthy, her power was sapped by unnecessary purchases of other societies' labor.

The impoverishment of India is a classic example of raiding through trading, backed by military might. Hand weaving was tedious and paid little, so the British, rather than producing their own cloth, purchased much of it from India. As India had no need or desire for British products, these imports could only be paid for with gold. But Britain did not make the same mistake as Spain. She embargoed Indian textiles and set about producing her own cloth with the evolving technology of power weaving machinery. After India was conquered, her import/export policies were controlled by Britain. Indian textiles were now not only banned from Britain but were taxed to a disadvantage within India. British cloth then dominated the Indian market. Through forced sales to India, the wealth immediately started flowing toward the "mother country." "It was [only] by destroying [the] Indian textile industry that Lancaster ever came up at all."[5] Other Indian industries were similarly devastated:

> In the name of progress, the limited but balanced economy of the Hindu village, with its local potter, its local spinners and weavers, its local smith, was overthrown for the sake of providing a market for the potteries of the Five Towns and the textiles of Manchester and the superfluous hardware of Birmingham. The result was impoverished villages in India, hideous and destitute towns in Eng-

---

[*] To a considerable degree, this constituted the capital that financed the Industrial Revolution.

land, and a great wastage in tonnage and man-power in plying the oceans between.[6]

One exceptionally rich sector of India was East Bengal (Bangladesh). When the British first arrived, they

> found a thriving industry and a prosperous agriculture. It was, in the optimistic words of one Englishman, "a wonderful land, whose richness and abundance neither war, pestilence nor oppression could destroy." But by 1947, when the sun finally set on the British Empire in India, Eastern Bengal had been reduced to an agricultural hinterland. In the words of an English merchant, "Various and innumerable are the methods of oppressing the poor weavers . . . such as by fines, imprisonment, floggings, forcing bonds from them, etc." By means of 'every conceivable form of roguery,' the company's merchants acquired the weaver's cloth for a fraction of its value.[7]

Later Bengal, still under British control, became a raw material (indigo and jute) producer for world commerce. Still later, the colonialists established the cultivation of poppies to provide opium for the enormous Chinese market. This foreign control devastated the once-balanced, prosperous economy, resulting in the extreme poverty of Bangladesh today. The destruction of their once thriving economy was so thorough that even the unique long staple, finely textured local cotton became extinct.[8]

As with India, China did not need or want British products. But since Britain consumed large quantities of Chinese teas, it was imperative that something be traded to avoid the loss of Britain's gold. Though it was done covertly and not acknowledged by the government, it became official policy to peddle opium to China. When this right was challenged by Chinese authorities (the Boxer Rebellion), their attempt at maintaining sovereignty was put down by British armed forces.[*] "Opium [sold to China] was no hole-in-the-corner petty smuggling trade but *probably the largest commerce of the time in any single commodity*"[9] (emphasis in original). With the sales of opium exceeding the purchases of tea, the latter cost Britain neither gold nor other currency. It did cost capital and labor, but this involved an internal circulation of money—no wealth was lost to another society. As a nonproductive expenditure of labor and capital, this is waste distribution. It looks productive because only the wealth gained or protected by Britain is considered. The much greater losses suffered by the Chinese are conveniently left uncalculated.

By controlling trade, Britain became the "workshop of the world," producing at its peak 54 percent of the manufactured goods in world commerce. As Great Britain's wealth and power grew through unequal trades, the countries plundered became impoverished.

Historian Charles Beard notes that the wealth of the American colonies was being similarly appropriated and credits the restrictions on trade as a primary reason for the American Revolution and the formation of the American govern-

---

[*] Actually there was a combined force of twenty thousand consisting of British, French, Japanese, German, and American troops (five thousand were Americans) led by a German general. This was a blatant attempt to carve up China between those centers of capital. (Samuel Flagg Bemis, *A Diplomatic History of the United States* (New York: Henry Holt and Company, 1936, pp. 1027–1142.)

ment. He writes, "The consumption of foreign luxuries, [and] manufactured stuffs, was one of the chief causes of our economic distress" and adds that our founders also recognized the connection between wars and the control of world trade:[10]

> In the harbor of New York there are now 60 ships of which 55 are British. The produce of South Carolina was shipped in 170 ships of which 150 were British. . . . Surely there is not any American who regards the interest of his country but must see the immediate necessity of an efficient federal government; without it the Northern states will soon be depopulated and dwindle into poverty, while the Southern ones will become silk worms to toil and labour for Europe. . . . The authors of the Federalist . . . regarded trade and commerce as the fundamental cause of wars between nations. . . . In the present state of disunion the profits of trade are snatched from us; our commerce languishes; and poverty threatens to overspread a country which might outrival the world in riches.[11]

The denial of freedom to trade led to our own revolution; the famous Boston Tea Party was only a particularly theatrical protest over a rather minor example of this systematic injustice. The colonialists

> could import only goods produced in England or goods sent to the colonies by way of England. They were not allowed to export wool, yarn, and woolen cloth from one colony to another, "or to any place whatsoever," nor could they export hats and iron products. They could not erect slitting or rolling mills or forges and furnaces. After 1763, they were forbidden to settle west of the Appalachian mountains. By the Currency Act of 1764, they were deprived of the right to use legal tender paper money and to establish colonial mints and land banks.[12]

The enormous prosperity we have enjoyed since we gained our freedom points to the cause of poverty in dependent Third World nations today. They are not free to develop and retain their own wealth because their commerce and trade are under the control of foreign powers.

Capitalism's leading philosopher, Adam Smith, recognized the importance of monopolization of trade in appropriating another society's wealth. He pointed out that "England had founded a great empire for the sole purpose of raising up a people of customers. . . . The maintenance of this monopoly has hitherto been the principal, or more properly perhaps the sole end and purpose of the dominion which Great Britain assumes over her colonies."[13] Historian Barbara Tuchman concurs:

> Trade was felt to be the bloodstream of British prosperity. To an island nation it represented the wealth of the world, the factor that made the difference between rich and poor nations. The economic philosophy of the time (later to be termed mercantilism) held that the colonial role in trade was to serve as the source of raw materials and the market for British manufacture, and *never* to usurp the manufacturing function.[14] (emphasis added)

If one were to calculate the wealth appropriated by colonization, trade, and war, then allow for the production forgone of destroyed local capital, it would be evident that colonial societies, had they not been colonized, could be enjoying prodigious wealth today. Even the developed countries could have been more prosperous. They have been destroying each other's wealth while battling over that of weaker societies.

## The Rationalization for Trade Raids

Those employed within economic territories rationalize their labor as efficient. The calculation of wasted labor outlined in this thesis exposes most of these rationalizations as nonsense. Those who profit from wars and international trades will also claim that their efforts are of value to society. If we are to understand waste in world trade, we must avoid such self-serving beliefs and look at the underlying causes.

Before World War II, citizens of the southern United States were considered backward and inefficient workers. After that war, corporations moved to the "Sunbelt" to take advantage of that cheap labor. As it became evident that these workers were as good as those in the north, the conventional wisdom still was that workers in other cultures were just too "uneducated, indifferent, and lazy to compete with American and European labor." When corporations decided to move their industries offshore to avoid the wages demanded by American labor, suddenly it was discovered that Third World labor clamored for work, learned fast, worked hard, and worked at a fraction of the wages of their sophisticated First World counterparts. The charges of incompetence were made when the Third World had not been given a serious opportunity to show what it could do.

Third World labor costs are 5 to 10 percent those of industrialized countries. Using the same technology, their production costs are far lower. If production costs were the only criteria, most Third World industrialists could undersell the industrialized countries on the world market. That this does not happen makes it obvious that monopolists have a firm hold on other choke points of world commerce. Hence Tanzanian economist Dan Nabudere's claim: "Imperialist monopolies have taken up all investment outlets and monopolized all markets."[15] Most Third World countries have enough resources and labor. What they need is access to technology, industrial capital, markets, and training—all now monopolized by industrialized countries. Breach those barriers and the Third World could produce just as efficiently and cheaply as anyone else.[*]

The Third World remains poor because monopolists strive to dominate every choke point of commerce. One key choke point is political control through the "co-respective" support of local elites. Where loyalty is lacking, money will be spent to purchase it. Protecting this complicated system of appropriation will be the descendants of those early raiding parties—the armed forces of the imperial country. The pattern has been established repeatedly throughout history and remains unchanged. To quote the well-known philosopher Bertrand Russell:

> An enormous proportion of the income of nations and individuals, nowadays, is blood money: payment exacted by the threat of death. Therefore the most prudent nation is the nation which is in the best position to levy blackmail. . . . Modern nations are highwaymen, saying to each other "your money or your life," and generally taking both.[16]

---

[*] Currently this is true only in coastal zones where transportation is cheap. Society is a machine and it requires a developed infrastructure (roads, railroads, electricity) to produce efficiently.

## Modern Methods of Unequal Trade

Most of the countries plundered by colonialism were once relatively wealthy. It is for this reason they were targeted for exploitation. If they could obtain industrial capital and equality in international trades, most could be wealthy again. However, once a society's economic and social structure has been shattered, it is at the mercy of external powers.

Japan was once closed to outsiders, but under the threat of Admiral Perry's naval task force was forced to sign a trade agreement in 1854. This contract distinctly favored the U.S.[17] It is from that experience that the Japanese learned the mechanics of becoming wealthy through unequal trades. They formed their trade policies in 1872 and since then have seldom deviated from those principles.[18] Through unequal trade practices being turned against us, "America is no longer such a rich country. And Japan is no longer poor. Much of our wealth has been transferred to the Japanese through the medium of exports and imports. *Their* exports and *our* imports."[19] Contemporary with Japan's enlightenment, Otto von Bismarck, the unifier of the German nation, deduced that "free trade is the weapon of the dominant economy anxious to prevent others from following in its path."[20] In spite of their lip service to free trade,

> virtually every country to industrialize after Britain did so behind a wall of protective tariffs. . . . In the classic Japanese model, the production of goods for export was accompanied by high protective tariffs to preserve the domestic market and strict controls to preserve domestic ownership of the national industrial plant.[21]

The methods of maintaining these unequal trades are quite simple. Both visible and invisible tariffs are used; these methods are being employed by Japan today with well-recognized success. Claims of "Japanese miracles"—parroted daily in the media—are misleading. Japan became an industrial power by selling on other markets while closing its own.

A common method of intercepting wealth through trades is contracting overseas labor at low prices. This is done by establishing overseas industries or purchasing products and services overseas that could be produced in a developed country (note that this led to Spain's downfall; see chapter two for a discussion of the dangers of this course). This requires some control over the policies of the low-wage countries:

> Production in developing countries takes place for the most part in "free production zones." These are enclaves designed to attract foreign capital by offering a range of commercial and financial incentives—exemptions from duties and taxes on machinery and raw materials, a five- to ten-year income tax "holiday," freedom from foreign exchange controls, preferential financing, preferential tariffs, furnishing by the local government of factory and office buildings, and a variety of supporting services.[22]

Another complicated maneuver for appropriating the labor of Third World countries is transfer pricing. The monopolists either manufacture in a Third World country or purchase directly from a local producer at the low values described. The product is then, theoretically, routed to an offshore corporation and invoiced at that low price. There the export invoice is increased to compare favorably with American labor prices and sold on the markets of the industrialized countries. The offshore company is nothing more than a mailing address and a plaque on a door. No products touch that offshore entity; even the paperwork is done in corporate home offices.

In 1980, there were eleven thousand such offshore corporations registered in the Cayman Islands alone, which have a population of only ten thousand. William Walker, whose firm held the record for the number of fictitious corporations, pointed out that, "We are directors of about 500 of them. . . . We funnel a lot of money out of Central and South America."[23] These corporations are doubly insulated from accountability. "Of the thousand American holding companies that control U.S. firms and their subsidiaries throughout the world, *six hundred have their registered offices in Switzerland.*"[24] (emphasis in original)

Besides the above described control of wages, corporations monopolize technology that is essential to industrialization:

> The market in which technology is transferred from developed to less-developed countries does not even roughly approach the theoretically and ethically ideal world of perfect competition, where multitudes of well-informed buyers and sellers mutually and fairly benefit from free and voluntary exchange. Rather, argument and evidence indicate a situation closer to the following analogy: a solitary man is standing on a dock, coiled life line in hand, trying to extract a commitment of financial reward from a helpless stranger floundering in the surf below, even though the man poised to pitch the lifeline is a millionaire and the drowning man is of only modest means. Understandably, the terms and conditions emerging from this bargaining may seem exploitive to the man in the water because the amount he pays for his life could well be onerous to him, more than the sum necessary to move his potential savior to action, and incrementally trivial compared to the riches the savior already possesses.[25]

Licenses for technology typically have severe restrictions that limit the benefits to the licensees. These include restrictions on research adaptations, use of personnel, and use after the expiration of a license, and obligations for continued use. There are also tie-in restrictions (required purchase from the licenser of unnecessary goods, services, or technology); tie-out clauses (against using competing products, technology, or services); price-fixing, export, and advertising restrictions; and more.[26]

There are also unwritten cartel-like agreements between transnational corporations. Some of their methods are collusive pricing; market or customer allocation; quotas; collective enforcement; refusing supplies; below-cost pricing to destroy competition; and excessive pricing to the competition. In contrast to the policies against weak Third World companies, multinational corporations pool their patents for use within their own industries.[27] While weakening dependent Third World producers by limiting their access to technology, they recognize the advantage among themselves of cooperatively using every innovation.

These subtle methods of control can be turned against us. Under the unwritten rules of monopolization we may well lose most of our advantage to cheaper overseas economies capturing markets through coordinated market plans:

> Japanese firms that control the market for videotape recorders regularly change technical protocols to prevent U.S. manufacturers from producing peripheral equipment for that market. *On a larger scale, today as a matter of policy, the Japanese and Europeans have begun to wire all their households in order to*

*achieve a base of sufficient scale to create telecommunications standards for the fu-*
*ture. By contrast, the U.S. industry is becoming fractured, uncoordinated, and*
*largely ignored by the government as well as subject to increasing foreign competi-*
*tion.*[28] *(emphasis added)*

## Unequal Trades in Agriculture

From the perspective of winning trade wars, the U.S. has an unsurmountable
advantage in agriculture. But sales of most U.S. agricultural products are not
only unnecessary, they are morally wrong. These exports destroy native agriculture by usurping their local markets. Overseas markets are developed because
we must sell rather than because they must buy:

A lot of attention is being paid these days to the Third World as a prime growth
market for American farmers. . . . The United States has become more dependent
on the Third World with more than 58 percent of total agricultural exports going
to these countries in 1986–87. . . . Virtually every trade analysis by the USDA
stresses the potential sales among developing nations in Latin America, Africa
and Asia. . . . Agriculture Secretary Richard E. Lyng said he most wanted freedom
for farmers "to produce what they want to produce" and that to accomplish that
would involve solving international trade problems. . . . [James R. Donald, chairman of the department's World Agricultural Outlook Board, said:] "The developing countries likely will continue to increase global grain imports and could be a
source of expansion for U.S. agricultural exports."[29]

The notorious selling of baby formula within poor countries eventually in-
spired a successful worldwide campaign to stop its promotion. This sounds in-
nocuous, but, besides being free, a mother's own milk is more nutritious and safer
than the powdered milk that led to many thousands of unnecessary deaths. This
is a particularly tragic example of needlessly importing foreign products.

These mothers were copying middle class American customs. They assumed
"being modern" must be better. When it comes to baby formulas, soda pop,
prepared breakfast cereals, and other processed foods, local foods are universally
better and cheaper. These people are just like people everywhere: barraged by
clever, misleading advertising, they too hunger for the prestige of modern consumer products. This is what Britain did when they were the workshop of the
world, namely sell other societies products they either did not need (opium and
luxury goods) or could very well produce themselves (textiles and pottery).

## Third World Loans and Capital Flight

Besides food products, there are the overseas purchases of luxury items by the
elite of these impoverished countries. To this must be added the consumer
products for these countries' middle classes that, if permitted the industrial capital, they could manufacture locally. This consumes large amounts of money. That
money represents labor appropriated from local workers, or the sale of their
countries' precious resources (such as oil, copper, or timber). Selling arms (always
to an elite who help maintain the colonial status) is another favorite method of
soaking up funds from these dependent countries and accounted for 40 percent
of their increase in debt between 1975 and 1985.[30]

Wealth skimmed off by the elite of these countries that ends up in foreign banks is another factor in the Third World debt burden. Mexico, with its $100-billion debt, saw $50 billion flow north between 1980 and 1985.[31] Forty-seven percent of Argentina's and 50 percent of Mexico's borrowed funds ended up in other countries. The average for eighteen of these impoverished countries was 44 percent. Howard M. Wachtel calculates the total as exceeding $200 billion, while Fidel Castro estimates the loss from Latin America alone at $10 billion per year:[32]

> As fast as the banks could wire fresh dollars to Latin American governments, the money was loaned to businessmen, after a suitable amount, of course, was skimmed off by venal civilian and military bureaucrats. The money in the bank accounts of both the businessmen and the bureaucrats quickly fled to safer havens, mainly in the United States. This mass flight of capital landed in Florida skyscrapers, New York apartments, and accounts in the most solid American banking institutions. It was not even necessary for the money to hide in Switzerland. The big American banks also maintained special departments that welcomed the money as savings, even though the lending officers in a different department had sent it to those same countries for supposedly productive uses.... 40 percent of Mexico's borrowed money leaked away, 60 percent of Argentina's, and every penny of Venezuela's. Like alchemists, the Latin American elite converted the debt of the public at home into their private assets abroad. . . . The figures mean that about one dollar out of every three loaned to Latin America by banks between 1979 and 1983 made that round trip. . . . no such capital flight is evident in loans to the industrious countries of Southeast Asia.[33]

Government loans are almost invariably tied to purchases from the creditor nation. Over 80 percent of America's foreign aid returns directly to us through our exports.[34] Commenting on such generosity, the prime minister of Malaysia pointed out that, "Although Japan furnishes loans, it takes back with its other hand, as if by magic, almost twice the amount it provides."[35] As of 1986, Cuban president Fidel Castro estimated that by these and various other methods the wealth drained from Latin America alone "has transferred more than $70 billion in a single year in the form of money or merchandise for which it didn't receive anything in exchange."[36]

If a loan is to be of value to the country to which it is granted, it must be put to productive, not consumptive or wasteful, use. A *60 Minutes* documentary on billions of dollars loaned to Brazil to clear jungle lands for homesteading was instructive. The World Bank's own agricultural experts testified that this plan was not feasible. Once cleared, rain forest soil would not be able to sustain agriculture. The bank was determined to loan this money anyway and did so. The result was just what the experts predicted: the fertility was quickly washed out of the soil, which was then unable to produce crops.[37] The waste in destroying forest for about seven years of grazing when it could be producing valuable timber, rubber, medicine, furs, and thousands of other products forever, and a standing forest's role in helping prevent the greenhouse effect, should be lost on no one.

The need to lend this money is rooted in monopolization. For example, the Arab oil cartel breached the monopoly of finance capital and intercepted billions of dollars once claimed by other monopolists. When this first occurred in 1973, Britain's most respected economic paper, *The Economist,* predicted that Kuwait and Saudi Arabia alone could "buy all the major companies on the world's stock exchanges in twenty-five years."[38] Instead much of this money was deposited in the safest haven, American and European banks, and reloaned to Third World countries. The simplicity of taking in immense sums of "petrodollars" (Arab oil money deposits) and lending this capital out in blocks of billions contrasts starkly with the other option. That would have required relinquishing the financial monopoly and spreading this investment money among local bankers who could work closely with productive industries of undeveloped countries.

Most of these loans to Third World countries did not develop industry (capital). The money was wasted through the various methods described above.* These unnecessary loans then became a mortgage on those nations' wealth. Uncollectable debts created by unequal trades and outright thefts now stand at $1.2 trillion. The interest that debt demands is a further claim against the wealth of the debtor countries:

> A debtor who repeatedly borrows more than the surplus his labor or business enterprise produces will fall further and further behind in his obligations until, sooner or later. the inexorable pressures of compound interest defeat him. . . . interest [is] usurious when the borrower's rightful share of profit [is] confiscated by the lender. . . . The creative power of capital [is] reversed and the compounding interest [becomes] destructive.[39]

One trillion dollars compounded at 10 percent per year will become $117 trillion in fifty years, and $13.78 quadrillion in one hundred years. That last figure is about $3 million for every man, woman, and child in the Third World. Their debt compounded at over 20 percent per year between 1973 and 1988—from under $100 billion to over $1.2 trillion. Most of these debts are incurred without the recipient country receiving any real benefits. The situation is comparable to the loathsome form of slavery known as peonage:

> In classic peonage, workers, though nominally free and legally free, are held in servitude by the terms of their indenture to their masters. Because their wages are set too low to buy the necessities, the master grants credit but restricts the worker to buying overpriced goods from the master's own store. As a result, each month the peon goes deeper and deeper into debt. For as long as the arrangement lasts, the peon cannot pay off the mounting debt and leave, and must keep on working for the master. Nigeria [and most other Third World countries] shares three crucial characteristics with a heroin-addicted debt-trap peon. First, both debts are unsecured consumer debts, made up of subsistence and spending-spree expenses, and with future income as the only collateral. Second, both loans are pure peonage loans, that is loans made not because of the potential of the project the loan is to be used for, but simply in order to secure legal control over the economic and political behavior of the debtor. Third, the only way made available for getting out of both debts is by getting into more debt.[40]

Third World capitalization would be catastrophic for First World monopolists. The development of productive capital with borrowed money capital would produce profits, pay the debt, and eventually eliminate the need to borrow. Without a place to export capital, interest rates (and the price of products) in the capital-accumulating country must fall. In short, the productive use of borrowed capital would eventually eliminate monopolization of capital:

---

\* Some oil money also went for essential things, such as purchasing oil for Third World countries, but we are only concerned with the loans which were spent nonproductively.

The ground rules of world trade produce ever greater inequality because of three basic facts of international life. The industrial nations are in a position to *keep the prices of commodities low and manufactured goods high.* They are unwilling to give special concessions to Third World countries that would enable them to overcome the inherent inequality that stems from the lack of capital, technology, and experience. *They refuse to permit the transfer of technology except under terms that perpetuate dependence.*[41] (emphasis added)

# 2

# World Wars, Trade Wars

## Commercial Wars

The commercial wars carried out almost without interruption from the end of the 17th century down to 1815, [were battles between societies for resources of neighboring countries.][1]

— Eli F. Heckscher, *Mercantilism*

At the peak of its trading power, Great Britain, with 2 percent of the world's population, produced 54 percent of the manufactured products in world commerce, and France produced much of the rest. The military power of the imperial nations controlled not only the resources of these colonies but their markets. This control was essential to market the enormous production from the ever more efficient industrial capital.

When Germany decided to industrialize in the late 1800s, "factories, machinery, and techniques were bought wholesale, usually from England."[2] At first, German manufactures were of inferior quality, just as later Japan's products were when she first industrialized and the Soviet Union's are now. However, it did not take the German workers long to learn—soon their industries were out-producing Britain's and with superior products. Britain's survival as a wealthy nation depended upon selling overpriced manufactured products and they could hardly afford to lose these markets. Control of trade through control of colonies led to World War I. Before that war

> [Europe] was "stifling" within her boundaries, with production everywhere outstripping the European demand for manufactured products. All Europe was therefore "driven by necessity to seek new markets far away," and "what more secure markets" could a nation possess than "countries placed under its influence?" . . . The rapid growth of German trade and the far-flung extension of German interests first encouraged in Germany a demand for a larger merchant marine, and then for a larger and more effective navy. . . . Without a strong fleet, Germany would find herself at the mercy of Britain, a "grasping and unscrupulous nation which, in the course of history, had taken opportunity after opportunity to destroy the trade of its commercial rivals."[3]

After that war, Britain thought that

> placing a ring of new nations around Germany (supported by proper guarantees)
> would do away with the immediate danger of a German-led economic union. . . .
> Once Germany's threat to British economic supremacy had abated the prewar
> crisis inside British politics would resolve itself.[4]

We can ignore the political explanations of the causes of World War I. Restrictive trade practices were strangling potentially wealthy countries and "everyone knew it would start, but no one knew how or when it would start until Archduke Ferdinand was shot."[5] Except for religious conflicts and petty wars of feudal lords, wars are primarily fought over trade.[*] Even President Woodrow Wilson recognized that World War I "was caused by commercial rivalry."[6] Germany was denied access to world markets much as Japan denies other countries access to her internal markets today. As with our revolution, the fundamental cause of the great war was that world trade was monopolized by the established powers:[7]

> It should be recalled that the practically universal use of sterling in international
> trade was a principal component of Britain's financial sway, and it was precisely
> into this strategic sphere that Germany began to penetrate, with the mark evolv-
> ing as an alternative to the pound. The Deutsche Bank conducted "a stubborn
> fight for the introduction of acceptance in overseas trade in place of the hitherto
> universal sterling bill . . . this fight lasted for decades and when the war came, a
> point had been reached at which the mark acceptance in direct transactions with
> German firms had partially established itself alongside the pound sterling". . . . "It
> seems probable that if war had not come in 1914, London would have had to
> share with Germany the regulatory power over world trade and economic
> development which it had exercised so markedly in the nineteenth century."[8]

Like Germany's Bismarck, Japan's rulers educated their people and developed industry. However, where Germany barely started on the road to becoming an imperial power and was stopped by World War I, Japan's empire was rapidly organized by force to build the Greater East Asia Co-Prosperity Sphere. Japan's appropriation of colonial territories cut powerful European traders off from what was once their private domain. This was the common bond between Germany and Japan in World War II.

There were other reasons for Germany's involvement besides trade, but her leaders were still burning over their humiliating defeat in World War I, a war fought over trade, and trade was still a component of this second struggle.[**] "The peace conference of 1919, held in Versailles, marked not the end of the war but rather its continuation by other means."[9] The injustice of controlled markets under the guise of free trade was never rectified. A resentful Germany prepared—at first secretly, then more and more openly—to employ military might to break those trade barriers and eliminate the humiliation of Versailles.

---

[*] Even most so-called religious wars have control of economies, people, and resources as an underlying purpose.

[**] The power brokers knew they were going to lose control of the governments by the vote. Thinking they could control the fascists, they turned over European governments to them to destroy the rising power of labor. Karl Polyani, *The Great Transformation,* paperback (Boston: Beacon Press, 1944), espec. p. 238.

William Appleman Williams, in *The Tragedy of American Diplomacy*, identified control of markets as the cause of World Wars I and II. He notes that free trade was then called the open door policy and "It was designed to win the objectives without recourse to war. . . . It does not prove that any nation that resisted (or resists) those objectives was (or is) evil, and therefore to blame for following conflicts or violence." While discussing markets, President Roosevelt and his advisors "explicitly noted as early as 1935 . . . that Germany, Italy and Japan were defined as dangers to the well-being of the United States."[10] This was reaffirmed in 1948 by Secretary of State Cordell Hull:

> Yes, war did come, despite the trade agreements. But it is a fact that war did not break out between the United States and any country with which we had been able to negotiate a trade agreement. It is also a fact that, with very few exceptions, the countries with which we signed trade agreements joined together in resisting the Axis. *The political line-up followed the economic line-up.*[11] (emphasis added)

Senior fellow of the World Policy Institute Walter Russell Mead, in an analysis of the gathering storm clouds of world trade during the 1980s, concurs that wars are extensions of trade wars. He warned that "the last time the world deprived two major industrial countries, Germany and Japan, of what each considered its rightful 'place in the sun' the result was World War II."[12]

Of course, Germany and Japan lost the war and were rebuilt as partners in the European/American/Japanese banking and trading system, and their success is well-known. Taiwan and South Korea did not have natural resources, developed economic infrastructures, or trained labor forces; however, both countries also became successful. We are too accustomed to self-serving explanations to trust the many pats on the back explaining this miracle. One need only study the postwar economic development of Europe and these countries and the real reason is all too obvious.

After World War II, Europe was devastated, and for the first two years of peace its reconstruction was stagnant. The intricate infrastructure of private wealth once operating the economy was in shambles. Eastern Europe was in much worse shape but, contrary to what we are told, community planning was steadily rebuilding their war-shattered societies. This frightened the powerful in the West, and plans were drafted to use American wealth to rebuild Western Europe. The Marshall Plan went into effect in 1948, and in about five years Western Europe was rebuilt. Even more shattered Eastern Europe had limited access to the world's resources and no wealthy country to provide industrial capital. As a result they took much longer to recover and, given such severe limitations and the continuing trade war against them (see chapter six), have not caught up yet. But note, under the threat of the latter's steady progress, Western Europe, Japan, Taiwan, and South Korea now have full trade rights within the system of monopolized capital.

A map provides the best insight on the prosperity of these nations. They are all on the fringes of the once rapidly expanding socialist countries which were considered our bitter enemies. They were given access to our capital, technology, and markets to develop prosperous societies that would be impervious to socialist ideology.[13] The old system of several centers of competing capital was abandoned for one collective system, and these countries were quickly industrialized. That these resource-poor countries became wealthy while naturally wealthy countries such as Indonesia, Malaysia, Zaire, Angola, Mozambique, and others remained poor effectively outlines the monopolization of world commerce.

## A Trap of Our Own Making

As opposed to the various trading blocs whose competition led to World Wars I and II, there has been put in place a single bloc to oppose socialist expansion. This has much to be recommended over the old system of separate centers of capital, but there are still problems. Losing industry to, and buying manufactured products from, overseas (beyond a balance point) will put the former industrial exporting countries into the same debt trap in which they have historically kept the Third World countries:

> "Until we get real wage levels down much closer to those of Brazils and Koreas, we cannot pass along productivity gains to wages and still be competitive." [Michael Moffitt quoting Stanley J. Mihelick, executive vice president for production at Goodyear. He goes on to explain:] With factory wages in Mexico and Korea averaging about $3 an hour, compared with U.S. wages of $14 or so, it looks as if we have a long way to go before U.S. wages will even be in the ball park with the competition. That the decline of U.S. industry is the natural and logical outcome of the evolution of the multinational corporate economy over the past 25 years has been a bitter pill to swallow and it will become increasingly distasteful as time goes on. *One consequence will be a nasty decline in the standard of living in the United States. . . .* we have the outlines of a true vicious circle: the world economy is dependent on growth in the U.S. economy but the U.S. domestic economy is [now] skewed more towards consumption than production and investment, and this consumption is in turn sustained by borrowing—at home and abroad. . . . The deal with surplus countries essentially has been as follows: you can run a big trade surplus with us provided that you put the money back into our capital markets. . . . The key lies in the explosion of debt, both public and private. Total debt in the U.S. economy (government, corporate, farm, and consumer) has risen from $1.6 trillion in 1970 to $4.6 trillion in 1980 and reached $7 trillion at the end of 1986.[14] (emphasis added)

This process is spreading havoc throughout the American economy. Many industries have been wiped out by Japanese, German, Taiwanese, and South Korean competition. For example, "America's machine tool industry is now targeted for extinction by Japan."[15] With $8.6 billion of overseas sales, Caterpillar Tractor of Peoria, Illinois, accounts for most of our machinery exports. Kamatsu of Japan is pricing their heavy machinery "10 to 15 percent below Caterpillar," and is building an excavator with "twice the horsepower of Caterpillar's biggest machine" and a bulldozer 30 percent more powerful.[16] Equally threatening has been the widely discussed potential for Japan to capture the market for computer chips. And in 1988 China offered to launch satellites at one-quarter of the price the U.S charged; under these conditions no private U.S. rocket industry can survive.

The above are reruns of earlier trade battles that Japan has won. By 1983, for example, the Japanese produced 96 percent of all imported motorcycles sold in the U.S.[17] However, if Korea and other low-wage countries continue their economic development, and free trade principles are followed, firms in both Japan and America will be destroyed. It is the simple logic of the cheapest producer capturing the market. Cheaper, however, normally means cheaper paid labor, not less labor expended.

A partial list of goods produced in other countries and their respective penetration of the U.S. market outlines the problem: table radios, 100 percent; video recorders, 100 percent; CB radios, 90 percent; shoes, 86 percent; black-and-white television, 85 percent; digital watches, 68 percent; stereo components, 64 percent; electronic calculators, 50 percent; phonographs, 43 percent; microwave ovens, 33 percent.[18] One-third of the automobiles sold in America are imported. At present 25 percent of all products purchased by the American people are manufactured overseas.[19]

This is economic insanity. Through so-called free trade the developed nations are destroying each other's industries, while 70 percent of the world's population is desperately short of industrial capital. There is no mechanism within the profit system to implant this new technology where it is badly needed while keeping the already producing factories operating. This vividly highlights the problems generated by monopolization of capital. Giant producers are so busy competing with each other, mostly for control of current markets, that no one stops to consider that this cannibalization of each other's industries might be both ridiculous and ultimately self-destructive. The destruction of capital by wars is well-known. What is unknown is that trade wars destroy and forgo production of even more capital.

This wasted capital could just as well produce industrial tools for sale to the Third World. (For that matter, why not give this capital away? It is wasted anyway—see conclusion.) With these tools and their own land and labor, these countries could build their own economic infrastructure. If it had been acceptable social policy, it would have been possible for the entire world to have been industrialized and its social capital brought close to the level of the industrialized countries during the last forty years.

When capital is diverted to an undeveloped country to produce for a developed country, the advantage of the latter's cheap labor destroys the already established industry of the developed country. The cheaper products will command more and more of the market, and the labor of the newly emerging countries will demand higher and higher wages. Japan's labor force has been docile, but the managers, knowing they would be forced to anyway, have been steadily increasing wages. There have been bloody battles in South Korea as workers there fight to increase their income. With true free trade, wages of developed and developing countries will equalize, and their integrated economies will eventually balance. This process is quite far along within Western European countries, the United States, and Japan, while it is only in the early stages of development in Taiwan and South Korea:

> With the growth of worldwide sourcing, telecommunications, and money transfers, there is no pecuniary reason for U.S. firms to pay Americans to do what Mexicans or Koreans will do at a fraction of the cost. This is why "elite" U.S. working-class jobs are being sent abroad and "outsourcing" is the current rage in manufacturing. As a result, American multinationals remain highly competitive and their profits are booming, while the United States itself is becoming less and less competitive. In the 1980s, U.S. capital goods exports have collapsed while imports of both consumer and producer goods have surged, no doubt in part because U.S. firms are now importing these products from foreign lands. In other words,

we once exported the capital goods used to manufacture our consumer imports; now we are also importing the capital goods to run what remains of our domestic industry. Even a growing percentage of output in "sunrise" industries like computers and telecommunications is moving offshore. At home, the result is downward pressure on wages and chronic job insecurity for the remaining manufacturing job holders, who are more docile as a result. Meanwhile, the castoffs from manufacturing and mining plus new labor market participants flock to low-productivity jobs serving coffee, making hamburgers, and running copying machines. Barring protectionism or a decline in U.S. wages to Korean or Mexican levels, this situation will persist and, in fact, will probably get much worse.[20]

Just as Britain one hundred years ago sold industrial technology to Germany who then used it to take over world markets, American labor has lost both industrial jobs and buying power by selling our technology. The miracle of "more Americans working then ever before" has been accomplished by reducing high-paying primary jobs and expanding lower-paying service jobs. The buying power of individual nonsupervisory American labor has declined by 17 percent from 1973 to 1987.[21] Again assuming true free trade, once it all balances, foreign labor and American labor within the power blocs monopolizing capital will receive roughly equal compensation.

## The Effects on the
## Industrialized Countries' Labor and Capital

This process is traumatic for the finance structure and workers within the countries whose economies are declining. (This, of course, is why countries go to war over trade.) It will be unsettling for America's monopolists when they discover that, once foreign industry with its lower paid labor is strong enough, they will be eliminated as intermediaries.* The current bandwagon approach—the appropriation of both foreign and American labor by American capital contracting cheap overseas labor—cannot go on forever. Foreign industrialists are getting stronger and will soon challenge U.S. monopolies. Once foreign producers crack the distribution barriers, they will claim most of the hitherto protected monopoly profits. Professor Lester Thurow outlines the problem:

> Our corporations once produced, but now they just distribute. They buy overseas, put their name on the product and distribute it through established channels. It is only a matter of time till those overseas producers distribute their own product and our corporations disappear.[22]

This scenario will only occur under continued free trade. While expounding the philosophy of free trade, we must abide by it. Of course, once these monopolists see themselves being eliminated, they will likely join forces with American labor and insist on protectionist legislation. All agree that, if this does occur, it will trigger a multidimensional crisis, in which chaotic financial markets will play a

---

* At this time Japan is investing the wealth (exporting capital) appropriated by unequal labor values in the U.S. at the rate of $1 billion per week. The products sold in the United States are priced much higher to the Japanese consumer (*NBC News*, 3 May 1989). This control of prices, as opposed to the rhetoric of free markets, appropriates the wealth of Americans.

major role. How do these finance monopolists get repaid if the industries they financed cannot sell overseas, and there is no local market? Many industries in the developed countries will have been eliminated (the destruction of capital through trade wars) and rebuilding the former balanced internal economy will be expensive. It would require enormous labor and resources without initially providing consumer products.

The least traumatic course may be to allow the economies to balance. But these economies will not retain that balance. Just now (1988) China has opened to outside investors coastal economic zones that encompass a population of two hundred million cheap laborers. With all the necessary political infrastructure in place to control labor and markets, capital will now flow to China. Initially there will be great profits for foreign investors as they take over other's markets. This will also be a large gain to China even at those low wages.

However, once China is developed and the skills learned by this organized labor force, the scene will change. Where most Third World countries are powerless to prevent the capture of their markets, China is not. Like Japan, they will insist on exporting a surplus and our rhetoric of free trade must allow it. Wages and profits will rise to just below those competing in world markets.

If this is allowed to reach its logical conclusion, much of the wealth of the U.S., Japan, and other countries will then be transferred to China. She would be like ten Japans and Hong Kongs competing on world markets. Even now China's textile exports to the U.S. have been climbing 19 percent a year. They have now reached 11 percent of the total U.S. market and China has agreed to limit increases to 3 percent a year.[23] These foreign workers received an average wage that was less than 6 percent of the wages received for identical work by American workers and, "without powerful unions overseas to limit corporate greed, competing on the world market means little more than a race to the bottom."[24]

We should make no mistake about this: integrating a high-wage developed economy with a low-wage developing economy—under free trade principles—will be traumatic. The wealthy society's labor income must take a severe cut. When labor costs between these countries equalize, monopoly capital will then reach outside the newly balanced economies for even cheaper labor and the downward cycle will continue.

It is unlikely that this process will continue unchallenged. Even now South Korea is copying Japan's methods of restricting imports. They are deflecting the negative effects of free trade and running a large trade surplus with the U.S. The American government, in turn, is threatening retaliation.

Within the vary narrow constraints of the prevailing ideology, attempting to integrate through free trade was done in good faith. The enormous profits being recorded by corporations and steadily increasing GNPs have been acclaimed by monopolists as proof that their theories are correct. These profits show up in corporate expansions, foreign purchases of American land and businesses, a climbing stock market, corporate takeovers, and the multiplication of billionaires.[25] This accumulation of wealth is occurring while the buying power of individual American labor has been falling. As the wealthy increase their share, Americans with no net share of the nation's wealth increased from 25 percent of the population in 1974 to 54 percent in 1988.[26] This enormous trauma to a developed society is not necessary; it is possible to capitalize the Third World while protecting the industrialized countries' labor and industries.

## Dependent Societies Can Be Held Hostage

The U.S. government and grain companies cooperated (conspired) to persuade the South Korean people to change their diet from rice to wheat. The effort was so effective that by 1978 South Korea was importing $1 billion worth of American products, mostly wheat. The Korean government then set the price of rice at about 60 percent of local production costs. Rice imports rose rapidly—from almost nothing in 1978 to 900,000 metric tons in 1980. From 100 percent self-sufficiency in food in 1960, South Korea imported 60 percent in 1986, and "now purchases over $2 billion in U.S. agricultural products each year."[27] In 1985 the Korean Christian Farmers group wrote to President Ronald Reagan:

> Due to the flooding of foreign agricultural products into Korea, our farmers have suffered chronic deficits in their farming operations, causing them to go deeper and deeper into debt. . . . [Of] these foreign agricultural goods which are destroying Korean agriculture and our farmers' livelihood, 90 percent or more are exported from the United States.[28]

Exporting that food may be profitable to the exporting country, but, when their land is capable of producing adequate food, it is a disaster to the importing countries. I wonder how the American farmers would feel if 60 percent of their market were taken over by another society. Not only American farmers would suffer; the entire economy would be severely affected. That imported food is not as cheap as it appears. If the money expended on imports had been spent within the local economy, it would have multiplied several times as it moved through the economy contracting local labor. (This is the multiplier effect.) If that $65 per ton paid for American wheat were spent internally, and assuming that the multiplier factor in South Korea is 5 (it could be higher or lower), it would create $325 worth of GNP. Instead that $65 multiplied within the American economy, allowing its magic to work here. This moving of money through an economy is why there is a lot of money in a high-wage manufacturing and exporting country and so little in a low-wage country "dependent" on imports.*

The Korean farm communities' loss of income drove thousands into the cities to work in the developing manufacturing, assembly, and export businesses. This followed the historic pattern of displacing agricultural labor to provide cheap industrial labor. This coincided with American planners' efforts to reduce their huge surpluses of wheat. The large grain traders naturally fulfilled the needs of both.[29]

South Korea's fledgling industries were designed for importing, assembling, and then exporting. This succeeded so well that "the total sum of its imports and exports are equal to 85 percent of its GNP, compared to 20 percent for Japan."[30] Eighty to 90 percent of these underdeveloped countries' exports are controlled by international corporations.[31] At present the Korean economy is "hostage" to im-

---

* The multiplier factor in different countries could be lower or higher than this example.

ports of food and assembly parts, while it is equally dependent on foreign markets for export. To be dependent is to be subject to blackmail.

It was the embargo of grain that created the greatest crisis for Chile when outside powers successfully masterminded the overthrow of its democratically elected government in 1973.[32] If a country wishes economic and political security, it must avoid dependency. Break that circulation of commerce at any point, and a dependent economy is in trouble.[*] Even now (1987 to 1989), there is protectionist legislation being introduced in Congress aimed at curbing South Korean imports.

These unequal labor costs result in some strange warps in the economies of trading countries. Coking coal is shipped twelve thousand miles from West Virginia to Japan to be used in the smelting of steel. This Japanese steel can then undersell American steel manufactured a few miles from the source of that coal.[33] Anaconda and Butte, Montana, lost fifteen hundred jobs when Anaconda Copper decided to close its local smelter and ship copper ore to Japan to be smelted, after which it is returned and sold in the U.S.[34] The closure of many steel mills and other industries faced with cheaper goods produced by foreign competitors is correctly labeled as the efficiency of a market economy. But as the automobile engineers said when they built those five-hundred- horsepower gas-guzzlers and suddenly the world wanted truly efficient cars, "We were working for the wrong kind of efficiency."

Free trade is a commendable goal. The problem in the past was that true free trade was only actively promoted within a predetermined production and trading group. The group members were usually bonded by racial and cultural ties. Those not covered by a fair trade agreement had to fight off monopolization of their industry and commerce. The American Revolution is the outstanding successful example. We have already discussed Germany, but Spain, Holland, and Portugal were once major powers, all eventually overwhelmed in the battle for world trade. Mutual support has now expanded to include other societies now perceived to be necessary for the security of Western nations; hence the plans to unite Europe into one solid trading bloc. The past practice of containing socialism with key allies and force could be replaced by example and support and bringing all nations within the world capital and trading structure. If that were to happen, rights would be extended to all countries.[**]

## True Efficiency in Developing Countries

Developing economies should be designed to be as self-sufficient in food and industry as possible. The industries that require economies of scale should be regionally planned and integrated and balanced with other undeveloped countries. Shipping products halfway around the world to an industrialized

---

[*] A key aspect of the effort to prevent the expansion of socialism is to make these economies interdependent. Once that is accomplished, a country's economy would be in immediate shambles if it tried to withdraw from the system.

[**] Keynes predicted that the world would be burdened by the inequities of capitalism for some time yet but, when the world became capitalized, the price of capital (interest) would fall drastically and essentially eliminate the appropriation of labor through monopolization of capital. (William Greider, *Secrets of the Temple*, pp. 173–74).

society that has the surplus capital and labor to produce its own when these same products could be sold regionally if all labor in local societies had rights to capital and were brought into a local production/trading system, is economic insanity. Instead of cooperatively extending capital to needy societies and developing those consumer markets, capital structures are cannibalizing each other battling for the limited developed market.

The labor and capital in developed countries should be protected from destruction by low labor costs of undeveloped countries. This, of course, requires the development of balanced economies in currently undeveloped countries and the necessary capital can only come from the developed countries. Once Third World countries are economically developed, they should then be integrated with other developed industrial economies using the maximum efficiencies of each society. This would cut deeply into monopoly profits but their present prosperity may be short-lived anyway. Unless they can maintain power over all governments, their crisis will come shortly after that of their workers and they can hardly start another war to protect this wealth, as with current military technology it will all be destroyed.*

Countries, like people, must have the right to productive work. If a country lacks natural resources, it should be assigned a higher level of industrial capital. This is what happened with our three miracle countries. Without resources, they were given access to industrial technology, capital, and markets and became wealthy.

Developing societies through rational planning—and following the principles of peace, compassion, and social justice—could create a world that is immensely richer than one based on monopoly capital and unequal trade. Once societies are developed with a balanced economy, then—and only then—will the efficiencies of free enterprise and free trade function for the benefit of all.

---

* With friendly money havens like Switzerland, wealth could escape control of all governments. This is happening now as the transnational corporations move their headquarters offshore. Whenever under threat from one country they simply operate from a subsidiary in another country. It would require cooperation of most countries they are doing business in to bring them under control.

# 3

# The Creation of Enemies

## Religious Wars Are Trade Wars

The creation of enemies to justify wars that erupt from trade wars has a long history. Even most so-called religious wars have control of economies, people, and resources as an underlying cause. For instance, the Crusades were fought for hundreds of years and we consider them ancient history. But that battle is not yet over. During the breaking up of the Ottoman Empire, the British and French with their military might gained control and decreed the borders and rulers of most of the Middle Eastern countries. Christianity won that war and has controlled those resources ever since. Whereas gentler religions have been overwhelmed by Christianity and their populations absorbed into the Christian belief system, the Moslems were an equally violent and socially protective religion. Their religion protected their race and culture and the Arabs could not be absorbed. The tinderbox of the Middle East is fueled by the hatred Muslims feel over the control of their resources and destiny by Christians.

The current civil war in Lebanon started when Israel invaded to provide the Christians with more muscle to control that government. The old Lebanese social contract under which Christians and Moslems shared the presidency but the real power remained in Christian hands was crumbling. Up to this time (1989) that attempt to maintain Christian control has failed. Meantime, as in all these conflicts engineered to maintain power, the civilian population is being devastated. The Crusades are far from over and the screaming rhetoric of enemies goes on as each religion battles to maintain control of its subjects' minds and gain the support of other societies—and the economic power to be realized from control of a society and its resources.

The destruction of the Templars in the Middle Ages was a classic example of destroying a group of people through accusations that they were immoral and a threat to the rest of society, when in reality they were only a threat to those in power.

The Templars were industrious and faithful servants of Christianity. Their history began in 1119 when nine knights formed an association to protect pilgrims in the Holy Land.* They fought so valiantly that

> gifts in abundance flowed in on the Order, large possessions were bestowed on it in all countries of the west. . . . By the Bull, *Omne datum optimum*, granted by Pope Alexander III in 1162, the Order of the Templars acquired great importance, and from this time forth, it may be regarded as totally independent, acknowledging no authority but that . . . of the supreme pontiff.[1]

The Templars fought many battles during the Crusades, and by 1302 they were spread all over Europe and were enormously wealthy and powerful. Much of the land owned by the Templars had been given to them by the ancestors of the local aristocracy and by the church; their successors resented and feared the power of this great order. The local bishops and clergy made many complaints to the pope about the Templars' refusal to recognize local religious authority.

When a French pope was consecrated in 1305, King Philip IV of France and other nobles instigated an intrigue against the respected Templars. The French secret service spread vicious rumors and,

> On the night of the 13th of October, all the Templars in the French dominions were simultaneously arrested. . . . They were accused of worshiping an idol covered with an old skin, embalmed, having the appearance of a piece of polished oil-cloth. "In this idol," we are assured, "there were two carbuncles for eyes, bright as the brightness of heaven, and it is certain that all hope of the Templars was placed in it: it was their sovereign god, and they trusted in it with all their heart." They are accused of burning the bodies of the deceased brethren, and making the ashes into a powder, which they administered to the younger brethren in their food and drink, to make them hold fast their faith and idolatry; of cooking and roasting infants, and anointing their idols with the fat; of celebrating hidden rites and mysteries, to which the young and tender virgins were introduced, and of a variety of abominations too absurd and horrible to be named.[2]

Like all inquisition charges, these fabrications could not be defended against and confessions were obtained by torture. King Philip then sent the findings to other countries of Europe. These preposterous accusations were at first rejected, but by 1308 the Templars were totally discredited and destroyed—many burned at the stake. In only three years the industrious defenders of Christianity who had been perceived as elite warriors and builders of the Christian world, commanding enormous resources and respect, were enemies cast into oblivion. The Second Estate—the church and the nobility, recognized throughout history as one collective power—had acted together to reclaim their wealth and power.**

All the essentials of a cold war are in that short three-year effort that destroyed the Templars. Of course, destroying them was the very purpose of the intrigue. When the war cry against an enemy goes out, the targeted people are denied the protection of others in society. Common people are busy with surviving and depend on their leaders to guide the ship of state; few will come to the defense of

---

* Pictures of crusading knights, each with a large cross emblazoned on his dress, depict Templars.

** The First Estate was the king and the Third Estate was the common people.

beleaguered and accused people. Even moral people in the higher echelons of power do not stand up to refute these atrocious lies. To do so is to risk being swept aside in the hysteria—the lies soon become reality to that society. The enemy belief system is then complete.

## Today's Fictional Enemies

The pattern of the current rhetoric of fear (our Cold War) begins much earlier in history than the rise of the Soviet Union as a world power; it goes back to the American and French Revolutions. As a result of these victories over aristocracy, rights were declared for all men.[3] This frightened the powerful and they immediately asserted their control by frightening the population into a witch hunt. The war cry went out: "Look out for the Illuminati! Look out for the Illuminati! They want to take over your country! Your church! The world!"[4]

But the Illuminati were not an enemy. They were a secret organization trying to stem the religious inquisition with its horrors of burning innocent people at the stake. They were defending the common people from the abuse of power by society's leaders. As a threat to the powerful right wing of the church, they were vilified as the enemy. The people, trusting their leaders and not having any other information, followed the war cry and supported the attempted destruction of those who should have been their brothers. The Illuminati had to remain secret or they would be burned at the stake. The Templars in the same situation, cast as enemies, had been well-known and respected and had no inkling they were targeted for destruction; they couldn't hide.

Fear gripped the monopolizers of wealth again after the Russian Revolution. More rights were being claimed by more people. The scourge of Bolshevism was substituted for the old Illuminati scare, but the basic message was the same— "Communism! Communism! They want to take over your country! Your church! The world!"[5] In the United States in 1920 this took the form of the Palmer raids in which, just like the Templars in the Middle Ages, thousands were arrested in the middle of the night, hundreds deported, and hundreds more sent to prison.

The powerful became frightened again after World War II; the Soviet Union now controlled half of Europe and the dreaded socialist experiment again looked as though it would spread. The second "Great Red Scare" went out and we witnessed the House Un-American Activities Committee and Senator Joseph McCarthy taking the lead in creating a national fever that destroyed tens of thousands of lives.[6]

The witch hunts of the McCarthy era have a remarkable similarity to the Inquisition. During those earlier trials, the first ones burned at the stake were rather defenseless people. But as the hysteria continued, the accusatory finger pointed higher and higher and eventually pointed towards those in power. When these powerful became the target, the hysteria died down. After a respite the witch hunts would start again. This cycle continued for four hundred years. In the same pattern, when McCarthy's witch hunts started destroying those in power, the powerful turned and destroyed him and the hysteria died down. Whenever the personal risk to those leaders is high, they are motivated to defend themselves. This demonstrates that the process can be controlled and the public protected if the leaders ever decide they wish to do so.

The use of these same lies and tactics by Hitler against the Jews is well-known history. However, the main thrust of Hitler's propaganda was against organized labor, which was poised to take over the government by the vote. The fascist takeovers of the governments of Europe were a sham:

> In no case was an actual revolution against constituted authority launched; fascist tactics were those of a sham rebellion arranged with the tacit approval of the authorities who pretended to have been overwhelmed by force. . . . Hitler was . . . put in power by the feudalist clique around President Hindenburg, just as Mussolini and Primo de Rivera were ushered into office by their respective sovereigns.[7]

When Hitler came to power in 1933 his police were ordered to shoot key labor leaders on sight and within a year one hundred thousand were in prison. The real target of this backroom political deal was labor.[8]

Although there had previously been much rhetoric against and individual persecution of the Jews within Germany, organized attacks against them did not start until November 9, 1938—"The Night of Broken Glass." Much of the onslaught against the Jews by fascists was undertaken to repay the super-secret Thule Society (roughly the same as our Aryan Nations) for its early financial support of Hitler. The symbol of this society was the swastika. This became the symbol of German fascism, and it is reasonable to assume that it was these fanatics who were put into positions of power by Hitler to repay them for their financial support.[9]

The persecution of the Jews has a long history—the Holocaust of World War II was just the climactic finale of a thousand years of hate rhetoric against them by religious extremists.[10] Just as the power of right-wing extremists in our society ebbs and flows, the power of these extremists ebbed and flowed. Where it was once common to openly persecute the Jews, the horrors of the Holocaust make it no longer acceptable. All who would advocate such a thing are now outside the permitted parameters of political or religious debate.

Today most Christians are very supportive of the rights of Jewish people. This stems from the positive statements of the church leaders, as opposed to the violent rhetoric of the right-wing minority that was once permitted. This again demonstrates that the process of creation of enemies is very controllable; social scientists would do well to study just how an entire society can be guided to commit such offenses against another innocent society. With nuclear weapons and with different enemies targeted, other far greater atrocities are possible.[*]

Jewish persecution was primarily religious, with economic jealousy and theft of their property secondary. The Moslem-Christian standoff is religious, but control of resources follows religious control of populations. If a society cannot be subverted religiously, it must almost always be controlled militarily. Politicians have simply copied the religious practice of targeting enemies by labeling them

---

[*]  See Jerry Sanders, *Peddlers of Crisis,* for an exposé of one group that admits to deliberately creating enemies in our society today. There are many more organized groups that practice this form of social control. See Milton Mayer, *They Thought They Were Free,* for a description of how the German people under fascism felt just as free as Americans today. Hitler guided the German people to kill with a cold war that, except for the attack on the Jews, was identical to the Cold War waged in the U.S. ever since World War II.

and accusing them of gross atrocities. It is a very primitive social survival mechanism practiced on a national and international scale.

## That Evil Empire

After the Bolshevik revolution, the Soviets had good reason to be paranoid. There were many powerful people inside the new Soviet Union who disagreed with that revolution, and there were powerful external allies ready to support them in a counterrevolution. These outside forces (fourteen countries) mobilized 180,000 troops and armed 300,000 anti-Bolshevik troops within the Soviet Union in a three-year intervention that almost overthrew the new government.[11] Those foreign powers have never abandoned their goal of destroying this socialist society and removing its threat to their centuries-old system of world domination. As in any society after any revolution, there were those within the Soviet Union who were sympathetic to, and subject to manipulation by, these outside forces; millions of innocent people (even many dedicated and loyal communists) were rounded up and sent to Siberia, and many were executed. Struggles for power became mixed with the legitimate battle to defend the revolution, and many within the power structure were swallowed up in that holocaust.

The Western press gave the numbers killed as forty million, then twenty million, then ten million, and the figures are still coming down. These are the same principles that "peddlers of crisis" have been functioning under for thousands of years. The greater the lie the more surely it will be believed by those who will become their followers. Even if it is done only verbally and the accuser is in no personal physical danger, the surest way to be recognized as a leader is to lead an attack against an enemy.

There has been so much fabrication that it is impossible to know what is true. I am satisfied that those searching for any who were a threat to the security of this new nation sent a minimum of six to seven million to Siberia, of which only a few hundred thousand survived to return, and a maximum of five hundred thousand were executed. Former Ambassador to the Soviet Union George Keenan, undoubtedly the most knowledgeable American of those times and one of the prime promoters of the Cold War, is quoted as saying it was in the tens of thousands. That is likely close to being correct though it could be in the low hundreds of thousands.[12] The Soviets are now opening those records, restoring the good name of these people, and historians are tracing what happened to each individual so their families can know their fate. Perhaps the world may someday know the true numbers of those unjustly persecuted souls.

While the Soviets were taking drastic measures to prevent counterrevolution, idealistic believers of Marx were restructuring the Soviet economy along his precepts. Like us after we gained our freedom, these people were proud of their revolution and worked hard to build their country. Their command economy worked well to build heavy industry and a basic infrastructure, which served them well in repulsing the onslaught of the German armies.

## A Cold War Is a Weapon

The hoaxes described above were all perpetrated by powerful people to slow down or, if possible, prevent gains in rights for the common person. It only required a change of names to fit whomever the power brokers perceived as a threat to their power. Once people obtained rights, how else could a power structure deal with any group that took those rights seriously and offered a greater share of the wealth to the common people? Powerful leaders put out the rhetoric about an enemy, which motivates a country's citizens to destroy what is only a threat to those in power.

In these battles for minds, it is certain that almost all except the originators of the hoaxes are totally unaware they are being manipulated to hate.[13] This includes the secondary echelons of power. Since they are unaware of the original fiction, when they move to the top the belief system is complete. Since they are not aware of the background, the threat looks real. At times it becomes real; the attacks by an enraged or frightened population upon those targeted as the enemy trigger fear and defensive action and that defense appears threatening to the deeply biased original aggressors.

Throughout history tens of millions of common people have died violently protecting not themselves but whoever was in power. Of course, while innocent people are slaughtering other innocent people, the hands of the perpetrators of these hoaxes remain spotlessly clean and their personal lives undamaged. However, in a war with today's nuclear weapons, most people may die and all will be very severely affected. It is time to analyze how enemies are created and, just as in the constitution of the Soviet Union, make it illegal to attack and degrade another society. Then whenever someone breaks out with the war cry of an enemy he or she should be taken to task for that disregard for our rights and the rights of others. That disregard for others' rights in the past has created the enormous waste of wars and cold wars.

# 4

# The Cold War

## The Long-standing Threat to the Soviet Union

Perhaps it is a universal truth that the loss of liberty at home is to be charged to provisions against danger real or pretended from abroad.[1]

— Letter from James Madison to Thomas Jefferson in 1798

No one would dispute that the arms race is wasteful. Nor would many Americans question that these arms are necessary if we are to prevent or repel an attack upon us. The enemy is, of course, the Soviet Union. We have already reviewed how cold wars originate, but to test the validity of the mind-set on this one we will review some simple historical facts that most Americans already know but do not put together into one picture. As all Americans have been exposed to "our" side of the story, I will concentrate on a few key facts that are practically unknown to the majority of Americans and are studiously ignored by those who interpret reality for us.

In 1916, at the beginning of World War I, Russia's industrial capacity was 13 percent that of the United States. During the turmoil of that war, Russian workers successfully overthrew the czarist aristocracy and installed a Bolshevik government.* Note the threat Americans feel upon hearing that word "Bolshevik"—yet in Russian it simply means "majority." This linguistic phobia is only the first of several distortions of reality carefully cultivated before our time and seldom questioned today. Would it not be a little silly to stand up and shrilly warn about the possible outbreak of majority rule in another country? The word "Soviet" also triggers some alarm, yet it simply means a council formed of a body

---

* In a holding action, Aleksandr Kerensky formed a government that lasted six months and it was this government that the Bolsheviks overthrew. Still under pressure to provide more rights to the people to hold off the revolution, Kerensky offered to institute a tax structure along the precepts of America's philosopher Henry George. It would be interesting to speculate on what would have ensued if this had happened. As it gives enormous rights to the people, no country in the world has attempted George's very sound principles of taxation, which were also those of the Physiocrats, the originators of the free enterprise philosophy. Of course, the revolutionists were following the philosophy of Karl Marx and were not interested in any delaying tactics.

of delegates. In theory, these delegates were to represent equal segments of the population and fulfill the goals of majority rule or Bolshevism. In the U.S. this is called democracy.

This reorganization to democracy had barely begun when fourteen countries sent in 180,000 troops and armed 300,000 more dissident Soviets to overthrow that revolution. This effort almost succeeded; nearly two-thirds of the Soviet Union came under interventionist and counterrevolutionary control before they were defeated. The effort was more successful than our history books acknowledge—Finland, Latvia, Lithuania, Estonia and the eastern half of Poland were carved from the Soviet nation by that intervention. Except for Leningrad, this barred the Soviet Union from Atlantic ports and restricted her access to world trade.

This invasion was undertaken under the guise of reinstating the lawful government and persuading the Russian military again to take the field in the war with Germany. Considering the initial intervention was undertaken just three months before the end of the war and lasted over three years, the latter was hardly a credible reason.

A famine then ensued and possibly 7.5 million Soviets died.[*] But note, with only a few thousand killed, the revolution itself was one of the least bloody in history. It was the intervention that disrupted the Soviet economy and compounded, if not directly created, this disaster. This key piece of history is rarely recited in the United States, not even in Montana, Washington, and Michigan—the three states that furnished the 17,500 American troops.[2] It seems the embarrassing chapters are conveniently left out of the history books. In the same way, external powers are destabilizing Angola, Mozambique, Ethiopia, and other countries and causing famines today.

Staggered by the chaos and destruction generated by World War I and the intervention, the Soviets did not regain their prewar industrial capacity until 1928.[3] Eleven years later, on the eve of World War II, their industrial capacity had reached 25 percent that of the United States. On June 22, 1941, Germany attacked with a modern, heavily motorized army designed to overwhelm the Soviets in six months. In those six months, Germany's offensive (Operation Barbarossa, named after the legendary emperor German myths proclaimed would return and establish a great German empire) took the invading troops to the outskirts of Stalingrad and within sight of Moscow, where they were stopped. In desperation, the Soviets moved their industrial machinery ahead of the invading army and rebuilt beyond the Ural Mountains. By 1942 these factories were, by a large margin, outproducing Germany in war materiel. That year, the Soviets produced

> 21,700 combat aircraft, 24,400 tanks and self-propelled guns, 127,100 guns of various other types and 230,000 mortars. Germany produced 11,600 combat aircraft during that year, 6,200 tanks and assault guns, 40,500 guns of other types, and 9,800 mortars. . . . In 1943, the U.S.S.R. produced 130,300 guns, 24,100 tanks and self-propelled guns, [and] 29,900 aircraft. . . . [That year, the Germans produced] 73,700 guns, 10,700 tanks and assault guns, and 19,300 aircraft. . . . In 1944, the Soviet munitions industry put out over 122,400 guns, 29,000 tanks and

---

[*] Some sources says thirteen million, others as low as three to four million.

self-propelled guns, and upwards of 33,200 combat aircraft. . . . Germany further expanded her war production in 1944. Output of guns was 148,200, tanks and assault guns 18,300 and combat aircraft 34,100.[4]

The above statistics came from Soviet historian Vilnis Sipols. A true accounting needs to allow for the weapons destroyed on either side, but all agree the early Soviet losses were several times greater than the Germans'. American historian Paul Kennedy of Yale University, an authority on the economic strength of countries at war throughout history, supports those Soviet figures:

> It is worth noting that Russia produced 4,000 more aircraft than Germany in 1941 and 10,000 more in 1942. . . . By the beginning of 1945, on the Belorussian and Ukrainian fronts alone, Soviet superiority was both absolute and awesome, fivefold in manpower, fivefold in armor, over sevenfold in artillery and seventeen times the German strength in the air.[5]

During 1942, the Russian front stalemated, but as the rebuilt factories came on stream the tide began to turn. The Battle of Stalingrad was won February 2, 1943, when the Soviets surrounded the German troops. It is estimated that over 1.5 million German soldiers were killed, wounded, or captured during that seventeen-month battle. The Soviet loss totaled 800,000 killed and hundreds of thousands more wounded.[6] The Russian victory was followed that summer by a six-week tank, artillery, and infantry battle at the Kursk Salient outside Moscow. This was the greatest tank and artillery battle in all history. Almost simultaneously there were the immense battles of Kharkov and Orel, which the Soviets also won.[7] The myth of German invincibility was shattered, and the Soviets cleared the Germans out of half their occupied territory by the end of that year.

For two years the Soviet Union almost single-handedly held off the German war machine and, in the third year, was rapidly driving the invaders from their land. Though it would take fifteen more months to complete the decimation of Germany's armies, World War II in Europe was already won in those first thirty-six months. Even after the Allied landing at Normandy (June 6, 1944), over two German soldiers out of every three were still on the Soviet front. It has been calculated that 85 percent of Germany's firepower had been expended against the Soviet Union.

This war was a terrible sacrifice for the Soviets. They lost 15 percent of their population (over 20 million) and millions more were severely wounded. These casualties comprised between 20 and 30 percent of their prime labor. One of every four Soviet citizens was killed or wounded in that war. By comparison, the United States had only 12.5 million men and women under arms and lost 293,000, and its homeland was untouched.

In this titanic struggle, 30 percent of the Soviet Union's national wealth was destroyed: "31,950 industrial enterprises, 65,000 kilometers of railway track and 4100 railway stations; 36,000 postal, telegraph and telephone offices; 56,000 miles of main highway, 90,000 bridges and 10,000 [electric] power stations." Damaged beyond immediate use were "1135 coal mines and 3,000 oil wells, carr[ied] off to Germany [were] 14,000 steam boilers, 14,000 turbines and 11,300 electric generators." Also destroyed in the scorched earth policy were 98,000 collective farms and 2,890 machine and tractor stations. Most of the livestock in the occupied territories—7 million horses, 17 million cattle, 20 million hogs, 27 million sheep and goats and 110 million poultry—was appropriated to feed Germany.

(Quite simply, the Germans were not going to repeat the disaster of 1917 when their food supply collapsed. This time their citizens were going to be well fed with protein from the Soviet Union. The Soviets could starve.) "They destroyed, completely or partially, 15 large cities, 1,710 towns and 70,000 villages. They burned or demolished 6,000,000 buildings and deprived 25,000,000 people [out of 88,000,000 in the occupied territories] of shelter." The Germans planned to destroy the budding new Soviet culture that, without the old privileged classes, was such a threat to the established power brokers. "They looted and destroyed 40,000 hospitals and medical centers, 84,000 schools and colleges, and 43,000 public libraries with 110,000,000 volumes." Along with these cultural treasures, "some 44,000 theaters were destroyed and 427 museums. Even the churches did not escape, more than 2,800 being wrecked."[8]

Soviet industrial capacity at the end of the war had fallen 8 percent and was once again less than one-fifth that of the United States. Their agriculture suffered even worse. While Soviet productive resources were being devastated, America's industrial capacity increased by nearly 50 percent and "annual output increased by more than a hundred and twelve percent."[9]

We need only one more piece of neglected history: the commander of the Manhattan Project (which built the first atomic bomb), General Leslie Groves, was reassuring President Truman that the Soviets were backward people who could not possibly explode an atomic bomb for fifteen to twenty years.[10] When the Cold War started, the U.S. was the greatest industrial and military power in the world; the U.S. alone had the atomic bomb, and there was no expectation that the Soviets, or any other nation, would develop one soon. Not only was the severely weakened Soviet Union not a danger, there was, at that time, no combination of formal military forces that could seriously threaten the United States or any area of the world we chose to defend. Just as with the Templars five hundred years earlier, the Illuminati after the French Revolution, and the Jews for a thousand years, the Soviet military "threat" was a myth.

To the above facts I would add a few more recently made available under the Freedom of Information Act. Michio Kaku and Daniel Axelrod published the names, dates, and analysis of now-declassified Pentagon war plans against the Soviet Union. Between 1945 and the Soviet Union's first detonation of an atomic device in 1949, there were at least nine such models for war. The names graphically portrayed their offensive purpose—Bushwhacker, Broiler, Sizzle, Shakedown, Offtackle, Dropshot, Trojan, Pincher, and Frolic.[11] The U.S. military knew the offensive nature of the job they had been ordered to prepare for and had named their war plans accordingly.[*]

Each of these plans was assessed for its feasibility to destroy the Soviet Union without damage to the U.S. (That analysis alone demonstrates that the plans were offensive, not defensive.)[12] For the first, the Pentagon's comments on the potential of destroying the Soviet Union were pessimistic; though the United

---

[*] Lower echelon officers and those promoted later would be victims of Cold War conditioning and, in keeping with all such perception control through control of information, would be largely unaware of this history. Thus the present military leaders, no doubt, are fully convinced of the right of their "defensive" stance. This is beyond the scope of this treatise, but only a small but powerful right-wing group is responsible. (See Book Two, chapter three, and the introduction to Book Three for a partial explanation.)

States would be untouched, there would be no way to keep the enraged and still powerful Soviets from taking all of Europe. It must be remembered that, besides the fighting spirit the Soviets showed during World War II, it is a long way to major targets in the Soviet Union. Those first bombs were huge, with only one to a propeller-driven B-29 bomber equipped with a special bomb bay door. In 1948, the U.S. had only thirty-two such bombers modified to deliver atomic bombs. It was expected that a large share would be shot down before reaching their targets. Many more would fail mechanically and still others would be unable to find their targets. Keep in mind, we did not know where most of their factories were. (This, of course, accounts for desperate measures such as U-2 planes photographing Soviet territory.) Any military confrontation must also be within the political constraints imposed by a population taught to be peaceful and just. Since we had just fought a dreadful war in which the Soviet Union was our major ally, and it takes time to condition a public to an enemy, these powerful restrictions were in place.

To back up these plans, bombers equipped with atomic bombs were deployed in Great Britain in 1948 and the North Atlantic Treaty Organization (NATO), comprising the U.S. and most Western European nations, was formed in 1949— six years before the Soviets responded *defensively* by forming the Warsaw Pact. The planners of these offensive schemes kept talking about the "Sunday punch." After studying these plans, Yale University Professor Bernard Brodie concluded that the Pentagon "simply expected the Soviet Union to collapse as a result of the bombing campaign."[13]

Just before the Soviets exploded their first atomic bomb in 1949, and when the United States arsenal was getting relatively large (250 bombs), the Pentagon's summaries changed. Victory without damage to the U.S. was now considered possible. Shortly after the Soviet's successful detonation, the summaries changed again. Pentagon comments for the first time mentioned possible damage to the U.S. By 1954, the analysis concluded that the U.S.S.R. would be destroyed and the U.S. crippled. From 1956 to the present, the sensible assessment has been that both superpowers would be virtually destroyed.[14]

After the formation of NATO and the early deployment of United States nuclear and conventional weapons, the American planners were "surprised and dismayed" when the Soviets exploded an atomic device in 1949.[15] In response to this unsettling news, the United States and its allies rapidly increased their offensive forces. By 1951 there were thirty-two Strategic Air Command (SAC) bases overseas, with plans for a total of eighty-two by 1961. When completed, these so-called *defensive* bases, along with others on U.S. soil, had 3,000 bombers capable of reaching the Soviet Union with hydrogen bombs. In that same year the Soviets had 190 bombers that could only reach the east coast of the United States on a one-way suicide mission.[16]

In addition to the bomber fleet virtually surrounding them in 1961, the Soviets faced forty intercontinental ballistic missiles (ICBMs), forty-eight submarine-launched ballistic missiles (SLBMs), and one hundred intermediate-range ballistic missiles (IRBMs) based in Europe. While watching this enormous buildup of nuclear firepower that could wipe out their civilization in minutes, the Soviets had exactly "four 'soft' non-alert, liquid-fueled ICBMs at one site at Plesetsk," although the official figure for public consumption in the U.S. was fifty.[17]

## Those Fictional Gaps

Naturally the common people don't want war . . . but after all it is the leaders of a country who determine the policy, and it is always a simple matter to drag the people along, whether it is a democracy, or a fascist dictatorship, or a parliament, or a communist dictatorship. Voice or no voice, the people can always be brought to the bidding of the leaders. That is easy. All you have to do is to tell them they are being attacked, and denounce the pacifists for lack of patriotism and exposing the country to danger.[18]

The above is German propaganda minister Hermann Göring's explanation of how popular support for World War II was accomplished in Germany. The right-wing organization, the Committee on the Present Danger (CPD), understood these methods well; they freely admit to organizing specifically to propagandize the American people about a Soviet military threat.[19] The purpose of this deception was to gain public support for building these enormous levels of "defensive" weapons.

Like most Americans, Daniel Ellsberg was taken in by this Cold War rhetoric. He was one of the planners for our "strategic defense" and a full-fledged Cold War warrior—he believed fully in the danger of a Soviet attack. While working for another right-wing think tank, the Rand Corporation, Ellsberg was commissioned to evaluate how our military leaders made their command decisions in times of crisis. The true dimensions of the ways in which our armed forces were preprogrammed to eliminate tens of millions of innocent people at the first hint of war were soon evident.[20] Ellsberg began to take a second look at this war hysteria. At about this time, he was commissioned to study the already prepared history that led to our involvement in the Vietnam War.[*] He concluded the entire process was based on paranoia and fabrication. The leaders were being told one thing, and they were telling the public something else. Unable to stand the deceit, he leaked the famous Pentagon papers to the news media. This is considered the turning point in the Vietnam War.

Noting that the Soviets had only four non-alert missiles when the American people were being told that fifty operational ICBMs were pointed at them, Ellsberg said:

> The true figure remains secret for the same reason as before: because public knowledge of the scale of the "missile gap" hoax would undercut the recurrently-necessary tactic of whipping up public fears of imminent U.S. "inferiority" to mobilize support for vastly expensive arms spending.[21]

Another public servant whose job permitted a view of the inner workings of government was George Kistiakowsky. Kistiakowsky's credentials include a position as head of the explosives division for the Manhattan Project that built the atomic bomb, Professor of Chemistry at Harvard University, and later science advisor to Presidents Eisenhower, Kennedy and Johnson. He, like Ellsberg, had a rude awakening as he observed the workings of the "defense" planners from the inside:

---

[*] Secretary of Defense Robert McNamara had commissioned this vast forty-three-volume study; Ellsberg had only to study this comprehensive work.

I attended all the National Security Council meetings, by order of the President. I began to realize that the policy was being formed in a way which really was quite questionable. It was being formed by people who didn't really know the facts and didn't have time to learn them because of bureaucratic preoccupation. . . . But it took time for all this to sink in. And then I began to see all of the lies, such as the so-called missile gap. I knew there was no missile gap, because our U-2 reconnaissance flights over the Soviet Union could not find any missile deployment. This was 1958—after the U-2's began flying. We put a lot of effort into detecting possible deployment sites. And we could find only one, north of Moscow. This was really a test site. It wasn't really an operational site. Those first ICBMs were so huge that you couldn't hide them.[22]

The U-2 surveillance planes had been spying on the Soviet Union since 1956 and could find no evidence of Soviet offensive missiles. Then in 1960 the spy-in-the-sky satellite proved that the Soviets had none pointed at the United States.[23] With the insight afforded him by his unique position as observer in National Security Council meetings, Kistiakowsky could see the pattern of deceit:

You will find our military has fed the populace, the taxpayers, and Congress with a sequence of false leaks—the bomber gap, the missile gap, the civil defense gap, the anti-missile missile gap. Now we have the missile accuracy gap—the latest one. We also had the MIRV (multiple independently targetable re-entry vehicles) gap.[24]

It was not until 1967 that the Soviet Union acquired the ability to threaten the United States by installing liquid-fueled intercontinental missiles in hardened concrete silos.[25] By contrast, the U.S. had threatened the Soviets with liquid-fueled missiles in the 1950s, and solid-fueled Minuteman missiles since the early 1960s. (Take note: we already had hundreds of missiles, including the medium-range missiles in Europe, pointed at the Soviets; these hundreds of pushbutton missiles were put in place immediately after the first spy satellite proved there were no Soviet missiles pointed at us.) The famous missile gap has always been wide, but in America's favor—until the late 1960s, we were the only country so equipped. The Soviet Union, which installed its first military missiles in 1976, had two thousand missiles to our seven thousand by 1970; by 1980 the gap had almost closed—the U.S.S.R. had increased to seven thousand and the U.S. to ninety-two hundred. At present (1987), the Soviets have about twelve thousand ICBM and SLBM warheads with a reliability of 40 to 60 percent, to our thirteen thousand with a reliability of 70 to 80 percent. Their ICBMs are still liquid-fueled, non-alert missiles of the technology the U.S abandoned in the 1950s.[26]

As the Soviets know the history we have just outlined, it is important to consider how they must feel. Despite having been so weakened by war, they are once again encircled by massive firepower directed by many of the same countries that attempted to overthrow their revolution in 1918. Given that the U.S. was relatively untouched by World War II, had five times the industrial capacity of the Soviet Union, had a virtual monopoly on nuclear weapons for the first five years of the Cold War, and had a devastating advantage in firepower until 1980, only one conclusion makes sense—the Soviets did not constitute a *military* threat. With the ruin and havoc they had experienced and given their limited productive capacity, peace was their greatest need, both emotionally and economically. They had touched the hot stove of war and were grievously burned. It is inconceivable that they would precipitate renewed suffering on such a scale when it would surely be themselves who once again would suffer the worst.

## Soviet Calls for Arms Reduction

While unknown to most of the American people, everything pointed out above was well known to our strategic planners. "An American intelligence report of November 1945 concluded that Russia would be incapable of any war for another fifteen years."[27] The myth of a Soviet "first strike" can be dismissed. They asked for "complete and general disarmament" for all sides back in 1927 and again in 1946.[28] They only armed under threat and have continually offered to abandon the arms race. The 1987 offer to President Ronald Reagan at Reykjavik to destroy all nuclear weapons by the year 2000 was only the latest of many; however, it was the first to get through to the American people. In 1952, the Soviets offered to permit Germany to unify under the condition she remain totally neutral. We refused.[29] In 1955 and 1956 they unilaterally reduced their forces by 1,840,000 men along with some military schools and 375 warships. At least twice they have unilaterally suspended testing of nuclear weapons while we continued.[30] A particularly comprehensive demilitarization offer was made again on August 8, 1962. (This was when the U.S. was embarking on the massive buildup of solid-fueled Minuteman missiles addressed above.) The Soviets again proposed complete and general disarmament for both sides, abolishment of all delivery systems, removal of all foreign troops from foreign lands, and completion of this in three stages over a four-year period.[31] We refused that offer.

While president of the International Physicians for the Prevention of Nuclear War, Dr. John E. Mack, Professor of Psychiatry at Harvard Medical School, met with General Secretary Mikhail Gorbachev. At that 1987 meeting the Soviet leader outlined and offered another comprehensive nuclear arms reduction. Returning to the U.S., Dr. Mack contracted with a public relations firm to get this information to the media. The result: nothing. Even though Dr. Mack shared a Nobel prize for his efforts, the media said, "You are not newsworthy." The American people were denied the knowledge of this latest peace offer.[32]

In early 1989, the Soviets were again unilaterally reducing their armed forces. The stated goals were a 14.2-percent reduction in military spending and "arms production to lower 19.5 percent as hundreds of military factories switch to civilian production."[33] This included a 15- percent reduction in the Soviet navy, which even then was but a shadow of the American fleet. President George Bush countered with an offer of a 10-percent cut in American troops in Europe, which would be about a 2-percent reduction of our worldwide forces against the Soviet's 14.2 percent. No sooner had the American offer been made then the Soviets countered with an announcement that in the next five years they would unilaterally cut their military expenditures by 33 to 50 percent.[34]

With a moment's sober reflection one would conclude that from the Soviets' more vulnerable position world disarmament is the safest and most logical course. Equally informative was testimony in Congress as this book went to press (July 26, 1989). Facing a hostile Congress that wanted to cut spending, a Pentagon general pointed out that building the B-2 bomber was a bargain because it would force the Soviets to spend far more to defend against it then it would cost us to build it. That should give some insight into the real purpose of this arms race.

## The Soviet Threat and American Politics

As a former U.S. senator, head of the State Department, and one of the prime architects of the Cold War, John Foster Dulles was in a unique position to know all this. At the start of the Cold War, his brother Allen was head of the CIA and both were members of that primary think tank on foreign policy, the Council on Foreign Relations.[35] At that time, Dulles said, "I do not know of any responsible high official, military or civilian . . . in this government or any other government who believes that the Soviet [Union] now plans conquest by open military aggression."[36]

Dulles should have been required to square that 1949 admission with a later speech that was analyzed by Michio Kaku and Daniel Axelrod:

> In Jan. 1954, John Foster Dulles had given his famous speech to the Council on Foreign Relations headquarters in New York, spelling out the strategic doctrine called "massive retaliation." According to Dulles, the U.S. would strike first with its full nuclear force if the Soviets started even a conventional war. However, given that Eisenhower still kept the option of pre-emptive first strike open, it would be more accurate to term the administration's nuclear policy Massive Pre-emption. As Eisenhower said on Nov. 7, 1957 in a secret briefing, "we must not allow the enemy to strike the first blow."[37]

Though these facts are part of the available historical record, they are almost unknown to most Americans. There has been such a drum beat of "The Russians are coming! The Russians are coming!" that Americans take it for granted that, not only are we threatened now, *but we were threatened first.* During the peak of our war hysteria, there was no such clamor for war in the Soviet Union.[38] In fact, it is against the Soviet constitution to propagandize for war.[39]

Certainly the power brokers felt a threat of some kind, or they would never have engineered this elaborate conditioning of our national consciousness. American leaders were being told that there was an imminent threat of a Soviet attack on Western Europe. This badly tainted information came from Hitler's secret service, the Gehlan organization, which the CIA took over after the war. These Nazis were trying to save their necks from an angry Eastern Europe, whose countries had had millions of innocent civilians slaughtered at their hands. The efforts of these killers proved quite successful. The CIA swallowed their stories, dutifully reported them to the president and, when there was no more use for their services, protected tens of thousands by scattering them around the world—including a substantial number sent to the United States.[40]

Our brief historical chronology proves that the Soviet threat was clearly not military. If the American people had the above information, it is inconceivable that they would have tolerated such an aggressive military posture or the immense toll it has taken on the nation's and the world's resources. How and why Americans were so badly misinformed by a free press is beyond the scope of this book, but the evidence is overwhelming.

The most important controlling factor is the public mindset. Once programmed to believe some other society is an enemy, there seems to be a need to believe the worst of that society and disbelieve anything else. Raising the specter of an enemy and the need for an aggressive hard line on defense is then the surest way to be elected. It becomes imperative to at least remain silent about any positive aspects of this mythical enemy; it would be political suicide to stand up for peace and common sense. Thus the enemy belief system becomes entrenched.

Though no U.S. presidents were intent on war, many were fully controlled by the enemy belief system. Some were not; President Franklin D. Roosevelt was certain he could get along with the Soviets and, like President Woodrow Wilson after World War I, was intent on building a postwar peaceful world. But President Harry S. Truman, who succeeded FDR, was fully under the control of those who were guided by belief in an enemy, and the Cold War began.

President Dwight D. Eisenhower expanded the arms race and it was he who first signed the order to target the Soviet Union with intercontinental missiles. However, before he retired he realized he had been controlled by the "peddlers of crisis" and it was this that led to the warning in his presidential farewell address for Americans to "beware of the military-industrial complex."

President John F. Kennedy was intent on winding down the Vietnam War and reversing the arms race. He, like all other peaceful presidents, was boxed in by the extreme right wing and their rhetoric of an enemy. Almost certainly his intelligence and popularity with the American people gave him the power to eventually outmaneuver those who were intent on a continued war posture, but he did not live to achieve his goals.[41]

President Jimmy Carter was certainly not pro-war; he is a classic example of how the rhetoric of an enemy controls public perception and even a president who is for peace. When Jimmy Carter first became president he started to wind down the Cold War; most importantly he almost totally dismantled the CIA. President Carter expanded other segments of the military in an attempt to appease the militarists. The extreme right never forgave him; it only took their war cry of "incompetence" and "soft on communism." Out went Carter and in went Reagan and the group who admitted they deliberately propagandized the American people about the Soviet threat—the Committee on the Present Danger. They then began the greatest peacetime military buildup this country has ever known. Using the specter of an enemy and the power of mass media, a small but powerful minority can control a country's military goals and much domestic policy.[42]

Certainly the Soviet Union also had their hardliners and passed up key moments in history when cooperation with the above named presidents could have reversed this Cold War. This treatise can only touch on the subject, but it is obvious that General Secretary Mikhail Gorbachev is now taking the lead in the search for peace and it is imperative that the American people recognize that. Their recognition will weaken the extreme right wing and give an American president not only the political freedom to negotiate for peace but the incentive to do so. Creation of en enemy controls social policy because it controls the vote; once the vote is for peace politicians can stand up for peace.

Noting that the Soviet Union rose from under 3 percent of the world's industrial capacity to 25 percent (almost equal to the U.S.), even as they fought off the intervention in 1918, World War II, and the Cold War, points to the real problem for the power brokers—the Soviets were rapidly developing capital outside the structure of monopoly capital. To permit that would contradict the very purpose and meaning of monopoly. Wars are extensions of trade wars. The potential control of resources and markets through industrial capacity outside the power brokers' control was the real threat.* Besides, there were enormous fortunes to be made from wars.

---

\* Equally threatening was the example the Soviet Union was setting for other undeveloped countries now under the control of capitalism.

# 5

# Those Peddlers of Crisis:
# The Arms Manufacturers

## Another Wasteful, Fiercely Defended Territory

The big bomber program of 1956 had been obtained by the use of inflated and alarmist estimates of Soviet power. The rivalry among the three services over missiles was getting completely out of control.... [Representative James L. Whitten of Mississippi pointed out] that we were "rapidly tying our domestic economy to the military" which had always been a threat to the safety of any nation. He recalled "that in Germany and Japan and every other major country, whenever the domestic economy got tied to the military, it led to war."[1]

— Testimony to the House Armed Services Committee

The arms industry is unlike any other competitive business. "The success of one firm does not mean the failure of another but rather increases its chances of doing business."[2] The buildup of one country's military capacity will appear as a threat to its insecure or paranoid neighbors. This, of course, epitomizes the present arms race that we have been leading. Sam Cummings, the world's leading free-lance arms merchant, points out, "It is almost a perpetual motion machine."[3]

The forerunners of today's corporate arms manufacturers (Krupp of Germany, Armstrong and Vickers of England, and others) were originally rejected by their own governments and had to depend upon foreign sales for survival. They often furnished arms to both sides in conflicts and even to their own country's potential enemies. Their practice of warning different countries of the aggressive intentions of their neighbors—who were supposedly arming themselves through purchases of the latest sophisticated weapons—yields a glimpse of the origins of today's mythical missile gaps.[4]

Stung by the horrors of World War I, world leaders realized that arms merchants had a hand in creating both the climate of fear and the resulting disaster itself. The League of Nations summarized the problem in six points:

1. That the armament firms have been active in fomenting war scares and in persuading their own countries to adopt warlike policies and to increase their armaments.

2. That armament firms have attempted to bribe government officials, both at home and abroad.

3. That armament firms have disseminated false reports concerning the military and naval programs of various countries, in order to stimulate armament expenditure.

4. That armament firms have sought to influence public opinion through the control of newspapers in their own and foreign countries.

5. That armament firms have organized international armament rings through which the armament race has been accentuated by playing off one country against another.

6. That armament firms have organized international armament trusts which have increased the price of armaments sold to governments.[5]

The arms merchants were not idle during the surge of sentiment for disarmament after World War I. As Anthony Sampson pointed out in *Arms Bazaar,* lobbyist William H. Shearer

> [reported] to Bethlehem [Steel] that, "as a result of my activities during the 69th Congress, eight 10,000-ton cruisers are now under construction." At the Geneva Conference held in 1927 he was paid $27,000 for six weeks' propaganda, to try to prevent agreement on restricting warships: he wrote articles and press releases stirring up suspicions of British intentions, and canvassed delegates and journalists. . . . As one of the British delegates, Lord Cecil of Chelwood, recalled afterwards: "I cannot help feeling that it would have been a decided advantage if Mr. Shearer had not been present at Geneva."[6]

It is evident that the Committee on the Present Danger designed their campaign of fear after that of those arms merchants. The public would never support the production and sale of arms without just such an avalanche of misleading information warning of imaginary threats, and the simultaneous suppression of information regarding other countries' peaceful intentions.

It is the logic of profits that drives arms manufacturers to produce weapons. After all, they own those factories after every war, weapons are what they were designed to produce, and the civilian economy is already saturated. This dilemma faced the aircraft industries after World War II—production dropped to one-half of 1 percent of their wartime peak. Even at the height of the Korean and Vietnam Wars, they only ran at one-third capacity.[7] Mumford points out the historic record of arms merchants when faced with this dilemma:

> In the long run they were forced back on the more reliable industry of war, and they loyally served their stockholders by inciting competitive fears and rivalries among the nations: the notorious part recently played by the American steel manufacturers in wrecking the International Arms Conference of 1927 was only typical of a thousand less publicized moves during the previous century.[8]

Lobbying governments and paying bribes to key officials have been normal business practices for arms merchants. They have been eager to increase their sales ever since the development of sophisticated, expensive killing machines. The simplicity of profiting by offering a government official a small fortune under the table to approve the expenditure of large sums of public money speaks for itself. This bribery and the much more sophisticated method, historically practiced by arms merchants, of fomenting suspicion between countries, are both still widely practiced today.[9] Their warnings are heard all the time but their bribery is only occasionally exposed. For example, in Italy during the mid-sixties Lockheed attempted to outbid rivals for the sale of Hercules transport planes. Lockheed president Carl Kotchian received this message from his agent:

> "I'm embarrassed, and I'm just chagrined, but I'm going to have to recommend to you that you make some payments if you wish to sell airplanes in this country." The payments were [Sampson continues], for the most part, to go to the ministry of defense, evidently for the minister's political party, the Christian Democrats.[10]

As the behind-the-scenes dealing continued, Kotchian returned to California, leaving the final details to his lawyer. In his advisory letter, lawyer Roger Smith wrote, "('Please hold onto your seat-belt'), that Lockheed's agent Lefebvre might now need $120,000 for each Hercules aircraft that was sold—because . . . he had to outbid the French and German bribes."[11]

Another Lockheed scandal occurred in 1972. Sworn testimony revealed that all the tricks of the trade had been employed. Lockheed admitted paying an intermediary $106 million in commissions. Key Japanese officials took bribes, and some went to jail.[12] Testimony at trials and hearings made it clear that the questionable past practices of arms merchants were still normal procedure all over the world. Sampson sums up the offhand attitude of Lockheed's president:

> There was nothing sheepish or reptilian in Kotchian's view of bribery: to him, payments to foreigners were business costs, or an insurance policy, as he put it, like fire risks or life insurance, which any prudent man would pay. The only criterion was the return on investment: . . . Such payments were part of the great battle for business, and for the free world.[13]

Centuries of experience in the arms trade have matured into a standard procedure for farming the public treasuries through arms sales. As the richest and most powerful country in the world, it is only logical that the U.S. is where the most money is to be earned procuring and selling arms. With each seasonal arms authorization and appropriation voted on in Congress, there are the predictably cadenced warnings of bomber gaps, missile gaps, and other dangerous gaps, including the "window of vulnerability" used to justify President Reagan's hoped-for trillion-dollar "Star Wars" arms buildup, the Strategic Defense Initiative. It was the recognition of this political control of public (and official) perception that led President Eisenhower to issue his stern warning to the American people in his farewell address, "In the councils of government we must guard against the acquisition of unwarranted influence, whether sought or unsought, by the military-industrial complex. The potential for the disastrous rise of misplaced power exists and will persist."[14]

Wars have primarily been fought to protect economic territories other than the arms industries, but power brokers are more than happy to let the weapons manufacturers be blamed. However, those who wield such vast political power could not wreak their havoc upon the world without the arms industries' voracious quest for profits.

## Governments' Vested Interest in Arms Sales

In order to maintain employment and protect their countries' balance of payments, governments also have a vested interest in arms production. Faced with severe problems in this area, the Kennedy and Johnson administrations, for example, proceeded to rectify it with arms sales:

> It was even given a name which was a masterpiece of Pentagon newspeak: International Logistics Negotiations. But the ILN was really unashamedly an organization for selling arms. . . . It was now the government that was urging companies to sell. Kuss (director of ILN), with his own staff of forty, set up four teams, Red, White, Blue and Gray, which divided the world market between them, to persuade foreign governments of the need to buy arms, and the American companies of the need to sell them. They soon produced results: from 1962 onwards Kuss could boast that the United States was selling an average of $2 billion in arms each year—more than twice the value of arms given away in grant aid. . . . the political parties and their agents were without scruple in exacting their full tribute, particularly from foreign companies. . . . it seemed almost an act of patriotism to fleece the Americans, who did not seem to mind; but in fact they were fleecing their own people. [It is the productive workers of the purchasing country who must pay for all those unnecessary sales.][15]

## Workers' Vested Interests in Arms Production

The livelihood of many American workers is also dependent on the production and sale of arms throughout the world. Describing the concerns over an arms embargo before World War I, labor historian Philip Foner explains how employment in arms production creates many loyal followers:

> It was becoming clear that supplying the markets created by the European war would soon restore prosperity and reduce unemployment. By April 1915, the depression did begin to lift as war orders caused mills and factories to rehire workers, and as farmers frantically increased the production of food supplies for Europe. . . . Even Socialist workers and farmers, much as they insisted on American neutrality and opposed American involvement in the European war, began to be concerned about the effect of an embargo on their own status.[16]

Boeing, Lockheed, and the other major arms manufacturers each point to their industry as the "keystone of prosperity" in their particular community. The employment given workers is always presented as proof of the benefits workers derive from arms production. Their representatives in Congress fight hard to maintain production in their home states.

In this context, all who protect their jobs in the arms industry add their political weight to the side of the scales promoting arms production and sales. Even if they do not support it individually, their representatives do. Ten labor leaders were members of the Committee on the Present Danger, whose leaders freely admitted they deliberately propagandized the American people about the Soviet threat.[17]

Many people are caught up in this contradiction. They are taught to be peaceful and avoid injuring others. This moral training is outweighed by their jobs in the arms industry. These people will vigorously defend the economic territory in which they obtain their livelihood and security:

> The economic reality of nuclear arms control is that no matter what form it takes, defense spending is not going to drop. . . . the money will almost surely be shifted from one nuclear program to another or to conventional weapons to make up for the loss of nuclear arms. Major defense companies by and large are so diversified that even if all nuclear weapons were eliminated—an unlikely prospect—they would not suffer much. But any changes would shuttle enormous sums of money around the country, impoverishing some communities and enriching others.[18]

## The Enormous Waste of Arms Production

In unjust societies, arms have always consumed a major share of capital and technology. Seven hundred years before the Industrial Revolution, China produced "125,000 tons [of iron] per annum [far more than Britain in the early years of the Industrial Revolution] chiefly for military and governmental use."[19] At the end of the sixteenth century, France had thirteen foundries, all devoted to building cannon along with a few scythes. Later, in the early nineteenth century, Robert Owen puzzled over what happened to the wealth produced by labor. He rightly concluded that the 2,400-percent increase in labor productivity in the textile industry in just the previous fifty years was largely being wasted in petty wars among the aristocrats.[20] The powerful continually appropriated the fruits of labor and expended them on war.

Between 1960 and 1985, this same process resulted in a $14-trillion increase in world military expenditures while economic product increased only $8.6 trillion, "in effect leaving a smaller civilian economy than there was in 1960." Much of this wealth was wasted on the Air Force, which "exceeded in wealth the resources of the fifty-five largest American corporations combined."[21]

Of this expenditure, NATO and the Warsaw Pact countries account for 86 percent of the world's $810- billion 1985 arms expenditures. The U.S. share was roughly $268 billion, or 33 percent of the world's total, while the Soviet Union spent about $237 billion.[22] In 1977, 34 percent of the producing capital resources of the U.S. was used for military purposes, and under President Reagan and his appointees it was higher.[23]

Arms races similar to those that led to World Wars I and II brought calamitous ruin to colonial powers. At present, the destruction from this continued belligerency is visited upon former colonies through proxy wars, while the costs of creating that destruction are borne by the taxpayers of the industrial countries. For example: SAINT SAINA'S SAY'S YELL !?

> The United States government . . . spent $150 billion and more than ten years prosecuting [the Vietnamese] war, dropping almost 8 million tons of bombs, 18 million gallons of defoliants, and nearly 400,000 tons of napalm. The Vietnamese, Laotian, and Cambodian countrysides were desolated by saturation bombings; several million Vietnamese, Cambodians, and Laotians were killed, millions more were maimed or wounded, and almost 10 million were left homeless; about 58,000 Americans lost their lives and hundreds of thousands more were wounded or per-

manently disabled. But the war did bring benefits to a tiny segment of the American population: corporate defense contractors like Dupont, ITT, and Dow Chemical. . . . not to defend these countries from outside invasion but to protect capital investments and the ruling oligarchs from the dangers of domestic insurgency.[24]

## Those Never-Mentioned Reasons

The productive capacity of modern technology is so enormous that the only way monopolies can be maintained is by wasting much of the production. When surplus capital cannot be used internally it must be wasted internally, exported, or consumed by war. To share the fruits of capital is to relinquish control:

An army is a body of pure consumers. . . . moreover the army is not merely a pure consumer but a negative producer: that is to say it produces illth, to use Ruskins's excellent phrase, instead of wealth—misery, mutilation, physical destruction, terror, starvation and death characterize the process of war and form a principal part of the product. . . . A thousand men mowed down by bullets are a demand more or less for a thousand more uniforms, a thousand more guns, a thousand more bayonets: and a thousand shells fired from cannon cannot be retrieved and used over again . . . quantity production must rely for its success upon quantity consumption; and nothing ensures replacement like organized destruction. In this sense war is not only, as it has been called, the health of the state: it is the health of the [social] machine, too. Without the non-production of war, to balance accounts algebraically, the heightened capacities of machine production can be written off only in limited ways: an increase in foreign markets, an increase in population, *an increase in mass purchasing power through the drastic restriction of profits. When the first two dodges have been exhausted, war helps avert the last alternative, so terrible to the kept classes, so threatening to the whole system that supports them.*[25] (emphasis added; that last alternative is increased sharing of the fruits of capital)

If the arms race were abandoned and this productive capacity used to capitalize the world, capital would no longer be monopolized. Justice would demand that the current excess claims of capital be reduced and productive labor's share increased. Monopoly capital (but not productive capital) would vanish. With everyone working productively, and all receiving the value of their production, an economy would balance and be productive.

The extension of such rights and the benefits that would accrue to the maximum number of people are not the goals of the powerful. Witness the comments of social scientist Sidney Lens on their plans after World War II:

The United States was now called upon to fill the void left by the disintegrating and impoverished British, French, Dutch, Belgian, German, Italian, and Japanese empires. Not only was the opportunity there, but the only way to avoid global imperialism was to stand by quietly while most of the world turned to socialism. . . . [Also], a War and Peace Studies Project of the Council on Foreign Relations [concluded that] . . . if we were to prosper under the present system . . . we would have to control the economic life of the Western Hemisphere, the former British Empire, and the Far East. [Addressing surplus capital, Lens continued:] According to the National Planning Association, *the capital equipment industry was "nearly twice the size which would be needed domestically under the most for-*

*tuitous conditions of full employment and nearly equal to the task of supplying world needs."* America, a market economy, needed outside markets to keep its great economic machine in operation. Under a different kind of social system, Assistant Secretary of State Dean Acheson told a congressional committee in 1944, "you could use the entire production of the country in the United States." But under the present free enterprise system the government "must look to foreign markets" or "we are in for a very bad time."[26] (emphasis added)

In short, instead of industrializing those other countries, the plan was to sell them our production. Of course the territory of the Soviet Union was also in those plans:

> The Soviets have a *closed* economy, not an open one, operating on the same principle as the United States did after the Civil War when it imposed large tariffs on foreign imports to protect less efficient American manufacturers. If the foreign trade monopoly in the Soviet Union were to be breached, as the United States wanted, and the door opened without restriction to Western imports, American corporations would easily undersell their Russian counterparts and drive them out of business. The Soviet Union in the end would have to deindustrialize and become a second-rate nation relying primarily on the sale of raw materials.[27]

Although there were several powerful support groups (the arms profiteers, fundamentalist religion, and reactionary right-wing groups), we have now found the underlying cause of the Cold War. Not surprisingly, it is caused by the same reason social scientists have concluded causes almost all wars—the efforts of powerful people to monopolize capital and trade to appropriate the production of others' labor.

## Conclusion

Though it was the excuse normally given for the production and sale of arms, at the inception of the Cold War there was no military threat from the Soviet Union. Those Hercules transport planes were of no use to Italy, unless the Italians were planning aggression. There was no need of pointing missiles at Soviet citizens who had suffered so grievously, who were desperately struggling to develop their country, and who had no missiles pointed at us.

The myth of a Soviet threat exposes most of the labor that went into the defense budgets of NATO and Warsaw Pact countries as wasted. The money paid to all labor from these defense budgets represented fictitious wealth—nothing of value was produced for society. The potential living standard of the entire world has thus been reduced by the amount wasted on arms. Those unnecessarily employed use their wages properly to provide for their families' living; useless labor is traded for productive labor. Those employed building unnecessary planes and other weapons could just as well have been producing useful products to trade for others' useful labor. There was no sensible economic reason to produce unusable products and trade them for usable ones, or unusable ones for others equally unusable.

There is, however, the need to distribute social wealth, and every wasteful contracting of labor does distribute this wealth. These people, lacking full economic rights, have no other way of asserting a moral claim to their share of social production. That a few powerful people are able, through this patronage and creation of enemies, to control a wasteful social policy for their gain, while billions throughout the world are deprived, points out the urgent need for reclaiming the last of our rights.

Even major companies do not save anything. Witness how Lockheed, the arms producer that Sampson chose as the archetypical modern arms merchant, went broke and had to be bailed out by the U.S. government.[28] With their capital invested in arms factories, major arms producers would suffer immediate bankruptcy if they lost control of public and official perception of the Soviet Union as a threat. If we had peace instead of continued hot and cold wars, the weapons factories would have all the value of Christmas trees the day after Christmas. The false value of this fictitious capital is the territory so vigorously and successfully being defended.

Every government statistic I can find on the total labor employed in defense is qualified by the phrase "directly employed," and the figure given is about six million. Economists Paul A. Baron and Paul M. Sweezy calculate the total directly and indirectly employed in 1966 was 9 percent of the labor force.[29] With the increase in military expenditures documented by Professor Seymour Melman, a 10 percent rate today is conservative.[30] The validity of this conclusion can be tested using the 1987 defense budget of $288 billion. If we allowed a 25-percent profit margin for the defense industries that would leave $217 billion for labor. Dividing this total by an average wage of $20,000 per year (while many in the arms industry are highly paid, soldiers are not), we arrive at about 10.8 million workers employed through defense production—almost exactly 10 percent of the labor force.[31]

Most of our fears of being attacked have been engineered by groups within our own ranks. With today's technology, a secure peace can be designed and ensured. Logically, 1 million should be an adequate number employed by the military and its support infrastructure. This would release 9.8 million workers to share productive jobs.

That these can be released will be obvious when one observes the desperate straits of the Soviet Union and Eastern Europe. The Soviet Union has offered for each side to eliminate nuclear weapons and disarm to the minimum necessary for defense. They have already unilaterally started to do so. The choice of a Cold War or peace is ours.

# 6

# The Economy of the Soviet Union

I have addressed the military background of the Cold War and will now turn to the enormous domestic problems that made the Soviet Union weak and vulnerable, hardly in a condition to threaten the world.

A part of the continued portrayal of an enemy is the image of incompetence—we hear much about the poor living conditions and shoddy consumer goods in the Soviet Union. To compare the Soviet standard of living with ours when they have suffered so is totally unrealistic and unjust. A proper comparison would be to visualize what the U.S. would have been like if, when our industrial development had just begun, powerful neighboring countries destroyed almost everything east of the Mississippi and north of Tennessee and 35 percent of our prime labor was killed in defeating the aggressors. From that destruction we would have had to rebuild while again rearming as powerful countries still made no secret of their belief that we should be destroyed. This nation could hardly have built quality housing and consumer products under such conditions.

The enormous cost of defending their freedom during the intervention, World War II, and the Cold War created a trap for the Soviet economy. After the war there were still few tools to work with, millions were homeless, and their work force was devastated. Their egalitarian ideology did not build elite housing examples that would later become a norm for a middle class, and not being permitted to build in peace created a housing disaster. The problems of production of consumer goods created by faulty ideology can be corrected relatively quickly (fifteen to thirty years) but to rebuild to a respectable housing standard will be an enormous strain on their economy, will require fifty to one hundred years to complete, and can only be done under conditions of peace.

In spite of their enormous problems, by the 1980s the Soviets' production of heavy industry was approaching that of the U.S. They are now ahead in steel, oil, coal, and a few other industries. However, like our production in the nineteenth century and the first half of the twentieth century, this production is extensive and not intensive. The substitution of light alloys and plastics for steel means we can produce many more products from a ton of steel or fuel than the Soviets.

But there are other problems. The destruction caused by the Great Patriotic War created great upsets in the Soviet economy. To rebuild, "the share of the Russian GNP devoted to private consumption, which in other countries going through the 'takeoff' to industrialization was around 80 percent, was driven down to the appalling level of 51 or 52 percent."[1] The Soviets had made the decision to bite the bullet and sacrifice the present to build for the future. If their economy had been weighted towards consumer items, this would have subtracted from the building of basic industries.

While such a command economy may be the most efficient way to build a developing country's basic industries, it cannot efficiently produce and distribute consumer goods. Only a rudimentary system for meeting basic needs can be designed and managed from above. Manufacture of millions of products and services necessary for a modern economy requires people with special talent, insights, and energy; the freedom to decide what the consumer wants; and the same freedom to produce and distribute.

The Soviet command economy was further complicated by idealism. They guaranteed a job for everyone without paying enough attention to the necessary incentives for a productive labor force. Workers who produced efficiently were paid no more than those who were apathetic. Since workers were secure and had no incentive to work hard or innovate, production kept gradually slowing.

By 1985 production had reached a plateau and no amount of planning and coercion could make it regain its momentum. So *perestroika* (restructuring the economy) began in 1985.[*] These new ideas included leasing land to the farmers. If this also provides for these farmers owning their own machinery, it is a sound idea. Only when it is theirs to be proud of, they incur the expenses of poor maintenance, and they reap the profits of good maintenance, will that machinery be well cared for.

They are also leasing industries to workers' cooperatives. This has the basic flaw of no incentive to modernize. For good care and efficient operation such machinery must be privately owned. This machinery, still owned by the government, will just be worn out and returned to the state.

The problem of both capitalism and communism is ideology. We believe fully in the philosophies that guide our economy, and it has led to the enormous waste of labor, capital, and resources outlined in this treatise. Likewise, the Soviets sincerely believe their philosophy, and it has led to the stagnation of their economy.

Under our philosophies most of the problems of production have been solved. It is the problems of distribution that have yet to be resolved. Our economy will expand, include a few more people than the last expansion, and then will stagnate. Ever since World War II it has appeared that we have avoided a crisis like

---

[*] In spite of the empty stores that seem to indicate a failed economy, at this time (early 1989) Soviet production has not fallen. (By the CIA's assessment the lowest point was reached in 1987, when the economy grew only 1.5 percent.) Soviet planning was faulty and the people ended up with more money than the value of consumer goods. It is likely this was an attempt to restart their economy which, without the civilian production to spend it and with controlled low prices, turned into a nightmare. (Abel Aganbegyan of the USSR Academy of Sciences' economic division, "We Made Some Serious Mistakes," *Newsweek,* 13 March 1989, p. 30.) Some Soviet economists are predicting a 4- to 5-percent drop in national income in 1989. (Grigory Khanin, "When Will the Ruble be Made Convertible," *New Times,* no. 30, 25–31 July 1989, p. 25.)

that of the 1930s, but this is only because the waste distribution territories (especially military waste) have kept the economy going.*

The Soviets, observing the industrial revolution, thought production was no problem. They planned on bypassing the nonproducing intermediaries by direct distribution. This may have solved the problem of distribution, but it stagnated the process of development and production of civilian goods and services. These Soviet ideological failures give enormous support to those who still would reclaim control of those populations, resources, or trade.

## The Cold War Is a Trade War

If someone says something positive about the Soviet Union, or for that matter anything negative about the United States, the immediate question that arises is, "Why then are the people fleeing those Eastern European countries?" It is quite simply because most of the capital and control of world resources is on this side of the border. It is with capital and resources that societies provide high-paying jobs and produce consumer products cheaply. Without capital, a society is relegated to low-paid labor and production of fewer, and inferior, consumer products.

Most common people do not concern themselves with the political processes that control capital and resources, produce consumer products, and thus control their life. They judge the world by the amenities of life they can obtain relative to those which their neighbors and friends have.

One must remember that, when all the rhetorical excesses are stripped away, all wars are to control populations, capital, and resources. Control of any one of those factors means some control of the others. They are trade wars and all the rules of war apply. This unacknowledged trade war has been waged against those whose social infrastructure was already shattered by World War II. (The destruction in some Eastern European countries was worse than that in the Soviet Union; Poland, for example, lost 20 percent of her population.)

President Franklin D. Roosevelt, who had plans for friendly relations with the Soviets and the attainment of world peace, died before World War II ended and before he could implement his goals. The next administration, that of president Harry S. Truman, proved to be guided by confrontation, not cooperation. One of the milestones of this Cold War which started under President Truman was British Prime Minister Winston Churchill's famous Iron Curtain speech at Fulton, Missouri, in 1946. That speech was the initial building of the curtain from this side and is officially recognized as the start of the Cold War.

Churchill's speech was the signal that an elite had made the decision to scare the people with the specter of an enemy. This was almost certainly an extreme minority faction within the total population, but by the time the masses were thoroughly indoctrinated with the rhetoric of fear, the enemy belief system was

---

* The inclusion of other countries in the monopoly capital system extended the benefits of capital and may have lowered the potential of collapse, but it has not eliminated stagnation.

complete. Almost the entire population would and did willingly follow the leaders to wage this Cold War against what was only a threat to that elite.[*]

The rhetoric of an enemy gained a large boost from George F. Keenan, who was holding a diplomatic post in the Soviet Union immediately after World War II. He had observed and was concerned about the enormous optimism and energy of the Soviets as they set about rebuilding from the disaster of World War II. There was no such optimism in Western Europe and they did not start energetic rebuilding until given the capital through the Marshall Plan. This optimism and energy was the threat; it was ideological, not military. This, of course, made no difference. A threat is a threat and the first rule of war is that one vilifies the enemy to gain the loyalty of the population. Here there is plenty of blame to go around. In their opinion of imperialism, the Soviets were being very blunt that their system would be the wave of the future.

Keenan's fears were voiced in his famous containment letter, published in *Foreign Affairs* magazine in 1947 under the pseudonym Mr. X. In this long dissertation, he described how it was essential that we contain the Soviets or their optimism, energy, and ideology would infect the entire world. Keenan's suggestions became American policy. Technology was simply denied to the Eastern bloc and markets were controlled by tariffs of 40 to 50 percent on anything imported from that bloc.

Eastern Europe was offered Marshall Plan funds but only on the condition they open their borders. Their already backward and now shattered industries could not compete with our modern undamaged industries, so they did not dare open their borders. This would have relegated them to being suppliers of cheap commodities to our factories, or allowed control of their capital by external capitalists, the examples of Japan, Taiwan, and South Korea notwithstanding. Capital is only shared when monopolists need allies. Even today, if they were to open their borders without special conditions their industry would collapse. The denial of markets automatically made Eastern European currency nonconvertible except at such an unfavorable rate that it amounted to direct appropriation of Eastern European labor. With a nonconvertible currency, they were effectively denied access to world resources and markets not directly under the control of the Western bloc.

## Technology and the Learning Process

To understand what being cut off from world commerce means it is necessary to understand that it is with tools a society learns to build more tools, with which they learn still more and build yet better tools, ad infinitum. Developing efficient tools is a learning process; each invention is an improvement on earlier inventions employed by a population. A late developing country can progress at a much faster rate because there are working examples but, unless it is given the technology and training, jumping from old technology to modern techniques without the learning experience of working with the latest machinery is a rare occurrence. An

---

[*] Many also followed blindly to the hot wars of Korea and Vietnam and what few were aware of the covert operations around the world approved of them as a defense.

undeveloped society must go through the same learning process that an advanced society has already gone through.

Compounding the Soviet problems is denial of access to markets to finance the production and learning process. Without markets, labor experience, and the inventions they engender, a country's industry will continually fall further behind. The current backwardness of other societies has much less to do with social systems than with access to technology, capital, markets, and experience. This is well understood and accounts for the desperate measures to embargo technology and deny markets to any society that is an economic threat. This is little different than the petty trade wars which for hundreds of years were waged by medieval merchants destroying the capital of the surrounding villages. The rules of trade have changed little; it is simply that industrial capital is now so complicated and expensive, with by far the greatest share on our side of the fence, that it is only necessary to deny an adversary access to technology and markets and they cannot compete.

The level playing field that one hears so much about in world trade is only between those within one trading bloc. Except for those countries necessary for allies, the Third World and any competing bloc will have to fight their way up a very steep economic slope before they are ever admitted into the club of world trade on an equal basis. Within that trading bloc, Americans are being far more honest than others. Japan practices severe trade restrictions while selling almost unimpeded on the American market. Europe also can sell over here quite freely but they do not let Japan's industry or ours take over their home markets. Through our more honest policies we are being decimated by unequal trades.

Poland, with an average wage of one thousand dollars a year, is in especially bad shape, and is a prime example of how destruction from war, denial of technology and world trade, and discriminatory banking retards a country's economic growth. Without thorough research and guarantees, Poland borrowed billions of dollars from the Western countries to build factories, supposedly to trade with the West. With better technology and full distribution pipelines in the West there was no market for those products. With a nonconvertible currency, there was no money in the Polish economy to purchase raw materials for those factories and turn that productive capacity directly to internal needs. Those factories remained idle. Poland is saddled with a $38-billion debt she cannot repay, identical to the imposition of debt on Third World countries.

Ever since World War II, cut off from trade with the rest of the world and totally surrounded by hostile countries, the Soviets and their satellites have had to learn technologies and build industrial capital from internal resources. To do this amid such destruction and from such a small industrial capital base while having to offset the fast-growing military threat virtually surrounding them was a formidable task.

## Resources, Production, and Capital

The Soviet nation spans seven thousand miles of some of the most difficult country in the world. Besides the great distance over which commodities must be hauled with expensive land transportation, much of the raw materials lies under many feet of permafrost. Compare this with the Western bloc, which obtains its raw material from the cheapest sources in the world, wherever they are. Copper mines in the United States that are much cheaper to run than those in the Soviet Union are shut down while copper ore in Zaire, sometimes running 10 percent pure copper, is mined with labor costs of less than a dollar an hour. Islands rich in ore in the South Pacific are similarly mined and the ore loaded directly on ships for cheap transportation anywhere in the Western world. The same control of resources in one form or another is evident in Chile, Brazil, and throughout the world. Book Two, chapter one, outlines the many techniques of that control.

Not only is production under such unfavorable conditions obviously far more expensive than in the developed West, but the Soviets set about providing their satellites with raw material and fuel at below world prices, this while they were themselves so heavily strapped to meet their own needs.

Though the excessive rights they gave labor seriously hampered initiative and production efficiency, the above considerations were their greatest problems. The decision to forgo consumer production to rebuild, to defend, and to simultaneously provide for Eastern Europe created a badly unbalanced Soviet economy. The financial and economic power of the West was just too great and the entire Soviet bloc is exhausted. They were unable to overcome all those enormous obstacles and simultaneously develop a consumer production/distribution system. By never allowing them into the game, the West has won that trade war and the cost to the Soviets is obvious. The costs to the West are not as obvious but are also enormous.

The fact that the Soviet bloc is consciously denied integration into world commerce (the fact that capital is monopolized) will be demonstrated if any satellite fully splits from the Soviet bloc. Capital will immediately flow to that country; they will not only be given access to technology and markets, but will be guided into world markets. Their economy and living standards will boom. Other Eastern European countries that have not yet broken away will still be denied technology, capital, and markets. They will lag far behind and the pressure to break away will rise to an explosive level.

There is also movement towards direct investment in the socialist bloc. If this continues this will bring rapid improvement in their economies. However, just how this is done will have great meaning for all societies. The key aspects to watch are the subjects of Book Three—land rights, patent rights, finance capital rights, and how those rights are protected through the structure of information systems. The socialist bloc has much leeway on land rights and communications but to attain technology and capital they will be pressured to privatize capital, patent rights, and banking. If they can keep control as they are integrated into the world economy they (and we) can restructure to utilize the most efficient aspects of both ideologies.

Where our problem is distribution, the Soviets' problems are in both production and distribution. Just as property owners have superior rights in this country, labor claimed excessive rights in theirs. Their philosophy required that the amenities of life be provided to all people by the government, so they kept the prices of basic commodities and services far below the actual cost of production. Highly productive workers were paid little more than those who produced only 20 percent as much. Labor simply relaxed and let the state make up the difference between what they produced and what they consumed, and labor productivity stagnated.[2] In short, waste distribution territories in the Soviet Union just developed in a different form than ours.

The Soviets are now drastically reducing arms, restructuring incentives, and increasing civilian production. However, it is far too early to claim they are defeated. Every society values its freedom, and they well know that to come under the control of monopoly capital is not freedom.

# 7

# An Offer the Soviets Cannot Refuse

## A Race for Peace

General Secretary Mikhail Gorbachev and President Ronald Reagan held a summit meeting in Reykjavik during October 1986. Gorbachev offered a multilateral elimination of all nuclear and chemical weapons and a reduction of conventional weapons to a level just necessary for defense. Later, on the seventieth anniversary of the Russian Revolution, Gorbachev spoke again:

> The Warsaw Treaty states have addressed NATO and all European countries with a proposal on reducing armed forces and armaments to a level of reasonable sufficiency. We have suggested comparing the two alliances' military doctrines in order to make them exclusively defensive. We have put forward a concrete plan for the prohibition and elimination of chemical weapons and are working vigorously in this direction. We have advanced proposals on devising effective methods for the verification of arms reduction, including on-site inspections.[1]

America's response:

> There was little reaction here to Gorbachev's proposals in early 1986 for the U.S. to join the unilateral [nuclear] test ban, for the removal of the U.S. and Soviet fleets from the Mediterranean, for steps towards dismantling NATO and the Warsaw Pact, for outlawing of sea-launched cruise missiles, and similar measures. But *matters could get out of hand.* Small wonder then, that Secretary of State George Schultz called on Gorbachev to "end public diplomacy," which was beginning to cause acute embarrassment in Washington; [specifically relative to this concluding chapter] . . . the U.S. alone boycotted a UN conference in New York called "to examine how money under future disarmament agreements could be used to stimulate economic development, particularly in the Third World."[2] (emphasis added)

The Soviet "peace offensive" puts the militarists in a bind; how are they to retain world approval while refusing such peaceful and sensible offers? Some will question the wisdom of trusting the Soviets and the reliability of on-site inspections and spy-in-the-sky satellites. In 1985, former CIA director Stansfield Turner addressed this problem:

I quickly became convinced that we had the capability of detecting any substantial buildup for war in any part of the world. For instance, in 1978 we were easily able to detect Cuban mercenaries massing with Ethiopian forces against Somalia in the Ogaden desert. We had forewarning when the Soviets prepared to invade Afghanistan in 1979, when the Chinese lined up against Vietnam in the same year, and when the Soviets positioned themselves to intimidate Poland in 1980. If even small conflicts broke out, we could keep track of the military action.[3]

With Gorbachev's offer on arms reduction, this is an opportune moment to reclaim the high ground. We could challenge the Soviets to jointly use our wasted industrial capacities to develop the Third World in a *race for peace.* * Whoever wins this race will gain the respect and loyalty of the world.

Immediately will come warnings from every entrenched mind that it can't be done. But it can. If we can build hundreds of billions of dollars worth of tools of destruction when they are not needed and are not used, we can build productive tools and loan (or give) them to needy societies. Tools lent for productive purposes can be repaid from the wealth they generate; tools for war can only subtract from the world's wealth. In the latter case, the value that could have been produced by that wasted land, labor, and capital is gone forever.

## The Money Is There

Seymour Melman, Professor of Industrial Engineering at Columbia University, has laboriously measured the squandering of public funds on the arms race:

> Without considering the full social cost to the American community, the combined Pentagon budgets of 1946–1988 represent a mass of resources equivalent to the cost of replacing just about all (94 percent) of everything manmade in the United States (excluding the land) [i.e. every house, railroad, airplane, household appliance, etc.]. But when we take into account both the resources used by the military as well as the economic product forgone, then *we must appreciate the social cost of the military economy, 1946–1988, as amounting to about twice the "reproducible assets" of U.S. national wealth.* What has been forgone for American society is a quantity of material wealth sufficient to refurbish the United States, with an enormous surplus to spare.[4] (emphasis added)

Melman's exposure only addresses our wasted industrial capacity. It does not allow for wasted Soviet capital, or that of other societies destroyed by wars either openly or covertly financed by these superpowers (wars in Korea, Vietnam, Afghanistan, Iran, Indonesia, El Salvador, Guatemala, Chile, Angola, Mozambique, and Ethiopia, for example.).

---

* In 1950, before the arms race was in full swing, this approach was advocated by Senator Brien McMahon of Connecticut, chairman of the Joint Committee on Atomic Energy (Fleming, *The Cold War and Its Origins,* p. 527).

Europe and the Soviet Union combined have spent on arms an amount at least equal to the U.S.* Given Melman's calculation of the cost of the military economy, this means that since World War II NATO and Warsaw Pact nations have consumed and/or forgone production of about four times the value of everything manufactured and built in the United States (excluding household goods and clothes). As the U.S. has 6 percent of the world's people, the wasted capital of the industrialized world is enough to have built homes, cars, and every other amenity of a modern country for 24 percent of the rest of the world. This would have required no effort beyond converting wasted land, labor, and capital to productive use.

The potential is even greater. Third World countries already have the resources and labor to build their own social infrastructure. They only lack tools of production (that monopolized capital) and the training and experience to use them. If that wasted industrial capital had built industrial capital for the Third World, they could have had adequate industrial capacity to manufacture their own consumer products in only a few years. As only 47 percent of American industrial capacity is being used for consumer needs (see below), rational planning would only consider industrializing the Third World to 47 percent of our level— less if the accepted living standards were lower.

We know from history that the powerful squandered resources, but we are unaware that social wealth is being wasted today on a scale never equaled in history. I have demonstrated above that, if it had been social policy, the world could easily have been capitalized since World War II. Using only a part of the money wasted on the arms race, it can still be done very quickly.

One-third of U.S. industry is wasted on arms; approximately 10 percent is used to support the infrastructure for the waste distribution territories within the civilian economy; and 20 percent has been idle in the slack economy of the 1980s, of which only half is down time for repairs.[5] This means that fully 53 percent of U.S. industrial capital (not social capital) is wasted, leaving only 47 percent producing for our actual needs (42 percent if one subtracts the down time for repairs of the nonproductive industry, but I will allow that extra five percent as being productively employed in a full employment economy.)**

Third World countries have their own land and labor and we have measured their per capita requirements for industrial capital at 47 percent that of the U.S. or less. We now only need to know how quickly they could be provided with factories by converting the industrial nations' wasted capital to those ends. The necessary calculations are quite easy. One-third of America's industrial capital is spent on arms; Western Europe, Eastern Europe, and the Soviet Union together squander at least an equal amount. The total capital wasted each year on arms by these developed countries is equal to at least 66 percent of the industrial

---

* The expenditure of arms is more heavily weighted towards the Western nations than is generally known. "America's NATO allies spend six times more on defense than Russia's Warsaw Pact allies; indeed, Britain, France, and West Germany *each* spend more than the non-Russian Warsaw Pact countries together." (Paul Kennedy, *The Rise and Fall of Great Powers*, p. 508).

** Homes, cars, roads, bridges, electric power, water systems, sewers, etc., are social capital. We are only concerned here with industrial capital—steel mills, factories, and so forth.

capacity of the U.S., or 140 percent of the U.S. capital currently producing consumer goods.

Production engineers noted in 1978 that "typical large-scale manufacturing activities yield sales of between $30,000 and $50,000 per employee and involve assets of $25,000 to $40,000 per [employee]."[6] These engineering statistics show that, on the average, each factory can reproduce its value in machinery every ten months. We will conservatively allow one year for our calculations. (As land values are included in those factory values and no one builds land, the actual time for capital to reproduce itself is well under ten months.)[*]

Allowing that 20 percent of the world's countries are industrialized and that the rest have 10 percent of the industries they need, 70 percent of the world's population is without modern tools (industrial capital) for efficient production. If only half the industrial capacity now wasted by the developed nations on arms were redirected to produce tools for the Third World, this would provide adequate industrial capital to over 4 percent of the world's people each year.[**] Dividing that 4 percent into the 70 percent of the world's people without adequate capital tells us the capital to industrialize the world to the level of that producing for U.S. civilian needs could be produced in eighteen years. It is likely that impoverished people would be quite satisfied with half the amenities of life of the average American. Using only half the wasted capital, the industrial tools for that standard of living can be produced in nine years, and using all the wasted capital in only four and one-half years.

Any engineer can quickly calculate this. Modern industries can spit out industrial tools just as fast as they can cars, refrigerators, airplanes, tanks, guns, or warships. (Most raw material is already available; in all those tanks, guns, and warships there is more than enough steel to produce the necessary machine tools.) This isn't done because profits are made by keeping capital scarce. Scarce capital means scarce consumer goods and high prices; that translates into monopoly profits. In short, monopolization of capital keeps these tools and the immense wealth they could produce out of the hands of the world's dispossessed. This is not done by conspiracy; it is the structure of capitalism. Each center of capital must defend its monopoly of capital or lose those monopoly profits. To share capital, technology, resources, and markets is to eliminate one's advantage. The waste exposed herein and the ease with which the Third World could be capitalized if it were only social policy is proof of the power of that monopoly.

Underdeveloped countries could not absorb these tools as fast as they could be built. This book, however, is only a broad overview. It is not meant to outline either the exact methods or a timetable for implementation. If they are authorized to

---

[*] This can be judged by anyone who has ever bought a chainsaw to replace the old hand-powered crosscut, power tools to replace hand carpenter tools, or garden tractors to replace shovels and hoes. Each of these will return its value in labor time in a matter of weeks.

[**] The industrialized nations waste 140 percent of U.S. industrial capital each year. Half of that is 70 percent of U.S. capital. Seventy percent of U.S. population is over 4 percent of the world's population.

proceed and given access to productive capital, engineers can solve these problems. It should be possible for the Third World to train workers and build the infrastructure (roads, sewers, electricity) to absorb this capital over a period of forty-five years.* Such a time span would only require 20 percent of the industrial capacity now wasted on arms by the developed nations, or 40 percent of that of the U.S. alone.

These calculations are proven credible by the Marshall Plan, with which the U.S. financed the reconstruction of Europe in five years. This cost $13 billion in 1953 dollars, which is roughly equal to $68 billion in inflated 1987 dollars.[7] Twenty percent of the capital wasted on arms by both power blocs would be $120 billion per year, or $5.4 trillion over a forty-five-year time span. These calculations are supported by Third World experts who point out that $5 trillion is "more than enough for our needs."[8]

Another comparison would be the cost of the world's largest engineering project—the Panama Canal. Calculated in 1988 dollars, it cost about $7 billion.[9] The $120 billion per year allowed above would finance the equivalent of seventeen such projects each year.

If this wasted 20 percent of industrial capital were turned towards building industrial tools for the Third World, there would still be about 33 percent of America's capital not producing useful products. The U.S. would have the option of finding a productive use for this excess industry or dismantling it. That means that, if we wanted to, the U.S alone could easily capitalize the Third World in those forty-five years, with plenty of labor and industrial capital to spare. I can think of no better way to develop respect and friends.

## The Politics of Economic Alliances

Every country is part of a natural, easily outlined region for production and distribution. The incorporation of economies on opposite sides of the earth, while simultaneously denying the inclusion of close neighbors, is economic insanity. This monstrosity can only be because of politics, and bad politics at that. The world's engineers obviously were not consulted.

As a mass market is essential for industries that require economies of scale, many people have recognized and championed the desirable efficiency of large economic regions. Production, distribution, and consumption can then be rationally integrated. These industries require a multitude of natural resources that are only available in certain regions of the earth. Planners can judge what countries form natural regional zones for efficient production and distribution. It only appears difficult because all past efforts have been to monopolize capital, not share it. After all, the definition of monopolizing is "to secure and retain exclusive possession."[10] The Central American states, for example, have long dreamed of forming an economic union, and all Latin American countries could logically form

---

* Society is a machine and every road, railroad, electric grid, water system, and sewer system makes this machine more efficient. These countries cannot compete in world trade until such time as their internal communication, production, and transportation systems are equal to those of the developed nations.

one or two integrated regions. There are many languages throughout Africa, but several efficient economic zones are conceivable.

There is nothing original in this. The small, fragmented, and weak Third World countries were established largely by imperial powers specifically to prevent their organization and power. Conversely, regional organization and development must have been the dream of progressive thinkers in every dependent country. Belatedly recognizing its efficiency, Western planners are organizing a "United States of Europe." More accurately, the long-term goal is to integrate Japan, Taiwan, South Korea, the U.S., Canada, the European countries, and a few other nations into a totally integrated production and distribution region.

To use these once wasted resources productively incurs no net increase in cost. The political framework under which this worldwide transfer of technology and tools can be carried out already exists: the United Nations. This organization has long been working on these problems and has collected most of the necessary statistics. The representatives of many of these nations are already cooperating, and industrialization is their shared goal. If the barriers of monopolized capital are breached, an agreement could be made between most countries within a region. There is no need to obtain the consent of every country, as the first capital can go to those that are amenable to a just society. Those were the rules under which the Marshall Plan that rebuilt Europe was established:

> Our policy was "directed not against any country or doctrine but against hunger, poverty, desperation and chaos. Its purpose should be the revival of a working economy in the world so as to permit the emergence of political and social conditions in which free institutions can exist." Any government that was willing to assist in the task of recovery would find full cooperation, but any government that maneuvered to block the recovery of others could not expect help from us. "Furthermore, governments, political parties, or groups which seek to perpetuate human misery in order to profit therefrom politically or otherwise will encounter the opposition of the United States."[11]

Few governments would endure for long if they rejected an offer to industrialize just because the conditions required a democratic government that recognized its citizens' full rights. Leaders who are now reluctant to surrender their dictatorial powers will—under these conditions—either do so quickly or risk losing power through a revolution. In any case, these dictators would already have been long gone were they not being kept in power by external support from "co-respective" monopolies.[12] As the goal of a *race for peace* would be winning the hearts and minds of people, continuing to support reactionary regimes would be self-defeating.

This would have worked well in Vietnam, where America experienced its only defeat. Ho Chi Minh asked for our support to throw out the French and wished to pattern the Vietnamese constitution after ours.[13] Only by our refusal were they forced to turn to the communists for support. We fear every democratic insurgency and label it communist but most have little to do with that philosophy and are really after only what we sought in our revolution—freedom. These insurrections could all be stopped in their tracks by honestly promoting democracy and capitalizing those countries. As shown, the true net cost would be nothing, as all that wasted production and devastation would be spared. At the officially recognized cost of $150 billion to conduct that war, we could have given every man, woman, and child in Vietnam almost $10,000. Of course, it would have meant giving up control of that capital.

## Conclusion

The math in this treatise calculates the wasted labor in the U.S. at about 60 percent, industrial capital at about 50 percent, and resources at possibly 40 percent. How the world deals with this potential depends on millions of powerful people, all exerting their influence to their own advantage. This power extends to everyone defending the "unearned" income from these waste distribution territories, including those who receive all kinds of welfare—business, agriculture, the middle class, and the poor. Though they are defending income that is not earned, they are locked into a system of distribution that is essential for their survival. Such is the system of patronage that has evolved slowly over time, entrapping almost everybody at least partially in some form of a waste distribution territory. Hopefully, this knowledge will eventually create a moral power greater than the political power that now protects these various economic territories.

The choice of capitalizing the Third World and achieving peace is ours. We have a developed social infrastructure and the surplus capital, resources, and labor. At this time, the Soviets would not stand a chance in competing with us. In another fifteen to thirty years it could be a different story. They could develop very fast and that developed capital and social infrastructure could challenge capitalism's right to control resources around the world. (Of course, they could also be overwhelmed by capitalism.)

Currently few countries in the world would choose communism but this could also change if capitalism continues to deny them freedom. People will always fight to control their own resources and destiny—their freedom. They will accept any ally to gain and maintain that freedom.

Of course, few would choose monopoly capitalism because by the very definition of a monopoly there can only be a few. If we decide to capitalize the Third World, there will be no monopoly capital, there will only be capitalism. Only when capitalized and on a level playing field in world commerce can these countries ever be free. As already demonstrated by postwar Western Europe and our three resource-poor miracle countries—Japan, South Korea, and Taiwan—this can be done very quickly. Scarcity of resources will be pointed out as a problem but, considering that possibly 40 percent of the resources we consume are currently wasted, there is enough within our own borders for most of our needs. The resources of the Third World would be available for their needs.

Armed with this knowledge, the citizens of the world can insist on policies that are efficient and provide true security. People who have that all-important right—the vote—can exercise this critical democratic power to insist on their economic rights: the right to hold productive jobs and to enjoy the fruits produced by their labor. This is only possible through access to their share of the world's tools (industrial capital). This reclamation of economic rights will result in an expansion of freedom, rights, and responsibilities for most people.

The powerful may feel they will lose, but if they insist on continuing the monopolization of capital they stand a greater chance of losing everything to waste, war, or revolution. However, they have also been trained to be moral and just; they are simply unaware of the waste and destruction caused by looking only at that bottom line—their profits. For every dollar of their profits, surely five have been wasted through the many waste distribution territories which evolved due to the excessive property rights designed to protect those monopoly profits. Once the enormous potential of a just social policy is realized, some of the wealthy will put their political weight behind the dispossessed people's struggle.

Detractors will attack this approach as simplistic, utopian, and idealistic. To be credible, they must address the fact that people throughout the world want peace, and ask where our moral authority will be if the Soviets keep the high moral ground in leading the world to disarmament.* With a world becoming aware that they have been deceived, the power brokers may have no other choice but to abandon their aggressive military posture. Capitalizing the Third World would provide the necessary economic activity to keep our economy functioning while we decide how to readjust the workweek so that all are working productively.

"Protecting the free world" with arms puts us at a disadvantage. Most countries do not perceive our attempt to maintain control as synonymous with their freedom. The people of the world have obtained too many rights for any country to keep them in bondage much longer under either communist or capitalist power brokers. In addition to the Third World's desperate effort to break free from monopoly capitalism, Eastern European countries are chafing under Soviet control.

No society willingly tolerates its economy or politics being dictated by another. Justice demands that they be free to decide their own course in history and those that offer true democracy should be aided in their economic development. If after World War II the decision had been made to capitalize the world instead of militarily surround and enclose the socialist world, there would be no communism as we understand it today. Of course, that would not be monopoly capitalism either.

The effort to prevent other societies from gaining control of their own resources or developing capital consumes enormous resources. This may impoverish the world, including ourselves. If the war hawks are not curbed, the world may even be destroyed. The only sensible choice is to abandon the monopolization of capital and resources and release the wasted labor, resources, and industrial capacity for productive use. To abandon the monopolization of capital and resources, along with the militarized, authoritarian governments this entails, should mean peace, freedom for the world, tools for everyone to work with and, most importantly, the elimination of world poverty.[14]

---

* In June 1989 the U.S. countered the unilateral Soviet reduction of military spending of 14.5 percent with an announcement of a 10-percent cut in Europe (2 percent of our total). The Soviets immediately countered with an announcement of a unilateral 33- to 50-percent reduction in the next five years. As of the printing of this book, we have not responded.

# Book Three

# Introduction

U nder the rules of its governing ideology, every society becomes locked into a system of production and distribution. This provides the emotional and physical security under which that society functions. The people become accustomed to the security provided by those rules and normally only under crisis will they change. Even then any change must be within the context of those familiar doctrines. To do otherwise is revolutionary and will cause enormous confusion and chaos.

These social rules are usually made by powerful groups and weighted towards their security and comfort. In our culture and under those rules, as industrial technology rapidly became more and more efficient, and produced more wealth, the powerful, under rules of their own making, claimed that increased wealth. In each person's scramble to find a niche within this production/distribution system, there evolved the system of distribution by waste described in Books One and Two. Book Three exposes the excess rights of property that past power brokers have carefully coded into our laws that monopolize land, capital, and finance capital to intercept the wealth produced. This monopoly system, possibly essential at one time to mobilize and concentrate capital, is now obsolete. It has become a sponge unnecessarily soaking up large percentages of others' production.

These excess rights claim an excessive share of social production and create an ongoing crisis as the rest of society struggles for its share. Such crises have always developed into severe crises in the past (wars, depressions) and they will again in the future. No one can predict what form they will take but here are some of the more likely possibilities.

*Economic collapse:* The excess claims of wealth can appropriate too much of the labor of others within Western society and without that buying power the economy collapses. In the Soviet culture, the same may happen for opposite reasons. Due to the concentration on rebuilding industry and social capital and building defensive arms, the citizens there have plenty of money and little to buy. The Soviet crisis is by far the more severe.

*Battle over world trade:* During the first half of this century there developed several competing centers of capital (Britain, France, Germany, Japan, etc.)— their wealth depended upon trade. The battle between those centers of capital for world trade erupted into World Wars I and II. The Soviet socialist experiment was both another emerging center of capital and an ideological threat. That threat can mean a loss of markets to capitalist production centers; the developing Soviet wealth could provide both an ideological beacon to the dispossessed people of the world and the tools (capital) with which they can free themselves from the bonds of our capital.

To oppose that ideological threat, today's managers of these once individual Western centers of capital are attempting to create one large center of capital. Being far weaker and with virtually hundreds of divided loyalties, there is the high possibility that the Soviet bloc may crumble. This is their great weakness and our great strength: they are fragmented under many ideologies and loyalties while we are united under one. But if the Soviets are able to handle their nationality problems and the restructuring of their economy they will be an economic power to reckon with. Thus the ongoing pressures of capitalism.

In the conclusion to Book Two, I outlined how, just since World War II, the Cold War has cost us twice the value of our current social wealth. Because of their limited capital, the relative cost to the Soviets was much greater. Fifty percent or more of their industrial capacity was spent to offset the external threat. It was their potential as a developing center of capital that fueled the ongoing Western effort to isolate the developing socialist centers of capital. The attempts at isolation and containment were failing; this led to a change of policy and acceptance of China into our trading system. Gorbachev's successes at disarmament and decreasing world tensions are forcing us to consider trading with that bloc also. This is as positive a development for world peace as I can possibly visualize. Wars are trade wars and only by equality in trades can they be avoided. Equality requires that each developing country have the opportunity to develop its capital (industry). If our barriers to trade and transfer of technology and their barriers to penetration of their markets are removed, our superior production technology will quickly overwhelm theirs.

But when brought within our trading bloc, if they can maintain equality for their industries, these countries are a continuing threat. With their developing capital and an ideology of the world's labor becoming free, they can offer technology and tools (capital) and be an example to the dispossessed people of the world. This will create an ideological crisis; to maintain the moral high ground we must also offer the Third World capital and this will be extending more rights to the world's dispossessed.

To be credible and to become truly efficient we must extend more rights to more people, including our own workers. This will require reducing the rights of property which have created monopolies which have, in turn, created this waste.

These monopoly rights are protected not only by law but by incomprehensible economic theories. These final four chapters will expose these excess rights. The exposure of the basic structures of monopolies will be a threat to many. They are not monolithic entities separate from ourselves: we are all tied into this production/distribution system. Monopolies' roots reach deep into and nurture our entire society. They also closely resemble these waste distribution territories I have been exposing. In fact, they are quite the same. They are structured in law and those employed within are working hard and producing little while intercepting a lot of social production.

Before we can understand how monopolization works, we must understand why a population so easily rejects what would be an increase in their rights and well-being. Communism and capitalism both function as religions as much as they do economic philosophies. In religion, those who dare to challenge the governing doctrines are ostracized—not only by the church but by their peers. That pressure to conform and be accepted is probably the strongest bond of a society. In our society, any ideas to the left of the governing ideology that threaten the powerful are labeled communist, socialist, or liberal: the C, S, and L words. To take such a stand is political (and social) suicide.

The American political spectrum is commonly described, and always viewed, as having full expression from right to left. That this is not so will be recognized if one asks politically aware acquaintances these three questions: Where in the American political spectrum is the Trilateral Commission—extreme right, right, middle, left, or extreme left? Where in that spectrum was President Jimmy Carter? Where in that same spectrum was the Committee on the Present Danger? For the Trilateralists, with few exceptions, you will get the answer that they represented the extreme right (after all, they are the organization of international business that some radical, and some not so radical publications, accuse of wanting to rule the world). Carter will be seen as extreme left; and few will have ever heard of the CPD.

Yet, as the Trilateralists were the power that backed President Jimmy Carter, they could hardly have been on opposite ends of the political spectrum. President Carter was a member and "incorporated 19 members of the Trilateral Commission" into his administration to institute that group's policies.[1]

The Trilateral Commission is comprised of business groups and intellectuals from the U.S., Europe, and Japan that were worried about the periodic economic crisis and its potential for creating revolutions (loss of their economic territory). Their agenda was to defuse this threat by sharing more of monopoly capital's wealth with both internal labor and developing countries.[2] Their commendable, but still too limited, goal was to reduce the tensions in the world. This angered the extreme right (the CPD) who cranked up their propaganda machine to destroy Carter's credibility and thus his power. Carter was portrayed as a weak president whose peaceful policies were leaving the U.S. vulnerable to attack. The American public, not having the slightest idea that the threat of imminent attack (that creation of an enemy) was a totally manufactured perception, voted Carter out and voted in possibly the most dedicated militarists we have ever known:

> After swamping Jimmy Carter in the 1980 election, Reagan appointed *thirty-one* members of the Committee on the Present Danger to high official posts. Policy shifts have seldom been expressed in such clear organizational terms. While the Carter administration had incorporated 19 members of the Trilateral Commission, the Reagan team completely shut out the trilateralists. Once in office, Reagan's team "hit the ground running," wasting no time in implementing the 1980 Republican platform, which called for "*overall military and technological superiority over the Soviet Union.*"[3] (emphasis in original)

It is the largely unknown CPD and similar groups that are the extreme right in American politics. (The lunatic right—Aryan Nations, Ku Klux Klan, and fellow travelers—are outside functioning politics.) In interviewing members of the CPD, Jerry Sanders found that they were easy to talk to, believed firmly in what they did, and were proud of it. They freely admitted they specifically and intentionally propagandized the American people about the Soviet threat.[4]

The well-known Trilateralists, viewed as an extreme right-wing organization, hold *relatively* moderate political views. It is groups such as the largely unknown CPD that are the extreme right on the American political scene.*

There have been no policies adopted or even seriously considered by any U.S. government since 1945 that are left of the most liberal of the above named political groups. Though it may surprise academics, politicians, and the public, in the proper meaning of the *full political spectrum,* there is no left and not even a functioning middle in American politics or economics. There is only a right and an extreme right. The most liberal of the two wishes to prevent the reclaiming of rights by sharing a little more with labor and the Third World. The extreme right is attempting to keep the lid on with military force.

This control of ideas is accomplished by attacking any ideas that threaten the powerful as being an extreme danger to society. The enemy, of course, is communism, even though most progressive ideas have nothing to do with that philosophy. D. F. Fleming vividly outlines the necessity of this enemy to control public perception.

> Forgetting that negation never built anything, we started building walls [military bases around the Soviet Union]. Then the global wall around Russia and communism has to be buttressed with all sorts of internal walls, until finally they stood around each American individual, silencing most dissenters. . . . A disease theory of communism was accepted, making each communist the carrier of a virus so deadly that a single Red was likely to infect the body politic. Then all engines of law and social pressure were operated to destroy all communists, and with them fellow travelers of fellow travelers, until *every person and idea not extremely conservative was in danger of attack.* . . . Stalin invented a brand name, "enemy of the people," with which he struck down all suspects and disarmed their defenders. For this purpose our counterpart was the brand "Un-American," administered by Congressional committees whose very existence was a negation of the central American principle that a man is free to think what he will. Nevertheless, these committees ranged through the country to expose anyone who had ever had any contact with communist ideas, even during the great depression, with heavy damage to lives and livelihoods.[5] (emphasis added)

The ideology that our society follows was created generations ago by the powerful to protect themselves. During its creation, they had firm control of what was taught but the remarkable thing about it is that, once established, it developed a life of its own and is largely self-perpetuating. It matters little whether this was planned or simply evolved. It now has perpetual motion.

In a society that theoretically gives its professors academic freedom to study and teach, to make the above statements appears contradictory. Most of these "free" intellectuals are unaware they are being well controlled by the methods described above:

> Slowly but surely one political economist after another moved closer and closer to the solution to the age old problem of poverty. The picture became clearer with each new writing of men like David Ricardo, N. W. Senior, James Mill and his son

---

John Stuart Mill, Frederic Bastiat, J. B. Say, H. C. Carey, and other political economists. The possibility of a world without poverty and war was within humanity's grasp, when quite suddenly the world's scholars stopped short—just as if they had come unexpectedly face-to-face with some terrifying, fire-spitting, blood-soaked monster blocking their path. . . . That it was very real, powerful, and dangerous cannot be doubted, because political economists even to this day have stopped prying into the possible causes of poverty—and gone back to less embarrassing Mercantilism.[6]

Of course, the few economists and political scientists who looked saw the excessive rights of property which our society was structured under. To speak out would incur the wrath of the powerful as well as the very people they were supposed to be educating. Any exposure would be branded heresy and heresies are not permitted to be taught. Those who professed beliefs outside those permitted parameters of debate would be branded the enemy and lose their authority, their income, and the respect of their peers. The National Association of Manufacturers even formed an Economics Principles Committee that censored all economics texts used in high schools and colleges.[7] There is an ideological "cordon sanitaire" keeping the alert from enlightening the public.

Due to this firm control of ideas, all views broadly distributed in the U.S. are on a very narrow ideological edge to the right of the political and economic spectrum. Having been conditioned to distrust any other ideologies, most will label this treatise "left" although it is actually in the middle of the full political spectrum.

The Populists of the last century were then the ideological threat and they were similarly pushed out of the political main stream. However, the Populist agenda

became a sourcebook for political reforms spanning the next fifty years: a progressive income tax; federal regulation of railroads, communications, and other corporations; legal rights for labor unions; government price stabilization and credit programs for farmers. The populist plan would essentially employ the full faith and credit of the United States government directly to assist the "producing classes," who needed financing for their enterprises. In effect, the government would *circumvent the bankers and provide credit straight to the users. . . . [and] provide "money at cost,"* instead of money lent by merchants and bankers at thirty-five or fifty or a hundred per cent interest.[8] (emphasis added)

Hardscrabble frontier farmers figured out banking reforms; Production Credit Associations; farm and home long-term loans; land reclamation and agricultural supports; credit unions; "a progressive income tax; federal regulation of railroads, communications, and other corporations; [and] legal rights for labor unions." With the exception of direct election of senators and women's suffrage, which became law in the early part of the century, these ideas were pushed outside the permitted parameters of debate. During economic crises, academia appropriated these Populist ideas without acknowledging where they came from and promoted them for solving the banking and economic problems of the Great Depression. Though Populism is degraded in virtually every textbook, the essence of their ideas has been appropriated and has been the law and custom of the land for the past fifty years.[9] They were in the middle of the full political spectrum all the time.

One of the rights gained at that time was purchasing homes on a long-term contract. Previously most homes were purchased by cash or with a one- to three-year note. This history is gone from social memory and most people think the masses have always had these rights. The old customs of cash purchases or season credits at over 50 percent interest are clear examples of monopolization of capital. It was the gaining of rights that severely curtailed that monopolization and created our wealthy society. It is the elimination of the last of those monopolies through the reclamation of the last of our rights, and becoming wealthier yet, that this book addresses.

Probably the best examples of controlling a population to vote against their own best interest are Social Security, Railroad Retirement, and unemployment insurance. Before these became rights for American citizens under the crisis of the Great Depression, there was nothing more communist or un-American than a paid retirement or being paid while unemployed. The right wing put out far more violent rhetoric against the passage of these laws than they did to the Soviet threat. Today, no one considers retirement pay and unemployment insurance as even socialist, let alone communist.

Of course, the reader will recognize that American citizens are also denied guaranteed health insurance and other rights covered in this treatise. It is interesting to note that rights such as Social Security, Railroad Retirement, and unemployment insurance were only extended to the masses when the economy was in crisis. When the economy is going strong and the country much richer no such rights are extended. That alone is proof that these rights could be reclaimed at any time but are not because of the control of public perception by the right wing.

Complex economic theories abound to explain how our economy works, but all that receive attention are within the permitted parameters of debate, to the right of the political spectrum. The problem of economists is not unlike that of philosophers during the Middle Ages. Once the church (or other powerful groups) established the governing ideology, no intellectuals dared challenge that gospel. If they did they were assured to be banned from the community or burned at the stake. Galileo just barely avoided that fate when he dared say the earth revolved around the sun. In order to state their thoughts, these philosophers developed a complicated language and wrote incomprehensible treatises that only the most highly educated could understand. Statements that could have been made in a few pages required volumes. This became an intellectual game which permitted some pure nonsense to be elevated alongside quality philosophy. Philosophies that supported the governing ideology were pushed and given free rein while others were ignored or even suppressed. Only a few people would be able to break through that philosophical barrier.

In the same way, today's intellectuals are boxed into a system of thought expression that protects the powerful. They must teach a philosophy acceptable to today's power brokers and the conditioned public. Failure to do so would assure that there would be no audience and no job (or if one has tenure, no promotion). This is what the political scientists and economists knew when they fled back to the classroom, never to speak of the excessive rights of property in our economic religion.

The waste distribution territories I have been describing are elaborate mechanisms for claiming one's share of the production of society. Likewise, the superstructure of ownership of land, capital, and finance capital is a complex system of intercepting social wealth under the claim of being fully productive.

It was these excessive claims of property that caused waste distribution territories to develop and reclaim some of the appropriated social production. The heart of those excessive rights is the ownership of three kinds of wealth-producing property. The first is land. Nature produced it, it is social wealth, and is properly held in *conditional* private ownership. Second are basic infrastructures, such as railroads and utilities, that are natural monopolies. This is social capital that is properly managed by *public authority*. These two forms of capital are mixed with a third form—that produced by individual labor which should be held in *unrestricted* private ownership. These three forms of wealth-producing properties are inseparable in our society today—they are all interchangeable through the medium of finance capital.

The monopolization of land, capital, and finance capital, and the excessive rights they incur, are structured in law. Their roots reach deep into America's middle class and function within our everyday normal commerce. All pay those monopoly charges and, except for the dispossessed poor, at times receive monopoly income. The overwhelming share of this unearned income is claimed by the 10 percent that own 86 percent of America's wealth.[10] From that point to the forty-sixth percentile, the unearned income declines steadily. Except through a waste distribution territory, the bottom 54 percent, on balance, receive no monopoly income. (That which is received is more than counterbalanced by excessive monopoly charges.)[11] Book Three defines those excess rights by outlining how land, capital, and finance capital are monopolized and the income distributed to those above that forty-sixth percentile.

If economists would just check their fundamental principles of economics they would find they know well the flaws in the system. They know there are only three physical foundations to production—land, labor, and industrial capital.* I have demonstrated in Books One and Two that in the U.S. 40 to 70 percent of these three elements is wasted so there is a large surplus of each. Poverty is rooted in ideology, not economics.

---

* All other elements to production are psychological and can be summed up under one heading—motivation. Honesty, morality, energy, and idealism all require motivation.

# 1

## Monopolization of Land

### Land Is Social Wealth

If I were to follow the normal pattern of avoiding anything threatening to the reader I would leave out this chapter, but it is here that monopolization of social wealth started. Hundreds of years ago the superior rights of the powerful were structured into ownership of land and it is now ingrained in law and custom. As you read how this was accomplished and how it can be corrected keep in mind that, once the monopoly rules are changed, all use rights will be retained and ownership of land for homes, businesses, and production will be far easier and cheaper. Removal of monopoly rules not only increases your right to land but ensures it.

If a person could be born with fully developed intelligence, physical ability, and judgment, but without social conditioning, one of the first confusing realities he or she would face is that all land belongs to someone else. Before this person could legally stand, sit, lie down, or sleep, he or she would have to pay whoever owned that piece of land. That this is absurd can be shown by reflecting on the obvious: land, air, and water nurture all life; each living thing requires, and is surely entitled to, living space on this earth; no person produced any part of it, because it was here when each was born; and its bounty belongs to all.

All human needs come from the land. Over time, the alert realized that if they claimed a piece of land and defended that claim others would have to ask permission and pay for its use. Jean Jacques Rousseau, in "A Discourse on the Origins of Inequality," wrote these incisive words:

> The first man who, having enclosed a piece of ground, bethought himself as saying "this is mine," and found people simple enough to believe him, was the real founder of civil society. From how many crimes, wars, and murders, from how many horrors and misfortunes might not any one have saved mankind, by pulling up the stakes, or filling up the ditch, and crying to his fellows: "Beware of listening to this impostor; you are undone if you once forget that the fruits of the earth belong to us all, and the earth itself to nobody."[1]

Rousseau's words outline the injustice of one person having *unrestricted* ownership to another's living space on this earth. This practice is only customary; it is part of the social conditioning that all receive while growing up. Being thoroughly conditioned, and having never experienced or imagined anything else, few ever realize that under the current structure of land ownership they may not have all their rights. Instead, the possibility of eventually owning one's piece of land is viewed as evidence of full rights. Being conscious of the not-so-distant past when common people did not have even this privilege, citizens view and celebrate these limited rights as full rights.

## Pride in Ownership Must Be Maintained

Land is, unquestionably, social wealth. However, the right to one's space on this earth, the pride it returns to its "owner," and the care normally given to one's personal property, are compelling reasons to keep most land under a *conditional* form of private ownership. Being socially efficient, private ownership that recognizes the equal rights of all to share the land and what it produces is fully justifiable. What is unjust is the unrestricted monopolization of what nature freely produces on and under this land. It is necessary to keep private ownership on land and its benefits while eliminating land monopolization and its unavoidable inequities.

## The Evolution of Private Ownership of Land

In the early formation of any society, to be required to pay another for one's living space was not customary. The bitter battle to retain rights to a family homestead, and access for everybody to nature's bounty, was fought for hundreds of years and in many civilizations—it continues yet today. In fact, the decline and fall of great civilizations has a distinct pattern. They start with everyone having rights to the land and end when a few powerful people have usurped all these rights.

The Roman Empire began with each citizen having inalienable rights to a homestead while the "general domain" was held for common use. It ended when, during Rome's last days, "only 1,800 men owned all of the known world" and the once-free dispossessed tillers of that soil were little more than slaves.[2] With "barbarians" offering the justice of each family again sharing the land as common property, the Romans could not hang onto their empire.

Earlier the Greek culture had collapsed when only "two percent of the Greeks owned the entire empire."[3] These idlers had to hide in the mountains when the farmers, shopkeepers, and peasants revolted, destroyed the mortgage stones, and reclaimed their lands. Many students of social evolution will recognize this revolution as the "birth of democracy."[4] (This was one of many bursts of democracy.) Later, the monopolization of land by the church and aristocracy was the primary injustice that led to the French Revolution. Though trumpeted as successful, it did not give the common people rights in property.

Before the advent of ownership of social wealth through ownership of capital, all sustenance for life and thus all wealth (rights) came directly from land. Money (wealth) is a symbol for ownership of land and capital. With wealth (rights) now produced by capital as well as land, powerful people undertook to monopolize these assets just as had historically been done with land. The cycle of appropriation of others' rights through appropriation of society's wealth, leading to dispossession and poverty, takes many generations. This has a long way to go in America but the well-documented trend suggests that fewer and fewer own more and more.

The Federal Reserve calculated that, in 1974, 25 percent of Americans had no net assets, and by 1988 this had increased to 54 percent.[5] These people have no share of what nature put on this earth. As full rights include economic rights, these people's rights are severely restricted. They are being denied through denial of a share of *productive* work or through working more than is necessary for what is received. This denial of the dispossessed to their share of social production is coded into the laws and customs of the land. With the right to vote and within the framework of our ever-flexible Constitution, these rights can be reclaimed through restructuring those laws and customs.[6] If the public ever realizes that we are wasting 60 percent of our labor, 50 percent of our industrial capital, and 40 percent of our resources, those rights will be reclaimed.

## The Origins of Our Land Titles

After the collapse of the Roman Empire, the common people regained their rights to the land, and the use of nature's wealth in common developed a powerful following.[7] (Their belief in freedom and natural rights resembles our claim to these same principles today.) Inevitably this reversion to social wealth in public ownership again came under attack by powerful clans. Petr Kropotkin, that unique historian, explains the repression of these rights as the origin of the modern state:

> Only wholesale massacres by the thousand could put a stop to this widely-spread popular movement, and it was by the sword, the fire and the rack that the young states secured their first and decisive victory over the masses of the people.[8]

As described by Kropotkin, the medieval roots of our culture grimly parallel the massive slaughter in many Third World countries today. These people fight to retain or reclaim their rights to a fair share of the earth's resources that are owned by and nurture the cultural descendants of that original violent theft. The resemblance here is not a coincidence; current struggles are a continuation of that medieval battle over who shall have rights to nature's wealth.

With the sharing of social wealth still practiced by local communities, the sixteenth century saw the beginning of a three-hundred-year effort to erase all trace of that form of ownership of social wealth. Kropotkin explains:

> The village communities were bereft of their folkmotes, their courts and independent administration; their lands were confiscated. The guilds were spoliated of their possessions and liberties, and placed under the control, the fancy, and the bribery of the State's official. The cities were divested of their sovereignty, and the very springs of their inner life—the folkmote, the elected justices and administration, the sovereign parish and the sovereign guild—were annihilated; the State's functionary took possession of every link of what formerly was an organic whole. Under that fatal policy and the wars it engendered, whole regions, once populous and wealthy, were laid bare; rich cities became insignificant boroughs; the very roads which connected them with other cities became impracticable. Industry, art, and knowledge fell into decay.[9]

The deliberate efforts to alienate the individual from common use of the natural wealth of the land, and the mutual support it automatically engendered, are documented in the nearly four thousand enclosure acts passed between 1760 and 1844 that effectively gave legal sanction to this theft.[10] For the powerful to further protect their title, it was necessary to erase from social memory all traces of the earlier custom of social ownership of social wealth. Kropotkin points out that, "It was taught in the universities and from the pulpit that the institutions in which men formerly used to embody their needs of mutual support could not be tolerated in a properly organized State."[11]

The alert will recognize the ongoing effort to prevent a rekindling of those old memories. Today we are taught by those who parrot this original disinformation that in an "efficient economy" virtually all property should be privately owned with each individual a "free" bargaining agent.

## Private Ownership of Social Wealth Moves to America

The classic descriptions of the evolution of capitalism explain how trade and industrial capital usurped the preeminent position of nobility with their historic title to all land. Yet in parts of Europe an elite social class still owns large tracts of land. As late as 1961, the Duke of Bedford, the Duke of Westminster, and the British Crown owned the most valuable sections of London, and large estates still abound throughout the countryside.[12]

The powerful, aware that wealth comes from control of land, originally structured land ownership in America under the same rules that were established in Europe. The origins of "the manorial lords of the Hudson Valley" were huge landed estates "where the barons controlled completely the lives of their tenants."[13] There were huge estates in Virginia. One covered over five million acres and embraced twenty-one counties. Such excessive greed contributed to the widespread dissatisfactions that fueled the American Revolution:

> Under Governor Benjamin Fletcher, three-quarters of the land in New York was granted to about thirty people. He gave a friend a half million acres for a token annual payment of 30 shillings. Under Lord Cornbury in the early 1700s one grant to a group of speculators was for two million acres. . . . In 1689, many of the grievances of the poor were mixed up in the farmers' revolt of Jacob Leisler and his group. Leisler was hanged, and the parceling out of huge estates continued.[14]

> . . . (by 1698, New York had given thousands of acres to the Philipses, Van Cortlands, Van Rensselaers, Schuylers, Livingstons and Bayards; by 1754, Virginia had given almost three million acres to the Carters, Beverleys, and Pages)— an early example of government "aid" to business men.[15]

Despite the egalitarian rhetoric of the American Revolution, only portions of these huge estates were confiscated and "speculation in western lands was one of the leading activities of capitalists in those days":[16]

> "Companies were formed in Europe and America to deal in Virginia lands, which were bought up in large tracts at the trifling cost of two cents per acre. This wholesale engrossment soon consumed practically all the most desirable lands and forced the home seeker to purchase from speculators or to settle as a squat-

ter." Moreover, observes Beard, "As the settler sought to escape the speculator by moving westward, the frontier line of speculation advanced."[17]

Some of America's famous leaders were deeply involved. "In the Ohio Valley a number of rich Virginia planter families, amongst whom were counted both the Lees and the Washingtons, had formed a land company and this, the Ohio Company, founded in 1748, was given a crown grant of half a million acres."[18] And Georgia had sold "over twenty-five million acres to three . . . land speculating companies for a total payment of less than $210,000."[19] Thus, "as the frontier was pushed back during the first half of the nineteenth century, land speculators working with banks stayed just ahead of new immigrants, buying up land cheap and then reselling it at high profits."[20]

While few who participated in this later land grab were members of the old aristocracy, they knew well that the route to wealth lay in claiming land so that those who followed would have to purchase it from them.

Mathew Josephson in *Robber Barons* and Peter Lyon in *To Hell in a Day Coach* document the greatest land grab in history when the railroads, through control of state and federal governments, obtained deeds to 183 million acres of land (9.3 percent of the land in the U.S.). By the turn of the century this included "more than one-third of Florida, one-fourth of North Dakota, Minnesota, and Washington and substantial chunks of 25 other states".[21]

> The state of Texas was the most generous of all: at one point they had actually given away about eight million more acres than they had in their power to bestow; as it finally turned out, they forked over to twelve railroad companies more than thirty-two million acres, which is more real estate than can be fitted inside the boundaries of the state of New York.[22]

Those who were parceling out this land only had that right through power (they took care to codify this power in legal statutes). The development of the railroads created easy access to these lands and thus made them valuable. Every landless immigrant had a more moral claim to a piece of that earth to earn a living. Yet, instead of simply being assigned it on a first-come-first-served basis so that they could use its rental value to develop the community, the land-hungry poor were forced to buy the land from these profiteers.

The celebrated Homestead Act of 1862 came after most of the choice land had already been claimed by speculators. Some six hundred thousand pioneers received eighty million acres under this act, but this was less than half that allotted to the railroad barons, who were only the latest of a long line of profiteers. These new lords of the land thoroughly understood the function of Ricardo's law of rent. They knew that all the surplus land had to be owned before their land could have significant value, thus the Homestead Act was vital to their plans.

Land sales by speculators were contracts that appropriated part of the future labor of those who bought the land. Any claim of need for that land by the powerful was dwarfed by the needs of the poor—likewise, any pretense of needing money for development and administration. As will be shown in chapter three, whenever labor, resources, and human needs coexist, there does not have to be any shortage of money—that is, if the rules for its creation and circulation are just.

## Unrestricted Land Titles Permitted
## the Mobilization of Capital

Under aristocracy, land could not be sold. It belonged permanently to the lord of that land and could only be lost through war. When English law changed to permit the sale of land this created the foundation for capitalism. Now that land could be sold, money could be borrowed against this natural wealth. When an entrepreneur wished to speculate by building a factory or ship his land could be mortgaged for that venture. This provided a far broader base of wealth to attract capital than did the old monopoly trade patents issued to favored friends by royalty. There is no question that the privatization of land and resultant mobilization of capital was a key stage in the development of capitalism that greatly increased the rights of many people. However, full rights were not attained for all as it left in place a subtle form of land monopolization.

## How Unrestricted Ownership Monopolizes Land

The French Physiocrats were the originators of laissez-faire (the philosophy of no government interference). They held as a cornerstone of their philosophy that society should collect the land rent. One of their most respected members, Mirabeau the elder, held that this would increase social efficiency equal to the inventions of writing or money. The respected economist John Kenneth Galbraith also accepts its justice and feasibility.[23] Now that the present tax structure is in place Galbraith disapproves of penalizing those who invested in land as opposed to those who invested in railroads and steel mills (those questions are automatically addressed later). Others include Thomas Paine, who is credited with promoting much that comprises our Bill of Rights; William Penn, the founder of Pennsylvania; Herbert Spencer, the noted philosopher, in his classic *Social Statics;* Thomas Sperry of the Newcastle Philosophical Society; and philosopher John Stuart Mill. These early economists "believed in the *sacredness* of private property, *particularly land.*"[24]

Later, David Ricardo formulated the law of rent which supports the logic of Mirabeau's statement. Put in simple terms, Ricardo's law of rent means that all income above that necessary to sustain labor will accrue to the owners of the land without the expenditure of their labor. A land monopolist only retains ownership of land until some innovative entrepreneur sees its potential for productive use.* The monopoly price demanded effectively appropriates a part of that entrepreneur's labor. In the price of American land we can observe Ricardo's law of rent in action.

*Commercial land:* Trading is one of the most valuable uses of land. The closer one approaches the center of commerce, the higher the price of land. Every transit line from the suburbs to a commercial district will raise its value a calculable amount. This high value represents the cheapness and quantity of trades within any population center and that savings (efficiency of trades) is recognized by the price business is willing to pay for that land. This rent value is very high in large

---

* The owner may be using it productively by past standards but not for its current most productive use.

population centers. It gradually lowers as the distance from the center of population becomes greater and the trades become less frequent and more expensive.

It is not unusual for commercial land to be valued at three, four, or even ten times the value of the buildings placed upon it.[25] Probably the highest priced acre in the world today is in the center of Tokyo, valued at $1.5 billion.[26] In a matter of minutes on that acre there may be millions of dollars worth of trades in grain, diamonds, stocks, land, finance capital, or consumer products. A small share of each trade is remitted to the landowner as rent. Thus the high value of land within population centers.

To visualize trading in primitive societies with someone standing by collecting tribute for trading on that piece of ground would show that the landowner did no productive labor—he only monopolized that land. Of course, to avoid paying tribute, that early trader needed only to move to another piece of land. Today that nearby land would also be claimed.

That $1.5-billion acre earning 5 percent interest could permanently retire 6,250 people from the labor force at one thousand dollars per month. Three acres of farm land on the outskirts of that city at $3 million could retire twelve. Thus the total acres in and around Tokyo and any population center produce an enormous amount of unearned income.

*Farm land*: Ricardo makes the rather simple evaluation that the value of land will be lower as the quality lowers. (The quality in commercial land is population and short distance.) Once the quality is such that one can earn only the wages expended in production or distribution the land's value is zero. American agriculture has evaded Ricardo's law of rent by exporting to countries that, if their lands were not monopolized, could just as well feed themselves; by converting grain into high-priced fat; and by farming the public treasury.[27] There is enough land in America to feed several times its current population; under true free enterprise and under Ricardo's law of rent the price of much of it should be zero.

*Home sites*: In Missoula, Montana, a typical $84,500 house will be on a $20,000 lot. In major population centers that same house would cost much more. It is not uncommon to pay double, triple, or even ten times that price. In Honolulu or parts of California a comparable home would be $400,000 and in Washington, D.C., $800,000. That price differential is the price of land functioning under Ricardo's law of rent. The price accurately measures the monopoly land rent charged for that lot.

The power brokers only took from the Physiocrats' free enterprise philosophy that which protected and further extended their wealth and power. As historically most members of legislative bodies were large landholders, naturally they did not accept that society should collect the land rent. If that were to happen, the dispossessed masses would have immediately regained their rights to nature's wealth. That we do not have that all-important right is evident when one observes what would happen if society did collect the land rent. The "divine rights" of private ownership of social wealth would be converted to "conditional rights" that protect all society.

Using homes for an example, real estate taxes are currently levied mostly on the improvements and only in small part on the land. That tax structure is the key to land monopolization. At 7 percent interest, the above described lot would return fourteen hundred dollars per year. The taxes on this home are twelve

hundred to fourteen hundred dollars. Removing all taxes on the house and placing them on the land would convert the taxes to land rent. This would create no
increase in costs for homeowners and the land purchase price would drop to zero
while its use value remains the same. As land speculation and all other taxes
would be eliminated (see below), the purchase price would be only the value of
labor and material that built the house; the homeowners would have even more
secure title to that land than with current unrestricted title rights.

It is this social wealth held in unrestricted private ownership that creates high
capitalized land values. True free enterprise requires breaking that monopoly
through restricted ownership—society should collect the rent. Distribution of
land by capitalized value (price) would then be replaced by distribution of land by
rental value paid to society—which is the same thing except there can be no
monopoly and no appropriation of another's labor through land rent. Whoever is
the better producer and willing to work his own land can easily outbid the incompetent, lazy, or absentee landowners. Thus those who use it for production or
distribution will, almost universally, have secure ownership of the land. The land
rent would go to society; the interest to the owners of capital (improvements,
machinery, livestock, or inventory); and wages to the farmer, businessperson or
entrepreneur.

Oil, copper, iron ore, etc. while still in the ground are land and can be very
properly privately owned so long as society is paid the land rent. We have a
surplus of most of these too. It is only that richer deposits and cheap labor in Third
World countries make those minerals cheaper and our more expensive deposits
can wait until these are exhausted.

Development of land—clearing, drainage projects, shaping the land, irrigation
dams, canals, etc.—are capital expenditures requiring special consideration. As
this is one of the most productive uses of labor, anyone who invests in such improvements should be well paid. However, unconditional title to land development is unconditional title to the land. Once the investor is well paid, the value
of those improvements should eventually be incorporated into the land rent.

The market has measured the rent value of that land and, with the exception
of homes, the land rent collected by society should equal that which is now collected both publicly and privately. Collecting land rent on homes beyond the basic
costs of running a community would intrude upon one's basic right to a share of
the land. However, the price spread between the choice home sites and lower
valued sites should still be maintained through the land rent tax imposed.

## If Society Collected Land Rent,
## All Other Taxes Could Be Eliminated

Countries today are far different than when early philosophers concluded that
society collecting land rent was the most efficient method of financing society.
Roads, airports, and harbors are all added expense. These, however, are directly
provided services and once built a user fee can be charged through a tax on gas,
airplane tickets, and harbor fees. With the exception of schools and governing
bodies, most public services authorized by law should not be supported by taxes.
There should be a charge to cover the cost, thus assuring that equal labor is

exchanged for providing that service. In this sense, a gas tax to cover highway costs is really a user's fee for the labor required to build and maintain roads.

Books One and Two show that welfare and most military expenses can be eliminated. (54 percent of every tax dollar is "defense" related.) Social Security, Railroad Retirement, health insurance trust funds, Federal Employees Retirement, etc. are, at this time, all improperly labeled government expenses—they are actually separate insurance funds.* This is an accounting trick—President Lyndon Johnson added the trust funds to the general budget to make the cost of the Vietnam War look smaller.

> In 1986 the gross revenue of the government was $794 billion. Of that amount, $294 billion was Social Security contributions, which should be subtracted from the National Security State. This leaves $500 billion. Of the $500 billion $286 billion went to defense; $12 billion to foreign arms to our client states; $8 billion to $9 billion to energy, which means, largely, nuclear weapons; $27 billion to veterans' benefits, the sad and constant reminder of the ongoing empire's recklessness; and finally, $142 billion to loans that were spent, over the past forty years, to keep the National Security State at war, hot or cold. So, of 1986's $500 billion in revenue, $475 billion was spent on National Security business. . . . Other Federal spending, incidentally, came to $177 billion . . . which is about the size of the deficit, since only $358 billion was collected in taxes.[28]

Land rent will not sustain government waste but will easily finance proper government services. Book One, chapter six, further outlines how society could be restructured to eliminate much government expense.

All farmers and businesspeople know that machinery and inventory are relatively easy to obtain; it is the price of land that restricts ownership of farms and businesses. With society collecting land rent, land prices would drop to zero while the use values would remain the same. Commerce would flourish as businesspeople, farmers, and other entrepreneurs—all true producers—would be able to start business with only the capital necessary to purchase buildings, machinery, and inventory. The land rent would be paid to society out of cash flow. The mechanism whereby one person appropriated the labor of others through unrestricted ownership of social wealth would be replaced by society's claiming the value. Society, not the landowners, put that value there by increased population, roads, water, electricity, sewer, etc.—the most important aspect being population. The wealth collected through land rent would then be returned to the people through social services—the same roads, schools, water, sewers, and parks. It must be emphasized that the landowner retains all rights to that land except the right to collect the unearned land rent.

Mortgages define the primary owner of specific properties and the mortgage interest represents the rent. If that *rent* is not paid, the land will be repossessed. Whether renting or making house payments, people are paying both land rent and house rent.

Land ownership has not changed much in the last two hundred years. It has been estimated that over 85 percent of Americans are paying rent to the fewer than 15 percent who really own the land.[29] The payment of interest in the form of rent to whoever produced that house (capital) is proper. The same is true of

---

* Edward Boorstein, *What's Ahead? . . . The U.S. Economy*, pp. 33–34.

farmers' and businesspeople's rent. Interest should be paid to whoever produced, and thus owns, the machinery, buildings, improved livestock, fences and so forth; the land rent properly belongs to society. Farmers and businesspeople in normal times (high land values are abnormal times) are not primarily collectors of rent. They are true producers.

## An Opportunity to Restructure with Society Collecting Land Rent

All within our Constitution, it would be possible to convert land taxes to land rent by gradually increasing land taxes while simultaneously eliminating other taxes. However, the political barriers to this approach are unassailable. Just as Social Security, unemployment insurance, Railroad Retirement, and banking reforms were all enacted into law under crisis, there will be an opportunity to restructure if the world economy should again collapse. Land values will again return to zero, and the search for answers will be paramount.*

From 1945 to 1966 the consumer price index rose a steady 1 or 2 percent annually.[30] True to Ricardo's law that land values rise to claim the production of labor, land prices increased around 6 percent per year. After thirty years of a land boom, which created astronomical land prices and their inevitable claim against labor, there have been five years of collapsing farm prices (1982–1987). This caused farmland and some development land to lose over half its value.

In a depression, characterized by inadequate income and collapsing values, ownership of bankrupt farms, homes, and businesses is normally relinquished to the counties in lieu of taxes. Almost all deposits and many loans are guaranteed by the U.S. government; in a collapse, the public will own those loan institutions and through them much of the land and capital (see chapter four of this book). Even now taxes diverted to support unnecessary agriculture production are all that keep the value of most farmland above zero.**

With such a collapse, and under Chapter 12 of the 1986 bankruptcy law, a farmer may erase all commercial debt above the value of his property.[31] In short, he may retain ownership and start over. Instead of using public money in the form of agricultural supports to protect a value that should not be there, this would be an opportunity to restructure land rent so that it is paid to the proper owners: society. This right, already in law for farmers, should be extended to commercial property and homeowners. After all, the old values would no longer be there and all that can be reclaimed by the lender is current values. In fact, foreclosure, maintenance, and selling costs would cause lenders greater losses than accepting this new *real value*. Instead of using public money in the form of agricultural supports to protect a value that should not be there, this would be an opportunity to restructure land rent so it is paid to the proper owners—society.

---

* In 1957, eighteen years after the end of the Great Depression and twelve years after the inflationary World War II, I calculated the value of the buildings on a farm I purchased as being equal to the asking price of the entire farm. The land was deeded free to whoever purchased the improvements.

** As documented in Book One, chapter four, 45 to 50 percent of the cropped acres are not needed at this time.

If ownership is relinquished to society in lieu of taxes or through loan and deposit guarantees, whoever could use that land could, just as now, purchase it by bid. The market value of the property would only be the value of the improvements. The land value would be zero but its use value would be as high as ever. With former owners having the right to meet the high bid, the sale should be made with the understanding that the use rights to the land and the improvements were the owner's but all land rent (not rent on improvements) would be remitted to society in the form of a land rent tax. This party could buy and sell both land and improvements but only the improvements would have value. They are the only part of the farm that required compensated labor, so only they can justly be unconditionally owned.

Thus, even as rights are reclaimed, mortgaged landowners have a better chance to attain and retain ownership of their land. The taxes on privately owned land could be converted to a land rent tax and all taxes on improvements and capital eliminated. With the elimination of waste, as outlined throughout this treatise, there should be no net increase in land rent for most people while doing away with income tax, sales tax, and other regressive taxes for all people. As values rise during a cyclical recovery or through an increase in population, the land rent tax should rise to absorb those values. This would eliminate claiming others' labor through future increases in the value of land. The "divine right" of private ownership of social wealth will then have been converted to "conditional rights" that protect all society.

Under this conditional ownership of land those who produce from that land (be it farm, home, industry or business) would be the owners. All income would go to land rent (society), labor (the farmer, industrialist, or businessperson), and capital (the owners of the buildings, machinery, livestock, or inventory). Absentee ownership of land (but not capital) would disappear. Production is the base of all wealth and there would be only productive, well-paid people on that land. This is the efficiency gain equaling the invention of money or writing the French Physiocrats spoke about. (Today there are many poor producers in farming and business that are there only through collecting land rent from inheritances, or economic windfalls, or through buying land at depressed prices and having its value increase as society [not those landowners] increased in efficiency.)

## Waste in Agriculture Wastes Capital

Where most waste distribution territories create unnecessary employment but no surplus products, unnecessary farming results in unnecessary production. This new title should carry the stipulation that only acres necessary to meet commodity needs would be farmed and the surplus planted to, and kept in, grass until it is needed for intensive agriculture. This control of surplus acres is preferable to selling excess production to the unfortunate people of other countries who are denied access to their own land. Justice, compassion, and common humanity dictate that we should use political and economic pressure to force the release of monopolized land in these poor countries to the people. This would conserve these countries' monetary resources, as well as our own soil, labor, and natural resources.

In 1987 the government planned to retire about 30 percent of the acreage of major crops.[32] This is close to our calculation of the excess acres being farmed. However, under this program, farmers will be paid an average of twelve thousand dollars for not producing. This is a true waste distribution territory and against everything for which farmers profess to stand, and it will not solve their problem. Once the payments stop, the land must be put back into production to maximize the earnings of those who own that land.

At present, government agricultural support is running about twenty-six billion dollars per year.* There are 2.2 million farmers, of which about one-third are free of debt, another third have a moderate debt, and the rest are in serious trouble.** The latter closely match the 35-percent excess farmers and farmland that we determined earlier. If this program were restructured to take farms that were in financial trouble out of production and place them in reserve, the 750,000 farmers now in serious financial trouble would be available to share in *necessary* work.*** There would need to be further readjusting of land farmed and land reserved, but this is only a general view of unnecessary farm production; it is not a treatise on the exact methods of implementing an alternative program.

The twenty-six billion dollars spent supporting farmers in 1986 averages thirty-five thousand dollars per *excess* farmer. If unemployed persons had rights to a negative tax (as outlined in Book One, chapter six), the immediate cost to society would be closer to ten thousand dollars per surplus farmer: less than one-third the current expenditure. This cost would decline rapidly and then disappear as the workweek was readjusted to assure everybody's right to *productive* labor and a share in social production. This can only be done with productive employment as a right—the elimination of nonproductive jobs and sharing productive ones. The 1.45 million remaining farmers could produce all necessary agricultural goods. As society's needs and production would now balance, these farmers would be well paid for their labor and capital.

There would need to be reserve storage combined with the right of society to control the surplus crop acres. This would protect against the chance of crop shortages and stabilize both production and prices. Without these controls and with unrestricted ownership of land, surplus production would again trigger low prices and bankrupt farmers. In normal times, they are impoverished because

---

* This is for 1986. There are different calculations on costs. For example, the government is considering an additional several-billion-dollar bail-out for the Farm Credit System which would increase this accounting. Other changes may lower it.

** These statistics are very subjective. For instance *ABC News* (31 March 1987) claimed that 85 percent of the farmers are financially solvent and that 10 percent produce 90 percent of the food, among other things. The math will change, depending on just what those statistics stand for, but the principle will stay the same. If that *ABC News* statement is accurate, far more than one-third of the farmers are unnecessary. In fact, I do not accept its accuracy, as it is likely measured in pounds or calories. This method of calculation ignores the fact that the enormous production of these few farmers is concentrated on wasteful fattening of beef and unnecessary exports. On the other hand, the labors of many are required for vegetable, fruit, and other specialty crops which put taste and variety—as well as more nutritious food—on our dinner tables.

*** As there would be a decline in beef produced from grain, livestock grazing should be acceptable on the reserve acres.

there is abundant land and thus abundant production—claims of world scarcity notwithstanding.

Placing this excess land in reserve creates a monopoly again (only this one under social control) and it will have a true rent value. If the land supply is balanced correctly, society will receive its proper rent, the farmer's capital its proper interest, and the farmer his proper wages while producing all the food society needs or demands.

Assuming the number of farmers with moderate or no debt holds at today's ratio and those in crisis are paid off and no longer farming, half of the 1.45 million remaining farmers would be debt free and the other half would have any debt above the value of their improvements and capital erased. All would be owners of their land but it would have no capitalized value. The land payments would be replaced by paying land rent to society. Owners would have all their past rights of ownership except the right to keep land rent. Depending on who owned that equity, they or their banker would earn interest on the improvements.

Once those values have collapsed, society's collection of land rents would mean everybody's right to nature's bounty would be reclaimed without appropriating anyone's equity.*

---

* Every tax restructuring that favors one group appropriates some from another. Those made in the 1980s have drastically favored owners of wealth over the less fortunate.

# 2

# Monopolizing Society's Tools

## Defining Capital and Finance Capital

Tools, which increase the productivity of land, are properly understood as society's capital. Early societies had tools to catch game, gather edible plants, store food, cook, and make clothes. Later ones had hoes, domestic food plants, domesticated animals, harness, plows, and forges. Besides the above, modern societies have factories, roads, railroads, and office buildings. It is the fruitful combining of land, labor, and capital that generates all society's wealth but it all originates with land.

It is this progression that is important: From what nature has to offer, labor builds tools and with these produces useful goods and even better tools; employing the latter, labor produces yet more goods and builds yet better tools. Productive capital is nature's bounty (land) molded by labor. Industries are produced by labor, and designed precisely for the same purpose as the simple tools of earlier societies. They are only a more complex and ever more efficient means of processing nature's wealth from the land. All true capital is productive, and created by labor in the process of reforming nature. Money capital is only the symbol of this actual capital.

Capital was first accumulated and mobilized through the capitalized values of unrestricted ownership of society's primary wealth: land. Monopoly capitalists are only modern land monopolists. They too demand to be paid for nature's bounty without productive labor. To deny some the right to work with capital (that productive job I always come back to) is identical to an early society denying some of their members the right to use tools to hunt, fish and otherwise transform nature to their needs. This was, of course, a very rare occurrence before the monopolization of land and capital.

Full rights include economic rights. If a society's capital were appropriated and people were pushed off their productive land into the desert, they may retain the right of assembly, free speech, religion of choice, and the vote, but they will have lost the most important right of all—the right to live. The right to a productive job represents a person's rights to land and capital.

# Labor Should Employ Capital

That capital is properly owned and employed by labor is recognized by no less an authority than Adam Smith. In his bible of capitalism *The Wealth of Nations*, he notes that, "Produce is the natural wages of labor. Originally the whole belonged to the labourer. If this had continued all things would have become cheaper, though in appearance many things might have become dearer." Smith defines 'cheaper' as "produced by a smaller quantity of labour,"[1] recognizing that it was monopolized capital that prevented labor from realizing its benefits.

If labor owned the capital it produced, then labor would employ—rather than be employed by—capital. Once monopolized, capital's use *can be denied* to labor at any time, and it *will be denied* if no profit is made. The natural order of labor employing tools (capital) is reversed. If land and capital were not monopolized, land, labor, and capital could freely combine to produce social wealth, and workers would receive their full wages from what they produced. This, again, is that increase in efficiency equal to the invention of money or writing that the French Physiocrats recognized was possible.

Just as with land, we are accustomed to wealthy people claiming ownership of the nation's capital (tools). We are taught that this is the proper and most efficient social arrangement. Therefore we do not recognize the obvious—capital is social wealth. It is comprised of all tools of production, and all should be entitled to the opportunity of employing it and receiving a fair share of what is produced.

However, capital is often more productive under private ownership and, when this is so, that ownership is justified. In such cases, this capital would be properly bought from those who produced it with the increased production from the entrepreneur's special talents. These talents are productive labor and a substantial share of our capital has been thus justly claimed. Any ownership of capital that is obtained by means other than trading useful labor (physical, innovative, or special talent) is an unjust appropriation of the production of others.

That which is more efficient under social ownership belongs there with all receiving the profits. What is properly social capital, "real" private capital, and *fictitious capital* are all lumped together and collectively treated as private capital. Ownership is considered proof that it was justly earned, and that the owner deserves compensation for its use. In these chapters, I will be distinguishing between social, personal, and fictitious capital. Once identified, the proper owners may claim their capital and their share of what it produces while eliminating fictitious capital altogether.

# Efficient, Socially Owned Capital

There are two basic differences between what is properly social or private capital. Social capital is used by everybody and forms a natural monopoly. Private capital is used only by the owner and his or her workers to produce for needs specific to a limited segment of society.

Capital that is required for society's basic infrastructure—which is in its nature a monopoly and used by all citizens—cannot properly be bought and sold as a commodity. This includes not only highways, airports, harbors, and post offices, but also railroads, electric power systems, banking, and the communications infrastructure. Most will recognize that our highways, airports, harbors, and post offices properly belong to all society. Although this is normal practice in most other Western nations, Americans are unaccustomed to railroads, electric power systems, banking, and communications being socially owned. These are nothing less than natural monopolies, and all claims of efficiency under private ownership are just a rhetorical cover to hide an enormous appropriation of labor.

This is shown in the electric power industries. Almost 24 percent of the population is served by consumer-owned electric utilities (13.4 percent are publicly owned, 10.2 percent are rural cooperatives). Privately owned companies charge 42.5 percent more for electricity than those publicly owned (7.17 cents per KWH as opposed to 5.03 cents). Yet, since they serve population centers with the highest density of customers per mile, their costs should be lower. The spread is even greater than these statistics show. The publicly owned utilities provide enough profits for some of those communities to build swimming pools, stadiums, and parks.[2]

Mathew Josephson's classic *Robber Barons,* Peter Lyon's even more complete *To Hell in a Day Coach,* and Edward Winslow Martin's *History of the Grange Movement* cover how the railroads were built at public expense and their appropriations were little more than theft of public wealth. Martin's description of building the Union Pacific Railroad is perhaps the most flagrant example but the pattern was typical:

> Who then was Crédit Mobilier? It was but another name for the Pacific Railroad ring. The members were in Congress; they were trustees for the bondholders; they were directors, they were stockholders, they were contractors; in Washington they voted subsidies, in New York they received them, upon the plains they expended them, and in the Crédit Mobilier they divided them. Ever-shifting characters, they were ubiquitous—now engineering a bill, and now a bridge—they received money into one hand as a corporation, and paid into the other as a contractor. As stockholders they owned the road, as mortgagees they had a lien upon it, as directors they contracted for its construction, and as members of Crédit Mobilier they built it. . . . Reduced to plain English, the story of the Crédit Mobilier is simply this: The men entrusted with the management of the Pacific road made a bargain with themselves to build the road for a sum equal to about twice its actual cost, and pocketed the profits, which have been estimated at about THIRTY MILLIONS OF DOLLARS—this immense sum coming out of the taxpayers of the United States.[3]

"By 1870 the states alone had given $228,500,000 in cash, while another $300,000,000 had been paid over by counties and municipalities." In the process of building those railroads, promoters skimmed off possibly one-half of this public investment and stockholders' capital, while simultaneously claiming 9.3 percent of the nation's land through land grants.[4] Thus Josephson's accurate description of them as robber barons. Obviously there was, and is, no savings to society from the private ownership of this natural monopoly. And, as will be shown in the next two chapters, when properly structured under a public authority the true cost of banking and communications would be only pennies on the dollar to what we are being currently charged by these monopolized industries.

Basic infrastructure (roads, water, electricity, etc.) is integral to a nation and used by all its citizens. *Society is a machine.* Even though these basic facilities do not directly produce anything, an industrial society cannot function without them. They are an integral part of production and are just as important to social efficiency as modern factories. To determine this, one only needs to compare the labor costs in a society with an undeveloped infrastructure to that in a developed one. For example, in the eighteenth century a letter traveling by U.S. mail traveling from New York to Virginia (four hundred miles) took four to eight weeks and cost sixty cents a page.[5] Today it is twenty-five cents for a dozen pages anywhere in the nation. Even today one can compare a society with a modern highway and railroad system with one that has dirt and gravel roads. The cost of transportation, and thus the products transported, would be far higher. A good share of the increased efficiency of labor outlined in this treatise is efficiency of this basic infrastructure.

## Efficient Privately Owned Capital

All other commercial activities besides basic infrastructure are used only by the owners and workers to produce for specific individual needs and are properly privately owned. The thousands of personal preferences (homes, clothes, furniture, jewelry, services, hobbies, and recreational activities of every description) cannot be provided by a public authority, as has been demonstrated in the Soviet Union. Such personal needs can only be assessed by perceptive and talented individuals close enough to recognize and fulfill those needs. The capital to provide such service will be more productive under private ownership. This increased productivity will produce the wealth to pay for the labor that produces that capital as opposed to its appropriation through monopolization of land and capital.

Most of the construction and production for basic social infrastructure operated under public authorization is quite properly provided by thousands of privately owned industries. This free enterprise, privately owned capital can, under contract, accommodate the needs of public institutions while also making available diverse consumer products and services.

## Fictitious Capital

Few economists agree on exactly what constitutes capital. Most will include all wealth which produces a profit (titles, stocks, bonds, etc.). But much of this wealth does not productively employ labor so cannot rightly be termed capital. Although it has a firm claim on part of society's income, because it is nonproductive it is properly defined as *fictitious capital*. Bonds used to construct harbors, deepen riverbeds, and build railroads represent true capital. The problem arises when a part of the monies raised by these bonds is not productively employed. In the above example of building the Union Pacific Railroad, only half the money was used to build; the other half was pocketed. The share of these certificates that was not productively used, yet had a claim on social production, was fraudulent. This fictitious capital may represent wealth to the owner, but it is not wealth to society.

The powerful issue these symbols of capital but, instead of employing them to build real capital, they use some and pocket the difference. That which is not productively employed becomes a debt the public or consumers must pay—it represents their appropriated labor.

Besides the fictitious capital embedded in debt instruments, there is fictitious capital directly involved in privately owned business in the form of unnecessary infrastructure and equipment—for example, the unnecessary insurance offices and equipment or the capital required to produce unnecessary agricultural products.

There are only three elements to production—land, labor, and capital. Land commands rent, labor is paid wages, and true interest can only be for the use of capital. Any savings (money capital) from these three sources properly represent physical capital, and interest on money capital is interest on this actual capital. Any interest above a fair charge on actual and necessary capital is labor appropriated by fictitious capital.

## "Robber Barons": The Appropriation of America's Capital

The efficiency of steam railroads was essential to the Industrial Revolution. In order to build these railroads, there were choke points of the physical landscape which had to be claimed if an entrepreneur was to beat his rivals and thus secure ownership of this developing social capital. The critical properties in question were gentle grades, mountain passes, harbors, barge terminals, and rights of way between population centers: none required labor to produce. To become owners of these critical crossroads of nature, the robber barons' agents converged on Congress and local legislative bodies. Armed with massive funds, they had no trouble finding enough corrupt legislators to help appropriate those key properties. Appropriated along with this were those 183 million acres of grants totaling 9.3 percent of the nation's land.[6]

In this country, the railroad, steel, and oil industries grew up together. Using the methods outlined above, a few powerful industrial monopolies appropriated these valuable tools of society. Their basic methods were quite consistent although repeated over and over again with slight variations and under different names. The first order of business was to control legislative bodies to structure the law in their favor and appropriate public money. Stock would be issued and touted to two, four, six, or even ten times any visible assets, then it would be unloaded upon an unsuspecting public—typically by selling short in a bear raid. After each collapse, the game would start all over again with the same or new promoters. Every swindle and promotion funneled money from those who produced to those who controlled. There was also much plunder from each other as the sharpest promoters managed to entrap the less agile in the web of their schemes. These master thieves could buy out their more honest competitors, and it is they who become the tycoons of American capital.[7]

Once most of the physical resources and capital were claimed, these unscrupulous men schemed to guide the flow of the nation's money through companies they controlled. Though the camouflage of names continued to change, the basic principles stayed the same—wherever possible monopolize the essential avenues of commerce, water the stock, and run the stock prices up and down so profits may be harvested from an unsuspecting and unprotected public. This was accomplished through intricate schemes called rings, corners, pools, syndicates, and trusts.

The most sophisticated scheme was a pyramid of companies formed under one giant holding company. The structural principle was quite simple: form an umbrella company with many investors, retain controlling interest, then use this pool of money to buy controlling interest in various other companies. The majority shareholder in the holding company controls it and all subsidiary companies. When profits are growing, the owners of the holding company guide any increase in earning power to themselves, thus claiming the increased production of that capital and labor.[8] They are "necessarily bad ... a mere exploitation of what may be termed the surplus earnings of operating companies during periods of prosperity and a temptation to rape the subsidiaries for the benefit of the holding company."[9]

Just before the great stock market crash of 1929 and the following Depression, these holding companies were able to claim about one-third of "all America's annual savings"—mute testimony to their success in intercepting the nation's wealth.[10] However, in a few months, Vanswergin's railroad holding company, the Allegheny Corporation, plummeted from $50 to 37.5 cents. Samuel Insull's Middle West utility holding company went from $57 to 25 cents.[11] The capitalized value, based on the ability to intercept the nation's wealth without producing, had vanished—it was fictitious capital.

The race to own the choke points of industry was fought in railroads, oil, steel, coal, iron, copper, and other essential commodities. During this Industrial Revolution, common men were also dramatically increasing their wealth and were unaware that, on the average, the entire nation could have been far richer. When combined with this virgin, wealthy country, technology was so efficient that we could waste vast wealth and still get rich.

## Invention: A Social Process

There is no isolated, self-sufficing individual. All production is, in fact, a production in and by the help of the community, and all wealth is such only in society. Within the human period of the race development, it is safe to say, no individual has fallen into industrial isolation, so as to produce any one useful article by his own independent effort alone. Even where there is no mechanical co-operation, men are always guided by the experience of others.[12]

These words from America's eminent philosopher, Thorstein Veblen, are well spoken. The long march of technology leading up to the present sophisticated level is based upon thousands of earlier discoveries—fire, smelting, the wheel, lathe, and screw—and untold millions of improvements on those basic innovations.[13] Many primitive, but revolutionary, technologies were discovered by Oriental and Arab societies. Greek, Roman, and other cultures improved upon these methods which were, in turn, appropriated by later Western cultures. Invention is a social process built upon the insights of others. Stuart Chase's list of such contributions of five thousand years ago barely touches the subject:

The generic Egyptian of 3,000 B.C., though unacquainted with iron, was an expert metallurgist in the less refractory metals. He could smelt them, draw them into wire, beat them into sheets, cast them into molds, emboss, chase, engrave, inlay, and enamel them. He had invented the lathe and the potter's wheel and could glaze and enamel earthenware. He was an expert woodworker, joiner and carver. He was an admirable sculptor, draftsman and painter. He was, and is, the world's mightiest architect in stone. He made sea-going ships. He had devised the loom, and knew how to weave cotton to such a fineness that we can only distinguish it from silk by the microscope. His language was rich, and he engrossed it in the handsomest system of written characters ever produced. He made excellent paper, and upon it beautiful literature was written. . . . He had invented most of the hand tools now in existence. . . . He had worked out the rudiments of astronomy and mathematics.[14]

There were also wedges, drills, wheels, pulleys, and gears—all were necessary before modern machines were possible. There had to be countless earlier inventions, back to the control of fire, before the Egyptians could have reached even that level of technology.

Not only does every modern invention rest on millions of prior insights going back to antiquity, but it requires thousands of people with special talents to develop it. For example, penicillin, which has benefited almost every person in modern civilization, was discovered accidentally by a British scientist. Even though penicillin was discovered by someone else, the research was funded by public money, and more people worked to develop and produce this drug for the wounded in World War II than worked on the atomic bomb, the drug was patented by an American who recognized its monopolized value.[15]

Every innovation is a part of nature. Just like land, oil, coal, iron ore, or any of nature's wealth, if something is to be discovered it had to have been there all the time. As a part of nature, the fruits of technology should be shared by everybody.

Inventions not only use the insights of millions of people throughout history and prehistory, they require the support and skills of millions of present workers as well. Stuart Chase estimated that at least five thousand were involved in contributing data to the writing of his book and those had millions of others to thank for their knowledge. These people provided tools, materials, and services: pencil, paper, graphite, rubber, lead, typewriter, telephone, car, electricity, typists, printing presses, book distributors, bankers, and so forth. The people directly involved in Chase's education required educators, authors of textbooks, and their educators, ad infinitum. Every one of these consumer items required the labor and skills of thousands of people, some in distant parts of the world (such as producers of rubber or tin). Though the labor charge of some of these is infinitesimal, each is real and definite, and collectively they accumulate a substantial, though incalculable, value.[16]

While the contribution of any one person to the pool of social knowledge is truly small, the wealth diverted to those who own the patent to that knowledge can be substantial. Normally these are people who neither invented anything, nor labored productively for this income, but they own these efficient technologies. They are commercial choke points and their monopolization permits huge overcharges. Inventors rarely receive much reward or even credit for their discoveries and innovations. The few who do receive only a small share of the tribute assessed society by those who own this social wealth. That a very small number of powerful people should monopolize the inventions of others—and ever afterwards charge the rest of society tribute—defies both decency and justice. This was well known to prominent inventors and industrialists such as Thomas A. Edison and Henry

Ford. Both "agreed that all patent laws should be repealed since they benefit the manufacturer and not the inventor."[17]

## The Process of Capitalizing Actual and Fictitious Values

Earlier we noted how robber barons watered their stock. These values appear to be real only if a company's monopoly position permits it to charge high prices to pay interest on that fictitious value. Today, the patent structure is one of the key methods of monopolizing that value and intercepting much of today's wealth. Where inventions once went unchanged for decades or even centuries, many are now obsolete before the seventeen-year life of the patent expires. By the time a key patent has run out, newer patents are able to boost efficiency yet more. As many of the technologies whose patents have expired are still essential to production, the owners of the latest patents monopolize both these technologies and the support technologies developed by society over thousands of years. Our earlier example of the monopolization of the stratified charge engine, even though the basic principles for this crucial technology were invented seventy-seven years ago, makes this all quite evident.

Patent monopolists are in such a powerful bargaining position that only occasionally will a new invention pose a threat to them. As monopolization limits the inventor's options, these patents are purchased for a fraction of their true value, or they are patented around and the inventor receives nothing. Controlling markets is also integral to controlling patents:

> Any move by the neo-colonial state to revoke the patent law as a defensive measure would have very limited results since the market belongs to the monopolies. This becomes quite clear when it is realized that the other markets to which such products would be exported would still have such legislation protecting the same patents, and the transnational corporation would be in a position to require compliance. The mere ownership without the actual know-how which is guarded by the monopoly at headquarters would be useless. This is the whole point about monopoly. The world imperialist monopoly market would not exist if such a system of market control were not in operation.[18]

Even though companies are in a continuous battle for markets, patents are leased to other companies. To monopolize this technology to the exclusion of all other producers would capture most of the market. But this refusal to share would expose the monopoly, and it would be eliminated by law.* However, this collective monopoly does not share those rights outside the political boundaries and alliances of a society. Just as with trade, it is societies outside these political alliances that are denied the use of this valuable social knowledge.

We view the inventions of four hundred to eleven hundred years ago as very primitive, yet in their time these simple inventions could produce—with less labor—both more and better products. Someone powerful enough to control these new techniques could trade one day's work for two, three, five, ten or as many days' production of other people's labor as the efficiency of his invention and political power allowed.

---

* In fact, that is what has supposedly happened. Antitrust laws are designed to prevent monopolizing any segment of the economy.

The invention of the windmill was so valuable (meaning its owner could appropriate enormous amounts of labor) that it created a dispute between the nobles, priests, and emperor "as to which of those three the wind 'belonged'."[19] A seventeenth-century French patent granted just such a right to selected owners of windmills:

> We have . . . permitted that he and his associates . . . build and construct mills according to his said invention . . . in all the towns and cities of our kingdom . . . We forbid all, of whatever quality or condition they may be, to build mills after said invention . . . whether in whole or in part . . . without his express permission and consent, on pain of paying a fine of 10,000 livres and having the said mill confiscated.[20]

However hard they tried, monopolizing the wind is quite difficult, but not so with other technology. The water mill, first used in Europe during the tenth century, permitted one worker to replace as many as ten others. A stone planer eliminated seven workers out of eight. One worker with an Owens bottle machine could do the work of eighteen hand blowers.[21] Modern technology has even greater efficiency gains. The steam engine is credited with the greatest gains, but Stuart Chase cites a study by C. M. Ripley of work that would cost $230 done by hand labor costing only $5 using electric power.[22] And in the final chapters, I will address banking and communications technology that, if they were not monopolized, could provide services for pennies which today cost dollars.

The owner of that first water mill may not have been able to trade his work grinding grain for ten days' production of a woodworker or blacksmith. But at a trade of seven days' labor, he will have been paid for seven days while working only one. The owner of a patented stone planer would likely gain five days' value for only one of his own. Any person lucky enough to own a patented Owens bottle machine could probably have claimed twelve days' pay for each day's labor. If the manufacturer in Ripley's study had been able to patent that efficiency, this would have monopolized the process, and he could have claimed twenty to thirty times the labor value in his product even while lowering the price. However, just like claiming ownership of the wind, it would be very difficult to fully monopolize electricity, which accounts for the drop in costs in Ripley's study.

The utilization of both windmills and electric machinery was due to the difficulty of monopolists claiming title. In small industries, most patent holders cannot own or operate the many businesses in which their inventions may be used. Typical of this inability to maintain control at the point of use would be power tools. The overcharge is then limited to the price charged for those sold, which is in turn limited by alternative technology. As we will see, there are efforts currently under way to extend those patent rights to *processes* of production, so some small industries may yet have to pay tribute to patent monopolies.

While it is very difficult to establish absentee ownership of technology used in small industries, it is easy to monopolize the efficiency of large industries. This process denies incalculable benefits to the dispossessed of this and other societies—witness the ease with which the world could be capitalized by bypassing monopolization.

That the owners of patents are entitled to *royalties* exposes the origin of the term. Patent rights to land and inventions were conferred upon favorites by kings and queens, with the understanding that the former would rebate a share of the earnings—royalties. In short, the origin of patents is indistinguishable from the paying of bribes for the privilege of doing business. Such bribes were the precursors of today's patent royalties.[23]

Long before patents were protected by governments, they were protected by violence. In the Middle Ages, early technologies for making and dyeing cloth were more efficient than ancient hand methods and thus more valuable. The larger cities used the former to appropriate the labor of the surrounding communities. In fact, "all through the fourteenth century regular armed expeditions were sent out against all the villages in the neighborhood and looms or fulling-vats were broken or carried away."[24] Those early claims to technology, enforced by violence, were the forerunners of today's industrial patent monopolies. They have just become more sophisticated by encoding those exclusive rights in law. Today, being accustomed to it and unaware of society's loss, we accept this as normal.

The efficiencies of textile machinery started the Industrial Revolution. The primitive looms were improved upon by inventions such as Kay's flying shuttle and the power loom. The owners of these technologies eventually dominated world trade.[25] Britain's famed navy was the muscle which controlled this trade throughout much of the world and, just as did those medieval merchants, their modern counterparts destroyed native economies in order to profit from their own production and sales. India and East Bengal (Bangladesh) are two of the best-known examples. The present scope of the usurpation of the production of others' labor, by monopolizing textile manufacturing technology, is dramatized by the spectacle of 150 power looms in Formosa weaving twenty-four hours a day under the watchful eyes of only one agile female operator on roller skates.[26] This is an efficiency gain of hundreds of thousands of times over handweaving.

The labor component in the price of a yard of cloth produced by modern industry is small. This includes the labor to smelt the ore, fabricate the machines, produce raw materials, and so on, which are stored in that capital. The powerful will say they are not appropriating anyone else's labor, as there is hardly any labor involved—but this is exactly how labor is appropriated. All society is denied the full benefit of cheap industrial goods by labor being charged more then they are paid to produce that product. If a product requires one hour's labor to produce and distribute, then sells for three hours' labor value, it effectively appropriates two hours of labor. It is by unnecessary work that labor reclaims a large part of that two hours' overcharge.

The technological advances in agriculture are well known. A bushel of wheat required three hours to produce in 1830 but only ten minutes in 1900.[27] A call to Montana State University in Bozeman revealed that, in 1986, it took only 3.2 minutes of labor to produce one bushel of dryland Montana wheat.

The introduction to Book One explained that technology would eventually lower rail labor to 4 percent per ton-mile of that required thirty-three years ago. This particular gain (of 2,500 percent), though spectacular, is dwarfed by the total labor savings in transportation during the past 150 years. Before the railroads, a man with a team and wagon could haul two tons twenty miles in one day. Now, in that same day's time, a train and six men (three shifts) can haul ten thousand tons one thousand miles. The present potential gain in transportation efficiency is 41,050 times (4,105,000 percent).

True, there are other workers besides the train crew involved—those who fabricate and maintain the tracks, cars, and engines. But wagon-freight drivers also needed support labor—those who bred, broke, and trained the horses, and built and repaired wagons, roads, and bridges.

The steam engine increased the efficiency of industry more than any other invention. The owners of steam-powered railroads were chosen by Josephson as the archetypical example of those robber barons who laid claim to America's wealth. Due to improved technology, textiles and agriculture also became thousands of times cheaper. The public did receive a large share of the labor savings. With the newly won rights that people had, the gains were just too great for the powerful to claim them all. However, there is much more production forgone and wasted than that which society so gratefully receives. Much of this waste is due to the excessive claims of these monopolized wealth-producing assets and the reclaiming of some of that wealth by the dispossessed through waste distribution territories.

As with the windmill in the Middle Ages, the steam engine in the Industrial Revolution, and electricity in modern times, when monopolization is impractical society can claim much of the gains. However, it is hard to visualize something so valuable escaping the powerful today. The patent laws, which evolved specifically to appropriate the gains of technology, are designed too well to benefit the monopolies. Their position permits them to buy patents at a fraction of their value and then to either withhold their use to protect their present industry or charge monopoly prices. A major example will be shown in the final chapter on communications. We think of communication as cheap and it is, yet dollars in tribute are paid for what would only require pennies if monopolization were eliminated.

Through patents, control of technology has come a long way since the medieval cities openly appropriated the labor of their neighbors by denying them ownership of technology and then selling them the production of those machines. Here is the power that separates an inventor from his or her rightful compensation and society from its rightful share of that efficiency gain. With multiple patents—occasionally with only one key patent and control of markets—monopolists have the power to appropriate large amounts of others' labor.

The fundamental creed of business—charge all the market will bear—justifies that monopoly charge. The reasoning is sound until it is shown that society produced that capital and is then denied its full productive potential. For example, Carnegie's new steel mills could produce for thirty-six dollars a ton and eventually for under twenty-two dollars, yet his steel was priced at sixty-five dollars. This was just under that of his competitors whose mills, using inefficient, older technology, required seventy dollars a ton. Assuming a 10-percent return above production costs, a price of forty dollars, later lowered to twenty-five dollars, would have represented proper compensation for land, labor, and capital. The difference of twenty-five to forty dollars represented appropriation of others' labor through monopoly ownership of land and technology.[28] During the capital accumulation phase this did concentrate capital. But today, as outlined in Book Two, almost as much capital is being destroyed in these trade wars as is being created.

Ownership of a key technology, the telephone, was Bell Telephone's advantage when that monopoly was established. (Inventions not controlled by Bell, such as the dial phone, were simultaneously suppressed.) The telegraph and telephone reduced communication costs an amount comparable to the savings in textiles and transportation.

Henry Ford's assembly line was a milestone in industrial technology. During the year of 1913 alone, the time required to assemble an automobile dropped from 728 minutes to 93. Up until that year, the wage rate averaged $2.50 for a ten-hour day. Influenced by Ralph Waldo Emerson, Ford doubled the daily wages of his workers, and reduced their hours from ten to eight, all while lowering the price of his cars.[29] This was unheard of in those times and drew much criticism from business and the press. What Ford knew, and others did not, was that the profits were so enormous the wages could have been increased to almost $20 per day. Actually it was all self-evident in that 770-percent increase in labor efficiency. Ford was strongly opposed by his managers and other investors. Had it not been for the influence of Emerson, it appears that the appropriation of labor from the innovation of the assembly line may have been much higher and lasted for a much longer period of time.

Perhaps we owe Ford another debt besides that unprecedented sharing of the wealth created by technology. George Baldwin Seldon, a lawyer specializing in patents, understood well that, as the law was structured, patents appropriate others' wealth. In 1899,

> he set his mind to working out the precise legal definition and wording of a patent that would give him the sole right to license and charge royalties on future automobile development in America. . . . Seldon had gone into partnership with a group of Wall Street investors who saw their chance to cut themselves in on the profits of the growing American car industry.[30]

The near success of Seldon and his partners in patenting the automobile outlines this position on patents. Neither Seldon nor these investors had anything to do with the invention of automobiles. The first ones had been built in Europe fourteen years earlier and virtually hundreds of auto companies were already in existence. Yet, if that attempt at claiming ownership had succeeded, every purchaser of an automobile would have had a part of his labor appropriated by that patent.

Those who design these titles to technology know what they are doing. Corporations are being formed to patent embryo transfers, gene splicing, and other advanced medical procedures. Any doctor who wishes to use this new knowledge will have to obtain a special license and pay a royalty.[31] This added tax, though common to medical equipment and drugs, has not, up to this time, been an added cost for an operation. If ownership of these procedures had been established years ago, every bill for an operation would have royalties tacked on to pay whoever owned the patent rights. Every future improvement in patented surgical procedures will also be patented; their monopoly would never run out. The stratified charge engine invented over seventy years ago and now tied up with over three hundred patents, as explained in Book One, chapter three, is a clear-cut example. The cost to society can be seen if one had to pay a patent holder for the use of fire, wheels, wedges, levers, and gears. Inversely, the savings are evident in their free use because they are not patented (monopolized).

Once inventors and developers have been adequately paid, inventions are a more or less costless store of knowledge [that] is captured by monopoly capital and protected in order to make it secret and a 'rare and scarce commodity', for sale at monopoly price[s]. So far as inventions are concerned a price is put on them not *because* they are scarce but *in order* to make them scarce to those who want to use them.[32] (emphasis in original)

There is one recent and remarkable exception to this rule. In certain remote parts of Africa, "as many as 60 percent of the people over age 55 are partly or completely blind" from becoming infected with a parasitic worm. Possibly eighteen million people are affected. The pharmaceutical corporation Merck and Company owned the patent on a drug (Ivermectin) used to kill worms in animals. In October 1987, however, Merck announced they would provide this drug free of charge for Africans afflicted with this parasite. The company chairman, Dr. P. Roy Vagelos, noted that, "It became apparent that people in need were unable to purchase it."[33] Here the loss to society from monopolization was so obvious that these corporate executives made a moral decision to save millions of peoples. The cost to them was negligible, while the gain to society is so large it is unmeasurable. There is a loss to society from monopolization of any technology; it is just usually not as obvious as in this dramatic example where the rules of patent monopolies were abandoned.

Innovation and technology thus create large reductions in labor costs in all segments of the economy. Most are more modest than the above examples but reductions of 90 percent are common. Witness the gains from satellite and digital technology. These are not even fully in place, yet further innovations, if they prove successful, will squeeze ten times the original signals into the bandwidth used by these communications satellites.[34] Such savings do not exert the immediate shock to the economy which these numbers suggest. It takes time to retool an industry, and these monopolies are in no hurry to destroy the value of their old production and distribution complexes.

There are endless variations of these basic methods of charging monopoly prices (such as appropriating others' labor through government subsidies), but they are all tools for the powerful to earn high profits and capitalize values. That such overcharges can exist while labor is fully paid for their work is a contradiction. It only appears proper because people are accustomed to a set wage for labor, equally accustomed to all increased profits going to owners, and unaware of their moral right to an equal share of the labor saved.

To make the contradiction clear we will do a little abstract reasoning using these high efficiency gains. Let's assume that all industry suddenly increased 50 percent in efficiency. (The final chapter will show that this example is here now.) Half of the work force would be unemployed and the owners of this new technology would rapidly claim all the production that was previously consumed or saved by those who were once employed. The monopolists' wealth, both actually and as a percentage of the nation's wealth, would increase dramatically; that of those still employed would remain the same; and those newly unemployed would be on welfare. It is only through distribution by unnecessary labor that our society has avoided facing this reality. An economy with 5 percent owners, 45 percent workers, and 50 percent welfare recipients is unthinkable in a country that claims equal rights for everybody.

To reverse this scene (sharing those savings equally) exposes the purpose of monopolies—appropriating others' labor through unequal labor exchanges. Ten percent of that theoretical 50-percent savings of the nation's labor is 5 percent of the GNP. This would adequately pay the inventors and developers for their labor and risk. The remaining 40-percent labor savings should properly go to society. Distributing this equitably would require each worker to have rights to a productive job. This, in turn, would require each worker reducing his or her working hours equally (40 percent in this example; Books One and Two have demonstrated that it could be reduced 60 percent at this time). Assuming this efficiency gain applied equally to all commerce, the price for these products and services should drop an equal amount—which is what happened with the windmill, steam engine, and electricity. Thus, with full rights to a productive job and assuming equitable pay, all citizens would automatically receive their share of technology's savings of labor. If everyone received a fair share of the savings of technology (i.e., if labor were both fully productive and fully paid), the capitalized, fictitious values would disappear.

Economists will quickly point out the importance of capitalized values in balancing the varying costs of different locations and industries. But location is a natural phenomenon—it is not built by labor. Its value should be balanced through paying society land rent.

## The Nation's Wealth is Measured by, and Appropriated through, Capitalized Values

Until late in the [19th] century, railroad securities were almost the only ones listed on the New York Stock Exchange. The man of speculative disposition was, perforce, limited in the play of his fancy.[35]

There have been stock markets ever since there have been stock companies. However, those early investors were almost exclusively wealthy people investing to produce for other wealthy people. Fulfilling the needs of the masses was not a great concern of those times. Early monopolists normally held ownership of their profitable industries within a close-knit group, but today's factories are so expensive that few people have such financial resources. Shares in these industries are sold with the price based on how profitable the industry is expected to be—its capitalized value.

This concept proved to be a real bonanza. All in one stroke, an alert individual or group may lay claim to the efficiency of a technology through capitalizing its value and selling shares to other investors. This appropriation of others' labor—through the mechanism of capitalized values—concentrated wealth in the hands of a few and gave capitalism its name.

The natural tendency for the wealthy was to appropriate an ever larger share of this wealth. Labor, just as naturally, tried to retain or reclaim what they produced. The rights gained in our revolution and enshrined in the Constitution, and the natural justice of those rights, eventually increased the power of labor. This and the expansion of waste distribution territories led to more people intercepting a greater share of society's wealth. With these savings more broadly distributed, there evolved the present diversified markets to sell shares in industry and concentrate that money capital.

The American public does receive a part of the increased efficiency of technology, feel enriched, and marvel at the higher standard of living it brings. They are unaware that they are being overcharged (their labor appropriated). Efficient producers lower their price to just under the production costs of those still using older technology. This lower price will draw business away from inefficient producers, and the patent-protected monopoly profits will rise accordingly. If the savings are 50 percent, consumers would normally receive about a 10-percent reduction in the product price, just enough to win them over as customers. The remaining 40 percent is appropriated labor. That which is not reclaimed by labor through unnecessary work becomes monopoly profits. These excessive profits, in turn, are capitalized into the selling price of the company's stock, creating fictitious values.

Even with such savings, businesses seem always threatened with insolvency. The cause is the income demanded by fictitious values; there is no labor expended to back up that excessive claim so the production of labor or real capital (stored labor) must go to satisfy that charge.* The claims of fictitious capital to income without producing are identical to that made by unnecessary labor; there is no production to back up that fictitious value. Only the past labor and price norms make this overcharge acceptable. Thorstein Veblen explains:

> The business concerns which have the management of industry on this plan of absentee ownership are capitalized on their business capacity, not on their industrial capacity; that is to say, they are capitalized on their capacity to produce earnings, not on their capacity to produce goods. Their capitalization has, in effect, been calculated and fixed on the highest ordinary rate of earnings previously obtained; and on pain of insolvency their businesslike managers are now required to meet fixed-income charges on this capitalization. Therefore as a proposition of safe and sane business management, prices have to be maintained or advanced.[36]

## The Stock Market

The battle for corporate ownership is centered in the stock market. Millions of hours are spent by speculators (called investors) trying to figure out which company is going to increase its capitalized value. The game is calculating profits that will translate into capitalized value. It is viewed as a simple method of keeping score. But appropriating others' labor—through owning shares in the nation's industry as technology continually replaces labor—is the underlying theme. Values which were once claimed by labor are now claimed by the shareowners of the new industrial technology.

If the innovators, investors, and underwriters of hot new companies are aware of the potential, they will print enough stock to absorb any foreseeable fictitious value. (Market psychology and speculation may inflate these values far higher yet, and the lucky or astute small investor may gain wealth.) This process takes

---

* This can also be compared to slavery. Here too the "owners" could go broke and have the slaves sold. It is the capitalized value of the slaves' labor that was mortgaged to the bank. Cannibalization of each other's industries as explained in Book Two, chapters one and two, is another prominent case of imminent bankruptcy. If there is no market, there is no value.

place in all companies where the owners become aware of the potential of capitalization to produce instant wealth.

Securities analyst and investment fund manager George J. W. Goodman, under the pseudonym Adam Smith, outlined the magic of capitalizing this unearned income. He christened this stock, and titled his book, *Supermoney*. He proves that this stock is in reality a "Supercurrency":

> In 1972 we have a good example of Supercurrency. The Levitz brothers . . . were furniture retailers whose company netted $60,000 or so a year. Then the company noticed that sales were terrific when they ran the year-end clearance sale from the warehouse: furniture right in the carton, cash on the barrelhead, 20 percent off. The idea was successful, they added more warehouses, and the company went public—in fact, superpublic. At one point, it was selling for seventeen times its book value . . . [They] banked $33 million of public money for their stock, and still held $300 million worth. . . . Now when they want to pay grocery bills, [buy a boat, a summer home, travel abroad or whatever] they peel off some of the [$333 million], as much as the market can stand. They have moved into the Supercurrency class.[37]

Smith's example of supercurrency is just another way of describing capitalization of fictitious values. There is the successful company, the underwriters, the innovation of a cheaper distribution system, investors clamoring for shares in this innovative company, and—at seventeen times tangible assets—94 percent of the stock value is sham. The overcharge to maintain that assumed value appropriates the labor of the consumer. If that illusory value cannot be sustained, then the wealth of the purchaser of that stock will be appropriated.

In this manner, "a $5,000 investment in Avon Products in 1950 would have grown to $2.3 million [by 1972], and $5,000 in the Haloid company, over the same time span, would be [in] Xerox and [worth] about $3 million."[38] The stock market abounds in such similarly successful investments—Liz Clairborne, Home Shopping Network, and Microsoft are several recent examples (1987).

While these fortunes were made, the Federal Reserve calculated that 25 percent of Americans in 1974, increasing to 54 percent in 1988, had no net assets.[39] Lester Thurow explains that this impoverishment of many while wealth is accumulated by a lucky few is due to "the process of capitalizing disequilibrium" (the capitalization of fictitious values just explained) and that "patient savings and reinvestment has little or nothing" to do with generating large fortunes.[40] Thurow concludes that

> at any moment in time, the highly skewed distribution of wealth is the product of two approximately equal factors—instant fortunes and inherited wealth. Inherited fortunes, however, were themselves created in a process of instant wealth in an earlier generation. *These instant fortunes occur because new long-term disequilibriums in the real capital market are capitalized in the financial markets.* . . . Those who are lucky and end up owning the stocks that are capitalized at high multiples win large fortunes in the random walk. Once fortunes are created, they are husbanded, augmented, and passed on, not because of "homo economicus" [economic man] desires to store up future consumption but because of desires for power within the family, economy, or society.[41] (emphasis added)

Of course, the small fortunes accumulated by upper middle class Americans are from these same disequilibriums in the value of land and capital. Except by violence or trickery, how else can wealth beyond what one produces be accumulated? The income demanded by these fictitious values is a private tax upon the rest of society, and quite accurately labeled *air:* "By reducing air to vendability, scarcity could be capitalized. Business would be richer—and every man, woman and child in the country would be poorer."[42]

A study of the market over a full boom and bust cycle will find these fictitious values developing in most stocks. The reasons given may be many but the underlying causes are clear—the steady rise in the nation's efficiency is captured by, and mirrored in, stock values. It is every speculator's dream to own some of those stocks and become wealthy, and the powerful and cunning, with far better than even odds, buy and sell in rhythm with the inflation and deflation of stock prices to appropriate most of this new wealth.

If successful, this frenzied attempt at owning the nation's industrial and distributive technology will free the owners from the necessity of laboring for their living. This is not a contradiction. Their frenzied efforts are certainly labor. However, when unnecessary, that labor is fictitious and all such earnings represent fictitious wages.

Capitalizing values is necessary to decide the sale price of a business. However, not only should everyone involved receive proper compensation for his or her labor, innovations and risk, but society should receive its share. Society not only provided tens of thousands of necessary preceding innovations, it also provided the schools, skills, tools, and labor, and the markets. Nature provided the resources, and the invention was there to be discovered. To monopolize it is to deny others the right to its use even when independently discovered. There is then great waste, as these waste distribution territories must expand to enable the dispossessed to reclaim their share. There will be even greater social costs if the appropriation of labor is so great that labor's buying power drops enough to stagnate the economy.*

This is no call for elimination of ownership of patents. It is only a call to eliminate the monopoly structure that denies the efficiency of technology to the world's dispossessed people, which can be accomplished while simultaneously increasing the compensation to society's invaluable innovators.

There is a necessity for a stock market. It has, however, gone far beyond its proper function of providing capital to the nation's industries through sale of stock. That the stock market's primary purpose today is financing the nation's business is pure fiction: "In 1980, gross business savings totaled $332 billion, or $33 billion more than the $299 billion in private nonresidential investment. The business sector was not only self-financing but a source of savings for the rest of the economy."[43]

Even though, on the average, businesses are self-financing, some will decide to finance through the market. Most of these times will be when they can convert those fictitious values into supercurrency as described above. For the most part, however, trades in the stock market have nothing to do with capital investment.

---

* Entrepreneurs and capital must not be denied their proper rewards. If a person has or develops a truly new idea, he or she is entitled to proper compensation. Most of the rewards, however, do not go to the innovators. They go to finance monopolists and a part is reclaimed by the dispossessed through unnecessary labor.

Buying a stock from a broker does not add one red cent to the corporate treasury and provides no investment capital except if the stock is newly issued. But new issues by major corporations are fairly rare because issuing new stock dilutes equity and depresses stock prices. As a result, the bulk of shares now traded on the stock markets were issued twenty or fifty years ago. Since then the shares have passed through many hands, and their prices have fluctuated over a wide range. Yet all these transactions have been strictly between the buyers and sellers of stocks, aided and abetted by stockbrokers trying to eke out a modest living. . . . speculators are not really interested in the company whose stock they temporarily own. They want to take their profits and get out. They are not investing in the proper sense of the word; they are simply gambling. Ownership of corporations has become largely a game of chance in which the individual players try to guess what the other players will do.[44]

The stock market is mostly a gambling spree; look, for example, at options. An option is only the buyer betting the stock will go up and the seller that it will go down. They do not have a stake in that stock beyond the gamble. Options may appear to have a legitimate purpose in takeover schemes but, when purchased by those attempting the takeover, they are not even gambles. The psychology of the market guarantees that almost surely it will rise, and this increase in wealth—and the company's own assets—provide the money for takeovers.

As if options were not enough gambling as opposed to investing, traders in 1980 introduced futures trading on these options. "They are not supposed to be venues for high stakes gambling. . . . [yet] today the trading volume in stock index futures is almost equal to the stocks themselves."[45] "Corporations have become chips in a casino game, played for high stakes by people who produce nothing, invent nothing, grow nothing and service nothing. The market is now a game in itself."[46] Capitalized, fictitious values are like chips on a poker table; they finance the game. But, unlike chips, when the game is over these inflated stocks cannot be traded in for full value.

The stock market is a high stakes, *low risk* (except at the peak of a bubble) gambling casino where these overcapitalized values are distributed. Everyone recognizes the high stakes; the unacknowledged low risk is due to the constantly increasing value of the nation's capital. This increase in value is the capitalized value of the labor appropriated by owners of the increasingly efficient technology. During the recent exposés of fraud in the commodities and futures markets, farmers have been recognizing this fact and some have clamored for closing the nonproductive futures markets down.[47]

A speculator is unaware that his gains are unearned. If the market wipes him out, he feels he has lost earnings when actually it was just the odds of the gamble and his turn to lose. Like the casinos they are, the stock markets are primarily a mechanism for the redistribution of wealth, not its production. It is a gambling game in which the rest of society's members are spectators—spectators who continually have their share of the nation's increased wealth thrown on the table of a game of chance they are not playing.

The danger of gambling with the nation's wealth was addressed by *Business Week's* cover story "Playing With Fire":

> By stoking a persuasive desire to beat the game, innovation and deregulation have tilted the axis of the financial system away from investment towards speculation. The U.S. has evolved into what Lord Keynes might have called a

"casino society"—a nation obsessively devoted to high-stakes financial maneuvering as a shortcut to wealth. . . . "Speculators may do no harm as bubbles on a steady stream of enterprise. But the position is serious when enterprise becomes the bubble on a whirlpool of speculation. When the capital development of a country becomes a byproduct of the activities of a casino, the job is likely to be ill-done."[48]

What is normally spoken of as speculation is only the appropriation of labor by rights of ownership that have gotten out of hand. Thus, in a market boom, the price of stocks tends to have no relation to either the value of the actual capital or the capitalized, fictitious value. History is replete with examples. Charles Mackay, in *Extraordinary Popular Delusions and the Madness of Crowds*, describes the tulip craze that broke out in Europe in the seventeenth century. Before that particular insanity dissipated, one rare tulip bulb cost "two lasts of wheat, four lasts of rye, four fat oxen, eight fat swine, twelve fat sheep, two hogsheads of wine, four tuns of butter, one thousand lbs. of cheese, a complete bed, a suit of clothes and a silver drinking cup." One wonders at the variety of commodities traded for that one flower bulb, but their total value of 2,500 florins serves as a guideline to the money value paid for other bulbs. Normally, prices ranged from 2,000 florins for an inferior bulb to 5,500 florins for the choicest varieties. "Many persons were known to invest a fortune of 100,000 florins in the purchase of 40 roots."[49] Although tulips are not stocks, the principle is the same.

During the eighteenth century, John Law implemented a plan to sell stock in enterprises in the Mississippi wilderness in order to pay off the huge debt of the French government. Though this scheme was seriously flawed, his banking reforms were quite sound, and the French economy prospered. The plan went awry when the money rolled in; those selling paper were so busy getting rich they neglected to invest in production anywhere. In a speculative frenzy, fortunes changed hands as some sold, and others bought, nothing but paper.[50]

The stock in this Mississippi scheme had no value because there was no investment and thus no production. Law's scheme seemed like such an effortless way to get rich that it caught the attention of the cunning in England. (Of course, the English also had to do something to protect their capital. It was fleeing to France to buy into Law's Mississippi scheme.) Stock companies were set up to trade with South America. Spain controlled most of this territory, and the English had limited or no trade rights within it. Visions of wealth stirred up a speculative fever, and companies were being formed for very unlikely endeavors. Soon, so many got in on the game that it got out of hand and the government finally called a halt to new issues. The intention of most of these promoters can be summed up by one audacious proposal. This promoter touted "a company for carrying on an undertaking of great advantage, but nobody to know what it is."[51]

Since the organizers of these companies had no intention of producing anything, their capital was 100-percent fictitious. Proof that this capital was not real was given when the speculative bubble collapsed, leaving no increase in capital, fictitious or real. There was no production to produce income in order to cover either expenses or profits—there was only the transferring of wealth from the naive to the cunning or lucky.

When wild speculation breaks loose, there is no relation between value and price. Even when the stock market behaves normally, there are always stocks whose prices defy all logic. This activity can only be attributed to crowd psychology, as described by Mackay, although sly promoters pull the strings.

When the psychology of the market is understood, it is possible to appropriate others' wealth using fictitious capital almost entirely. The psychology of crowds and peer pressure create loyalty to brand names and the desire to possess what one's peers own. This is accounted for on corporate ledgers as good will and creating this fictitious value is the cornerstone of advertising. For example, Levi jeans, once used as everyday work clothes, suddenly became the rage as society sought to adopt the Western look. The retail price of Levi's jumped from three or four dollars to twenty dollars, and the value of Levi Strauss stock can only have multiplied as they capitalized these fictitious values. As peer acceptance and identity are important to those consumers, this is proper. However, only the wealthy can effectively use that route to instant supercurrency.

## Mergers, Takeovers, and Greenmail
## Are Largely Fictitious Wages

We are told that management compensations of hundreds of millions of dollars yearly to key individuals are due to the recipients' special talents. Howard M. Wachtel, Professor of Economics at Washington University, describes it otherwise:

> American corporations have become primarily managers of money and only incidentally organizers of production . . . production is what is done to justify the manipulation of money. With legal and financial backgrounds that are interchangeable among enterprises, their time span with any one company is brief. The talents of these financial administrators can be sold wherever there is a new financial war chest to manage. They gain little knowledge, therefore, of the products made in corporate holdings before moving on to another company in an entirely different line of production to do more of the same: manage the symbols of production but never organize the actual fabrication of goods and services. The big stakes are in high finance and legal legerdemain.[52]

To the calculation of fictitious wages can be added the "golden parachutes" given managers of companies that are takeover targets. These lump sum payments or lifetime salaries are nothing more than bribes to simplify takeovers. Allowing corporate managers to determine their own salaries, retirement plans, and stock options is like permitting students to mark their own examination papers. The large sums involved in the former can only come from stockholders and consumers. These executives' wages—both real and fictitious—amounted to $500 billion in 1980 and are much higher today (1989).[53] Mike Milken, the junk bond king, is known to have received $1.1 billion in three years in salary and bonuses and investigators feel "that may be only the tip of the iceberg."[54]

That $500 billion was one out of every nine dollars of America's $4.5-trillion GNP for that year. The measurement of how much of corporate managers' income is fictitious wages is very subjective. They say they earn every penny of it. As shown, many very astute intellectuals disagree. With the economy being capable of the same production level with less than half the current capital and labor force, these corporate managers may be doing a terrific job making paper profits but a disastrous job of running the economy. Their manipulations create immediate profits for certain individuals and companies, but this money is just being appropriated from others less fortunate in this gambling casino.

A more careful examination of the above machinations would conclude that many of our most respected financial managers are little more than promoters and speculators—they produce nothing. It is also evident in the wasted labor and capital documented throughout this treatise. To earn such enormous sums at the very moment America's productive capacity is declining proves the fiction of their claims.

Felix Rohatyn, the well-known Wall Street investment banker, criticizes nonproductive paper profits created in the process of using market funds for mergers and acquisitions:

> Very large pools of money are managed by arbitrageurs looking for rapid returns; some of these pools of money are created by issuing junk bonds. Equally large pools of money, similarly financed, are in the hands of corporate raiders. . . . the result, in virtually all cases, is more and more substitution of debt for equity and less and less stable financial structures. . . . this in turn requires cut backs in research and development, capital-spending, and usually, significant reductions in employment. Some companies may be leaner and more competitive as a result; some may have to sacrifice the future.[55]

"In the real world, it is usually the competently managed companies that are the targets."[56] "Our best and brightest are just shuffling paper, using somebody else's money, producing nothing and getting rich at it."[57] Financial analyst William Greider concurs:

> It was a transaction in which everybody seemed to win immediately (except, of course, the defeated management). When they sold their shares to the raider, the company's stockholders got a windfall—freed up capital they could now invest elsewhere at a higher return. The investment-banking house that promoted the deal collected staggering fees. The new owner got control of a valuable company, and often proceeded to cannibalize it, selling subsidiary parts that were less profitable to help pay off the debt that he'd incurred to purchase it. Only the corporation itself lost. It was now saddled with new debt—often a huge amount, which would collect a toll far into the future. Even companies that successfully fended off raiders sometimes used similar techniques. The net consequence was to convert corporate equity into corporate debt on a vast scale, providing immediate profit for the present owners and putting additional burden on the future.[58]

Leo Cawley, host of a show on political economy on WBAI in New York City, outlines the problem:

> It is stagnation that causes speculation and not speculation that causes stagnation. Stock repurchases, the merger and acquisition wave, the arbitrageurs and the takeover artists are simply aspects of the tendency to buy financial assets rather than new plant and equipment. American capitalists considered that they had nothing better to do with their funds. Going to the factory or research lab was risky and difficult, so they went to the casino instead. . . . the lack of channels for investment in plant and equipment is the underlying reason they chose to buy stock instead of expand productive capacity. . . . But since everywhere companies were looking for companies to buy, share prices rose and everybody looked like geniuses.[59]

There is a unique resemblance between our debt structure and the debt trap of Third World countries. "Corporate borrowing, which, properly invested would have been self-liquidating, went into stock acquisition. Now all this debt must be repaid with a productive capacity that has not expanded."[60]

Speculation is replacing the proper use of money capital's financing of production and distribution. Not only is this damaging to the American economy, it directly employs labor unproductively, which is the crux of our thesis. "Employment in many investment banking firms, law firms, arbitrage firms, investment advisors, etc., has grown tenfold over the last few years."[61] The ability of managers to earn money is recognized; yet it is their skill in developing a productive society that is the proper measure of their competence. They are hardly passing the entrance exam when it is considered that America's engineers, technicians, and skilled workers—along with entire industries—are disappearing. Many other industries were never even started (video recorders and high-speed railroad passenger equipment, for example). Even though our industry leaders claim to be able to divert production back to these neglected products, it is "absurd on its face. A ten- to twenty-year major effort to enlarge the labor force and equipment of the industries directly responsible for the society's fixed capital formation would be needed to accomplish such a conversion."[62]

The devastation of America's productive and competitive ability hardly deserves the millions of dollars our senior corporate executives earn as they extract those impressive short-term profits. It is like a farmer not maintaining equipment or the fertility of the soil—sooner or later production will fall.

The public has learned that these takeovers mean large rises in stock prices. Crowd psychology makes this an easy method of fleecing other investors. T. Boone Pickens acquired $968 million of Gulf Oil stock and "his well-publicized campaign led to a big increase in Gulf's stock value. The bluff worked and Pickens sold his stock for $1,760 million."[63] The rapid advance in stock prices is normal in a takeover bid. This is the powerful using the herd instinct to appropriate others' wealth; there is no increased production.

One of the newer wrinkles in appropriating labor through stock market manipulations is a payoff to the raiding corporation's management called greenmail: a bribe not to go through with the takeover. Some management is more principled; they attempt to avoid a takeover by becoming so indebted they are no longer desirable targets:

> To help pay off the $2.6 billion it borrowed to buy back its stock, the company must trim its size and concentrate its resources on its core tire business. Goodyear put up three subsidiaries for sale: . . . It hopes to raise $2 billion by selling what amounts to 25% of its assets. . . . Goodyear has already eliminated nearly 3,900 jobs from its payroll by closing two tire plants and trimming jobs from its corporate headquarters staff. Goodyear will also cut spending on research and development, advertising, and promotion by $170 million annually. (You'll see less of the Goodyear blimp floating around.) Capital expenditures for the remaining tire business will be reduced by $275 million annually to provide cash needed to service its debt.[64]

It makes no difference whether a corporation is raided or incurred so much debt they are raider-proof—manipulation and speculation have been substituted for sound management and production. Companies borrow whatever their credit will permit (usually with junk bonds) and use this money for takeover ventures or to prevent a takeover. "Debts [are] piled upon debts and leveraged buy-outs [are] pyramided into thin margins until it became hard to distinguish legitimate corporate debt from a so-called junk bond."[65] Junk bonds of course explain themselves by their very name. When the promoters are offering twice the returns of treasury bonds sophisticated investors know well they are high risk.

Sound business requires conservative financing, but these once properly managed businesses are trapped. To be conservatively financed invites takeover attempts through speculative financing, as the takeover artists typically use the companies' own assets as collateral for the loans. Thus every industry is forced into risky financing and the net result is that the entire American corporate structure becomes speculatively financed. This heavy borrowing creates money, much of which is put right back into the stock market, generating the well-known stock inflation on pyramided debt.

## Capital Can and Does Go on Strike

During the stable phase of an economic cycle, corporations have normal levels of capitalized, fictitious stock values. When these fictitious values claim too much of the nation's income, the income of workers begins to drop. Businesspeople are constantly calculating labor's buying power by estimating potential sales. When they determine that the buying power is not there and that direct capital investments are too risky, they withdraw their financial capital—capital goes on strike.[66] What appears as excess capacity is really the other side of the coin: monopoly control appropriating too much of labor's production. Awash in liquidity, finance monopolists must invest their once productive capital elsewhere:

> A strike of capital, like a strike of labor, is simply the withholding of a factor of production from the process of producing commodities and services. As a result, less is produced than would otherwise be the case. It exists because there are alternative ways to earn a return on capital that do not involve production. The owner of private capital can simply refuse to reinvest in an existing productive apparatus and instead put all the financial resources into paper assets. Today [1986] there has been a proliferation of such paper assets, and they have grown considerably in the last decade. This represents hoarding: the complete withholding of financial resources from productive use and their transformation into paper assets. The value of these paper assets can increase due to short-term speculation and long-term increases in the demand for them, as more wealth holders move their assets out of production and into paper.[67]

## Mergers and Acquisitions Are Also a Strike of Capital

> The extraordinary growth in mergers and acquisitions is a second way in which capital can be withheld from productive investment. Such activities create no new productive assets but simply rearrange existing wealth among different owners, while sequestering vast sums of money that could be used productively to create growth and employment.[68] [It can also cause serious harm to those companies.]

> . . . During the conglomerate drive a lot of mismatched companies found themselves floundering uncomfortably in the same corporate tent. . . . Extreme diver-

sification diluted, and in some cases simply swamped, management abilities. In the process a lot of fine businesses were ruined.[69]

Michael Moffitt, investment advisor and author of *The World's Money,* sums up the cause and process of mergers and acquisitions:

> As they were at the end of the last century, the financiers, raiders, and latter-day robber barons are now in charge of the U.S. economy. . . . Increasingly, corporations are taking on more debt not to invest in bricks and mortar but to finance acquisitions, to go private, or to fend off unwanted suitors through stock repurchases or greenmail. . . . As attractive productive investment opportunities dried up in recent years, it became cheaper and less risky to buy capacity than to build it. So virtually all publicly traded companies became legitimate takeover targets. As company after company was either acquired or forced to pay greenmail to raiders, the practice of making quick and enormous profits from takeovers became an accepted way of doing business. Soon the mergers and acquisitions boom was feeding upon itself. Nowadays, before raiders have even deposited the greenmail or buyout checks, their investment bankers are already busy lining up the next targets. Using the profits from the last deal, they take positions in new and vulnerable companies. Then they start leaning on management to agree to a takeover or to pay some greenmail.[70]

The capitalization of fictitious values ends where our story started: the appropriation of society's productive wealth by powerful robber barons. In earlier times the only productive wealth was land. Its appropriation led to the eventual impoverishment of weaker peoples, their eventual revolt, and the reclaiming of rights in land. Today capital is the major producer of wealth. When too much of it is appropriated, monopolies are strengthened, prices relative to *productive* wages will rise, the circulation of money will slow down, and the economy will recede or even collapse.

Though there are other winners among shareholders besides raiders, specific appropriation of wealth through mergers and acquisitions is roughly measured by both the increase in stock values and the increase in corporate debt—with no corresponding increasing in productive capacity. "While investment was going nowhere fast, as a percentage of net worth, corporate debt has gone from less than 95 percent in 1980 to over 115 percent in 1985."[71] In the first quarter of 1984, "nearly 20% of the dollar volume of new bank lending in the U.S. went to finance [these] mergers and acquisitions."[72] As the merger mania is increasing, that percentage is higher today (1988). This expansion is only to intercept wealth; the ranks of corporate managers could be trimmed over 50 percent with no loss in production.[73]

Every gambler knows the odds are against the players when the deck is stacked. "Insider trading is a big thing in the present merger mania and the SEC detects less than 1 percent of it."[74] "The papers are full of stories showing that even the high and mighty are tracked down. But the truth is that most people who get caught are dumb or naive or careless."[75] And *U.S. News and World Report's* article, "Stealing $200 Billion the Respectable Way," speaks for itself.[76] This and other white-collar crimes add an average of 15 percent to the price of all consumer goods—which is only another way of saying they collectively appropriate 15 percent of all labor.[77] When we add that 15 percent of wealth stolen outright to that immorally, but legally, appropriated we start seeing the dimensions of labor appropriated by management's fictitious wages.

The present frenzied stock market activity has nothing to do with production—there has been no such increase in useful products, services, or profits.[78] But it has lots to do with distribution since employment in stock-related firms has increased "tenfold over the last few years."[79]

## Commodities and Futures

In 1980, the futures market in metals was estimated at "more than five times annual world production."[80] In 1979, on only two commodities markets—the New York Commodity Exchange and Chicago's International Monetary Market—thirty-four times the world's annual production of gold symbolically changed hands.[81] One speculation, the Hunt brothers' attempt to corner the silver market, "consumed nearly 13 percent of new business loans."[82] To this would have to be added the unknown number of other speculators borrowing to purchase futures in silver, gold, platinum, wheat, soybeans, corn, cotton, cocoa, beef, pork, and the stock market. It is obvious that an enormous amount of finance capital is being diverted to gambling instead of production. When thus used, it is fictitious capital.*

Every farmer, miner, and businessperson recognizes that stability is crucial to efficient production and distribution. Compare this with the statement of a member of the Chicago Board of Trade—"stability, gentlemen, is the only thing we can't deal with."[83] These fluctuating markets are needed by speculators and this instability is largely created by them to intercept a part of that value. This creates boom and bust cycles for producers, while it inflates and deflates prices for consumers, the claims of the players that it smooths out the highs and lows notwithstanding. So long as there are world surpluses, planning could regulate steady production at stable prices. Since speculators are intermediaries between producers and consumers, their income and expenses can only come from the rise and fall of commodity prices and are ultimately derived from the added cost averaged into the final sale.

As outlined in Book One, chapter four, a large surplus of farmland exists in the U.S. and every country in the world has adequate land to feed its own population. Their stability and security can only come with control of their land and for American agriculture there can be no stability until the excess acres are removed from production and a reserve is established to cover production fluctuations. Unlike food, reserves of oil, coal, iron, copper, gold, and other minerals are concentrated in a few fortunate countries. Only a well-designed system of production and trade could guarantee that all countries would have access to these naturally monopolized resources.

The knowledge and skills of labor are now divided into minute segments of the production process. How a society retains that knowledge and skills has become as important as an inventor's creative ability. The collection, organization, and

---

* The gamble is eliminated for many of the insiders as there is also much insider trading and fraud in the commodities market. "The Sting in The Pits," *Newsweek,* 30 January 1989, p. 54.

maximization of the use of this critical knowledge are managed under patents—the private ownership of intellectual property. The incentive to preserve and use this knowledge lies in the amount of other people's labor which can be claimed under the heading of profits. These claims are made through investments in shares of industrial technology in the stock market. This system appears efficient because most of the calculations are done in terms of profits, and there is no calculation of the lost potential we have been describing. Another tracking system, one accounting for all the potential efficiencies of technology and the quality of life, would give far different conclusions on that bottom line.

## Myths of Corporate Inventions and Efficiencies of Being Big

> I know of no original product invention, not even electric shavers or heating pads, made by any of the giant laboratories or corporations, with the possible exception of the household garbage grinder. . . . The record of the giants is one of moving in, buying out and absorbing the smaller creators. [Quote from T. K. Quinn, a former vice president of General Electric. Mr. Quinn was later informed that the garbage disposal he had in mind was also an appropriated idea.][84]

Seymour Melman's book title, *Profits Without Production*, speaks for itself; profiting without producing is a waste distribution territory:

> The imaginative managers of conglomerates have developed myriad methods for maximizing their profits, with or without production. Milking a subsidiary, one of the more common devices, involves severe restrictions on maintenance of plant and equipment, reduced outlays for research and development, and no spending for new plant and equipment. Thus, operational overhead is restricted to wages, salaries, power and materials. As long as the subsidiary can survive on this starvation diet, it functions as a "cash cow". . . . Thus, what is described in economic theory as mobility of capital translates into shattered lives, decaying communities and a net loss of production competence in the nation as a whole.[85]

Appropriating others' wealth through holding companies, as exposed by Josephson, is still the bread and butter of the powerful.

The U.S. steel industry is commonly thought to be unable to compete internationally. Many U.S. steel companies sold their furnaces and bought into higher profit companies. Those who were after those easy paper profits—instead of productive profits—were proven wrong by Nucor Corporation of Norfolk, Nebraska, which was able to "produce steel at a lower cost than any steel company in the world, including the Japanese." And they did this while paying above average wages.[86]

Just as Nucor has been taking back some of the steel market lost to Japan, it follows that U.S. Steel and Bethlehem Steel could also have followed this path instead of shutting down dozens of mills and laying off over twenty-five thousand workers. But, instead of producing, they preferred to join too many others in producing profits through speculative purchases of paper.[87]

Even though they abandoned the local steel mills these companies will not abandon them to serious competition. Employees of one company sued to purchase several abandoned steel mills. Management must not have felt they could win such an obviously conservationist position, so they dynamited the furnaces, making the suit irrelevant.[88] Monopolization is clearly visible in that successful effort. Those jobs were evidently going overseas to lower wage workers and the steel companies were not about to leave these mills to produce in competition with them. The math must have shown that those workers could earn their wages, pay for that capital, and still compete. Otherwise the company would have sold the mills and then destroyed the value by underpricing steel produced elsewhere. There was more capital destroyed than those steel mills. The homes, businesses, utilities, and infrastructure of that town had much lower or even no value without that industrial capital as a primary producer of wealth. This is the destruction of capital through trade wars described in Book Two, chapters one and two.

## Restructuring Intellectual Property Rights

Inventions and innovations are the cornerstone of prosperity. To establish them in social memory and reward the inventors and innovators, intellectual property rights must be privately owned. It is, however, necessary to eliminate the monopolization of patents and reward those who have the original innovative ideas. This includes development patents for those who put others' ideas to work. The present policy of restricting access to technology should be changed to one of easy access with proper compensation for inventors, developers, and producers while returning the maximum savings to society.

All patents should be required to be recorded in simple, easily understood language. People with knowledge of production and distribution needs can then browse through these patents and spot those which could be useful. (Many patents are now filed in deliberately obscure language in order to delay any possible use by competitors.[89]) Many innovations are never patented; instead they survive only as closely held trade secrets. The law should protect a corporation's trade secrets only as long as is reasonably required to perfect their innovation. Patentable ideas which are now protected as trade secrets should then be registered and available for all the world to use. Trade secrets should no longer be enforceable under the law. Failure to record the innovation would risk someone else's publishing the information and becoming its owner. If the patent is useful, the present holders of these trade secrets would not lose proper compensation; they would be entitled to royalties.[90]

To analyze and catalog these inventions and innovations would require an Intellectual Property Rights Authority and an extensive "national network of regional assistance centers" for the orderly registration of innovative ideas.[91]

The expense and risk involved in product development and market penetration are far greater than those associated with invention. These efforts should receive the largest share of the patent royalties. Once a product is brought to market, a *development patent* would be established by filing with the regional patent office. At that point the patent holders would be entitled to royalties, but others would be free to use that innovation by filing notice of their use of this technology. Thus owners would be adequately protected and properly compensated for those risky efforts. The inventors, developers, and producers would all be adequately paid for their ideas, capital, labor, and risk. Society would be paid through low-priced products and services. Note that this is all within the framework of the Constitution. Each one's labor and property is fully protected and no one's is appropriated.

The first thing this process would expose is that most inventions are only slight improvements on technology that already exists. With everybody having the right to use these innovations, the charges for fictitious capital and fictitious wages of the present monopoly system would be eliminated. This would do away with the present policy of industries buying up and shelving patents that threaten to destroy the value of obsolescent industrial capital—every producer would have rights to their use:

> There are countless numbers of patents which, if in operation, would much cheapen the articles they could produce, but they are intentionally shelved to prevent competition. Concerns operating under old inventions for which they have expended great sums to erect plants, buy up these new and cheaper methods to prevent competitors from getting hold of them. They then tuck them away in their safes never to be used.[92]

"Technical knowledge in a functional society would be free." Without it,

> new inventions may not only be suppressed, they may be pre-suppressed. A concern may get patents on a whole series of processes in order to tie up the field for the next generation or more. . . . If scientific advance could be kept free and accessible, with proper reward for the inventor duly secured—a large amount of labor power which now trades on the processes of patenting and mystification—lawyers, "fixers", patent clerks and the like, would be released to useful service, a large amount of duplicated scientific research would be saved, and above all the way cleared to let society benefit at once and directly in the new discovery.[93]

Producers would register with the Intellectual Property Rights Authority all patents used in their production process, where they are being used, and the gross sales of products or services using these ideas. The royalties, determined on a sliding scale, would then be calculated and distributed to the patent holders.

Once the producers register their use of patents, it would be a simple job to calculate proper royalty payments. The ideal source for these royalties is through consumer purchases, just as now, but collected and distributed by society through the databanks addressed in the final chapter. Using computerized databanks, any interested person can cheaply have access to and study every patent. There would be much competition to gain a development patent and put this innovation to work in places the inventor never thought about. Being paid by society would eliminate any incentive to conceal the use of another's patent. Patent holders should have a clear idea who is using their ideas, and a simple check of the patent files would ascertain if such uses were properly filed. This would greatly reduce the cost of bookkeeping, while guaranteeing the patent holder proper compensation. In this way, all costs (labor) would be reduced for the inventor, developer, producer, administrative authority, and the public.

## Competitive Monopolies and Developmentally Mature Technology

A vast range of intellectual pursuits are required to develop the tens of thousands of inventions involved in the manufacture of most consumer products.

The most efficient way to develop new inventions or techniques is through competition. Inventors must be free to invent and develop products as they see fit. There will, however, come a time when a technology will be developmentally mature. At that time society should consider standardization. Once standardized, development and production costs will drop to a fraction of that for competitive monopolies. Automobiles are a good example. There were at least 502 automobile companies formed in the U.S. between 1900 and 1908. There has been a great rationalization of this industry and only three U.S. manufacturers are left. In Book One, chapter three, I outlined in depth how labor expended in production and distribution of these automobiles could be further reduced through standardization. Once it is standardized and patent monopolies are eliminated, competitive monopolies will disappear, but there still remains the problem of efficient distribution, which will be addressed in the final chapter. By passing the efficiencies of standardization on to the consumer, U.S. auto makers would have a competitive edge over foreign auto makers and could regain superiority.

Computers have taken the place of the automobile as the glamour industry. The high cost of competitive monopolies in developing computers is unintentionally shown by William H. Davidow in *Marketing High Technology—An Insider's View*. Davidow, a former executive for Intel Corporation, points out that most markets end up with only two or three consistently profitable suppliers, the others being unable to compete. The cost to an outsider wishing to penetrate that market is an ongoing

> 70 percent of the sales of the leader. [This cost] creates a *segment* or *entry* barrier. The total cost of doing business decreased 20 to 30 percent every time business experience [production] doubled. All of these things created barriers to market entry. . . . [One] business started with a $500,000 investment, long ago passed $100,000 in revenues and enjoyed profit margins above the corporate average. Multibus's market share passed DEC's [Digital Equipment Corporation], and Intel is far and away the leading supplier of Multibus products. Semiconductor companies, such as NEC, National, and Advanced Micro Devices (AMD), who raced Intel for the market, have dropped out. Intel now stands almost alone in this maturing market segment, protected by barriers difficult to cross.[94] (emphasis added)

In describing the marketing of a bit processor called the 8080, Davidow further outlines the principles of competitive monopolies. This device replaced the 8008 priced at $36:

> Since the 8080 had ten times the performance of the 8008 and was probably hundreds of times more useful, I decided the market would, initially, be willing to pay ten times the price [$360]. . . . We recovered the development cost of the product in the first two months it was available. . . . [The just price was exposed when] the 8080 ultimately sold for just *two dollars*.[95]

Though highly successful in the short run, this monopoly price gave competitors an opportunity to penetrate their market. The public was denied a possible price break, and had to pay for the competition to develop a similar product. Only then did the full advantages of the new technology become available at a fair price. The technology is developing so fast that by this time the industry would have advanced to another, more powerful bit processor. Davidow argues that if Intel had planned their pricing strategy correctly, the market penetration barrier would have prevented the competition from being able to develop a competing product and penetrate that market. This would have permitted Intel to continue charging a *competitive* monopoly price.

The cost of research and development for the first color TV was $125 million, while a new generation of computers in 1985 required $750 million. The development of many incompatible systems was necessary to sort out which technology would be the most efficient. But there comes a time when a decision must be made as to when society will be served by standardizing parts. The cost of research, development, manufacturing, consumer education, and distribution of several incompatible brands is roughly the cost of one multiplied by the number of brands. If the producers are roughly equal in economic strength, they will divide the market between them and effectively establish a competitive monopoly. To their duplicated costs would be added the loss of social efficiency resulting from these computers' inability to communicate with each other and the smaller number of citizens who could afford them.

While this technology was immature, the above costs to finance innovations may have been proper. However, once developmentally mature, a properly structured patent law, as outlined above, would have allowed competitors access to technology and the framework to agree on standardization. This would eliminate the overcharge to the public, while simultaneously protecting the investment and risk of the inventors and developers.

TRW Incorporated is now developing a computer chip with the capacity of a million transistors. This is thirty-five times more powerful than the most powerful computer chip. This chip in a personal computer will give it the capacity of some supercomputers now in use.[96] This technology will permit the development of a personal supercomputer and may represent the point at which computers are developmentally mature. When calling up a local computer salesman to hear his opinion it was amusing to note that, without any inkling of this thesis, he pointed out that

> the development of these powerful new super-microcomputers is threatening to IBM and other major computer manufacturers. Their development will likely be delayed, as these powerful personal computers are already infringing upon their multi-user mid-size computers. Their political power, patent monopolies and market control will determine when this latest technology will be marketed.[97]

Computers are part of the communications industry, and may be approaching developmental maturity. If the use of this technology is to be efficient, society must make the decision to stay with one basic computer technology and language. From that moment, it would be impossible to bring to market an incompatible computer. All producers would then expend their efforts on developing and producing compatible hardware and software, and the cost of computers and communications would drop precipitously.

Once the experts of all affected industries make the decision of standardization and what standards, innovators need only develop computer hardware and software in compatible form and offer it to society. Each additional innovation would be welcomed into an already functioning and efficient system. The savings on labor and capital should properly accrue to all society in the form of lower costs. This savings would permit generous compensation to the nation's creative talent and risk-takers. The relatively few people who produced this product would be well rewarded, while the cost, as a percentage of the consumer price, would be negligible.

This analysis of the need for competitive monopolies in the early development of the computer business has been conservative to the extreme. Experts feel the computer industry should have been standardized from the beginning:

> The computer industry is tackling this problem decades later than it should have—after selling 50 million computers that work pretty much alone, much like isolated islands with little or no connection to the outside world. Just the opposite happened with telephones. There the standards—established in 1885—came first. Every country in the world adopted them. That's why you can pick up the phone and call anywhere in the world—and why manufacturers of telephones, answering machines and fax machines can build their products to plug directly into the phone network and go right to work. "The world's 600 million phones are interconnected," says Doehler [executive director of Siemens AG]. "Computers should be too". . . . Computers from all vendors will [then] be able to exchange information easily. The "global village" envisioned by Marshall McLuhan in the 60's finally will become a reality. You'll be able to sit down at any computer terminal anywhere on the globe, and send a message or electronic file to any computer, regardless of its make.[98]

## Conclusion

The changes in law governing ownership of technology outlined above would properly pay the inventors and developers, while allowing the rest of society to retain rights to their share of these labor savings. There would be no more free ride: no more appropriation of society's share of technological efficiency. The stock market should remain for the legitimate financing of industry and as a market in which to sell those shares—any activity above that would be pure gambling.

Through high capitalized values, monopolies periodically appropriate too much of labor's production and throw the economy into a severe depression. Then there are calls for stock market reforms.[99] The only real reforms have been the outlawing of pools, rings, corners, and other organized assaults on the public.

The use of public money to finance gambling for takeovers, futures, and options is a privilege for those who gamble with the nation's finance capital. With the exception that a money monopolist's appetite is insatiable, it is much like giving children the keys to a candy store. Besides a 100-percent tax on short-term profits on stocks, there have been proposals to "ban all forms of stock market manipulation and rigging."[100] However, eliminating the lending of society's savings for these games of chance would be a much more effective strategy. Borrowing to invest in first issues of stocks or company expansion should be permitted as this is true investment. Gamblers would be free to do as they wished with their own money but could not gain leverage through the use of others' capital.

There is a need for stock and commodities markets. The countless opportunities to use industry and technology to fulfill social needs can hardly be taken care of by a central authority. When an entrepreneur sees such an opportunity he must have access to capital. The subject of the next chapter is how to free these true entrepreneurs from the clutches of money monopolists who have staked out a territory between the savers and consumers of capital.

# 3

## Money, Money Capital, and Banking

### Money

Before money evolved, trading involved the simplest form of commercial transaction—barter. This involved the exchanging of two or more products of roughly the same value, thus limiting most trading to others having equally valuable items. This led to cattle, tobacco, salt, tea, blankets, skins, and other items being used for money, such commodities being the most desirable, the least perishable, the most portable, and the most readily exchangeable, and having the most recognizable common measure of value.

Products intended for consumption typically have one or two owners on their way from producer to consumer. Those that are used as money may have dozens or even hundreds of owners. Whether a product is used for exchange or consumption distinguishes it as money or a commodity. The products listed above were imperfect as a medium of exchange, and the limited extent of their use dictated a limited amount of trade because not everyone wanted these commodities. They created problems of storage, transportation, and protection.

Only highly desirable, useful items could represent money. No one would accept a piece of paper, brass, copper, or other common item in trade for what he or she had worked so dearly to produce. Such a trade would effectively rob one of hard-earned wealth.

Gold and silver have been highly esteemed and accepted as money in every culture, and coins of measured value were routinely minted from these precious metals. The labor required to produce a given amount of gold, silver, or precious stones was roughly equal to the labor required to produce any other item that this treasure could buy. (The scarcity value of any item in a trade is due to monopolization of land, capital, or finance capital.) As accustomed as we are to viewing gold as money, it is still commodity money—it is desirable and useful and requires roughly equal labor to produce.

Inequality of money values is only inequality of exchanged labor values. Whenever a ruler became strapped for cash (usually because of war), he resorted to debasing his currency by lowering the gold or silver content and replacing it with inexpensive metals such as copper. The labor value represented by these debased coins was less than the labor value of the items purchased. Assuming the labor cost of gold was five hundred times that of copper, each day's production of copper substituted and traded as gold would appropriate five hundred days of labor spent producing useful items. Thus it was the universally recognized value of pure precious metals that became the first readily acceptable money.[1]

With gold (or any precious metal) divisible into measurable value, a trade could be made for products of any value. This convenience fueled world trade, for it was only with handy, universally accepted money that commerce could flourish. Trades were still clumsy, however, as these precious metals had to be located, mined, delivered, and protected before society could have money.

The handicap of gold's weight, bulk, and protection against debasement was eventually eliminated by printing paper money that could be redeemed for a stated amount of gold or silver (the gold standard). Even with paper money backed by gold, there remained the complication of finding, mining, smelting, and storing this expensive commodity.

From using gold- and silver-backed paper money our society evolved to the use of pure paper money. (Paper money was almost universally resorted to in revolutions, although it usually had little value once the banking systems returned to the gold standard.) Benjamin Franklin had proposed paper money, and, while it was used less successfully in the New England colonies, it was used productively in the middle colonies in promoting production and commerce while controlling inflation and deflation. English monopoly capitalists recognized the threat to their control and outlawed the printing of money in the colonies. This effectively dictated who controlled commerce and who would profit, and was a contributory cause of the American Revolution.[2]

World Wars I and II weakened many belligerent countries, eroding the monopoly of the gold standard.[3] As most of their gold had been traded for war materiel, these countries had to keep printing money in order to rebuild their shattered cities and industrial plants. To have returned to money backed by gold would have been to leave their economies at the mercy of U.S. bankers. Thus the monopoly of the powerful, controlling societies through the gold standard, was partly broken. The arms race that followed almost totally eliminated gold-backed money as nations continued to print money wastefully for war.

Paper money, used productively and not backed by gold, was true money. Printed at little cost, it could be traded for as much wealth as its stated value. Society now only required one finished product to make a trade. Those who sold this labor and received in return the paper symbols of value needed only save this money until they wished to purchase products produced by others. Once freed from its bondage to gold, paper money *represented* rather than possessed value. Being simpler to produce, it was traded more extensively than gold-backed paper money.

As simple and light as paper money was, however, it was still too clumsy for most trades. Most of these units of value called money were deposited in a bank (just as gold had been) and trades were then consummated with checks. These were more efficient than cash, because each check was a symbol that the signer had produced, saved, or borrowed that much wealth, and that its money form, safely deposited in the bank, was now being traded for equal value in other products or services. Most family, business, corporate, and international trades are done with these symbols of deposited savings—checks, drafts, notes, bills of exchange, and the like.

Commodity money had dozens, possibly hundreds, of owners before this trading medium returned to its status as a commodity to be consumed. Gold (still commodity money) retained the status of money much longer and had thousands of owners. Gold-backed paper money traded more conveniently and had many more owners. Deposit money, traded by check (via debits and credits in a bank), can have an endless number of owners, as this representation of value keeps moving from owner to owner. Modern computer money (still deposit money) is but a blip on magnetic tape or disks that can be instantly debited from one account and credited to another. This is the ultimate in efficient money.

Paper money and checks are familiar to everybody. Even a child learns quickly what they are and how to use them. When most of the historical and ideological mystique is eliminated, money is easy to understand. The banking system collects all production (symbolized by money deposits); completes society's trades through debits and credits; and loans the surplus production (savings) to those who, at any particular moment, have capital or consumer needs greater than their savings. Money is no more complicated than this.

What makes money appear mysterious is that the powerful have always controlled it. Its secrets are protected by governments, bankers, and finance monopolists of every shade trying to intercept others' wealth. Their appropriation of another's labor is quite simple. In a trade, symbolized by money, the actual value of products or services, purchased or sold, could be higher or lower than its actual labor value (higher priced or lower priced). Labor may be appropriated either by underpaying for labor, by overcharging for products or services, or both.

## Credit or Trust Money

People accept money because they trust that the value represented can be replaced by equal value in another commodity or service. Credit (pure trust) is both the oldest and most modern currency. When credit is given, nothing is received for the item of value except a promise. Each month families and businesses are provided with products or services (value) and then billed. This is a procedure based on trust. On a deeper level even cash money is based on the trust that it can be redeemed in equal value.

When money is controlled with equality and honesty, there is trust. Money then exchanges freely and all mystery disappears. I will be describing money and banking in the everyday language that would apply if the remaining flaws in money's creation and control were eliminated.

## Different Meanings of Money

To the layperson, money is always explained as a medium of exchange. This it is. However, a medium of exchange implies equality and, as noted earlier, it is precisely the *inequality of exchange* that is the greatest problem.

Money is first and foremost a *contract against another person's labor*. With the exception of land, value is properly a measure of the time and quality of labor spent producing a product or service. Both monopoly overcharges and unnecessary labor increase prices and create fictitious values. If the difference between the price received for productive labor and the price paid by the consumer is greater than fair value for expediting that trade, either the producer was underpaid, the final consumer was overcharged, or both. When intermediaries in the process of distribution underpay producers or overcharge consumers, they are appropriating the labor of one or the other, or both. This process is seen in the notorious and once common practice of forced shopping at the company store. The underpaid workers' meager wages were further reduced by their compulsory purchasing of overpriced merchandise.[4]

Savings implies that something has been produced and not consumed. But even if a commodity is for consumption, it is properly understood as capital until sold to the final consumer; then it is his or her wealth and no longer capital. Products are normally sold and their money form deposited in a bank, manufacturing and personal expenses are paid, and any surplus is lent to others for investment or consumption. This savings has become money capital. The parties who labored to create this capital are only lending their surplus production in its money form along with the promise to be paid interest for what their stored labor produced. Interest is the money form of wealth produced by that capital.

## Money Improperly Used to Contract Labor

The improper use of money occurs when labor is contracted to destroy others' capital (war), or on endeavors from which neither the present generation nor their descendants will benefit (waste). In 1800, Robert Owen, manager of a family cloth mill in Scotland, began his famous social experiment of paying workers well, giving them decent housing, educating their children, and doing this all profitably. He calculated that this community of twenty-five hundred persons (workers and families) was producing as much as a community of six hundred thousand did less than fifty years before.

Wondering where the wealth from such a large increase in efficiency was going, Owen studied the problem and concluded it was being consumed by the petty wars continually fought by aristocracy.[5] The mill workers were being underpaid for their work, the customers were being overcharged for their cloth, and the appropriated labor (monopoly profits symbolized by money), was being used to contract materiel and soldiers for war. Labor was being paid to fight because this generated the greatest rewards for those who controlled the use of money. This use of money was wasteful to the rest of society—nothing useful was produced, and much of what existed was destroyed. Earlier, in the sixteenth century, "about 70 percent of Spanish revenues and around two-thirds of the revenues of other European countries" were employed in these wars.[6] Most of this revenue came from a country's own citizens:

> Until the flow of American silver brought massive additional revenues to the Spanish crown (roughly from the 1560s to the late 1630s), the Hapsburg war effort principally rested upon the backs of Castilian peasants and merchants; and even at its height, the royal income from sources in the New World was only about one-quarter to one-third of that derived from Castile and its six million inhabitants.[7]

The treasure pillaged from the Americas was only a small share of the wealth destroyed in European wars. The massive destruction of agriculture, transportation, homes, businesses, and factories (society's capital)—because labor and capital had been employed for war—has become even greater in recent history. World Wars I and II, the Vietnam War, and the waste of the Cold War testify to the improper employment of labor for war by a money aristocracy today.

The monopoly of the nation's money capital is apparent when comparing the high employment during times of war with the unemployment during times of peace. In the latter, monopolists cling to their wealth (in the form of the nation's money capital) and only employ it under conditions in which it is secure and will earn monopoly interest. When war threatens, this capital is immediately used to employ labor for defense (or offense).

Although it is to fulfill military needs that the original products are contracted, the newly employed workers use their wages to contract for their needs. As this process releases the monopolized money, this appears to create a prosperous civilian economy. However, if society, instead of money monopolists, controlled money capital, it would also be available to employ labor productively and fully during times of peace.

The contracting of labor forces should only be for productive goods and services and full value should be paid for that labor. If each had rights to a share of those jobs, every laborer would have the money to bargain for his or her needs. There is nothing more important in any economy than that the rules of money be equal and just. If they are, if the country has industrial capital, and if there are sufficient natural resources, the country will be wealthy. Every nonproductive or selfish contracting of labor by the powerful denies the use of this capital for truly productive uses. Though other nonconstructive uses are not as wasteful as war, their cost to society is still high. All unnecessary work outlined in this treatise is labor improperly contracted by money.

To use one's own *earned* money for speculation is properly one's privilege. But borrowing society's money capital for speculating on land, gold, silver, or commodities is an attempt to intercept social production through monopolization—there is no intent to produce. The use of society's savings for corporate takeovers usually only involves a battle between the powerful for monopoly control. Whether the takeover is successful or not, these unproductive uses of social capital continually milk money from the economy. All this unnecessary activity diverts money capital from its true purpose—production and distribution. By taking the easy way out (financing unnecessary labor for distribution) society is being irresponsible. More appropriately, it is an exercise in insanity. Of course, insanity is often the only appropriate response when reasonable options are blocked and, in this case, the monopolization of money capital precludes alternative courses.

## Money Properly Contracting Labor

Because money is always controlled by those who rule, all major revolutions resort to printing money to finance their insurrection. Successful revolutionary wars, like those of the United States, France, the Soviet Union, and China, were fought for freedom and were productive expenditures of labor—and all were fought with paper money.[8] Every battle for freedom requires large expenditures. Most labor is donated by those directly involved, but much of the weaponry, clothing, food, and medicine must be paid for with money. Money is thus a tool for mobilizing society's labor to produce great things—in this case freedom.

Money properly employing labor is seen every day in farming and in building homes, roads, schools, shopping centers, factories, and consumer products. The rebuilding of Europe after World War II was a productive use of labor employed by American capital, as was the industrialization of Japan, Taiwan, and South Korea. However, a careful analysis of the politics of their capital development would point more towards the powerful protecting their interests than to meeting humanitarian needs.[9]

## In a Modern Economy There Must Be Money Before Wealth

Dissertations on finance teach that first wealth is produced, and that money is then created to expedite trade. This is true of commodity money but not credit or paper money. In a modern economy it is credit money (trust) that must be available first. People would not produce beyond their immediate needs unless they knew they could safely loan that production (savings) and reclaim it when they wanted it. Just like a powerful train or modern roads, money expedites the transfer of commodities between producers and consumers. With it representing a set value of labor, a person can trade that value for equal value of any of the millions of items or services produced by other people. Every acceptance of money in trade for products or services is the completion of that person's share of the contract to produce or distribute that product or service.

We view here the enormous power of money. So long as there are land (resources), labor, capital (industrial tools) and unmet needs of society, it is only necessary to print money to contract labor to produce for society's needs. If there are not enough savings to fully employ the resources, labor, and capital, it is a simple matter to print more money. So long as this money contracts labor to produce needed products, the value represented by that money is real. First printed to contract labor for increased production of wealth, this money continues through the economy employing more labor for the needs of whoever passes it along the economic chain, or it is lent to others to finance their needs. Once an economy is fully employed and in balance, there is a continual circulation of these contracts against labor we call money, and there is no need to print more. It is worth noting that the Federal Reserve does expand the money supply, supposedly for the reasons suggested above.[10] It is, however, usually done for the wrong reasons—arming for and fighting wars; sustaining, rather than employing, those on welfare; and paying interest on its own internal "debt trap."

If there is to be trust, and if the financial machinery of a society is to function smoothly, there must be strict observance of the rules of equality and honesty. This means fair pay for one's productive labor. But with land, capital, and money capital monopolized, it is not surprising that these rules are not observed. Whoever controls the money has the power to employ workers, to deny them employment, or to shift them within the economy, whether it be for productive or nonproductive uses. Thus much money is spent on the interception of more wealth, graft, high living, and wars. All such nonconstructive contracting of labor creates inflation, deflation, recessions, depressions, unemployment, poverty, social unrest, and crime.

If the best possible living standard for every person were society's goal, resources (land), labor, and industrial capital would be used to capacity through efficient contracting of all labor for true production. Adequate money would be employed building more and better tools (industrial capital), which would ensure large gains in efficiency and a rapid rise in everyone's living standards. As the technological and social efficiency gains continue, and if the decision is made that living standards are high enough or the resources are inadequate to employ more labor, the working hours could be continually reduced in step with that gain in efficiency without lowering living standards.

Here monopolization becomes highly visible. Let us assume that society wrenched control of government away from the monopolists. They could then print the necessary money to employ the idle labor and resources to produce the amenities of life many people are unable to obtain. Immediately there would go up a cry of "foul" from those who control land, capital, fictitious capital, and money capital. They would point out that they have the idle capacity to produce for those needs. This would be true, but monopoly rent, monopoly profits, and the fictitious wages of waste distribution territories consume at least 60 percent of productive labor's efforts without having produced anything of value to trade. This creates unnecessarily high costs, and leaves the underpaid and unemployed with insufficient money to contract for their needs. If the monopolization of land, capital, and money capital were broken by guaranteeing everyone the right to a productive job and if money were strictly used to contract only for such useful employment (that is, attaining full rights and equality), the cost of living would fall rapidly. Those previously paid while idle, or paid for nonproductive labor, would then have to produce, and the overcharges of monopolies and unnecessary labor would disappear. The savings would be apparent in both higher living standards and shorter working hours.

For those who take the rhetoric aimed at the creation of enemies seriously and look at every progressive move as communist (which is the purpose of the rhetoric) take note: communist philosophy specifically has as its ultimate goal the elimination of money and this philosophy has it as an indispensable tool for modern society. I would only maximize its efficiency as any businessperson would his or her tools.

## The Creation of Money

When savings deposited in a bank are lent, this money is spent and returns directly to the banking system through the deposits of those who sold products or labor to the borrower. After allowing for reserves (normally about 20 percent), this money is again lent out. From this continuous circulation, reduced somewhat on each cycle, every dollar of the original loan will normally create five dollars in subsequent loans, though under uncontrolled banking conditions it can go much higher.[11]

When financial capital is monopolized, banks do create money as just described. But if money contracts only productive labor and full value is paid for their work, then all money will represent true and full value and will trade freely as a symbol of true wealth. Money will then be only a tool, a symbol for the trade of productive labor. There would be no difference between the last money created and the first: all of it brought wealth into existence by credit employing labor.

Under conditions of equal rights (when each person is fully paid for his or her fully productive work), money lent combines land, labor, and capital to produce full value in needed goods and services. These fully productive workers will trade their production and what is left unconsumed is accumulated as wealth lent to others for consumption or production. When this loan is repaid, the created money disappears. It has been consumed or converted to real wealth owned by those who produced more than they consumed.

If labor is underpaid; charged interest on capital that is rightfully theirs; overcharged by nonproductive labor in these waste distribution territories or by monopolists controlling land, capital, and money capital; then it is these intermediaries who end up owning the surplus production (i.e., money capital). If that nonproductive interception of others' labor were eliminated there would simply be a continual circulation of symbols of productive labor.*

It is the current banking structure that permits the lending of money for nonproductive uses. This could be eliminated if we were to restructure (see below) and the caretakers of the nation's savings learned to lend the nation's capital for truly productive labor. (Within reason, consumer loans will automatically be productive.) True, this would require a complete restructuring of loan policy from one of almost exclusively lending against equity to the bankers being knowledgeable about community needs and lending to produce for those needs.

## True Money Is Not a Commodity

Land and labor have been discussed as being improperly treated as commodities. The same is true of money:

> The commodity the banker handles is money. The scarcer the commodity the higher the price, that is, the interest rate. He protects his business and his profit by keeping this commodity relatively dear. Thus he clings to a position taken by money-lenders centuries ago, when all cash was metallic; when gold and silver were genuinely rare metals and highly prized. For all his downtown urbanity, the banker is still at heart a goldsmith, with a sideline in usury.[12]

As society's most powerful tool, money can hardly be permitted to be monopolized as a commodity by those whose stated purpose is profits, not production. Since modern money requires almost no labor, it should have no value itself; it should only *represent* value. It is properly only a tool to contract labor for the production and distribution of useful commodities (i.e., true value). When money is monopolized and earns profits without producing, this is identical to labor's being paid without doing productive work. After all, money capital is only a sym-

---

* There may not be any net surplus production for society as a whole, because the laborers within the waste distribution territories and the monopolists together are consuming and society may consume all surplus production. It is also possible for a waste distribution territory to exert a more powerful claim than the primary monopolists and thus end up with some of society's finance capital.

bol for real capital, which is but stored labor. We can thus understand why the powerful own—and jealously guard—the institutions of financial control.

## Evasive Banking: Bidding for Rights to Society's Most Powerful Tool

In the early development of money capital, the rights to its use were apportioned by power. During the developing years any American was free to be a banker, but in practice this was still those who monopolized land and capital. Because of the many abuses of money capital and the consequent social disasters, restrictive banking rules were developed. These rules included adequate deposit reserves and limits on interest that could be paid on its money form (savings).

After the banking crisis of the Great Depression, the Federal Reserve Board established Regulation Q. This was designed to hold down interest rates by eliminating *bidding* for deposits. Banks eventually avoided this control by segregating loans, putting them in a holding company, and issuing commercial paper. This, too, was thwarted by imposing reserve requirements "on any paper sold to fund such loans." Yet the loopholes were not fully closed, and bank holding companies still funded commercial paper through "credit card receivables purchased from the bank, assets leased, and loans extended through a nonbank sub[sidiary] of the holding company."[13]

Before the crisis of the 1930s, banking systems had been funneling the nation's money towards large money centers where it was used for speculation and not production. As this destroyed the public's buying power, this was a prime cause of the Great Depression. Laws were then passed forbidding intrastate branch banking. The powerful devised devious ways to evade this regulation. "[P]rior to the 1960s bank holding companies were used primarily to surmount restrictions on intrastate branching." The government tried to control these holding companies by passing the Bank Holding Company Act of 1956. But, through a loophole in the law, banks formed "one-bank holding companies which were not subject to the provisions of the 1956 act . . . The bank's ability to achieve such diversification was, however, severely limited by the Bank Holding Company Act of 1970."[14] Yet in 1980, "Congress repealed virtually all the remaining government limits on interest rates and political regulation of lending that had existed since the New Deal. The price of money was free at last—free to seek whatever level the marketplace dictated."[15]

The combination of uncontrolled bidding for savings and branch banking (collecting and diverting funds to the money centers) was a sure formula for the powerful to monopolize most of the nation's money capital. This, along with wild speculation with these social funds, was considered the cause of the economic collapse in 1929 and was the reason controls were installed in the first place. Efforts were made to pass laws to bring banking under control, but bankers just designed schemes to evade that control. Control of banking has been sidestepped by eliminating the ceiling on interest rates and guiding money out of banks into money markets:[16]

> What we actually have here is a giant Ponzi scheme on a global scale. Nobody planned it that way, but there it is. Just like water seeks its own level, money

seeks freedom. As western governments evolved currency controls in the 1960s and 1970s, so there also evolved a mechanism by which the money could escape.[17]

Perhaps the best example of banking taking place outside of banks is commercial paper. In 1946, commercial paper, as structured in today's money markets, was "virtually nonexistent." In 1966, it comprised 12 percent of banks' investments and loans; in 1970, 19 percent; and by 1980, fully 45 percent was these unsecured loans avoiding federal reserve regulations. These money market funds are simply unsecured IOUs.[18] In search of higher interest, a large share of the nation's finance capital is being lent without any security or government guarantees. Granted, these loans are to the nation's largest corporations, but as already described takeover artists are forcing these corporations into risky financing.[19] In support of such practices, money traders are getting sophisticated in their bidding for society's savings by offering higher interest and creating new debt instruments. One investment house, Salomon Brothers, "alone put out 30 'innovations' last year [1987] with catchy names such as COLTS, CARDS, SPINS, TWINS AND M-CATS."[20]

Though these money market funds go by many names to avoid banking laws, they are all part of the banking system that has escaped social control. The money market is "a wholesale market for high-quality, short term debt instruments or IOUs" consisting of

> short-term government securities, short-term federal agency securities, state and local notes, repurchase agreements (loans collateralized by money market instruments), bankers' acceptances, commercial paper, bank certificates of deposit, and Eurodollar deposits.[21]

These money market debt securities finance essential elements of commerce, and in a normal economy they are not risky investments. As the banking system is now structured, they provide essential finance capital and move money instantly to any point around the world. These intermediaries bid high for the nation's savings, secure in the knowledge that they can demand yet higher rates, as borrowers have nowhere else to turn.

The Eurodollar money market is the latest and largest wrinkle in the many efforts to evade regulation. We only need to examine it briefly to observe the danger to society of unregulated money markets. Eurodollar accounts

> are not subject to such reserve set-asides. The full dollar can be lent out, raising the theoretical possibility of unlimited dollar creation. The total value of Eurodollars in circulation has grown at a rate of about 25 percent a year since the mid 1970's, compared with a growth of real trade of only 4 percent annually. By comparison, the total number of U.S. dollars has grown only 10 percent a year. Starting from a base of about $50 billion in 1973, the "stateless" Eurodollar system today [1987] is approaching $2 trillion, almost as large as the domestic monetary system of the United States, which comes under the Federal Reserve and Treasury regulatory authority. ["Total liquidity" potential of all financial assets in the U.S. in 1987 was just under $2.1 trillion.] It is as if we have been transported back to an earlier century, when private bank money operated around and in spite of government.[22]

A large share of the increase in Eurodollars originated from 375 billion surplus petrodollars that were deposited in large U.S. banks that held them in "offshore banking sanctuaries" in order to evade U.S. taxes and regulation. Searching for a profitable outlet for these funds

> the banks first moved Eurodollars into Third World countries, saddling them with a $1-trillion debt burden by the end of 1986, compared to less than $100 billion in 1973. . . . After Mexico and other large Latin American borrowers effectively defaulted on loan servicing, Eurodollars were shifted into funding the U.S. budget deficit, into mergers and acquisitions, and finally into the U.S. stock market. Very little of this huge flow of funds—more than $2 trillion—went into investments that expanded production.[23]

These dollars on deposit outside our borders are supposedly, but not actually, beyond the reach of Federal Reserve regulations.[24] The "uncontrolled Eurodollar" is only an accounting and political trick. No dollar from the U.S. deposited in a Eurodollar account ever leaves the U.S. Those dollars—whether spent, deposited, or lent—must end up in a dollar account somewhere, and all these transactions only change the dollar reserve account at the Federal Reserve.[25] That the Fed has the ability to control these dollars was quickly shown when Iranian dollar assets in European banks were frozen during the Iranian hostage crisis in 1979.[26] That these dollars are in the U.S.—can be controlled, and all evasion eliminated—should be remembered when we are addressing the simplicity of money used properly as a social tool.

These uncontrolled money markets, designed for monopolization through the payment of higher interest, began to withdraw deposits rapidly from the conventional banking system. This forced a relaxation of the restrictions on bank deposits (Regulation Q). Not to have done so would have caused a rapid disappearance of all bank funds, and money markets would have replaced banks. The Fed's control of the money supply was destroyed. Money, society's most important tool, was available to the *highest bidder*. Without controls, the financially and politically powerful and the speculators could outbid the established rates for home, business, and consumer loans. Those usurious interest rates transferred enormous wealth from those who borrowed to those who monopolized money capital.

Evasive banking has dismantled banking controls in order to reassert monopoly rights for the powerful (and correspondingly reduce rights for the weak). This bidding for money has led to an interest rate war that extends from local banks giving prizes, to the paying of higher interest at savings banks, all the way to an international scramble for funds in the Eurodollar market.[27] When the U.S. raised its interest rates in the 1970s and 1980s to attract overseas money,

> this led to a competitive ratcheting up of interest rates worldwide. Other countries sought to maintain relative parity with U.S. interest rates; otherwise their currency could come under attack. . . . This worldwide race has led to the highest real rates of interest in history . . . and the most severe economic stagnation in the industrial economies for fifty years.[28]

Financial power is exerted by bidding for the right to use society's savings. Though all have the right to bid, those already economically strong and speculators, who are notoriously careless with society's security, can outbid the weak. The economically weakest are deprived of the right to use capital, and those who do meet that bid are, through that high interest rate, serving as a conduit, diverting part of the produce of labor to those who monopolize capital. Thus high interest rates represent both the true earnings of capital and monopoly interest demanded by monopoly capital and monopoly finance capital.

Though they cannot carry out all the functions of a regular bank, money markets are still just banks. Banking can be brought under control by bringing the money markets into the banking system, applying reserve requirements, standard banking controls, and regulated interest. All the labor that is now wasted as money markets evade supervision—and the attendant speculation in paper—would disappear. The powerful would still exercise much authority, but the worst abuses would be curbed by these regulations money monopolists are so busy avoiding. Howard M. Wachtel, a perceptive writer on world financial structures, supports this approach and more:

> It is time to bring them under the same regulatory umbrella that exists for dollars inside the United States. In particular, money center banks should be required to observe the reserve set-asides that constrain U.S. banking. This will make it possible for governments to coordinate such economic parameters as interest and exchange rates by regulating the rate of future growth of Eurodollars. In the absence of such regulation . . . speculative money will continue to hit and run, moving from treasury bills to foreign exchange to mergers and acquisitions. Continuing instability will breed worse economic imbalances until another financial crisis occurs requiring an even larger bailout from the federal reserve than the one engineered to save the market in October [1987].[29]

## Monopoly Control of Money Capital

We would again quote Josephson's introductory remarks:

> When the group of men who form the subject of this history arrived upon the scene, the United States was a mercantile agrarian democracy. When they departed or retired from active life, it was something else: a unified industrial society, the effective economic control of which was lodged in the hands of a hierarchy.[30]

By definition, the control of capital means control of its symbol, money capital: through this control monopolists dictate the very form of society. This was accomplished before the Great Depression by money center banks controlling regional banks and bringing money to that center. It is accomplished today by these same monopolists outbidding the rest of society:

> [M]any of these sums come from the deposits of regional banks, deposits whose source is regional business and regional salaries. With a beautiful and maddening kind of circularity, these deposits are then used to bankroll the local business' most powerful competition, either regionally, in another area like the Sunbelt, or even abroad, to the growing disadvantage of the place where the money came from to begin with. It is a game that can even be played within the narrow confines of the money centers themselves, as for example in the progressive disinvestment by the banks in the industrial base of Brooklyn or the South Side of Chicago. . . . What one witnesses here is a form of pillage.[31]

Michael Moffitt concurs:

The banks reduced the availability of credit to noncorporate borrowers in order to maintain credit commitments to their top corporate customers. . . . The multinationals have had access to all the credit they need, whereas small businesses, home buyers and consumers have been clobbered.[32]

When regional businesses do have access to loan funds, they are still at a disadvantage. "The larger the loans, the greater the likelihood of borrowing below the prime. Meanwhile, small businesses are paying the prime, plus stiff markups."[33]

The surge of borrowing to support M & A [mergers and acquisitions], as it is known on Wall Street, was particularly strong in the summer of 1981. Though only half of the credit lines were actually drawn down, this large-scale borrowing increased the demand for credit, keeping interest rates high and draining credit from more productive uses. For the economy as a whole, it was a high price to pay to ease summer boredom on Wall Street.[34]

To further outline the monopolization of money note that the vast sums of Arab oil money now in the banking system never escape. Every trade financed by that money capital just creates a change in bank reserves at the Federal Reserve. Lent to Third World countries, Arab money capital continues to finance not only production and distribution but waste throughout the world. It is spent on arms, elite consumption, and importation of necessities for the masses.* The crunch will come when that borrowed money cannot be returned, because the wealth it once represented has been squandered. Not wanting to lose their wealth, and having control of social policy, the powerful will expect the American public to make good that loss. This gives a hint to one reason for the high interest rates today. The earnings of American labor are being taxed to replace those squandered funds.

This potential for abuse of money as it is used to contract for labor points to the need for strict controls. As time and labor expanded to intercept social production—the wasted labor exposed in previous chapters—they required the use of money capital. This occurred without either this capital or added workers being fully productive. Money thus used is fictitious capital. That this distributed social production only makes it *appear* productive. Eliminating the wasted labor without redistribution of the productive work would eliminate the workers' moral claim to their share of production, while it would increase monopoly profits. This is an extreme contradiction, as it would also reduce purchasing power, which in turn would reduce production. Ultimately those monopoly profits would shrink, and the economy would be in one of its periodic recessions or depressions.

We are so accustomed to rhetorical assertions about the efficiency of capital, and so unaware of its unrealized potential, that this argument will fall on unbelieving minds. But note the many common characteristics of these waste distribution territories we have observed: those who work within them feel productive; they are unaware that much of their labor is unnecessary; and they all must deny their redundancy, or lose the territory within the economy from which their claim to productivity is asserted. Since people have secured enough of their rights that their labor cannot be arbitrarily claimed, those who monopo-

---

* They normally could better produce for themselves, if only this capital were directed towards that goal.

lize society's money capital must maintain the fiction of being fully productive while providing an essential service, or their claim will lose its moral backing.

## Monopoly Money Capital May Easily Go on Strike

When faced with "a situation not to its liking" capital will go on strike through selective strike, capital flight, mergers and acquisitions, or hoarding. A selective strike is choosing not to invest unless the advantage is in monopoly capital's favor—meaning labor must turn over some of its wages to be converted to monopoly profits. Capital flight is when local labor cannot be persuaded to give up its claim to that extra production, so capital goes elsewhere. Mergers and acquisitions involve using money capital to cannibalize existing industry instead of investing in other productive enterprises. Hoarding is management's decision to "put all the financial resources into paper assets."[35] Money thus employed would be part of a "pure money complex" having nothing to do with production.

"The value of these paper assets can increase due to short-term speculation and long-term increases in the demand for them, as more wealth holders move their assets out of production, and into paper."[36] In short, they are just bidding for each other's paper symbols of wealth with surplus money capital. A specific dramatic example of such nonproductive use of this valuable tool would be in 1980 when Bunker and Herbert Hunt were granted 13 percent of the nation's new business loans (9 percent of all new bank credit) in their effort to corner the silver market.[37] To this must be added the loans to other commodity speculators. If the loans to all speculators—commodities, stocks, and land—were considered, this would outline one dimension of the enormous waste of society's money capital. After the acceleration of credit that financed the Hunts' speculation, the economy went into a steep decline, and millions became unemployed when credit restrictions were tightened.[38] In fact, that recession of the early 1980s was by far the worst since the Great Depression.

The redirecting of finance capital from productive employment to purchase of paper assets is evident in the slackness of the world economy during this decade (1980s) while the stock market is booming. Values are rising as more and more managers move money out of production into paper. This will likely produce substantial profits to monopoly capital as the price of paper assets climbs, or even as it falls if the historic pattern holds true that a substantial portion of this paper will be distributed to the public before the price collapses. Monopolization of money is highly visible in this setting, because, if unneeded for investment, this money should never have been appropriated from labor. Labor would then either have been better paid, or consumer products would have cost less (which is the same thing).

## Society Is Being Held Hostage to Monopoly Capital

An especially onerous function of monopoly capital is currency speculation. International financiers, like all speculators, have a herd instinct. They receive their information about countries' economic status from common sources, such as key banks, financial journals, and scholarly economic treatises. When they collectively move out of one currency, its drop in value verifies the reports, and they stampede to get out of that country's money.

Though termed speculation, these mass movements are very predictable. Whenever a country's currency is under attack, the central bank buys back its currency in an attempt to maintain stability, but the transnational pool of money usually overwhelms it. Monopoly capital's investments in currency are more a sure win than speculation:

> When a trader gets a call from the Fed to buy or sell currencies for the Fed's account, the cry goes up around the trading room: "Feds in." More importantly, it is usually not hard to guess which way the Fed is going. Thus the Fed, unlike any good poker player, telegraphs its hand to the other players.[39]

While "nothing in the fiscal and monetary policies of the United States and other governments can justify gyrations in exchange rates of 40 percent or more," it is the country whose currency is under attack that is openly subsidizing that speculation. The enormous financial power of monopoly capital, tapping the treasuries of besieged economies, is part of the reason for the wild currency value swings of recent years:

> Exchange rate instability is a major cause of high interest rates. They are the only effective weapon against short-term exchange rate fluctuations, and countries play the interest card whenever their currencies are under attack. The result is a competitive world ratcheting up of interest rates that reduces economic growth, makes debt repayment out of reach for many debtor nations, and is generally dysfunctional for nearly everyone. . . . The vast war chests of Eurodollars [move] around the world in an instant, attacking weak currencies and forcing nations whose currencies [are] under attack to change their policy direction. "Eurodollars," says international relations expert Susan Strange, "may prove to have been the most important single development of the century undermining national monetary sovereignty."[40]

The extent of this currency speculation can be gauged by world trade being $2 trillion and the currency swaps—supposedly to finance that trade—being $50 trillion in 1977 and climbing to $200 trillion by 1988.[41] The speculative activity for 1987 can be guessed at when the value of bank wire transactions every four days equaled the nation's total economic activity for one year. The greatest share of that activity is the movement of money through the hands of many bidders until it finally reaches either a producer or a consumer.

It seems that conservative economists and bankers expect the Fed (the public) to be the lender of last resort to protect monopoly capital's speculative binge. Marcia Stigum, in her masterly work *Money Markets,* says that "runs on banks are a thing of the past." However, her later statements give strong support for other conclusions. On the Federal Home Loan Bank securities, which pool money for savings and loan institutions, Stigum notes that, "FHLB securities are not guaranteed by the U.S. government. However . . . it is inconceivable that the U.S. government would ever permit the FHLB to default on outstanding securities." The same statement is made about Federal National Mortgage Association securities: "Fannie Mae debentures are not backed by the federal government . . . [but] it seems highly improbable that the government would permit a default on Fannie Mae obligations." Regarding the Government National Mortgage Association, she notes that "they carry Ginnie Mae's guarantee of timely payment of both principal and interest and are backed in addition by the full faith and credit of the U.S. government." This faith that the U.S. government would protect them from loss was expressed in almost identical terms for Federal Home Loan mortgages, Banks for Cooperatives, Federal Land Banks, and Federal Intermediate Credit Banks—in fact, for the entire U.S. credit system. To Stigum's list of shaky loans guaranteed by the government can be added Guaranteed Student Loans, the Export Import Bank, the Commodity Credit Corporation, the Pension Benefit Corporation, and the Overseas Private Investment Corporation.[42]

The Federal Deposit Insurance Corporation (FDIC) is a congressionally chartered private insurance agency for bank deposits. This $16-billion (1987) private insurance fund is about 3 percent of total insured deposits. One large bank failure can deplete it. Yet the name "federal" is so convincing as a government agency that even sophisticated financial writers refer to it as a government guarantee.

Added to those burdens, the U.S. Federal Reserve is being counted on (though it has not accepted) to be "lender of last resort" for Eurodollar deposits.[43] Marcia Stigum believes that each central bank will be expected to care for its own offshore banks. Dollars are the dominant trading currency, however, and will receive the greatest pressure in a financial crisis.

Savings and loan banks are similarly hard-pressed. In April 1987, the Federal Savings and Loan Insurance Corporation (FSLIC) reported $2 billion in reserve against an estimated $8 billion in expected losses. Just three months later, they reported the latter might be as high as $26 billion. A year later the official estimated cost had climbed to $36 billion and six months later to $100 billion. These estimations are while the same analysts are saying the economy is going strong. If there is a severe recession, the cost could be much more. "Taxpayers have to realize: They're going to pay."[44] Eight months later (June 1989) Congress is voting to bail out six hundred savings and loans; analysts predict the eventual cost could be anywhere from $125 billion to $325 billion depending on the interest rates and time spans used in calculations. The higher figure is fourteen hundred dollars for every man, woman, and child in America.[45]

It was bidding for finance capital that created this debt trap. "Even S and Ls with huge losses can easily raise more money by offering above-market interest rates on their savings accounts."[46] Then, "to obtain operating funds the solvent thrifts were forced to bid one percent over market rates."[47]

Though the proper function of banks is to finance essential commerce while paying reasonable interest on savings, their present purpose is to maximize earnings for their shareholders. To do this, they must have money to lend and they must bid for it. Each participant is forced into the game as there are no other sources—it is monopolized by bidding power.

This process can make money market instruments risky speculations. This became apparent during the bankruptcy of the Penn Central Railroad, which had borrowed heavily through commercial paper. The railroad's collapse created a $6-billion selloff of commercial paper. This was absorbed by the Fed's lending of funds to any bank to cover loans normally serviced by the money markets. As Adam Smith describes it:

By Monday night, phone calls had gone out through the twelve Federal Reserve banks to every bank in the system—not just to big city banks, but to small-town banks all over the country. The Fed's index finger was beginning to bleed from all the dialing. The message was the same: if anyone comes into your bank and wants to make a loan, *give it to him.* Then if you're all loaned out, come to us and we will see that you have the money.[48] (emphasis in original)

The need for the Fed to be lender of last resort was again demonstrated during the collapse of the Continental Illinois National Bank in 1984. The total rescue costs came to $7.5 billion.[49] And Federal Reserve Board officials admitted that there were now ten a year of these "breathless moments."[50] Further strains in credit markets are evident, with Congress considering "whether to invest a further $6 billion to save the country's primary farm lender, the farm credit system, which is teetering on the brink of failure."[51]

These public savings are going through a complex bidding process. Much is ending up in risky speculation when it could be providing homes and employment for family, neighbors, and friends. Most money market funds have four things in common which create high risk when the economy enters one of its periodic severe recessions: they are unsecured IOUs; they evade the regulatory requirements of the Federal Reserve; when included as part of the banking system, these exterior bank loans cause the parent banks to exceed the normal reserve requirements; and they are financed by "hot" money that zips back and forth across the financial landscape but which will disappear if the market appears risky.

All central banks are trying to protect themselves from the consequence of this speculation by inserting money into their economy each time a part of this pyramid starts to collapse. In this effort, "the FDIC went from a corner drug store to being Sears and Roebuck in three years."[52] During these breathless moments, although it can later be redeemed through taxes, the Fed must print any money not covered by insurance reserves.*

"Interest on the national debt is transferred from the ordinary taxpayer to the rich, who hold a disproportionate amount of the treasury notes."[53] The $2-trillion national debt in 1986 equaled $10,048 for every man, woman, and child in the U.S. The pyramid of government-guaranteed loans just described raises this another $3.6 trillion. If we conservatively assume 50 percent of that debt would be uncollectable in a severe depression, each American citizen, from cradle to nursing home, will owe the money monopolists almost $20,000, or $60,000 per average family. As values will have collapsed, they will have received nothing in trade for this debt. They would be in the same predicament as most Third World countries—they would be in a debt trap.**

The above was computed only on the federal debt. The total of all debts as of 1986 was about $8 trillion.[54] Generally there were values received for these debts, but not necessarily full value, and in an economic collapse much of these values

---

* It is interesting to note that those who loan money almost always have first mortgage; when borrowers default, the lender will promptly repossess the mortgaged property. When these money monopolists get in trouble, Uncle Sam (the public) is asked to bail them out. But repossession is never contemplated.

** The total national debt held steady for the first three decades after World War II at roughly 135 percent of GNP, but it "is now 180 percent and rising." (William Greider, "The Money Question," *World Policy Journal,* Fall 1978, p. 585.)

disappear but the debt remains. For every debtor there must be a creditor and it is interesting to speculate as to whom would be owed all that money in an economic collapse. One can only conclude that the nation's capital would be monopolized by few people.

Interest on the federal debt took one out of five tax dollars in 1981 and two out of five in 1986; savings has dropped from 18 to 19 percent of earnings to 14 percent in those same five years (Japan's is 30 percent); and "average real incomes have been stagnant for more than a decade," while consumer debt has tripled. From 1981 to 1986, the nation's debts have been growing twice as fast as both values and national income. That "five year spending spree" added five hundred dollars per year per taxpayer until it is repaid; and "three cents of every dollar spent in the United States was borrowed from foreigners."[55] Where total debt has normally been 40 percent greater than GNP, by 1984 it had climbed to 60 percent. The share of the national income that went to interest was 3 percent in 1960 but climbed to over 10 percent in the 1980s.[56] The evolution of our own debt trap is becoming quite visible.

## The Potential for Economic Collapse

As only by production can value be generated and only from that value can those debts be honestly repaid, the burden all falls on the shoulders of producing workers. Of course, if unemployed in a severe recession, the workers would not be producing and therefore could not repay such a debt. When the economy retrenches, repossessions appropriate others' labor. If the retrenchment is severe enough, eventually such a large share of labor's income is appropriated that the economy collapses.

The process is quite simple. There is first the appropriation of labor by unequal labor trades; this surplus capital is then lent back to the people from whom it was appropriated; and by the magic of compound interest this wealth continues to expand and claim an ever larger share of this nation's wealth. The rate of interest on this unjust debt, and the rate of production of wealth produced by labor, determines when this process of appropriation unbalances the economy.

Laypeople can make these judgments themselves. If $10,000 were put in a tax-exempt investment at 10 percent interest,* compounded yearly, and left untouched for 50 years it would increase to $1.17 million; in 100 years to $137.8 million; in 150 years to $1.6 billion; and in 200 years it will have multiplied 189,000,000 times to become $1.89 trillion. Those figures should adequately show the unjustness of the 10 to 24 percent interest charges of monopoly capital and the justness of a reasonable 5 percent. Excess interest charges are simply a method monopoly capitalists use to appropriate the surplus production of others. There will be circumstances, such as the need to control consumer spending, when high consumer interest rates are justified. But these excess profits belong to society and should be returned to the people in the form of services or capital investments.

To rephrase Greider's explanation quoted in Book Two, chapter one, when an economy is thus unbalanced the underpaid must borrow from the overpaid. "This

---

* Many higher incomes escape all taxes.

process [cannot] function indefinitely if the creditors [get] most of the rewards.... The creative power of capitalism [is] reversed and the compounding interest [becomes] destructive." The American people should look carefully at the interest share of the national income being 3 percent in 1960 and 10 to 11 percent in the 1980s.[57]

The potential for an economic collapse (due to this appropriation of labor) is a continuing subject of grave concern for economists and laypeople alike. The power of the central banks to print money and finance any problem areas is, up till this time, being used effectively to protect the present pyramid of debt instruments. But society is being held hostage. The governments must print money and tax the people to support these speculations in order to protect the country's entire financial structure.

To permit a collapse—and the attendant unemployment, hunger, social unrest, even potential revolution—is unthinkable. Society is trapped; even the most knowledgeable and conscientious of the country's leaders must protect these money monopolists and speculators in order to protect the nation. It is possible for an economy to limp along indefinitely under the weight of all these nonproducers. However, there is the likely possibility that these speculators will lean on the security provided by government guarantees. They could then pyramid this speculative paper to such a high value that the governments can neither finance it by printing money because of the risk of inflation, nor finance it through tax collection because of the risk of destroying the public's buying power.[58] Government officials understand well that they are at the mercy of these monopolists. If any of the reforms described in this book were attempted in any country, monopoly capital would go on strike and collapse the economy enough to create severe distress and force a change of political leaders. With that entire nation held hostage, they would reclaim their control of social policy.

Throughout the decade of the eighties, real interest rates were over double their historic norms and bankruptcies were rising fast. Yet the Federal Reserve did not dare lower interest rates to take the pressure off the real economy. Whenever they tried, the signals from the bond markets indicated the bondholders were dumping their bonds.

The share of the nation's income received by creditors rose from 3 percent in 1960 to over 10 percent in the 1980s and, if it is not corrected, the magic of compound interest will appropriate ever more of the nation's wealth, the debtors will incur ever higher debts, and the economy will become unbalanced and collapse.[59]

A nation should not be able to go bankrupt when it owes the money to its own citizens. National bankruptcy is just another way of saying that one segment of society has appropriated more than its share of the nation's money capital. Though this may be hard to grasp within one country, it is easily visible in an international collapse. Those debts are owed to others outside a society.

These excessive debts are because of the relentless expansion of claims upon society's production through monopoly land rent, monopoly capital, fictitious capital, and fictitious wages. This wasteful expenditure of labor and capital appropriates too much of society's income, creating the imbalance just described. These overpaid segments of the economy are the powerful few who will not accept a reduction in their present share. As they control social policy, they will continue to insist that any savings be taken from the weaker sectors of society: thus the

17-percent drop in buying power of individual labor from 1973 to 1987 and an even greater loss for those on welfare. Meanwhile the earnings of the top 1 percent rose 67 percent (from $301,000 to $452,000) in 11 years.[60] With an increase of fifteen million in the labor force, that is possibly only a 2-percent loss per family for all labor. To prevent the impoverishment of families to levels that could not be papered over, the earnings of labor have been quietly redistributed by employing more family members at lower wages.

The threat of a strike of unregulated international finance capital is influencing the decisions of even the developed countries. To regain social control of capital it is

> time to bring Eurodollars under the same regulatory umbrella as dollars inside the U.S. . . . This stateless reserve of capital exerts a transnational effect on national policies, seeking the lowest common regulatory denominator as it travels around the globe in search of the best rate of return. . . . While government and public policy remain confined to national boundaries, the new supranational economic order recognizes no geographic borders for its financial and commercial activities. Money is moved with the press of a button on a computer console and bounced off communications satellites, leapfrogging national borders. As a result, there is tension between the bounded public policies of nation-states and the unbounded economic imperatives of supranational enterprises. . . . The globalized financial system allows the money center banks to make end runs around governments and then leverage their influence to promote the same deregulated and privatized environment within nation-states that they have been able to create for themselves supranationally.[61]

The "free enterprise" economies of the U.S., Japan, Canada, Great Britain, France, West Germany, and Italy have many different degrees of private and public ownership. Within the latter four, utilities, basic industries, and banks keep changing from public to private ownership, depending on which political group is in power at the moment. (As of 1980, France's industry was about 33 percent under public control and Italy's was 40 percent.[62]) Sometimes these governments are labeled socialist but they are so in name only. Their options are severely curtailed by the power of monopoly capital to go on strike.

Those who create these crises by speculation in social funds are normally unaware that this is an excessive right of property and that they are creating a crisis for all society. The are compartmentalized within the economy and are only aware of the effect on their wealth and power. Just as in feudalism, from which capitalism evolved, the aristocrats were unaware they had excessive rights and fought bitterly to retain their privileges, those with excessive property rights view these as their proper rights and fight to retain them no matter what the cost to the rest of society. This is evident in the control of public perception to wage the Cold War and the waste it created in all societies. All that ever mattered was the economic territory and power of the nation's power brokers.

This battle between ideologies prevents societies from experimenting with the most efficient methods of operating their economic systems. Monopolists invest only when they have reasonable assurance of monopoly profits. When industries are nationalized, those with substantial money send it out of the country—i.e., capital goes on strike—and the economy inevitably suffers. Most will not do this but it only requires a small percentage of a nation's capital to flee to cause a crisis.

Due to the multiplier effect, every dollar sent abroad instead of invested at home subtracts from the local economy several times that amount. The public, unaware that capital flight is an excessive right of capital and the cause of the crisis, blames the political leaders and their new policies instead of the monopoly capitalist. This financial sabotage denies societies the right to experiment in economic reorganization. Never has a Western society gained full control of its finance capital to experiment with it as a social tool. Thus, we do not just have individual monopolies within a free economy or even one country monopolized, *we have an entire world economy monopolized.*

Government employees responsible for controlling society's money would like to have full employment, price stability, low interest rates, and stable exchange rates. If this could be managed, there would be no inflation, deflation, recessions, or depressions (except from natural disasters or war). How to achieve this is no secret. It just conflicts with the privileges of powerful people—the money monopolists.

## Money, Banks, Computers, and Borrowing Rights

A cornerstone of Populist philosophy in the nineteenth century was banking reform. I would repeat William Greider's description of Populist thought. Their agenda

> became a sourcebook for political reforms spanning the next fifty years: a progressive income tax; federal regulation of railroads, communications, and other corporations; legal rights for labor unions; government price stabilization and credit programs for farmers. . . . The populist plan would essentially employ the full faith and credit of the United States government directly to assist the "producing classes" who needed financing for their enterprises. In effect, the government would *circumvent the bankers and provide credit straight to the users. . . . The government would provide "money at cost,"* instead of money lent by merchants and bankers at thirty-five or fifty or a hundred per cent interest.[63] (emphasis added)

There have been many reforms since those days of blatant extortion by money monopolists but "the money-creation system that Congress adopted in 1913 . . . [and reformed during the Great Depression] preserved the banking system as the intermediary that controlled the distribution of new money and credit."[64] An efficient society demands the complete elimination of monopoly finance capital and replacement of it with a banking authority to collect society's savings and use this money as a social tool.*

This could happen by default. In an economic collapse the public, through loan guarantees, would own most loan institutions in the country. Continental Illinois National Bank is already owned by society and the current effort to sell hundreds of bankrupt savings and loans will likely end up with the buyers "mailing the keys back to the government".[65]

---

* For a pragmatic look at how some banks could be publicly owned and the rules of banking changed to eliminate speculation while preserving the efficient aspects of private banks see William Greider, "The Money Question," *World Policy Journal*, fall 1988, espec. pp. 602–4.

... many European countries have already nationalized the banks. ... In France, Italy, Austria, and Greece, the state owns all major banks. Even in a country like West Germany largely seen to have a classic liberal economy, about half of the banking apparatus is government owned.[66]

Banking should function as an efficient tool for society to contract labor for productive work. If this were so it would eliminate most nonproductive claims on society's wealth and the periodic economic stagnations or collapses they create.

The thrift of the early bankers in Scotland is so well known that even today a person careful with his or her money is called "Scotch." The universal practice of Scottish banks in the early nineteenth century was to set interest on loans between 1 and 2 percent above that paid depositors. Their innovative practices are considered to this day to be a model of banking stability.[67] The proper banking service charge has thus been well established at 1 to 2 percent for small-volume banking using expensive hand accounting. One percent would seem to be a proper service charge for large-volume banking using inexpensive computerized accounting.

During most of the years of stability since World War II, the real rate of interest in the U.S. (allowing for inflation) hovered between 1 and 2 percent. Previously the normal world rate had been 2 to 3 percent.[68] Although the real rate of interest during what were considered the best years the American economy has ever known was under 2 percent, I will allow a 4 percent real rate of interest in my calculations as a fair rate. As stored labor, capital should be well paid and this allowance of 4 percent assures it will be.

## Rights to Credit

Under a Banking Authority, consumer credit (within limits) should be a right instantly available, just as it has been pioneered by computerized credit cards. Risks are minimal once there is thumbprint scanning: everybody gains full rights to productive employment; waste is eliminated; each person's right to credit is tempered by being subject to standards, much as they already are; and the local credit union (now an integrated member of the banking system) is in a position to know a member's creditworthiness. The local bankers—under the guidance of social policy—will be in the ideal position to know both the needs of society and the creditworthiness of those who borrow to build and produce for that society.

The present American economy is dynamic due to the hopes and dreams of its citizens. These hopes are the motivation for the millions of small businesses that spring up all over the country. Though 90 percent of them fail, some do succeed, and the economic health of the nation requires that all with ideas, talents, and energy have access to credit to bring together land, labor, capital, and technology at the right time and in the right place to fulfill society's needs.

Historically, capital has been accumulated by appropriating the production of others' labor. The problem of channeling individual savings into productive investments, and still having them retained by the producer, is largely solved by the suggestion of true interest on savings being two to three times higher than the historic norms. Society will receive a useful product or service; it will receive land rent from the increased economic activity; and the loan will be repaid with interest. With these triple benefits to society, bankers should pay close attention to, and be generous with, requests for investment credits. They are the sinews of capitalism.

Only individuals operating under free enterprise and competition can develop the millions of ideas necessary for the progress of science, industry, and society. In order for citizens to fulfill these visions of providing their special expertise, it is necessary to have access to credit. With banking personnel trained to be generous, yet careful, and with the right to borrow these tools (capital), speculation in actual production by business and industry is still unhampered.

Credit is now rationed by the simple method of lending up to a certain percentage of the borrower's equity. Access to this investment capital should be a right based on maximum potential for production. Loans should be made on the basis of productive merit as well as collateralized equity. Thus credit for productive people in their first ventures would be easier to obtain. With employees of the Banking Authority trained to be alert to productive investment requests these loans would be quite simple. When a loan request was received, an evaluation would be made on the feasibility of its financial success and if it looked reasonable the loan would be approved. Even though innovations are risky, they are the key to our prosperity. For this reason the banking community should be trained to be cautiously generous on these loan requests.

With the elimination of capitalized values in land, monopoly capital, and fictional capital, there will not be these artificial values against which to lend. But neither will money capital be needed to purchase these fictitious values. These smaller loans will be backed by a smaller, but more secure, true value. A loan would, of course, require financial accountability by the borrower just as it does now.

With elimination of wasted labor, the potential workweek would be about two days, or one-seventh the time an entrepreneur would have available to dedicate to a personal business. The well-known sixteen-hour days, seven days per week, put in by those developing their dreams will produce a larger labor income to protect their effort. Note the incentive this would be to produce through free enterprise.

As these loans would have first mortgage on the industry, seed money can be lent to get a project organized. With this initial capital, an entrepreneur may issue stock for the rest of his or her financial needs and this primary bank loan would be secure. With elimination of communications monopolies (addressed in the next chapter), those who buy this stock will be investing risk capital directly into production rather than having to go through finance monopolists who will claim most of the physical and intellectual labors involved in this endeavor.

Few economists will challenge the assertion that "The 'gales of creative destruction' made famous by Joseph Schumpeter that once swallowed up inefficient companies have been replaced by the modern corporation having immortality."[69] Using techniques of mass advertising, corporations today create a market for their products. Many people have great ideas but, as few have the financial resources to promote their idea, most are ignored or taken over by a corporation.

Assuming that the monopolization of land, capital, and finance capital were eliminated, putting creative ideas to work and retaining earnings from those ideas should be easy. Those with insights need only prepare a prospectus describing the product or service, market potential, profit expected, financial requirement, and labor needs; the loan institution would study the proposal and, assuming the idea was sound and of benefit to the community, would approve the loan; workers would have access to that prospectus and those who were hired should agree to 10 to 20 percent of their wages being deducted to purchase 60 to 80 percent of the stock; the managers would also deduct from their earnings to pay for their 20 to 40 percent share; this, plus profits, would be used to pay off the loan. The owners of this capital would be true producers, not monopolists.*

Society's collection of land rent could and should permit it to accept a larger share of the risks of new entrepreneurs. Every success increases the rental value of that land.** There are thus three sources of income for society to protect that loan—land rent, profits, and a share of wages. The risk of uncollateralized investment loans could be further offset by a higher interest charge to go into an insurance fund. With these reclaimed rights, many more people would qualify for investment capital than under equity loans. If an entrepreneur were successful in an endeavor, he or she and the workers would honestly own that capital, as opposed to the current custom of appropriating social production through monopolizing social wealth.

Those searching for a higher return—and confident they have found good investments—could directly employ their capital. Those who wish, and who can find the opportunity to lend their savings at a higher rate, are free to do so. But they would have to find a productive niche in the economy that would pay the higher profits, high administration costs, and the risk. They could no longer obtain the extra profits by simple tribute for the use of monopolized capital. Those who once bid for money market funds would now have to compete for loans on their projects' productive merits. This would eliminate speculation with social funds, while retaining that right with personal funds.

## Security, Liquidity, and Fine-tuning the Economy

Investors sacrifice profits for security and liquidity. Under a Banking Authority, depositors would have total security and immediate access to their savings. This is unheard-of under monopoly capital. There need be nothing more than checking accounts paying 4 percent interest. This would eliminate all money market instruments and their attendant labors competing for deposits, opening accounts, accounting, and closing them out. There will be those detractors who would decry this as a loss of their rights. But the only right lost is that of the powerful to appropriate labor. With savers receiving over double the historic real interest rate, there would be a great gain in real rights.

In every banking system, total debits and credits should balance, and the total withdrawals nationwide should roughly match all deposits. With an integrated banking system, any deviation from that balance could be quickly corrected by loan policy. The visible flow of funds would respond to the economic pulse of the nation every day. Any unexplained deficit in one bank could be immediately

---

\* The methods of distributing ownership are endless and this only outlines one simple plan.

\*\* It is from that same land rent (but privately collected) that much risk capital has been obtained in the past.

looked into. The economy would be easily balanced by increasing the interest rate for consumer credit and decreasing it for investment in productive capital, or vice versa. There would always be the additional mechanism of increasing or decreasing the equity requirements of the borrower. As a tool under a Banking Authority, money can fine-tune an economy to the maximum capacity of resources and labor.

## Money: A Measure of Productive Labor Value

Citizens judge the value of most commodities by imperfect memory and comparison, as witness our exposure of unnecessary costs built into the price of products and services. Using money to contract only for productive employment would give a true measure of labor value to every product and service. It is the responsibility of the leaders of society to maintain an honest relationship between the compensation paid labor to produce and distribute commodities and services, and the price charged the final consumer. This can only be done by eliminating monopoly land rent, monopoly capital, fictitious capital, and fictitious wages—all inflate costs and appropriate others' labor. This in no way conflicts with a person's right to contract out his or her labor, or to contract to themselves others' labor. It only eliminates the nonproductive element of these contracts, i.e., appropriating the labor of others. If the labor value of the production of wealth were protected from these inflated fictional values, the value of the symbol of wealth (money) would always be stable. Then the public could much more accurately judge values, and society would be enabled to function both more efficiently and equitably.

## Honest Brokers: Society's Most Productive Workers

Money market monopolists claim their knowledge, expertise, and judgment are socially beneficial, and that they are therefore entitled to large remuneration. This is hardly the case; witness the enormous waste that has been documented above. These money monopolists are little more than superfluous intermediaries demanding excessive tribute for brokering society's trades. Borrowers are made to feel that these monopolizers of social capital are doing them and all society a great service by lending society's own savings back to them.

Borrowing against and selling appropriated social wealth (land and capital) constituted the original mobilization of capital. But with society collecting land rent, labor collecting interest on their production (capital), and society controlling money, capital is even more mobile. None of the savings of society have to go through the barricade of money monopolists demanding their tribute before they will let it pass to those who need this capital.

The highest education, motivation, and incentives are needed by employees of a Banking Authority. Their job would be to maximize production, consumption, and free time within the reasonable capacity of the nation's resources. Theirs should rightly be one of the most honored and best-paid of all professions.

# Conclusion

Bank transactions are society's trades, accomplished through the medium of money (debits and credits). Daily trades are cleared (balanced between different accounts) within each bank and between local banks at the end of the day. Taking one or two days longer, banks within a region clear all drafts drawn against each other. Only then can central clearing banks of one region clear trades with central clearing banks of other regions of the country or with foreign countries. It may take up to ten days to complete some of these trades through the banking system.

The Clearing House banks of New York have installed a computerized Clearing House Interbank Payments System (CHIPS). This computer clears over $50 billion in interbank trades every day, and it has been integrated with a European computer called Society for Worldwide Interbank Financial Telecommunications (SWIFT). Together, these computers automatically clear national and international trades between member banks.[70]

All institutions with banking functions could and should be integrated into one system and brought under a single banking authority. An expanded CHIPS, or a similar computer system, should be installed to instantly debit and credit every transaction locally, regionally, nationally, and internationally. Each person should be paid 4 percent true interest on his or her deposit. Society may decide this should be higher or lower but two key criteria should be met. All capital should be equally and well rewarded. (The problem of risk has been addressed above.) Each bank should cover expenses by charging an average of not over 1 percent above interest paid the depositor. Also, there should be automatic accounting between surplus and deficit banks. Surplus funds should be available to the deficit banks under a prearranged formula that recognizes the greatest social needs. Deficit banks should pay 4 percent interest on the surplus funds used, and the surplus funds banks should be credited with this 4 percent interest so they can pay their depositors.* Borrowers should pay the interest on these savings plus the bank's costs of 1 percent. The previous bidding for social funds would be replaced by a stable, 5 percent interest charge. This is nothing radical; it is close to what was the law for years.

Society could pay higher or lower interest to capital (savings) than that 4 percent, but there is no room for a greater spread between interest on savings and interest on investment loans than the 1 percent to cover administration costs. There is simply no one there doing productive labor to justly claim that income. Substantially higher consumer loans may be justified but only as a tool to regulate demand. The substantial profits this would generate properly would go to the social fund. These social earnings, along with land rent, add up to enormous sums available for productive investment and consumer loans. Land rent should be stable and predictable, and income from consumer loans could be regulated exactly to balance supply and demand in an economy.

When any financial instrument was cashed or deposited at any bank anywhere in the country, the account of the party that issued this draft would be

---

* Except for the variable interest rate created by bidding for these federal funds, this is the same procedure as now. If those surplus funds are not lent, they must be deposited with the Fed at no interest, which is why the federal funds market evolved.

instantly debited, while the depositor's account would, at the same instant, be credited. Banking costs would be low and overdrafts nonexistent. The computer would not honor a draft on any account with insufficient funds. Modern computers are quite capable of recognizing thumbprints and thus eliminating bad checks. In fact, that potential is being installed right now. Super smart credit cards are being developed that will debit and credit with your computer-memorized signature as authorization.[71] A hint at the potential efficiency of computerized banking under a public authority is given by credit card labor costs. When VISA was the nation's largest credit card service, it functioned substantially as we have outlined and required only three hundred workers.

This system can only be used in a society that guarantees full rights of privacy for personal transactions. In a society that permitted surveillance of its citizens, a master computer could track a person's every move. Today these records are supposedly private but are hardly so. This abuse of privacy can be eliminated by the simple legal requirement that all computers be programmed to record who requests what information.

Investors would still be free to search out direct equity investments but would do so only if it is productive. Only through production can true value be produced. Interception of social production through monopolized capital and finance capital would be eliminated.

Marxist economists estimate this interception at 50 percent of America's surplus value. Their conclusions may be correct by their interpretation of appropriation of labor. By my interpretation their calculations are too high. These waste distribution territories are no more productive than finance monopolists, and they appropriate even more labor.

Both conventional and Marxist economists assume every worker on a job is productively employed. This thesis disagrees with their view. The potential efficiencies of industrial technology have been appropriated both by monopolists and wasted labor, and unnecessary labor now exceeds the appropriation of the monopolists.

This is not to say that most are not entitled to the share they receive. All are entitled to a fair share, only each should be employed and fully productive. The result would be a prosperous nation, with all that wasted time converted to enjoyable free time.

True money requires nothing to produce; has no value of its own; and should be strictly a tool to increase the efficiency of society's trades. It should be printed and circulated only to produce and distribute wealth, not to be monopolized, demanding tribute for its use. When this is done, money will always represent true value—nothing more nor less than the value of the labor that produced that product or service. Bankers should be well-paid agents of society, not extortionists barricading the most important highway of commerce and exacting tribute from all who would pass.

# 4

# Monopolizing the Communications Industry

## The Television Industry's Capitalized Value

$B_y$ 1967, scientists had determined they could build a satellite powerful enough to broadcast directly to home television sets. This satellite could simultaneously handle transoceanic phone calls for ten cents (about sixty cents in 1987 dollars).[1] However, *U.S. News and World Report* predicted at the time that, "The big decision will be made by statesmen and politicians, not by scientists."[2] With every TV program made available to every home, monopoly control of broadcasting would have been eliminated. This, of course, was not acceptable to the powerful who control the communications airways.

These statesmen and politicians were influenced not only by owners of broadcasting and cable television stations but by major corporations who monopolize advertising time and manipulate consumers' purchasing choices. These territories are so successfully protected today that only a few viewers receive direct broadcast TV. The use of large dish antennas to intercept satellite TV signals was a technological end run to bypass their monopoly. This could not be tolerated and monopoly control has been reclaimed by scrambling many of the signals.

The primary reasons for monopolizing television channels are to concentrate the audience for advertisers and maximize profits. Corporations will not pay premium rates if TV broadcasting is so cheap that there are one hundred to three hundred program choices available at any one moment. The audience would be so fragmented that any one channel might provide consumers only in limited numbers.*

In communications, as in other industries, the appropriation of social wealth is accomplished via the time honored method of monopoly title and capitalized values. For example, in 1973 "television stations in major markets earn[ed] 90-

---

* Ben Bagdikian, the nation's best informed and best known media critic, saw the need for a "different system of announcing new products, prices, and specifications, under the control of the consumer and at lower cost than present media ads." (Ben Bagdikian, *Media Monopoly,* updated and expanded, 1987, pp. 138–40, 148, 229.) This is an outline of just such a system.

to 100-percent return on tangible investments annually."[3] A TV station in Tampa, Florida, which had been purchased in 1979 for an already inflated $17.6 million, sold six years later for $197.5 million. The average price of all TV stations doubled between 1982 and 1984, yet one year later they were still earning 40- to 60-percent profits. For those that encompass major markets, a typical station and license worth $10 million in 1959 was worth $400 to $500 million by 1987.[4]

The true dimension of this appropriation of wealth through monopolized technology can be gauged when, "in comparison, one major-market PBS broadcasting station will cost $1.5 million."[5] That $1.5-million actual cost of capital as opposed to the $400-million to $500-million value the market places on these stations accurately measures the fictitious capital and its appropriation of labor. It also outlines monopoly capital's control of the media.* The conservative periodical *U.S. News and World Report* recognized this when they headlined:

> Who Will Control TV? This Battle Has It All—Power, Money, Politics. On the Outcome Rides the Future of America's Most Pervasive Medium and the Programs it Brings into Homes. . . . Wall Street has discovered that ownership of TV stations is tantamount to running a money machine that churns out profits in good times and bad.[6]

## The Public Paid for Satellite Development

During the fifties and sixties the American public paid $24 billion (about $140 billion in inflated 1987 dollars) to develop satellite communications.[7] The cost of building and launching each satellite is less than $100 million, or under $1.9 billion for the nineteen satellites now in use. There are now (1987) about nine hundred television stations in the U.S. Having already noted that only $1.5 million is enough to establish a PBS station in a metropolitan area, I will generously allow an initial cost of $5 million per station; the total actual cost of these nine hundred American TV stations is then $4.5 billion. The entire system with its 436 satellite channels could have been constructed for $6.4 billion. That is about $73 per American family, or a 4.6-percent addition to the $140 billion they have already paid.**

Only about 15 percent of the 436 existing satellite transponders (signal relays, 24 per satellite) are now being used for TV signals. Even with telephone and electronic mail being transmitted simultaneously with the TV signals, there is a large surplus communication capacity. This was proven in 1961 when Hughes Aircraft Company designed the Syncom satellite that alone could "handle twenty-two times the [then] existing volume of long-distance telephone service in the United States."[8] Even as this book goes to press a technological breakthrough may have been made that squeezes ten times the original signals into the

---

* There are no more radio frequencies to be had and, as radio has proven its ability to target narrow audiences, the values of stations have climbed into the tens of millions of dollars and are rising fast. Their high capitalized values may soon parallel television.

** As direct broadcast TV signals will not go through walls and require relatively expensive dish antennas, cable TV is required to reach consumers efficiently in areas of high population density. But those cost will not be included as, with the use of recently developed technology, both cable TV companies and dish antennas would be obsolete.

bandwidths used by these communications satellites.[9] If the traffic were there to use this capacity this multiplies the value of those systems many times with almost no investment. As this technology is not included in the calculations, it also means the cost of communication could be much lower than outlined below.

## A Totally Integrated Communication System

Great strides have recently been made in communications technology. The old analog signals, sent over four-inch copper communication cables capable of 4,200 simultaneous conversations, are being replaced by digital signals, sent over fiber-optic lines and satellites, that will be capable of transmitting "data at 1.7 gigabits per second, enough to transmit the entire contents of the *Encyclopedia Britannica* in two seconds or to carry 169,344 simultaneous telephone conversations, all on a glass strand that looks like a very thin fishing line."[10]

The initial installation of both digital satellites and fiber-optic lines has already begun. Together with computerized communication equipment the technology is here to communicate across the country, or around the world, as cheaply as we now telephone a neighboring town. Using local computerized switching terminals, each covering several city blocks, these same fiber-optic lines are capable of transmitting those hundreds of TV channels described above to every home so wired. Upon electronic command from a home TV set, any channel on any satellite could be instantly routed to that home. It is anticipated that replacing the present copper lines and switching equipment with fiber-optic lines and computerized switching will cost about $2,500 per business and home.[11] The nation will require about one hundred million of these consumer communication terminals to replace telephones, at a cost of about $250 billion.

The immense capacity of satellite communications for long-distance, point-to-point, and all point-to-multipoint communication, and the equally large capacity of fiber optics for point-to-point and local service (under four hundred miles), can be combined with compatible computerized telephones, personal computers, software, database supercomputers, laser recorders, and high-resolution picture tubes. This would form a totally integrated communication system.

With this technology, communication would be practically instantaneous. Information would be stored in a databank computer, and when specific information was requested, route codes would be automatically encoded thereon. This "packet switch" (the almost instantaneously transmitted signal), all in split seconds, would find its way through many switching terminals, satellites, and trunk lines to the requesting communication terminal, there to be stored in an electronic buffer of a computerized telephone, laser recorder, or computer.

With fully compatible computers and software and all producers having access to technology, the above home equipment and databanks should cost society no more than another $250 billion. A totally integrated communication system would thus cost about $500 billion.

The normal reaction is that this is not feasible because the cost is not valid. *Cheaper* means specifically that *less labor* is required. Proper costs are nothing more than traded labor. As it requires less labor, it is only necessary to share the work to obtain one's proper share of income. If each person had rights to *productive* employment, each would be able to share in the benefits of technology.

Though this equipment may be initially expensive, it has such a large capacity that even long distance will be inexpensive per unit of information transferred. This will create great savings in other segments of the economy—predominantly in distribution, as here the major costs are in obtaining information. Only if this technology is monopolized will it be beyond the reach of anybody. A properly structured communication system operated by a publicly mandated authority would be even more accessible than highways. The savings to society could be enormous as it would permit bypassing the intermediaries I have been outlining throughout this book.

## Communication's Competitive Monopoly Costs

According to then-retired President Truman, "The public spent $25 or $30 billion developing satellites and the communication system ought to be publicly owned."[12] Michael Parenti explains what happened instead:

> . . . through its extensive influence in the White House and Congress, AT & T managed to have the entire satellite communications system ("Comsat") put under its control in 1962—after U.S. taxpayers had put up the initial $20 billion to develop it. Then AT & T decided not to extend the benefits of Comsat to its U.S. customers, the reason being billions of dollars of the company's equipment would have become obsolete overnight if satellites were put into use in the United States. The big savings for long distance customers would have meant huge losses for AT & T owners. In order to preserve its obsolete but highly profitable investment, AT & T withheld satellite service from the very U.S. public that had financed it.[13]

The Intelsat satellite, owned by 109 nations, faced the same denial of business, and it appears to be destined for obsolescence due to lack of enough communications traffic.[14]

Control of public policy, and thus control of wealth-producing assets, surfaced again when AT & T's Bell Telephone monopoly was divided into several Baby Bells. AT & T kept the profitable long-distance communications which consisted of one-third of the assets and two-thirds of the income. The local consumers have been left with the high-cost, local distribution systems.

At present AT & T controls 80 percent of long-distance communication traffic. Two upstarts, MCI Communications and US Sprint, realized the potential and have claimed 15 percent of the market between them while other smaller companies split the remaining 5 percent.[15]

With multiple duplication of services, the present communications capacity is far underutilized. AT & T could handle all the traffic, while MCI and US Sprint could, with little or no increase in cost, handle much more than 15 percent. AT & T, MCI, and US Sprint's long-term strategy is evident. It is nothing less than the collective monopolization of communications between producers and consumers. They wish to totally control this potentially efficient social tool. The anticipated profits from monopolizing communications technology are truly enormous.*

---

* Much of the anticipated labor savings will be paid right back out through these competitive monopolies (another waste distribution territory).

Where digital replaces analog signals, the capacity of transmission lines and satellites increases by several times with no increase in costs. Communications companies will lower their rates to attract customers, but the expensive duplications, as new companies install matching equipment, will demand competitive monopoly charges. Being used to the older, higher rates and pleased at the new lower rates, the public will be unaware that communications could be far cheaper yet.

We are taught that a monopoly is formed either by a single corporation or a few in collusion. This is true, but competing groups can just as easily—or even more easily—form a monopoly by wasted input. Normally the surviving competitors are roughly equal in financial and political staying power. Most of their efforts are wasteful duplications that must be paid for. All this unnecessary activity creates an excessive cost that amounts to no less than monopoly charges, and it is done without direct collusion. A competitive monopoly is a standoff between roughly equal competitors for control of economic territory. However, competition turns to cooperation when efforts to lobby government bodies are coordinated to ensure the laws protecting them stay intact. If society completes this communications system without planning—and with multiple duplications as different companies battle to control territory—the unnecessary costs will be quite large:

> . . . each of the Big Three must meet the enormous cost of financing and maintaining its own nationwide transmission network. AT & T already owns such a network, and the other two are building them. Industry experts think that for long-term health, national network operators need at least 7% of the total long-distance market.[16]

At the price these competitive monopolists expect to be able to charge, 7 percent of the national market is enough to build and maintain a national communication network. There is the measurement of monopoly charges. If the market were equally divided, 14 companies could profitably duplicate AT & T's already installed system. A single, consumer-owned, integrated communications system could deliver these messages at a fraction of those competitive monopoly costs. I would again quote what communications experts say on the current fragmented system:

> The computer industry is tackling this problem decades later than it should have—after selling 50 million computers that work pretty much alone, much like isolated islands with little or no connection to the outside world. Just the opposite happened with telephones. There the standards—established in 1885—came first. Every country in the world adopted them. That's why you can pick up the phone and call anywhere in the world—and why manufacturers of telephones, answering machines and fax machines can build their products to plug directly into the phone network and go right to work. "The world's 600 million phones are interconnected," says Doehler [executive director of Siemens AG]. "Computers should be too". . . . Computers from all vendors will [then] be able to exchange information easily. The "global village" envisioned by Marshal McLuhan in the 60's finally will become a reality. You'll be able to sit down at any computer terminal anywhere on the globe, and send a message or electronic file to any computer, regardless of its make.[17]

When every computer can talk to every other—using digital signals over satellites and fiber-optic lines at the rate of "the entire *Encyclopedia Britannica* in two seconds"—communication efficiency will rise astronomically. With such large communications capacity, society has the opportunity to reduce its labors by possibly half, with no loss of food, fiber, shelter, or recreation.

## Communication Eliminates Intermediaries and Reduces Trading Costs

*Two-thirds* of all the expense of running . . . stores is loss and waste. . . . In other words, for each necessary store, there are two superfluous ones. . . . The retail trade as conducted on this plan of self-help and equal opportunity has the stocks, equipment and man-power which will unavoidably exceed what is required for the work by some 200 to 1,000 per cent . . . The retail trade always and everywhere is something like three-quarters to nine-tenths idle waste, to be canceled out of the communities' working efficiency as lag, leak and friction.[18]

— Thorstein Veblen

As discussed in the last chapter, the first trades involved face-to-face bartering for commodities of roughly equal value. But as these trades required traveling long distances to—and long waits at—markets, it became more efficient to use intermediaries. From this humble beginning developed the wholesale and retail sales forces of today. Sixty-five years ago that venerable economic philosopher, Thorstein Veblen, estimated that

one-half the price paid for goods and services by consumers is to be set down to the account of salesmanship . . . But in many notable lines of merchandise the sales-cost will ordinarily foot up to some ten or twenty times the production-cost proper, and to not less than one hundred times the necessary cost of distribution.[19]

The difference between manufacturing cost and the consumer price measures the major cost of most products—distribution. With mail order shipping charges from 2 to 5 percent, no one would pay intermediaries 2 to 3 times the production cost if it were feasible to contact the producer, purchase the item, and have it shipped directly. With an integrated communication system employing the latest technology, it would be possible for producers and consumers to trade directly again, just as with those first trades thousands of years ago. The monopolization of distribution, now exploited by an army of intermediaries, could be largely eliminated.

Shopping is searching for information and those intermediaries are in the information business. Take insurance for example; if Andrew Tobias and others had access to the mass media to present their case efficient social insurance would be quickly adopted. It would be computerized, and society would then have been both informed and served by this modern technology. The same holds true for law, transportation, agriculture, health care, the welfare system, and banking. So the savings estimated here for communications overlaps—and possibly fully duplicates—the potential savings of labor that we have covered up to this point.

# Expensive, Big-ticket, Infrequently Purchased Items

Autos, appliances, furniture, farm equipment, industrial equipment, and tools are all big-ticket, infrequently bought consumer items whose purchase requires accurate information but not the promotional/persuasive advertising that hammers at us incessantly.

We all trust and get information from direct experience and consumers make the most important decisions by observing products in daily use. For the final decisions, customers need only code into a computerized telephone their requests for a master index of all who manufacture the particular product in which they are interested. This computerized telephone would be totally compatible and integrated with personal computers, software, laser recorders, and database supercomputers. This index would include the basic information required to make an informed decision—energy efficiency, noise level, hours of useful life, price, and other features. (Note the pressure this would put on manufacturers to make the most efficient products and stand out in this all-important master index.) From this index, the consumer would choose brands and models for visual inspection. The precoded, computerized telephone would dial the product databank, request the information, and receive it in an audio-visual electronic buffer, laser recorder, or computer—all in seconds.

Buyers could, at their leisure, study the engineering specifications and styling on their television. Once a decision was made, they need only punch in the code for the desired order—model, color, and accessories—and a databank computer would instantly note the closest distribution point where that item is available. If there was not one close by, buyers could choose delivery from the factory. Their bank account number and thumbprint could be verified by a master computer so that their account could be instantly debited. If a credit line had been established at the local credit union and recorded in an integrated computer, credit needs could be handled simultaneously. The entire process need not involve advertising, sales, or banking labor. Product guarantees could be handled much as they are now, while maintenance and repairs could be taken care of by local private enterprise, under standardized guarantees.

From the initial information request to the completion of a trade, the communication arteries would only be in use for that communication for a few seconds; there would be tens of thousands of simultaneous communications. Both seller and buyer save time and labor, as verbal explanations and mailing of information are largely eliminated. The current time-consuming exchange of information could be handled in split seconds. This automatic and instantaneous transfer of massive amounts of information means there is an infinitesimal labor cost per communication.

Monopolization of information could be eliminated. Every qualified producer could enjoy the right to place his or her product or service in the databank and pay the charges (a percentage of gross sales) out of cash flow. In place of millions of dollars up front to advertise through the present monopolized TV system, there would be only a small charge for entering the product information in a retail database computer. To eliminate clogging the databanks with the useless information of producers no longer in business, regular payments would be required to retain the privilege of selling through this integrated communication network.

Note the above closely. It is this that could break the monopolization of our production and distribution system by wealthy corporations. Starting up a truly productive industry could be quite simple. This company's advertising would have full billing alongside any others, whereas currently only those with large financial backing can pay the charges of the monopolized media and have access to the public; all others are financially excluded. Corporations deciding what the public wants and what is good for them could be replaced by consumers having easy access to all choices. Several large corporations are establishing just such databanks. They are, however, individual databanks for each corporation and this is an extension of monopolization.[20]

## Inexpensive, Small, Frequently Traded Items

The markup on perishable groceries is about 50 percent while the markup on small, nonperishable consumer durables is several hundred percent. There is a competitive sales monopoly at work in the latter. These proposals would remove all purchases above an intermediate price range out of the wasteful, duplicated retail outlets. Simultaneously the consumers' choices are increased through access to these products through databanks.

With a properly structured communication system, one need only transport oneself to and from his or her job to produce his or her share of the nation's wealth and then search for and order electronically his or her share of what others produce. This would substantially reduce the 1.9 people distributing for every one currently producing.* A study starting from the point of potential efficiency of communication technology would arrive at the same labor savings described in this treatise.

If traded directly between distant producers and consumers, individual shipping and handling costs would be too high for small, frequently purchased items. Thus, though computers will provide some savings, groceries, household supplies, cosmetics, knickknacks and most small, inexpensive consumer items would be most efficiently distributed through the present retail outlets. The breakeven point would be in the lower range of the intermediate-priced, occasionally purchased items.

Even now companies in Japan are planning computer shopping. "A housewife can switch on her personal computer and scan the list of goods available for sale. . . . The order will be delivered strictly on time." With high capacity communication, plans are also under way for offices at home. Together these plans are perceived as reducing traffic congestion and needing fewer expensive buildings on valuable land.[21] This is moving towards these suggestions and the savings are quite apparent.

Wholesalers of small-ticket consumer items could keep the quality and price of all products posted in a databank computer. Purchasing agents could periodically analyze the quality and prices of all products. Once initial trust has been established, a retailer need only check these updated bulletin boards for the best buys. This would eliminate many jobbers and other sales forces.

---

* This returns us to the importance of reclaiming the right of each citizen to a share of the remaining productive jobs as outlined in chapter six of Book One.

## Shopping as a Social Event Entails a Cost

Shopping is recreation to many people and a status symbol for others. Direct communication between producers and consumers would change society's psychological profile. If enough people decided they wished to do their shopping socially and expensively, that would be their choice. This is a personal decision, and they would have no trouble finding merchants to accommodate them. Those products would cost more in order to compensate for the additional labor. The added unit costs are properly accounted for under socializing and recreation (like Tupperware or Avon) or social status. The majority would surely choose to save their money on the most direct and least labor-intensive (cheapest) method of completing a trade. As direct trades would be only for intermediate to big-ticket items, this would in no way impinge on local coffeehouse-type trades where socializing is the primary activity.

## The Actual Distribution

When a manufacturer produces a product, it is normally ready to use, and the customers already understand the use for which it was designed. All that is missing for potential consumers is complete information on where the best quality product is available at the lowest possible price. Once direct contact is established between producer and consumer, it would only require roughly 100,000 railroaders, 1.5 million truckers, and a system of organized freight terminals to distribute the nation's production. It would be quite simply a freight postal system just as is done with Christmas packages today. Consumers would receive notices of arrival of their purchases and pick them up at the local freight terminal or make arrangements for delivery.

As it requires a central dispatching office, most truck freight is handled by moderate to large trucking companies. They may either own all their trucks or sublease from independent truckers who own and drive their own rigs. There are normally several trucking companies in any moderate-size city, each complete with loading docks, storage capacity, and dispatching equipment and staff.

If it were the decision of a society to be efficient and the communications system were in place, the following scene would be possible. Shippers need only punch into their communication terminal the information on loads to be shipped; an independent trucker would stop by a computer terminal and dial a computer programmed for dispatching all loads; he or she would punch in his or her location and freight preferences and where he or she would like to deliver the next load; the computer would tell instantly where the loads are, what type of freight, the required pickup and delivery times, the rate per mile, etc.; the trucker would choose a load, inform the computer, and record his or her identification number; the computer would record the acceptance, remove that load from the databank, provide a contract number to the trucker, and inform the shipper. The minimal dispatching costs would be included in the freight charge. Recording and billing would be handled automatically by the computer—there need be but few intermediaries.

There would be no need for duplicated dispatching services, loading docks, storage facilities, equipment, and personnel. This would not restrict any trucker or company from signing contracts outside the national computerized dispatching system. It would, however, break the competitive monopoly created by the minimum capital requirements for a trucking company. Each independent trucker would be on an equal footing with corporate trucking companies: another monopoly is broken.

When producers and consumers trade directly over publicly owned communication arteries, just as they now transport over publicly maintained transportation arteries, costs will drop precipitously. The competitive monopolies of retail outlets for intermediate- to high-priced products will be eliminated. The nation's freight would quickly settle into flow patterns and be moved as regularly as mail by the cheapest combination of rail, truck, water, and air.

It might take a consumer from one day to a week to receive a purchase, but at possibly one-third the price, he or she would be well paid for this time. As there are no intermediaries, the actual transit time between producer and consumer would be dramatically reduced and those who formerly bought, stored, and sold these products would be available to engage in productive labor. American society would attain an undreamed-of efficiency. Possibly 50 percent or more of these intermediaries between producer and consumer could share the remaining work. If equally shared, this would create a corresponding increase in free time for everybody. That small amount of time necessary to labor for one's share of the nation's wealth would be the proper measure of the price of products and services.

Except for unlimited TV channels, the present communication infrastructure is already capable of handling this long-distance information transmission. With that exception, these efficiencies could be used once the databanks are in place. The system would pay for itself as fast as, and most likely much faster than, the fiber-optic lines and computer switching terminals are installed.

Detractors will point out that it is taxpayers' money that will be used to eliminate businesses and jobs. This is true. However it was this taxpayers' money which developed the technologies to be used, and it is the same taxpayers who will provide even more dollars for the much more expensive, fragmented, nonintegrated, duplicated, competitive monopolies. It is also these same taxpayers who would be working only two days per week if the potential efficiencies of technology were fully used.

Only with full and equal rights for everybody could this efficiency be realized. This would require sharing the productive work. Not to do so would either subvert the economy and put many people out of work, or the waste distribution territories would have to expand to reclaim a share of social production.

## Trades Should Still Pay for Our "Free" TV

The same computer that routed the requested TV program to the consumer could record what programs are watched and for how long. This accounting would determine the pay for entertainers and programming, which would be directly relative to the number of viewers their talents commanded.

The programming and transmission costs per TV show would cost only pennies for each viewer. But with the average American family watching seven hours of TV daily, those pennies would add up to dollars per day, tens of dollars per month, and hundreds of dollars per year. Consumers willingly pay more than this through the painless (for the unaware) yet expensive method of advertising (one thousand dollars per household) which is priced into consumer products.[22] Those for whom it is painful currently can do nothing about it. However, if billed directly, money-conscious consumers could do something. They would promptly restrict their TV viewing time which would, in turn, raise the unit cost.

The natural tendency towards conservation mandates that TV for the masses must have other than direct viewer financing. These costs could be financed from tax revenues, but this is still too visible and arbitrary. As most families watch TV, the fairest source of funds is to, just as now, collect them through consumer purchases. Even though none of a company's products or services would directly sponsor these programs, for the privilege of advertising and selling through society's integrated communications system they would be collecting the television charges from the consumer.

Producers using this service need only calculate the price markup necessary to cover a communications surcharge on gross revenues. The communication system required for these direct trades would be capable of simultaneously carrying TV programs with minimal additional equipment. The TV transmission charges should also be minimal, and most of these funds would go towards programming and entertainers.

Consumers are making heroic efforts to avoid being force-fed promotional/persuasive advertising. One-third have remote-control TV and change channels when the commercials come on, and 90 percent of all buyers of new TVs insist on this feature.* Monopolization of advertising will monopolize any market. With direct access, instead of a few wealthy producers and distributors spending hundreds of millions of dollars supporting (monopolizing) TV, consumers—collectively through their purchases—would pay for their TV viewing. In the process, all producers would have access to every consumer. Only if the intention were to monopolize a market could more than that be expected. Impulse buying would be greatly reduced and create more savings for society. When people wanted or needed something—and assuming they could afford it—they would buy it without being pressured.

While innovations on a familiar product are readily presented to the public through a databank, a totally new product is very expensive to market. These innovators would require special access to the public. To complement other methods of familiarization, some TV channels should be specifically reserved to promote such innovations. Novelty buffs comprise a large segment of the population, and there are few of us who do not have some interest. A program demonstrating these creations should be quite popular.

An undeveloped society needs promotional/persuasive advertising to alert a population to the standard of living possible with developed capital. There must be demand before the industries and distribution arteries can be established. The Soviet Union is recognizing that now and permitting advertising on their state owned communications channels. However, once the production/distribution infrastructure is in place and a society energized to produce and accustomed to that standard of living, promotional/persuasive advertising can become wasteful and

---

* *NBC News,* 5 October 1987; however, stations may be thwarting the public by synchronizing their ads.

confined to a predetermined group within the loop of money circulation. Those not within the loop can hardly purchase the products they see on their TV screen. Rather than titillate a well-to-do group with thousands of toys that they will play with, discard, and abandon for the next, it would be much more socially efficient to break that corporate control of social policy which would permit people to advance to a higher level intellectually and socially. The basic living standard within the capabilities of this earth has long been set. Socially mature individuals could decide what products they want by observing them in use or scanning the databanks of new products. Any item that is truly useful for society will be desirable and become a common household item. Those unessential products currently purchased due to promotional/persuasive advertising would not be produced. That capital currently wasted on these titillating toys could then be diverted to the dispossessed.

If it is such a thing that people are so dull that a society with a respectable living standard could not function without promotional/persuasive advertising (which I do not believe), society can break it down to essential and unessential products for the desired standard of living. After all, many items such as cigarettes, alcohol, and chemical-laden processed foods lower the quality of life and to spend social funds in their promotion is economic insanity.

When radio first came on the scene its most prominent use was for public education programs. When cable television arrived with its potential for eighty channels, idealistic planners also tried to establish an education medium. In both cases powerful interests subverted the public interest and monopolized this valuable media for commercial interests, and the chance for society to become truly informed was lost.[23] Rather than being radical, the following suggestions are similar to the original plans for radio and cable television and are only one of the many ways these hundreds of TV channels could be organized.

Only 35 percent of the 436 current satellite channels (152) would be more than adequate for satellite TV if organized along the lines outlined below. *Newsweek* reporters Harry F. Waters and Janet Huck noted that TV has the "power to deliver mass audiences to programming . . . [but] commercial television makes so much money doing its worst, it can't afford to do its best."[24]

## Music, Sports, Movies, and Game Shows

Music, sports, movies, and game shows have an established market and draw large audiences and fifteen to twenty channels could be reserved for these program. Only pennies per viewer would bring in millions per broadcast to the investors, stars, directors, managers, and support labor. Auditions and introductions to the public by established entertainers are well-established methods of deciding who has the opportunity to present their talents on stage, screen, or TV. There would be adequate channels to guarantee all promising entertainers the opportunity to present their shows for a probationary period of time. If successful, as shown by automatic computer recording of viewer interest, their shows would be made permanent. With communication channels now open there would no longer be monopolization through high-priced promotion. With these equal rights, it would be talent that counted. There would be many more able people investing, designing, producing, and starring in many more shows.

Viewer choices would rise, and the truly talented artists would be well paid for their efforts. All would have had a reasonable opportunity to prove their abilities.

Equal pay per viewing hour would entail monopolization again. The overwhelming share of income would be appropriated by a few with loyal followers due to popularity and early market entry. A formula of gradually reduced pay per million viewing hours as a show increased in popularity would compensate performers relative to their popularity; this would be little different from now. The exception would be that, with a designed program of access to the public for new performers, the monopolies that control the entertainment industries would disappear, along with the appropriation of labor their substantial income represents. There would then be direct trades between the producers and the consumers of entertainment.

## Investment

Earlier I addressed the problem of monopolization of technology through capitalization of fictitious values in the stock market. We noted the necessity of eliminating the gambling casino atmosphere of stock trading. Several TV channels could be reserved for direct communication between those offering investment opportunities and investors looking for opportunities.

An entrepreneur who had obtained community approval and initial investment capital from the local bank need only present proposals over these channels and deposit a prospectus in a databank. Investors could then study the various investment plans, buy shares in the most promising ventures, and have their accounts automatically debited—all without intermediaries.

As everyone with savings would have access to this investment information stored in a databank, the money monopolists could be totally bypassed. Individual investors would put their risk capital in productive innovations that went unrecognized by regular loan institutions. If their insights and talents are truly productive (as they now claim), they would receive much higher than average returns. However, if their claim is not valid, they would not be able to hide behind the protective shield of monopolization.

Every segment of the economy essential to provide that new or cheaper production would be properly compensated. For their risk, the original innovators and investors would receive the initial, higher profits plus royalties. Workers and management who bought stock through deductions of 10 to 20 percent of their wages would be well compensated and have incentive to maximize their efficiency. Assuming society had eliminated patent monopolies, others would quickly analyze and duplicate the process. Those who copied this innovation would compete for sales. With monopolization eliminated, prices would fall to just that required to properly compensate the patent holders, labor, and capital.

If communication technology reduced production and distribution costs 60 percent, and adequate compensation to the patent holders was 10 percent, the public would quickly benefit by a 50-percent reduction in costs. This savings would have to be matched by sharing productive jobs or there would be no savings, as waste distribution territories would have to expand to reclaim income or the economy would collapse.

# Education

Educating children is quite simple. Copying parents and peers is the basis of all learning. They all want to imitate their elders and other children. They wish the approval of their parents, love to excel, and *must* be equal with their peers. They are curious and, if not discouraged, love to learn. The present educational system just puts too many barriers in their way. At present "half of all gifted children float through school with average or worse grades, never realizing their potential . . . [while] almost 20 percent will drop out."[25] There are many reasons: a child may be timid and terrified of school; an inferiority complex may prevent a student from functioning; pressure to do well may paralyze one's mind; the school district may have obsolete books and teaching aids; a local peer group (gang) may replace parents and teachers as role models; and the curriculum may be so slow it is boring. With elimination of these barriers, many who now maintain low grades will blossom, right along with their peers.

Allowing 40 to 60 reserved TV channels for education, every subject now taught at elementary and secondary schools, and at the college and university level, could reach every home at no charge. Logically, each subject would have several teachers and be broadcast at various hours of the day. The competition would be enormous for the teaching positions on these programs, and, once picked, these best educators in the nation could be well paid. Each taped course would be edited for maximum clarity, simplicity, and comprehension.

The minimum equipment required for each student would be a TV set, while the local education system would provide workbooks to match the TV lessons. A recorder would be desirable, as these same lessons should be in a databank and accessible through the computerized telephone. With recorders and society providing incentives (see below), students could tape the lessons and study when they have the free time and are emotionally ready. They can replay the lessons as many times as necessary for maximum comprehension. The much lower education costs would be paid for from the same funding sources as the present education system.

So long as a student maintained a certain grade average, a share of the money society saved on maintaining the present school system could be paid to each child's family. Allowing, of course, for each child's ability, it would be logical to pay this incentive for each subject and on an average of all subjects. This would be high motivation for families to restructure their time for home education.

This treatise documents that there could be adequate time for parents to stay home and monitor their children's education. Private or public day-care education centers could be operated for the few who could not function under, or who were unable to arrange for, home self-education. Those who were intellectually capable but who failed to maintain a minimum average would lose their incentive funds and should also be required to attend these specially structured classes.

Few six-year-old children will be able to relate their school work to incentives to be received at some future date; however, most will want to learn. A formal school setting will be necessary for the first few grades for some—but not all—students. Those who feel they and their children are capable of home education should be required to prove this through testing to determine basic education skills. Well-designed children's TV programs could have most of them already above first grade entry level.

Children can be just as easily culturally trained to quality as they can to trash. All society would gain from this cultural training so it would be logical to eliminate the senseless violence in today's children's programs. At the least, the quality programs can be assigned a block of channels so that conscientious parents could maximize their children's intellectual and moral growth.*

The compensations received by siblings and friends for schooling would be noticed by these younger children and this along with peer pressure would provide motivation to avoid the formal school setting. With motivation for home education high, by the third grade most students would easily see the advantage. Possibly between the third and fifth grades—and likely much sooner—all students who were capable would have chosen the option of home education with incentive compensation.

Actually a first-grader would be quite proud going shopping with those earnings. It is hard to visualize many children being irresponsible towards their education if it were to mean losing both their freedom of choices and spending money. They would quickly learn responsibility when it meant both financial and emotional rewards. Once in operation, society would quickly become accustomed, and the need for formal schools would be minimal above first or second grade. Reasoning is quite natural and nothing can beat a good educator whose lectures anticipate and are carefully structured to answer most questions.

It is doubtful if excess spending money helps develop character and responsibility. The incentive funds paid young students should undoubtedly be in script, redeemable in essentials such as clothing. Independence is a powerful motivator and with years of cultural training using this script, older students would be ready to handle money responsibly and should then be paid in standard currency.** Incentive funds, as a right, would in no way impinge on other rights of society. That right could only be exercised by obtaining a set grade average. Holding that average with inexpensive home education would save society more than the cost of those incentive funds. In fact, those funds cost nothing—they go right back to the people from whom they came. Over time, society would become accustomed to this, and these incentives would be looked upon as being as normal as wages earned from a job. This would go a long way towards balancing per capita earnings between families with children and those without.

Older students would soon learn to structure their flexible education time around the nonflexible time required for a job. Thus there need be no sharp cutoff between school years and entering the work force. This would greatly increase the options of both education for a career and earning one's own living. Instead of

---

* These are public channels and rules of courtesy should apply. How groups are taught to hate has been explained in Book Two, chapter five, and the introduction to Book Three. Where any should be able to logically and calmly explain their views, no hate messages should be permitted. Society would then have the maximum breadth of views without being stirred to violence and hate.

** Currently and very justifiably there is an assumed responsibility to obtain an education. To provide incentives such as educational comic books would be all right in the lower grades but candy and other such treats that are bad for the child's health and can lead to obesity by labeling food as a reward should in most cases be avoided.

a division between students and workers, the two would overlap until the young adults opted for a career. This would also increase the labor force substantially and reduce the average workweek even more.

Motivated children, youths, young adults, and adults could obtain most of their education at home and at their own pace. Curious children with a desire to learn—which is most of them—would find the field wide open. Left to their own devices, they would quickly learn that it is their own time and labor that is being conserved by dedication and attention to the subjects being taught. Many talented children's potential, now lost through boredom and diversion to socially undesirable activities, would be salvaged. The brightest could probably attain a twelfth education in as little as eight years; the middle level, in possibly ten; and, with these motivations, even the slower group, which currently sets the pace of a classroom, would learn more quickly. There would be adequate resources and time to give special support to those who are unable to cope for various reasons. This would not only conserve society's labor, it would economize students' energy and time. This potential was proven by interactive videos. These taped educational videos reduced learning time and increased comprehension 30 percent.[26]

A central testing facility should be maintained that would issue scholastic-level certificates and incentive funds. Lab experiments, dissecting, and other classes that require hands-on learning would be held in a classroom setting just as now. The savings to society would be substantial, and the increase in the nation's educational level would be equally dramatic. Millions who dreamed of additional education would find it freely available in what was previously their idle time.

As no one's knowledge is complete, every educator would be subject to review and correction by his or her peers. Much of history and other beliefs would be revised as thousands of people with critical knowledge would prove the official record was incomplete or in error and be in a position to correct it. Educators would themselves become better educated. This would be a great gain for students, who, armed with a more accurate view of the world, would be able to make more-informed decisions. Motivated intellectuals, educators, and scientists would have the latest and most accurate information with which to decipher the mysteries of the world. Virtually all segments of society would gain by the increased accuracy of information.

Learning is fundamental to everyday life. Every day we view the world we learn something new or reinforce what we already know. To create enormous waste along with injustice and poverty while continually affirming nice-sounding slogans about efficiency and justice can only seriously limit true knowledge. Viewing this waste distribution system for what it is, and rationalizing production and distribution to eliminate it, would give children a better cultural education. Such an education would provide a much firmer foundation for the further evolution of society towards its stated goals of justice and freedom from want.

It would never be possible to get every student to enjoy learning and probably is not desirable. After all, given a choice, most people will choose to study those things that best support their need for identity and security. They can't all crowd into academia. For most there is a lot more room for identity in work, sports, and hobbies than there is in intellectual pursuits. There will be those who, though unable to compete across the board in education, will take great interest and do well in one field. The above suggestions would eliminate as many barriers as possible and give the maximum incentive to learn in the field or fields of one's choice.

Those within one segment of the economy are normally unable to accept that their job might be either eliminated or accomplished with more satisfactory results, while having no problem seeing the redundancy of others' labor. Educators will undoubtedly be no different. They may be capable of providing a superior educational structure but only to a narrow segment of the population.

School as now structured does perform a babysitting function. But, if that is the criterion, society should be aware that there is a loss in building the potential of many children and that babysitting is what they are paying for, not education.

## Culture and Recreational Learning

Fine arts and recreational learning, such as are produced by public broadcasting stations (and increasingly on for-profit shows), are enjoyable to many people and add to their knowledge. Fifteen to twenty TV channels could be blocked out and reserved for these high quality shows. The social benefits of learning while relaxing are self-evident. The popular, educational talk shows and good recreational educational TV command a loyal audience. However, most of these are public broadcasting stations outside the system of collecting costs through consumer purchases: they depend on grants and donations. One live show can easily exceed one PBS station's yearly cost of all its taped shows.[27] With their fair share of TV funds through a restructured media still financed by sales, the present financial struggles of these quality programs would be eliminated. This income would permit expansion of these programs as the costs of these taped shows would be minuscule compared to sports and large, live shows.

New methods of distribution and governing skills that contribute to social efficiency are as much a matter of inventing as the well-known mechanical devices. Among the cultural and educational programs should be one introducing and demonstrating these innovations and inventions. Alert, imaginative minds would relate their special expertise to other machines, production processes, distribution methods, and social policies, and would devise simpler methods of governing, producing, and distributing.

## Minority Cultures

Five to ten TV channels could be reserved for ethnic minorities. They are now inadequately represented and are participating in our national culture only to a limited extent. With these new rights, they could quickly develop outstanding media and political personalities to articulate issues essential to their cause. With their own communication channels, equal access to land and jobs, and the right to retain what their labors produce, minorities could share the nation's work, its wealth, and the prestige of national decision-making. Every American might at last attain and exercise the full rights of equal citizenship.

## Foreign Cultures

Guaranteeing representation of their views should apply also to foreign cultures. Not being present to defend themselves and with no right of presenting information, another culture can easily be portrayed as an enemy. Eight to twelve channels could be reserved for their contact with Americans. With all sides presenting their views of events, any society would be hard-pressed to falsely accuse another of aggressive intent or camouflage an aggressive buildup. It would be equally difficult to hide aggressive intentions.

By mutual agreement there should be reciprocal presentations of cultural programs between countries to provide cross-cultural information. As each would be a guest in the other's home, the rules of courtesy and agreements between governments would limit propaganda. Beamed to every home, these programs would show people throughout the world at work and play. All people would begin to appreciate—and thus respect—both what we have in common and what is distinctively different. There would be intense pressure to extend full rights to all people once all societies were open for the whole world to see.

## Local TV

Most local TV stations now pick up national programs from satellites and rebroadcast them to local viewers. With a totally integrated system, these stations would broadcast nationally when a local event was of national interest. Their primary purpose would be for transmitting local shows and events. What has been advocated for national TV is applicable to local TV as well. It should be a source of community information and culture—ideally a medium for citizens to share ideas and experiences with each other. Local elections and community development could have complete coverage. There would be adequate time to broadcast local sports, concerts, plays, parades, and community information forums on a broad range of issues. Meetings of governing bodies, normally open to the public by law, could be beamed over local TV.

The rights to a share of the TV fund would give adequate income for popular local events. Having already paid their share, through being consumers, all may watch for free in the comfort of their living rooms. Talented local people would have their chance at national exposure without the time, expense, and risk of leaving their local area and the security it provides.

## Elections

Many leaders are so busy leading that they have or take little time for a sincere research of ideas. In fact, politics as now contrived is hardly amenable to new ideas. As explained in the introduction of Book Three, society is kept to the right of the political spectrum. Political rhetoric is then kept within those permitted parameters of debate. To move outside those parameters is political and social suicide. Here is where the power brokers reap the rewards of ideological programming. Assuming there is no crisis, an ideologically programmed population is guaranteed to vote in support of the social policy the power brokers promote, as there are no choices outside those parameters. To move to what is a true middle position is to be instantly attacked as liberal, socialist, heretical, un-American, or even communist. Thus few leaders can be pinned down to what they believe, and they avoid in-depth analysis and commitments.

These politicians should not be too heavily criticized for their evasions. To openly admit that the Soviet military threat was not real or to promote truly progressive social policies would cost them their political life. If they suggested even moderate plans to restructure any of the wasteful segments of the economy we have been outlining, the big guns of the many monopolies would collectively and immediately sink their political ships.

Ten to twenty reserved TV channels would be ideal for every serious leader to present his or her views. Serious, in this instance, means having a substantial segment of the population to represent—corporations, businesspeople, farmers, labor, women, the poor, conservationists, peace groups, etc. If there is anywhere politicians must be, it is in the spotlight. They would have to attend these in-depth background discussions or relinquish their claim to leadership. With authorities such as those cited throughout this book invited to those forums, it would be difficult to duck the issues. There would just be too many questions for which they must have reasonable answers. Those who presented a consistent and accurate view of reality, and promoted a policy for the maximum good of the maximum number of people, would gather a loyal following.

Most of the public would not watch these in depth discussions, but those who did would be gaining the knowledge of these experts. Interested people would be making value judgments on the history that led up to the present problems, the different solutions that were presented, and the intelligence and integrity of the leaders proposing these solutions. It is these people and their opinions that guide the thinking of the nation. These opinion makers (intellectuals, leaders, and the news media) must watch these information forums in order to inform themselves and, in turn, inform the public. To do less is to be uninformed and lose one's followers. With elections structured for the electors to prove their mettle—like the famous Lincoln-Douglas debates—the now-informed citizens would be enabled to make responsible voting decisions.

With every politician having direct access to the public, there is no need to spend private funds for elections. Most such money carries with it a price—it makes the recipient beholden to that supporter. There are no reasons such funds cannot be prohibited by law. If the channels of communication were open and the public conditioned to be distrustful of those who would spend large sums to be elected, the candidates themselves would avoid these attempts to buy elections. With the elections becoming commonsense debates of the issues, the advantage would be to those who are most knowledgeable and articulate.

Due to the structure of power, without a crisis few of the above reforms can become social policy. However, knowing they are possible, progressive citizens and politicians may insist on some reforms and power may eventually shift to permit reclaiming these rights.

It is possible that the dispossessed may yet gain control of adequate channels of communications to organize and gain power. New communications technology is being invented so fast and becoming so available that the monopolists are having a hard time controlling it all. Even now local TV stations could be almost as cheap as their radio counterparts. Low-power TV transmitters (LPTV) are available that can transmit up to fifteen miles and as of 1989 there were over five hundred licensed in the United States. The government pays about 75 percent of the roughly ninety-thousand-dollar start-up costs for each station:[28]

> The FCC awarded the first 23 licenses for LPTV stations in September 1983 by drawing the names of applicants from the same plexiglass barrel used by Selective Service officials to pick draft registration numbers during the Vietnam War. One can only hope that the second drawing bodes better for activists than the first. Chances are that it will. Eight of the first 23 licenses went to minority firms. Both the lottery method and the sheer number of potential stations seem to favor greater access by radicals and reformers to LPTV than to standard TV, where the purchase price of a station in a major metropolitan area can run into tens of millions of dollars. Low-power television should increase access to the airwaves by minorities, women, left activists, environmentalists, workers, and other elements of the broad, loose coalition of the disenfranchised that has, of necessity, invented alternative media.[29]

Such stations should be established with bylaws limiting them to ownership and control by the community. If not, whenever they develop an audience monopolists will offer such a high price that few would ever survive to provide alternative information to the nation.

This is happening to radio today. Corporations have discovered they can target specialty markets with radio ads and, as the profits climb, the price of radio stations has soared. There are no more channels available and, once the charges climb high enough, the low income groups will again become dispossessed of the opportunity for cheap communication:

> Doing without information is tantamount to being excluded from the democratic process. Still it is this principle that now is being introduced across the informational spectrum—from pay TV, to 'deregulated' telephone services, to charges for on-line data bank services, to the disappearance of modestly priced government and academic information. . . . The *kind and character* of the information that will be sought, produced and disseminated will be determined, if the market criteria prevail, by the most powerful bidders in the information market place—the conglomerates and the transnational companies. . . . [In this process] Americans are forever being congratulated by their leaders for being the beneficiaries of the most technologically advanced, complex, expensive, and adaptable communications facilities and processes in the world. This notwithstanding, and this is the paradox, people in the United States may be amongst the globe's least knowledgeable in comprehending the sentiments and changes of recent decades in the international arena. Despite thousands of daily newspapers, hundreds of magazines, innumerable television channels, omnipresent radio, and instantaneous information delivery systems, Americans are sealed off surprisingly well from divergent outside (or even domestic) opinion. . . . There is a demonstrable inability to recognize, but much less empathize with, a huge have-not world.[30]

As the laws controlling the communications media are now structured, the rights of corporations to decide the nation's future are firmly in place. We can only hope that communication becomes just like the windmill, steam engine, and electricity. It will be so cheap that the monopolists will lose their control. It is then that the dispossessed may be heard and reclaim their full rights.

As seen in the three previous chapters, it is bidding for control of land, capital, and finance capital that monopolizes these wealth-producing segments of the economy. It is this same *sale to the highest bidder* that monopolizes information. Control of information controls people (albeit without their realization), which protects these monopolies. This process ensures that the distribution of wealth will remain in the same channels among approximately the same people. Wealth will circulate among a predetermined group as they each intercept a part of social production. This, of course, is the pattern of excessive claims of property and the reclaiming of a share through waste distribution territories I have been describing. Lacking power or information (information is power), the world's dispossessed are forever excluded.

# 5

# Conclusion

Societies have made great progress in extending rights to all people. With our cherished rights and the efficiencies of technology we have become very rich even as we waste at least 60 percent of our labor, 50 percent of our industrial capital, and possibly 40 percent of our resources.

This waste distribution evolved under the realities of past power structures, their ideologies, and the inertia of customs locking society into a production/distribution system. A key stage in reforming older power structures into the current ones was the historic mobilization of finance capital through unrestricted private ownership of land; this concentrated capital.* But we are now overcapitalized and, even though we have most of our rights, those excessive rights of private property are embedded in our laws. Though there are restrictions imposed after exposures of excesses, these superior rights are continually being updated and reinforced through the law-making process. Witness the steady erosion of banking reforms and the takeover of the publicly financed innovation of satellite communications. The above along with the unnecessary labor in insurance, law, the health care industry, and all other waste distribution territories carefully code their rights to intercept social wealth through structuring these excessive rights in law. One has only to note that every *landmark* law or Supreme Court decision that extends rights to more people becomes the law of the land as proof that previously some of the people did not have all their rights. I have been outlining some very important economic rights that we do not yet have.

During the Industrial Revolution, the holders of wealth became more numerous than before that gaining of those cherished rights enshrined in our Constitution. But the well-to-do were still a small percent of the population and our economic rights were not a reality for the majority of the people until after the Great Depression. It was then that middle class America claimed its share. Even some from both the middle and bottom strata of society became wealthy. The gain in wealth paralleled the gain in rights.

However, even as we waste half our potential, one-third of American children grow up in poverty. The problems of production have been solved; it is the

---

* An early society that gave equal rights to all its citizens might have consumed most production and never built capital. Also, without a model to copy from, only by philosophy and trial and error can societies evolve.

problems of distribution that have yet to be mastered. Academics are still debating on how to produce when they would do well to study seriously on how to distribute. The model to study is the true efficiencies and productive capacity of industrial technology, how it is being wasted in the frenzied competition for economic territory (especially international trade), and how quickly the world could become industrialized if this waste were eliminated and that energy turned to those goals. Of course, a workable hypothesis threatens entrenched powers and is outside the permitted parameters of debate.

The enormous waste that I have outlined, created even as we became wealthy, was possible because modern technology is far more productive than we ever realize. Measured by how many consumer goods our industrial capital could have been producing, if built and used only for that purpose, we could be at least twice as wealthy; the production could be halved without any loss of food, fiber, shelter, or recreation; or this excess capacity could be used to capitalize the Third World in a few short years. However, we feel so proud of so much more wealth spread to so many more people, and are struggling so hard to survive within this complicated system of distribution by waste, that we are unaware that half our labors are wasted.

Considering its productive potential, our economy is at present gridlocked by unnecessary labor and capital that have a claim on production but do not produce anything useful in return. In the past, this was partially broken by depressions. It may be that enough rights (Social Security, unemployment benefits, farm supports, and the like) have been gained that these waste distribution territories will circulate the money and the economy will limp along without collapsing. This is doubtful. There is unprecedented debt, both foreign and domestic, and the war economy that has been distributing much of this wealth is being brought into question.Though there may no longer be any danger of a run on the banks by the public, there is danger of a run from the top. Instead of using depositors' funds directly for loans, major banks bid for this money and collect it in blocks (called managed liabilities) which are then reloaned throughout the system. If ever a major problem developed these funds would be immediately recalled by the managers of those funds and this process would rip through the world's financial markets in a matter of hours.[1]

Disaster can be averted by reclaiming our economic rights: the right to work productively with land and capital for one's rightful share of our production. Other societies should also have that right and can only obtain it with productive capital and control of their own land and resources. Producing the tools to capitalize the Third World would replace weapons of destruction as a distribution mechanism while we restructure to an efficient society. None of this can occur on a large scale until enlightened people break through the communications monopoly and power shifts from the controllers of wealth to those with progressive thoughts. Normally this only happens under crisis conditions.

Over time, every social system develops customary channels of production and distribution. Even small changes in those production/distribution channels create havoc for some citizens. Those feeling insecure about such changes are not only those who intercept the nation's income through monopolization but those who reclaim their share through equally unnecessary labor—these waste distribution territories. Everybody's income flows through these interconnected economic channels.

However, past systems such as slavery and feudalism were also methods of distributing social production. The change from any of these methods of distribution also caused enormous upheavals. Conscientious leaders of the time foresaw the short-term damage to the people and were very hesitant to change, but looking at the benefits today no one would say the changes should not have taken place. The same holds true if our economic rights are ever reclaimed—no one will want to return to the past. Besides, we now have most of our rights and the necessary changes to reclaim the last of our rights are not radical like those that reclaimed our well-recognized current rights. In fact those last rights are already inferred in the Constitution and can be reclaimed under that Constitution.

Unbending ideology prevents experiments in different social structures. This is especially unfortunate because societies are social production machines and experimenting with different methods of producing and distributing can be just as productive as experiments that produce other inventions. In either capitalist or communist societies, only by each sharing fully productive and fully paid jobs can unnecessary jobs be eliminated and incentives to produce maintained.

An economy can reach its maximum efficiency only if the job of each individual is fully productive. The universal belief that our present jobs are productive prevents honest analysis, the development of alternative social policies, or any experiments with different social structures. Tragically, the preservation of the status quo through ideological control, as outlined in Book Two, chapter five, and the introduction to this third book, locks out all feasible alternatives. This is especially distressing because time and resources are limited. If through a system of monopolization and distribution by waste we exhaust the world's cheap fuel, minerals, and other resources, it will not be possible for the Third World ever to become capitalized. In our society, the elimination of the monopolization of land, capital, and finance capital and the sharing of productive jobs would allow production and distribution to soar while eliminating this waste. That increased productive potential should go to capitalizing the Third World while simultaneously restructuring American society to a relaxed lifestyle.

The Soviet command economy worked well to build basic infrastructure and large industries. After World War II the consumer share of production was reduced to 52 percent as opposed to a normal of 80 percent for other countries during their industrialization. At great sacrifice, industrial capital was built from internal sources faster than ever before, in spite of the handicaps outlined in Book Two. However, once their basic capital was built, their command economy could not efficiently produce and distribute consumer goods. They must change (and are changing) to allow free market decisions for production and distribution. Most important, their citizens must be permitted to own capital and retain the profits from the gains in efficiency of free enterprise. Whereas in our society it would be difficult, it would be a simple matter for them to deed the land and capital to those working it and collect the land rent and interest.*

---

* The sale of the buildings, machinery, and other capital integral to that land on contract would be an ideal source for further investment capital, all paid for out of the increased efficiency of a market economy.

Those in agriculture are now being offered fifty-year leases (ownership within time parameters) but the greatest gains will be if and when commercial land is privately owned and society collects the land rent. The ownership of land and capital by those who produce would remove an enormous bureaucracy while increasing both consumer and state income.

Even under rules of privatized patents and capital it is possible to capitalize and integrate the rest of the world into the production/distribution system—witness Japan, Taiwan and South Korea. It only requires the decision of power brokers to do so. Once they are capitalized, if they decide to do so and retain enough freedom of action, the socialist bloc can divert capital to the Third World. If this is done with sincerity (i.e., the Third World owns this capital) we must respond likewise. Likewise, if we decide with sincerity to capitalize the dispossessed, the socialist bloc must respond with their effort. Failure to do so is to relinquish one's claim to being the better and more moral society. There is also the possibility that the two centers of capital will merge and together plunder the Third World through monopolization of technology and industry. Given the ideology of each, competition is the more likely scenario. Of course there is also the possibility that socialism will be overwhelmed. If that should happen there would be no incentive to share capital and woe to the world's dispossessed, including those within the industrialized countries.

The heart and sinews of capitalism have been the capital concentrated from the monopolization of land, capital, and finance capital. Control of this concentrated finance capital allowed alert and energetic people to build more real capital and produce for more people. However, now that we are 100-percent over-capitalized only a small share of land rent, monopoly interest, and interest on fictitious capital is used for that purpose. It now operates like a huge sponge sucking up the surplus production of others' labor, which is then consumed in the living standards of upper and middle class Americans or wasted in the many claims to social production through unnecessary labor. This monopolization needs to be eliminated so that every innovative producer has access to capital and markets and retains the fruits of their labors.

We give excessive rights to property and are paranoid of any infringement on those rights. The Soviet paranoia is opposite ours. In their ostensibly egalitarian society, a large gain in wealth from the ownership of productive capital appears unjust. Whenever a cooperative succeeds under the free enterprise rules of *glasnost* and *perestroika,* their philosophy causes them instinctively to restrict that freedom and appropriate the profits. This does not permit the accumulation of capital by talented, creative, and hardworking people so they can produce even more with that land, capital, talent, and energy. Only by being allowed to retain the profits from their efforts will they be motivated to be productive. Once that is allowed, the successes of these entrepreneurs would be quickly duplicated by others, and competition would increase production. As still others figured out still more efficient methods of production and distribution, commerce would soar. To create an efficient society, both systems are faced with uprooting an entrenched system of production and distribution.

The economic religions of capitalism and communism were each right for their moment in time—capitalism to bypass the then-current power structure and accumulate capital, and communism to catch up with capitalism's example. Just as Joseph Campbell, the great student of the world's myths, recognized, religions are essential to all mankind and those that are successful are right for that moment in time to guide a society. But in step with changing technology reality changes fast and religions only slowly or not at all.*

Technology is so productive that distribution is no longer efficient under the old system of rights. Our economic religions, right for their moment in time, must change to the reality of these times.

If either society is to become truly efficient, the U.S. must give more rights to labor and the Soviets more rights to capital.** Each society could eventually be not that much different. Either can function well to the left or right of this model, but that will create waste or inefficiency that can only be a loss to the world. Of course, as each moves towards that central position they will claim it as being within their ideology and each will also point to the other's change as moving towards their ideology. Under the pressure of crisis, each compromise with reality moves both societies towards that central position. If under the continuing pressure the socialist centers of capital collapse, capitalism will be home free and will not have to compromise any further. Of course, the reverse is true. If communism had overwhelmed the world quickly no one could have told them they did not have the full answer and, not being under threat, they would not have had to change.

In most societies it is normal that wealth accrue to the powerful. It matters little if a society is ruled by religious, military, or political powers. Witness the wealth of the Egyptians—all surplus labor went to build a shrine for the leaders. Aristocracy in its heyday claimed all surplus production and today those who are politically powerful are normally soon wealthy and those wealthy pay much attention to politics through their lobbies in the legislatures.

Those who have a reasonable share of American's income point to it as proof they are productive when most was really gained through monopolization of land, capital, and finance capital or by unnecessary labor. Those same fingers point to others' poverty as proof that they cannot or will not produce when it is only that they do not have rights to land and capital through a *productive* fully paid job.

The income of many U.S. workers is high enough that they feel well satisfied and fiercely defend the ideology through which their security is obtained. The lower paid keep struggling and almost all point their finger at the lowest paid and welfare recipients as nonproducers. These impoverished people are embarrassed and discouraged. If, in their confusion, they rebel by drugs, theft, violence against others or against each other, or by violent protest, they are controlled by the justice/prison system. In short, most are well enough paid to keep them satisfied, many are discouraged and apathetic, and the others are controlled by violence. Almost none are aware that enough resources are wasted to give all a good living and simultaneously provide far more free time.

However, people are trained to be, and are, compassionate and just. If the monopoly of communications by the powerful is ever breached, and Americans

---

* This is roughly what Campbell said in a PBS series on his life hosted by Bill Moyers. He started studying at ten years of age when his father took him to a museum of Indian religious artifacts. He studied all his life and has many books on mythology that outline what he learned in his lifetime of study.

** This can only be done by abandoning the arms race and trade wars.

become informed of this wasted labor, capital, and resources, they and the rest of the world will insist on changes. Once the population becomes aware, the old control by creation of an enemy will no longer work so easily. There are many good leaders in America and, with the power of the peddlers of crisis reduced, they could now surface with progressive ideas. That wasted capital, resources, and labor could be put to productive work.

American capital is now overbuilt; there should no longer be any need to claim the labors of others to concentrate capital through monopolization. Free enterprise and free markets are a theoretical cornerstone of our ideology and monopolization is a direct contradiction of that philosophy. The accumulation of wealth through those past rights of property, necessary in the early accumulation and mobilization of capital, is now counterproductive. Within the framework of the Constitution power brokers are continually strengthening their property rights: witness the steady expansion of the interception of wealth by the insurance industry, AT & T's legal appropriation of the wealth-producing potential of the satellite communications industry, and the steady expansion of other waste distribution territories within the economy. That monopoly power reaches down to all in middle class America who are able to claim a share of production without having produced an equal share. Within that same Constitution, these appropriated rights can be reclaimed.

That the powerful are claiming excessive rights is not visible because the enormous efficiency of technology permits a continued increase in living standards for most people even as most of this efficiency potential is wasted. That true potential is lost through wasted labor, capital, and resources—these waste distribution territories. To eliminate that waste the rights of property and the rights of labor must be rebalanced. To eliminate the waste and not rebalance those rights would leave roughly 60 percent of the people with no economic rights and the 40 percent working productively would have to share with them through direct support (welfare) or the economy would collapse. Of course, this cannot happen as the ridiculousness of the situation would be fully visible. The waste distribution territories through which production is currently claimed are just as ridiculous today but acceptable because they are invisible. With those rights rebalanced, society can be truly efficient just as the designers of the free enterprise system planned.

# Endnotes

## Book One

### Introduction

[1] "Change," *Railway Age*, Nov 1984, p. 34; during the six years it required to write this book the labor force dropped another thirty-five thousand. One hundred tons hauled one mile is one hundred ton-miles.

[2] Ralph Borsodi, *The Distribution Age* (New York: D. Appleton & Co., 1929), pp. 7–8.

[3] Lewis Mumford, *Pentagon of Power* (New York and London: Harcourt Brace and Jovanovich, 1964 and 1970), p. 152.

[4] Thorstein Veblen, *The Vested Interests* (New York: B. W. Huebesch Inc., 1919), p. 83.

[5] Bertrand Russell, *The Prospects of Industrial Civilization,* second edition (London: George Allen and Unwin Ltd., 1959), p. 40.

[6] Lewis Mumford, *Technics and Civilization,* paperback (New York and London: Harcourt Brace Jovanovich, 1963), p. 405.

[7] Stuart Chase, *The Tragedy of Waste* (New York: Macmillan Publishing Co., Inc., 1925), p. 270.

[8] Stuart Chase, *The Economy of Abundance* (New York: Macmillan and Company, 1934), p. 14.

[9] Olga Popkova interviewing Professor Nikolai Shmelyov, "Not By Money Alone," *New Times* 50:87, p. 19.

[10] Georges Lefebvre, *The Coming of The French Revolution,* translated by R. R. Palmer (Princeton, NJ: Princeton University Press, 1967); Olwen Hufton, *Europe: Privilege and Protest,* paperback (Ithaca, NY: Cornell University Press, 1980), pp. 299–347, espec. p. 347; Albert Soboul, *Understanding the French Revolution* (New York: International Publishers, 1988).

[11] Lefebvre, *French Revolution,* p. 156.

[12] Charles A. Beard, *An Economic Interpretation of the Constitution* (New York, Macmillan Publishing Co , Inc , 1913, 1935, 1941), pp. 154, 161–2. See also the earlier work of J. Allen Smith, *The Spirit of American Government,* 1907.

[13] Aric Press, "The Blessings of Liberty," *Newsweek,* 25 May 1987, p. 66.

[14] Ben Bagdikian, *Media Monopoly* (Boston: Beacon Press, 1983), p. 52. These were free family vacations.

[15] "The Logic of Stagnation," *Monthly Review,* October 1986, p. 7. (Introduction to Paul Sweezy and Harry Magdoff's forthcoming book, *Stagnation and the Financial Explosion.)*

## 1. Insurance

[1] Andrew Tobias, *The Invisible Bankers* (New York: The Linden Press/Simon and Schuster, 1982), p. 12.

[2] Tobias, *Invisible Bankers*, p. 72. Six categories listed return over 50 percent and ten pay under 50 percent; legal costs must yet be deducted.

[3] "Oasis," *Social Security Reference*, December 1983, pp. 16–17.

[4] Tobias, *Invisible Bankers*, p. 72.

[5] Tobias, *Invisible Bankers*, p. 72.

[6] Tobias, *Invisible Bankers*, p. 72.

[7] At present, Michigan, Minnesota, and New York have plans that approach pure no-fault and fourteen other states have modified no-fault laws. Jeffrey O'Connell, *The Lawsuit Lottery* (New York: The Free Press/Macmillan Publishing Co., Inc., 1979), pp. 158–61.

[8] O'Connell, *Lawsuit Lottery*, pp. 157–175.

[9] O'Connell, *Lawsuit Lottery*, pp. 157–175.

[10] O'Connell, *Lawsuit Lottery*, pp. 157–175.

[11] O'Connell, *Lawsuit Lottery*, p. 166.

[12] O'Connell, *Lawsuit Lottery*, p. 166.

[13] Walter S. Kenton, *How Life Insurance Companies Rob You* (New York: Random House, 1982), chap. 3.

[14] Ronald Kessler, *The Life Insurance Game* (New York: Holt, Rinehart and Winston, 1985), p. 1.

[15] Tobias, *Invisible Bankers*, p. 65.

[16] Kenton, *Insurance Companies*, p. 72.

[17] Kenton, *Insurance Companies*, p. 73.

[18] Kessler, *Life Insurance Game*, pp. 8–9.

[19] Michael Jacobson and Phillip Kasinitz, "Burning the Bronx for Profit," *The Nation*, 15 November 1986, p. 512.

[20] William M. Welch, "Insurance Bills Rock Officials," AP, *The Missoulian*, 19 August 1985, p. 10, col. 1; Walter Shapriro, Richard Sandza, Peter McKillop, Mark Miller, and Elisha Williams, "The Naked Cities," *Newsweek*, 26 August 1985, p. 22–3.

[21] Laramie and Natrona Counties in Wyoming, along with the cities of Laramie, Cheyenne, and Casper, and the Laramie County Community College, are looking into insuring themselves. Gregg Livovich, "Self-insurance Plans May be Delayed for at Least One Month," *Star Tribune*, Casper, Wyoming, 5 August 1985, p. A3. Sixteen counties in Washington state have formed a pool and more are considering joining. Kim Crompton, "Self-Insurance Lets the County Save $1 Million," *The Spokesman-Review*, 19 March 1989, p. C1, col. 3.

[22] Tobias, *Invisible Bankers*, p. 46.

[23] Tobias, *Invisible Bankers*, pp. 59, 72.

[24] Steve Shirley, "Lawyers' High Fees Push Work-comp Bills to the Edge," *The Missoulian*, 13 October 1986, p. 2, col. 3.

[25] Mark Reutter, "Workman's Compensation Doesn't Work or Compensate," *Business and Society*, Fall 1980, pp. 33–44, quoted by Michael Parenti in *Democracy for the Few*, fourth edition (New York: St. Martin's Press, 1983), p. 131. No doubt these figures are because most job-related illnesses are not counted as such.

[26] Edward J. Bergin and Ronald E. Grandon, *How to Survive in Your Toxic Environment*, paperback (New York: Avon Books, 1984), p. 130.

[27] Michael Isikoff, "Lawyers Gain From Defective-product Suits," *Washington Post*; reprinted in *The Missoulian*, 1 September 1985, p. 2, col. 2–5.

[28] *Nightly Business Report*, 3 November 1986.

[29] Tobias, *Invisible Bankers*, p. 72, and the *Nightly Business Report*, 3 November 1986.

[30] "16,000 Died and 8,000 Were Born without Arms and Legs." *Multinational Monitor*, August 1984.

[31] *CNN News*, 22 January 1986.

[32] Ivan Illich, *Medical Nemesis,* Bantam edition. (New York: Bantam Books, 1979), p.23.

[33] Speech by Ralph Nader at the University of Missoula reported on *KPAX News,* Missoula, Montana, 29 January 1987.

[34] James H. Rubin, "Chief Justice Says Legal System 'Painful, Inefficient'," AP, *The Missoulian,* 13 February 1986, p. 6, col. 1–4.

[35] Tobias, *Invisible Bankers,* p. 50.

[36] Tobias, *Invisible Bankers,* p. 48.

[37] Robert Goodman, *The Last Entrepreneurs,* paperback (Boston: South End Press, 1982), p. 196.

[38] Tobias, *Invisible Bankers,* pp. 35, 36; Kenton, *Insurance Companies,* p. 74.

[39] *CNN News,* 5 August 1988; Bill Zimmerman, "$60 Million War in California," *The Nation,* 7 November 1988, pp. 449–51.

## 2. Law

[1] Grant Gilmore, *The Age of American Law,* quoted by Jerold S. Auerbach in *Justice Without Law* (New York: Oxford University Press, 1983), p. 13.

[2] Fred Rodell, *Woe Unto You Lawyers* (Littleton, CO: Fred B. Rothman & Co., 1987), p. 7.

[3] Auerbach, *Justice Without Law,* p. 9.

[4] Rodell, *Woe,* pp. 7–8,16.

[5] Rodell, *Woe,* pp. 16–17.

[6] John Stromnes, "Denman's First Law: Be Your Own Attorney," *The Missoulian,* 24 April 1984, p. 9, col. 3.

[7] Norman F. Dacey, *How to Avoid Probate,* updated (New York: Crown Publishers, Inc., 1980), p. 15.

[8] Dacey, *Avoid Probate,* p. 15.

[9] Quoted by Dacey, *Avoid Probate,* p. 24.

[10] Quoted by Dacey, *Avoid Probate,* p. 5.

[11] Dacey, *Avoid Probate,* pp. 16–17.

[12] Dacey, *How to Avoid Probate.*

[13] Katherine J. Lee, "Justice Has Broken Down," *Americans For Legal Reform* 4:2, 1985, p. 5; and other issues of *ALR.*

[14] Richard Hebert, "Rosemary Freed," *Americans for Legal Reform* 5:2, 1985, p. 10.

[15] Jan Nordheimer, "Rosemary's Baby Has Nation's Lawyers Worried," *New York Times,* reprinted in *The Spokesman-Review,* 13 August 1984, p. 3, col. 1–6.

[16] Rodell, *Woe,* p. 10, 19, 171. See also Karen E. Klein, "Party of the First Part Favors Plain Talk," *Los Angeles Daily News,* quoted in *The Spokesman-Review,* 6 February 1988, p. A1, col. 2–5.

[17] Rodell, *Woe,* p. 130.

[18] Rubin, "Chief Justice Says Legal System 'Painful, Inefficient'."

[19] George Milko, "It's Hassle Free Down Under," *Americans for Legal Reform* 6:3, 1986, p. 3.

[20] Auerbach, *Justice Without Law,* preface.

[21] Elizabeth J. Koopman, E. Joan Hunt, and Virginia Stafford, "Child-related Agreements in Mediated and Non-mediated Divorce Settlements: A Preliminary Examination and Discussion of Implications," *Conciliation Court Review* 22:1, June 1984, p. 20.

[22] Dacey, *Avoid Probate,* p. 7.

[23] John A. Jenkins, "Corporations Find 'Minitrials' Nice Way to Kiss and Make Up," *Americans for Legal Reform* 5:1, 1984, p. 18.

[24] Lawrence J. Tell and Paul Angiolillo, "From Jury Selection to Verdict—In Hours," *Business Week,* 7 September 1987, p. 48.

[25] Dacey, *Avoid Probate,* p. 9.

[26] "Tomorrow," *U.S. News and World Report,* 23 September 1985, p. 14.

[27] *CBS News,* 12 Feb 1984.

## 3. Transportation

[1] Paul A. Baron and Paul M. Sweezy, *Monopoly Capital,* paperback (London: Monthly Review Press, 1968), pp. 135–7; derived from *The Journal of Political Economy,* October 1962, and *The American Economic Review,* May 1962.

[2] "Autos: Engine of the Future?," *Newsweek,* 11 November 1974, pp. 103–6.

[3] Jan P. Norbye and Jim Dunne, "Honda's New CVCC Car Engine Meets '75 Emissions Standards Now," *Popular Science,* April 1973, p. 79–81; Jim Dunne, "Stratified Charge: Is This the Way Detroit Will Go," *Popular Science,* July 1975, p. 56–8, 124–5.

[4] Information provided by a Michelin tire dealer in Missoula, Montana, who had been employed by the Firestone Tire Co. in those years.

[5] Seymour Melman, *Profits Without Production* (New York: Alfred A. Knopf, 1983), p. 115.

[6] Insurance Institute for Highway Safety report, "Highway Death Rate Cut in Half," *The Missoulian,* 13 September 1986, p. 8, col. 1–3.

[7] National Highway Traffic Safety Administration, *Spokane Chronicle,* 17 December 1987, p. A1. This was further confirmed in their 1988 year-end report.

[8] "Million Mile Bug," *The Missoulian,* 15 July 1987, p. 2.

[9] *CBS News,* 9 March 1987.

[10] Tom Icantalupo, "Average Car in 1995 Could Cost $13,800," *Newsday,* reprinted in *The Missoulian,* 12 March 1987, p. B4, col. 1.

[11] The classics on this subject are *Robber Barons* by Mathew Josephson; *To Hell in a Day Coach* by Peter Lyon; and *The History of the Grange Movement* by Edward Winslow Martin.

[12] Peter Lyon, *To Hell in a Day Coach* (New York: J. B. Lippincott, 1968), p. 8. As those statistics are twenty years old the labor savings are much greater today.

[13] Chase, *Tragedy of Waste,* pp. 226–7.

[14] Brian Dumaine, "Turbulence Hits the Air Carriers," *Fortune,* 21 July 1986, p. 101.

[15] Eugene Linden, "Frederick W. Smith of Federal Express: He Didn't Get There Overnight," *Inc.,* April 1984, p. 89; *60 Minutes,* CBS, 6 June 1984.

[16] *ABC News,* 28 October 1986.

[17] Paul Stephen Dempsey, from the University of Denver's College of Law, "Fear of Flying Frequently," *Newsweek,* 5 October 1987, p. 12.

[18] Mumford, *Technics and Civilization,* p. 272.

[19] Marty Jezer, *The Dark Ages* (Boston: South End Press, 1982), pp. 139–40; Lyon, *Day Coach,* pp. 7–8.

[20] David Morris, *Self-Reliant Cities* (San Francisco: Sierra Club Books, 1982), pp. 21–2; Parenti, *Democracy for the Few,* pp. 124–5; Kirkpatrick Sale, *Human Scale,* paperback (New York: G. P. Putnam and Sons, 1982), p. 252; Jezer, pp. 138–44; Edward Boorstein, *What's Ahead? . . . The U.S. Economy* (New York: International Publishers, 1984), pp. 71–2.

[21] Sale, *Human Scale,* p. 253.

[22] *Statistical Abstract of the United States,* 1986, p. 405.

[23] *Statistical Abstract of the United States,* 1986, p. 405. This is conservative. Carl Icahn took over Transworld Airlines and reduced labor costs by $350 to $400 million per year.

## 4. Agriculture

[1] Frances Moore Lappé and Joseph Collins, *Food First: Beyond the Myth of Scarcity,* revised and updated (New York: Ballantine Books, 1979,) p. 486; Susan George, *Ill Fares the Land* (Washington, D.C.: Institute for Policy Studies, 1984), pp. 8–9; Susan George, *How the Other Half Dies* (Montclair, NJ: Allen Osmun and Co., 1977), p. 36; David Goodman, "Political Spy Trial in Pretoria," *In These Times,* 19–25 September 1984; "The Buffalo Battalion—South Africa's Black Mercenaries," *Covert Action Bulletin* 13, July–August 1981, p. 16; "Hunger as a Weapon," *Food First Action Alert,* undated.

[2] Susan George, *How the Other Half Dies*, p. 36.

[3] Lappé and Collins, *Food First*, p. 20.

[4] Lappé and Collins, *Food First*, pp. 14–19, 48.

[5] Richard Barnet, *The Lean Years* (New York: Simon and Schuster, 1980), p. 153.

[6] Lappé and Collins, *Food First*, pp. 42, 71.

[7] Lappé and Collins, *Food First*, pp. 238–9, 289.

[8] James Wessel and Mort Hartman, *Trading the Future* (San Francisco: Institute for Food and Policy Development, 1983), p. 4.

[9] *ABC News*, 27 June 1986.

[10] Lappé and Collins, *Food First*, p. 27.

[11] *Statistical Abstract of the United States*, 1985, charts 1136 and 1160, for the year 1983.

[12] Lappé and Collins, *Food First*, p. 46; "The Plowboy Interview," *The Mother Earth News*, March/April 1982, pp. 17–18.

[13] Frances Moore Lappé, *Diet for a Small Planet*, revised edition, paperback (New York: Ballantine Books, 1978), pp. 66–7.

[14] Lappé, *Diet*, pp. 7, 17–18. Ranchers will claim seven to nine pounds but that is for live weight and Lappé's is for dressed weight; Lappé's calculation is conservative. Prime-fed cattle have 63 percent more fat than standard grade, and much of it is either trimmed off, cooked away, or left on the plate. Even the fat that is eaten is usually not wanted, so the true usable meat produced requires much more than sixteen pounds of grain.

[15] Lappé, *Diet*, pp. 7–10, 40. Poultry and hogs are not ruminants and convert grain to meat two to three times more efficiently.

[16] Lappé, *Diet*, p. 10.

[17] Lappé, *Diet*, p. 17.

[18] "Low Cholesterol Beef Produced on State Ranches," AP, *The Missoulian*, 15 October 1986, p. 18, col. 1.

[19] Lappé, *Diet*, pp. 17–18.

[20] Wessel and Hartman, *Trading the Future*, p. 158; Sale, *Human Scale*, p. 244.

[21] Barnet, *Lean Years*, p. 151; George, *Ill Fares the Land*, p. 48.

[22] Annual report of the Department of Health and Human Services, "American Life Today: Longer and Healthier," AP, *The Missoulian*, 23 March 1985, p. 3, col. 4; *1987 Heart Facts*, American Heart Association; Don Kendall, "Meat-Eaters Consuming Less Fat," AP, *The Missoulian*, 4 February 1987, p. 18, col. 1.

[23] Barnet, *Lean Years*, p. 168.

[24] William H. McNeill, *The Pursuit of Power* (Chicago: University of Chicago Press, 1982), p. 6.

[25] Lappé, *Diet*, p. 47; Kevin Danaher, Phillip Berryman, and Medea Benjamin, *Help or Hindrance? United States Economic Aid in Central America* (San Francisco: Institute for Food and Development Policy, 1987), pp. 3–4, 72; see also Jon Bennet, *The Hunger Machine* (Cambridge, England: Polity Press, 1987).

[26] Frances Moore Lappé, Joseph Collins, and David Kinley, *Aid as an Obstacle—Twenty Questions About Our Foreign Aid and the Hungry* (San Francisco: Institute for Food and Development Policy, 1980), pp. 93–102, 107–10; Frances Moore Lappé, Rachel Schurman, and Kevin Danaher, *Betraying the National Interest* (New York: Grove Press Inc., 1987), chap. 4; Danaher, Berryman, and Benjamin, *Help or Hindrance?* pp. 3–4, 72; see also Jon Bennet, *The Hunger Machine*. Cheap American grain destroyed the traditional Russian grain market and diverted that wealth to the United States. This permitted us to buy industrial tools and thus we became wealthy and they stayed poor.

[27] Harlan C. Clifford, "Exploiting a Link Between Farm Debt and Soil Erosion to Aid U.S. Farmers," *Christian Science Monitor*, 31 July, 15 August, and 5 September 1984; Clifford, "My Turn," *Newsweek*, 4 June 1984; Wessel and Hartman, *Trading the Future*, pp. 128–9.

[28] Clifford, "Exploiting a Link," *Christian Science Monitor,* 5 September 1984, pp. 16–17.

[29] Estimate based on the *Western Livestock Marketing Information Project,* table 6.506, and *Statistical Abstract of the United States* 1985, chart 1188.

## 5. The Health Care Industry

[1] *60 Minutes,* CBS, 15 July 1985; "Health, Wealth and Competition," *U.S. News and World Report,* 10 November 1986, p. 59; Gregg Easterbrook, "The Revolution in Medicine," *Newsweek,* 6 December 1987, p. 74.

[2] Tom Shealy, "The United States vs. the World: How We Score in Health," *Prevention,* May 1986, pp. 69–71.

[3] Vicente Navarro, "What Is Socialist Medicine," *Monthly Review,* July–August 1986, p. 64. Also see David U. Himmelstein, M.D., and Steffie Woolhandler, M.D., M.P.H., "Sounding Board: Cost Without Benefit: Administrative Waste in Health Care," *The New England Journal of Medicine,* 13 February 1986, pp. 441–5. Though their statistics are slightly different they describe "both the British and Canadian systems [as] immensely popular."

[4] "Nation's Health Bill Expected to Triple," *Washington Post,* reprinted in *The Missoulian,* 9 June 1987, p. 8, col. 1.

[5] Richard Bandler and John Grinder, *Frogs Into Princes,* paperback, (Moab, UT: Real People Press, 1979), p. 102.

[6] *The MacNeil/Lehrer Report,* 16 February 1989.

[7] *CBS News,* 20 June 1986.

[8] *Cultural Crisis of Modern Medicine,* John Ehrenreich, editor (New York: Monthly Review Press, 1978), pp. 4–5.

[9] *Sally Jesse Raphael Show,* 30 May 1988. Patient advocates Bill Johnson and Tom Wilson.

[10] Paul Raeburn quoting Steven Gustein, director of the nonprofit Houston Child Guidance Center, "Too Many Children Being Hospitalized for Psychiatric Problems," AP, *The Missoulian,* 2 October 1987, p. 19, col. 1–3.

[11] Nino Darnton, "Committed Youth," *Newsweek,* 31 July 1989.

[12] Easterbrook, "Revolution," pp. 43, 49.

[13] Easterbrook, "Revolution," pp. 43, 56.

[14] Sale, *Human Scale,* p. 267.

[15] "Unnecessary Operations Reported," *New York Daily News,* reprinted in *The Spokesman-Review,* 15 March. 1985, p. 6, col. 1–2. The carotid artery facts were from a Rand Corporation study published in the *New England Journal of Medicine* and aired on the *Today Show,* 25 March 1988.

[16] Sale, *Human Scale,* pp. 267–68; Gorz, *Ecology as Politics* (Boston: South End Press, 1980), p. 161.

[17] Andre Gorz, *Ecology as Politics,* p. 159. The authoritative book is *The Castrated Woman* by Naomi Miller Stokes. She points out that only a tiny fraction of the 750,000 operations performed each year are necessary and the problems created by depriving these women of those hormones are staggering.

[18] Matt Clark, "Still Too Many Caesareans?," *Newsweek,* 31 December 1984, p. 70.

[19] Barbara and John Ehrenreich, *The American Health Empire,* paperback (New York: Vintage Books, 1971), p. 17.

[20] *60 Minutes,* CBS, 7 May 1989.

[21] Harvey Wasserman, Norman Solomon, Robert Alvarez, and Eleanor Walters, *Killing Our Own,* paperback (New York: Dell Publishing Company, 1983), pp. 132–6.

[22] *60 Minutes,* CBS, 23 March 1986; Stanley Wohl, M.D., *The Medical–Industrial Complex* (New York: Harmony Books, 1984), pp. 56–7; *ABC News,* 13 May 1985.

[23] Parenti, *Democracy for the Few,* p. 127; taken from Bernard Winter, M.D., "Health Care: The Problem Is Profits," *Progressive,* October 1977, pp. 16, 27; Gorz, *Ecology as Politics,* p. 159.

[24] Gorz, *Ecology as Politics,* p. 159.

[25] Gorz, *Ecology as Politics,* pp. 161, 167; Wohl, *Medical–Industrial Complex,* pp. 56–57; *ABC News,* 13 May 1985.

[26] John Braithwaite, *Corporate Crime in the Drug Industry* (London: Routledge & Kegan Paul, 1984), as quoted in the critique "Corporate Crime: The Underbelly of the Drug Industry," *Multinational Monitor,* August 1984, p. 21.

[27] Michael Parenti, *Inventing Reality* (New York: St. Martin's Press, 1986), p. 55.

[28] Michael Unger, "Drugs for the Mentally Ill Can Ravage Body," *Washington Post,* reprinted in *The Missoulian,* 17 July 1985, p. 8, col. 1.

[29] Samuel Epstein, M.D., *The Politics of Cancer* (San Francisco: Sierra Club Books, 1978), pp. 216–26.

[30] It was approved for use as a palliative for kidney cancer; doctors could prescribe it for any purpose. Amy Goodman, "The Case Against Depo-Provera," *Multinational Monitor,* February/March 1985, pp. 3–12.

[31] Illich, *Medical Nemesis,* p. 69.

[32] Marc Lappé, *Germs That Won't Die* (Garden City: Anchor Press/Doubleday, 1982), pp. 3–15, 21.

[33] Illich, *Medical Nemesis,* pp. 66–69; Gorz, *Ecology as Politics,* p. 167; Marc Lappé, *Germs,* pp. 3–15,21; Lesley Doyal, *The Political Economy Of Health,* paperback (Boston: South End Press, 1981), p. 192.

[34] Marc Lappé, *Germs,* p. 167.

[35] Marc Lappé, *Germs,* espec. pp. 161–71.

[36] *ABC News,* 19 July 1985.

[37] Donald Robinson, "The Great Pacemaker Scandal," *Reader's Digest,* October 1983, p. 107.

[38] Robinson, "Scandal," pp. 106–9; "Pacemakers Often Useless," AP, *The Spokesman-Review,* 30 May 1985, p. B6, col. 1.

[39] The conclusions of federal investigators. "Pacemakers Often Useless," p. B6, col. 1; Robinson, "Scandal," pp. 105–6.

[40] *Nova,* PBS, 18 February 1985.

[41] Jane Gross, "Desperate AIDS Patients Seeking Cure or Comfort," *New York Times,* reprinted in *The Spokesman-Review,* 15 May 1987, p. 37, col. 1–3; Charles W. Hunt, "AIDS and Capitalist Medicine," *Monthly Review,* January 1988, p. 17.

[42] Gorz, *Ecology as Politics,* p. 166–7.

[43] Doyal, *Political Economy of Health,* p. 192; Illich, *Medical Nemesis,* p. 66.

[44] "Health, Wealth and Competition," *U.S. News and World Report,* 14 November 1985, p. 59; "Same Drug, Higher Price," *Time,* 1 December 1986, p. 57.

[45] Easterbrook, "Revolution," p. 50.

[46] Wohl, *Medical–Industrial Complex,* pp. 69–71; Illich, *Medical Nemesis,* p. 245.

[47] "Four of 10 Hospital Stays Are Unneeded," AP, *The Missoulian,* 13 November 1986, p. 25, col. 1.

[48] Easterbrook, "Revolution," pp. 57, 62–63; statement on "everybody knows who the bad doctors are" is by Puyallup, Washington, surgeon Dr. Jacob Kornberg.

[49] Wohl, *Medical–Industrial Complex,* p. 45.

[50] Easterbrook, "Revolution," pp. 50, 71.

[51] Illich, *Medical Nemesis,* pp. 98–99.

[52] *60 Minutes,* CBS, 5 January 1986; Roland Do Ligny, "Voluntary Euthanasia Estimated at 5,000 Annually in the Netherlands," AP, *The Missoulian,* 8 April 1987, p. 18, col. 1.

[53] Brenda C. Coleman, "Competitive Hospitals Cost More, Study Says," AP, *The Missoulian,* 5 February 1988, p. 8, col. 1–4. Her information obtained from *The New York Journal of Medicine.*

[54] Easterbrook, "Revolution," p. 43.

[55] Wohl, *Medical–Industrial Complex,* p. 3. See also pp. 27, 46–59, 94–97, 179, and Doyal, *Political Economy of Health.*

[56] Wohl, *Medical–Industrial Complex,* p. 3.

[57] *ABC News,* 30 December 1986; by 1988 it dropped to 60 percent.

[58] Wohl, *Medical–Industrial Complex,* p. 4.

[59] Gorz, *Ecology as Politics,* pp. 161, 167; Wohl, *Medical–Industrial Complex,* pp. 56–57; *ABC News,* 13 May 1985.

[60] Peter Downs, "Your Money," *The Progressive,* January 1987, pp. 24–5; Wohl, *Medical–Industrial Complex,* pp. 7–9, 15, 28–32, 44, 49–53, 73.

[61] Downs, "Your Money," pp. 24–8; Senate hearing to outlaw the dumping of patients, reported on *CNN News,* 28 October 1985; *60 Minutes,* CBS, 17 March 1985 and 28 July 1985.

[62] Illich, *Medical Nemesis,* p. 23.

[63] Illich, *Medical Nemesis,* p. 23; Gorz, *Ecology as Politics,* p. 160.

[64] *20/20,* ABC, 11 December 1986.

[65] Joshua Hammer, "AIDS, Blood and Money," *Newsweek,* 23 January 1989, p. 43.

[66] Gorz, *Ecology as Politics,* p. 174–75.

[67] Gorz, *Ecology as Politics,* pp. 153–6; Ehrenreich and Ehrenreich, *American Health Empire,* p. 12.

[68] Gorz, *Ecology as Politics,* pp. 151–57, 182–83; *ABC News,* 12 March 1988.

[69] Easterbrook, "Revolution," p. 59.

[70] Gorz, *Ecology as Politics,* p. 169.

[71] *Vital Statistics of the U.S.,* 1981, vol. II, Mortality, part A, table 1–5, shows 75 percent, but degenerative disease is dropping rapidly with the interest in nutrition and exercise.

[72] Department of Health and Human Services, "American Life Today: Longer and Healthier," AP, *The Spokesman-Review,* 23 March 1985, p. 3, col. 3.

[73] *1987 Heart Facts,* American Heart Association.

[74] Easterbrook, "Revolution," p. 64–8.

[75] "Half of Children Avoid Tooth Decay," AP, *The Spokesman-Review,* 22 June 1988, p. A–1, col. 4.

[76] Tamara Strom, "Dentistry in the 80s: A Changing Mix of Services," *JADA* 116, May 1988, pp. 618–19.

[77] Strom, "Dentistry," p. 618.

[78] Gorz, *Ecology as Politics,* p. 151.

[79] Gorz, *Ecology as Politics,* pp. 166–7. Perhaps one of the best examples of simple as opposed to high-technology medicine would be the medical community's treatment of the most common cause of infant death in the world—dehydration from diarrhea. Over twenty years ago, scientists discovered that a simple water, salt, and sugar solution, costing almost nothing, was as effective as the standard practice of intravenous feeding of liquids costing hundreds of dollars. However, even though the mother could easily treat the child herself, intravenous treatment is still the choice of almost all physicians.

[80] Deng Shulin, "Leprosy on the Way Out," *China Reconstructs,* May 1986, p. 20.

[81] Quin Xinzhong, "How China Eliminated Venereal Disease," *China Reconstructs,* June 1985.

## 6. Poverty and Rights: The Struggle to Survive

[1] *60 Minutes,* CBS, 2 July 1986; 10,000 children—NBC News, 10 August 1987.

[2] Parenti, *Democracy for the Few,* pp. 33–5; "Kidneys Worth $13,000," AP, *The Spokesman-Review,* 4 November 1985, p. 1, col. 1.

[3] Barry Bluestone, "Deindustrialization and Unemployment in America," *New Perspectives on Unemployment,* Barbara A. P. Jones, editor (New Brunswick: Transaction Books, 1984), p. 32; citing the work of Dr. Brenner of John Hopkins University.

[4] William Greider, *Secrets of the Temple,* paperback (New York: Simon and Schuster, 1987), p. 458.

[5] *60 Minutes,* CBS, 20 July 1986; *ABC News,* 19 June 1987; "Tomorrow," *U.S. News and World Report,* 29 June 1987, p. 25.

[6] One of the three network evening news programs, 9 November 1987.

[7] *60 Minutes,* CBS, 27 March 1988.

[8] *Statistical Abstract of the United States,* 1985, charts 592–593.

[9] *Statistical Abstract of the United States,* 1985, p. 355, and other charts leading to that final $592.6-billion figure.

[10] Charles Murray, *Losing Ground* (New York: Basic Books, 1984), p. 68.

[11] Frances Fox Piven and Richard A. Cloward, *New Class War,* paperback (New York: Pantheon Books, 1982), p. 15.

[12] Eugene H. Methuin, quoting Charles Murray, "How Uncle Sam Robs the Poor," *Reader's Digest,* March 1985, p. 136. Although the math seems to support Murray, that seems high. However, that is the only figure I can find and is the one many conservatives use. I will use Murray's figures. If they prove to be wrong, it is only necessary to allow a part of the obviously much higher numbers of those intercepting wealth that are outlined in the conclusion of Book One and in Book Three. The waste from their labors is not included in my calculations.

[13] Milton and Rose Friedman, *Free to Choose,* paperback (New York: Avon Books, 1981), pp. 110–15; see p. 99 for Friedman's analysis of the poverty program that, though it was arrived at somewhat differently, came out stronger than my conservative figures. They calculated that if only that which was classed as welfare reached the poor and no earnings were included, the average family would have an income of twice the poverty level.

[14] Ben Bagdikian, *Media Monopoly,* updated and expanded, paperback (Boston: Beacon Press, 1987), p. 209.

[15] Victor Perlo, *Super Profits and Crisis,* paperback (New York: International Publishers, 1988), p. 169.

[16] Bertram Gross, "Rethinking Full Employment," *The Nation,* 17 January 1987, pp. 44–8; Stanley Aronowitz, "The Myth of Full Employment," *The Nation,* 8 March 1986, p. 135–7; Anna DeCormis, "Cooking the Books on Joblessness," *The Guardian,* 20 August 1986, p. 2; Bertram Gross, *Friendly Fascism,* paperback (Boston: South End Press, 1980), p. 145; Michael Harrington, *The New American Poverty,* paperback (New York: Penguin Books, 1984), pp. 68–71.

[17] DeCormis, "Cooking the Books on Joblessness," p. 2; Boorstein, *What's Ahead?,* p. 199.

[18] *The Week in Review,* PBS, 15 December 1983.

[19] *NBC News,* 16 December 1987; Dukakis election campaign speech 1988.

[20] Boorstein, *What's Ahead?,* p. 202.

[21] Robert Lacey, *Ford,* paperback (New York: Ballantine Books, 1986), p. 136.

## 7. Conclusion

[1] *The Public Power Directory and Statistics for 1983* (Washington, D.C.: American Public Power Association); Jeanie Kilmer, "Public Power Costs Less," *Public Power Magazine,* May/June 1985, pp. 28–31. The late Montana Senator Lee Metcalf and his executive secretary Vic Reinemer presented an in-depth study of this phenomenon in their aptly named book—*Overcharge* (New York: David McKay Company, Inc., 1967).

[2] *60 Minutes,* CBS, 2 May 1988; Craig Baker and Amy Dru Stanley, "Incarceration Inc.: The Downside of Private Prisons," *The Nation,* 15 June 1985, pp. 728–30; Konrad Edge, "Free Enterprise Behind Bars," *The Guardian,* 9 October 1985, p. 7; Loren Siegal, "Law Enforcement and Civil Liberties: We Can Have Both," *Civil Liberties,* February 1983, pp. 5–8; Russ Immarigeon, "Prison Bailout: Can Business Run a Better Slammer," *Dollars and Sense,* July/August 1987, pp. 19–21; William D. Marbach, William J. Cook, and David L. Shapiro, "Punishment Outside Prison Walls," *Newsweek,* 9 June 1986; Deborah Davis, "Prisons for Profits," *In These Times,* 17–30 August 1988, pp. 12–13, 22; "The Far Shores of America's Bulging Prisons," *U.S. News and World Report,* 14 November 1988.

[3] The classic on chemical pollution is Rachel Carson's *Silent Spring.* See also Lois Marie Gibbs, *Love Canal;* Jim Hightower, *Eat Your Heart Out;* Jonathan Lash, Katherine Gillman and David Sheridan, *A Season of Spoils;* David Wier and Mark Schapiro, *Circle of Poison;* William Longgood, *The Poisons in Your Food;* and Jonathan

Kwitney, *Vicious Circles.* The nuclear pollution is well explained by Harvey Wasserman, Norman Soloman, Robert Alverez, and Eleanor Walters, *Killing Our Own;* McKinley C. Olson, *Unacceptable Risks;* Dr. Helen Caldicott, *Nuclear Madness;* Jonathan Schell, *Fate of the Earth;* and Karen Dorn Steele, "Cleaning up Hanford: Who Will Pay the Bill," *The Spokesman-Review,* 28 August 1988.

[4] Gregg Easterbrook, "Cleaning Up," *Newsweek,* 24 July 1989, p. 37.

[5] Charles P. Alexander and Christopher Redman, "A Move to Ease Death's Sting," *Time,* 14 May 1984; "The Cost of Dying," *Consumer Research Magazine,* October 1983; Tom Post, "Growth Business: Death on the Installment Plan," *Fortune,* 30 April 1986.

[6] Seymour Melman, *The Permanent War Economy,* revised and updated, paperback (New York: Simon and Schuster, 1985), espec. p. 13. I specifically asked him what his estimation of unnecessary administrators was, and he answered that it was two-thirds.

[7] William Greider, *The Education of David Stockman and Other Americans,* paperback (New York: New American Library, 1986), p. 6; for a look at bureaucratic waste also check Mark Bisnow, "Congress: An Insider's Look at the Mess on Capitol Hill," *Newsweek,* 4 January 1988.

[8] Greider, *Stockman,* p. 17.

[9] "Snags in Working Part Time," *US News and World Report,* 28 July 1986, p. 24; *CBS News,* 19 June 1986; DeCormis, "Cooking the Books on Joblessness," p. 2.

[10] The Council on International and Public Affairs, a nonprofit research organization headquartered in New York, just came out with an analysis of the true percentage of unemployed as 15.8 percent ("In Short," *In These Times,* 10–16 February 1988, p. 4.) They include in their calculations part–time workers who want to work more. Our calculations assume all part–time workers would be fully employed under a proper sharing of jobs. As this thesis will show, it would likely require no increase in their working time but would mean a full-time paycheck. See also William Serrin, "Playing Down Unemployment," *The Nation,* 23 January 1989, pp. 73, 84–8.

[11] Perlo, *Super Profits and Crisis,* p. 74.

# Book Two

## Introduction

[1] Karl Polyani, *The Great Transformation,* paperback (Boston: Beacon Press, 1957), p. 277.

## 1. Trading Can Be Raiding

[1] Lewis Mumford, *Technics and Human Development,* paperback (New York: Harcourt Brace Jovanovich, 1967), p. 279.

[2] William H. McNeill, *The Pursuit of Power* (Chicago: University of Chicago Press, 1982), p. 6.

[3] Lloyd C. Gardner, *Safe for Democracy* (New York: Oxford University Press, 1984), espec. chap. 1. Gardner clearly points out that colonialism was only a method of controlling trade and wars are battles for that trade.

[4] Eric Williams, *From Columbus to Castro,* paperback (New York: Vintage Books, 1984), pp. 46–7.

[5] Dan Nadudere, *The Political Economy of Imperialism,* paperback (London: Zed Press, 1977), p. 86; see also pp. 35, 68. See Betsy Hartmann and James Boyce, *Needless Hunger,* revised edition (San Francisco: Institute for Food and Development Policy, 1982) for a graphic account of how this happened.

[6] Mumford, *Technics and Civilization,* pp. 184–5.

[7] Hartmann and Boyce, *Needless Hunger,* pp. 10, 12.

[8] Hartmann and Boyce, *Needless Hunger,* provide the story of this devastation.

[9] Michael Greenberg, *British Trade and the Opening of China 1800–1842,* paperback (New York: Monthly Review Press, reprint of 1951 edition), p. 104. Jack Beeching's *The Opium Wars* is another good book on the Boxer Rebellion.

[10] Beard, *Economic Interpretation,* p. 46.

[11] Beard, *Economic Interpretation,* pp. 46–7, 171, 173.

[12] Philip S. Foner, *From Colonial Times to the Founding of the American Federation of Labor* (New York: International Publishers, 1982), p. 32.

[13] Quoted by Herbert Aptheker, *The Colonial Era,* second edition (New York: International Publishers, 1966), p. 23–4.

[14] Barbara Tuchman, *The March of Folly* (New York: Alfred A. Knopf, 1984), pp. 130–31.

[15] Nadudere, *Political Economy,* p. 247. A further barrier to industrialization in Third World countries is their inability to achieve steady production. There is no market in their primitive economies.

[16] Russell, p. 193.

[17] Steven Schlosstein, *Trade War* (New York: Congdon & Weed, 1984), p. 55.

[18] Schlosstein, *Trade War,* p. 99.

[19] Schlosstein, *Trade War,* p. 13; see also p. 9.

[20] Schlosstein, *Trade War,* p. 9.

[21] Walter Russell Mead, *Mortal Splendor* (Boston: Houghton Mifflin Company, 1987), pp. 304, 306.

[22] The Max Planck Institute of Germany's analysis of the control of a Third World country's industrial and export policies. Barnet, *Lean Years* p. 246.

[23] Anthony Sampson, *The Money Lenders,* paperback (New York: Penguin Books Ltd., 1981), chap. 16, espec. p. 283.

[24] Jean Zeagler, *Switzerland Exposed,* paperback (New York: Allison & Busby, 1981), p. 35.

[25] The Columbia University Center for Law and Economic Studies treatise on monopolizing industrial capital: Oscar Schachter and Robert Hellawell, *Competition in International Business* (New York: Columbia University Press, 1981), p. 42; Douglas Greer's chapter, "Restrictive Business Practices Affecting Transfers of Technology."

[26] Schachter and Hellawell, *Competition,* pp. 106–20, 166.

[27] Schachter and Hellawell, *Competition,* pp. 5–6, 109.

[28] Jeff Faux, "The Austerity Trap and the Growth Alternative," *World Policy Journal* 5:3, Summer 1988.

[29] Don Kendall, "U.S. Farmers Look to the Third World," AP, *The Spokesman-Review,* p. B5, col. 1–4.

[30] Ruth Leger Sivard, *World Military and Social Expenditures* (Washington, D.C.: World Priorities, 1986), p. 5.

[31] *Adam Smith's Money,* PBS, 6 July 1986; see also Lawrence Malkin, *The National Debt* (New York: Henry Holt and Company, 1988), chap. 9.

[32] Howard M. Wachtel, "The Global Funny Money Game," *The Nation,* 26 December 1987, p. 786; Castro, *Nothing Can Stop the Course of History,* p. 68; Howard M. Wachtel, *The Politics of International Money* (Amsterdam: Trans National Institute, 1987) p. 42; Greider, *Temple,* p. 517.

[33] Malkin, *National Debt,* pp. 106–7; see also David Pauly, Rich Thomas and Judith Evans, "The Dirty Little Debt Secret," *Newsweek,* 17 April 1989.

[34] Nadudere, *Political Economy,* p. 219; Michael Moffitt, "Shocks, Deadlocks, and Scorched Earth," *World Policy Journal,* Fall 1987, p. 558.

[35] Quoted by Nadudere, *Political Economy,* p. 220.

[36] Castro, *Nothing Can Stop,* p. 69.

[37] *60 Minutes,* CBS, 20 April 1987; Bruce Rich, "Conservation Woes at the Bank," *The Nation,* 23 January 1989, pp. 73, 88–91.

[38] Sampson, *Money Lenders,* p. 152.

[39] Greider, *Secrets,* pp. 707, 581–82.

[40] Chinweiezu, "Debt Trap Peonage," *Monthly Review,* November 1985, pp. 21–36.

[41] Barnet, *Lean Years*, p. 288.

## 2. World Wars, Trade Wars

[1] Eli F. Heckscher, *Mercantilism* vol. 2, pp. 23–4; Gardner's account of modern wars demonstrates that wars are still over these resources and trade.

[2] Kurt Rudolf Mirow and Harry Maurer, *Webs of Power* (Boston: Houghton Mifflin Company, 1982), p. 16.

[3] Nazli Choucri and Robert C. North, *Nations in Conflict* (San Francisco: W. H. Freeman and Company, 1974), in part quoting other authors, pp. 58–59, 106–7. Again, read Gardner, *Safe for Democracy*.

[4] Gardner, *Safe for Democracy*, p. 98.

[5] Malkin, *National Debt*, p. 11; and Gardner, *Safe for Democracy*.

[6] George Seldes, *Never Tire of Protesting* (New York: Lyle Stuart, Inc., 1968), p. 45; Gardner, *Safe for Democracy*, chapters one and two, describes many of Wilson's concerns about world trade and war.

[7] William Appleman Williams, *The Tragedy of American Diplomacy*, revised (New York: W. W. Norton & Company, 1972); Williams' and Gardner's books outline how World Wars I and II were trade wars. See also Fritz Fisher, *Germany's Aims in the First World War* (New York: W. W. Norton & Company, 1967), pp. 38–49; Dwight E. Lee, *Europe's Crucial Years* (Hanover, NH: Clark University Press, 1974), pp. 1–18; D. F. Fleming, *The Cold War and its Origins* (New York: Doubleday & Company, 1961), p. 1084.

[8] Harry Magdoff and Paul M. Sweezy, *Stagnation and the Financial Explosion* (New York: Monthly Review Press, 1987) p. 167. Quotes are from H. Parker Willis and B. H. Beckhart's *Foreign Banking Systems,* and from J. B. Condliffe's *The Commerce of Nations.*

[9] D. J. Goodspeed, *The German Wars* (New York: Bonanza Books, 1985), pp. 267–8.

[10] Williams, *Tragedy*, pp. 128–9, 172–3; see also pp. 72–3, 134–5, 142. This is not a defense of Germany's motives or conduct in World War II. The supporters and goals of fascism represent the antithesis of this treatise. We would expand rights; they would restrict them.

[11] Williams, *Tragedy*, pp. 163–64.

[12] Walter Russell Mead, "American Economic Policy in the Antemillenial Era," *World Policy Journal,* Summer 1989, p. 422.

[13] An analysis of this, citing Japan's enormous dependence on U.S. technology, has been made by Nadudere, *Political Economy*, pp. 157–58, and by Jerry Sanders, "America in the Pacific Century," *World Policy Journal*, Winter 1988–89, pp. 47–80, espec. p. 52.

[14] Moffitt, "Shocks, Deadlocks," pp. 560–61, 572–3.

[15] *CBS News,* 13 October 1987.

[16] Lewis and Allison, *The Real World War* (New York: Coward, McCann & Geoghegan, 1982), pp. 161–2.

[17] Schlosstein, *Trade War,* p. 118.

[18] Schlosstein, *Trade War,* chap. 28.

[19] *NBC News,* 30 December 1987.

[20] Moffitt, "Shocks, Deadlocks," pp. 359–60.

[21] Walter Russell Mead, "After Hegemony," *New Perspective Quarterly,* quoted in "As Reagan Crumbles, Who Will Pick Up the Crumbs," *In These Times,* 28 October 1987, p. 14. We can trust this is accurate, as the 1980 Economic Report to the President put the loss from 1973 to 1980 at 8 percent; an editorial in *The Nation* (19 September 1988, p. 187) puts the loss at 16 percent in weekly income and 11 percent in hourly earnings.

[22] *Nightly Business Report,* PBS, 21 January 1986.

[23] "China Maneuvering Around Quotas to Market Textiles to United States," *The Spokesman-Review,* 10 January 1989, p. B6, col. 1–3.

[24] Daniel Cantor and Juliet Schor, *Tunnel Vision* (Boston: South End Press, 1987), p. 16.

[25] There were over 140 worldwide in 1987, increasing to approximately 160 in 1988; Harold Seneker, "The World's Billionaires," *Forbes,* 5 October 1987, p. 83; *Forbes,* 25 July 1988.

[26] Lester C. Thurow, *Generating Inequality,* paperback (New York: Basic Books, Inc., 1975), p. 14; "Worker's State," *The Nation,* 19 September 1988, p. 187–8.

[27] Wessel and Hartman, *Trading the Future,* pp. 169–77; Tim Shorrock, "Disappearing Act for the Economic Miracle," *Guardian,* 11 December 1985, p. 16.

[28] Frances Moore Lappé, Rachel Schurman, and Kevin Danaher, *Betraying the National Interest* (New York: Grove Press, 1987), p. 94.

[29] There are six largely family-owned international grain traders whose monopolistic practices are thoroughly examined in *The Merchants of Grain* by Dan Morgan; see also Wessel and Hartman, *Trading the Future,* p. 91.

[30] Shorrock, "Disappearing Act," p. 16, col. 2.

[31] Fidel Castro, *The World Economic and Social Crisis,* paperback (Havana, Cuba: State Publishing Office, 1983), p. 16.

[32] Barnet, *Lean Years,* p. 157.

[33] Barnet, *Alliance,* p. 394.

[34] Howard M. Wachtel, *Money Mandarins* (New York: Pantheon Books, 1986), pp. 5–6.

## 3. The Creation of Enemies

[1] James Burnes, *The Knights Templar,* second edition (London: Paybe and Foss, 1840), pp. 12–14.

[2] Charles G. Addison, *The Knights Templar* (London: Longman, Brown, Green, and Longman, 1842), pp. 194–203, espec. 203.

[3] Georges Lefebvre, *The Coming of the French Revolution,* R. R. Palmer, translator (Princeton, NJ: Princeton University Press, 1947). These rights were not yet extended to women or minorities.

[4] David Caute, *The Great Fear,* paperback (New York: Simon and Schuster, 1978), pp. 18–19; Arkon Daraul, *A History of Secret Societies* (Secaucus, NJ: Citadel Press, 1961); James and Suzanne Pool, *Who Financed Hitler* (New York: Dial Press 1978); and Heiko Oberman, *The Roots of Anti-Semitism* (Philadelphia: Fortress Press, 1984).

[5] Caute, *Great Fear,* pp. 18–19.

[6] For a fuller description of how this has happened throughout history read Caute, *Great Fear,* espec. pp. 18–19. There are many other sources on this phenomenon.

[7] Karl Polyani, *The Great Transformation,* paperback (Boston: Beacon Press, 1944), p. 238.

[8] F. L. Carsten, *Britain and the Weimar Republic* (New York: Schocken Books, 1984), espec. chap. 8; also Michael N. Dobbowski and Isodor Wallimann, *Radical Perspectives on the Rise of Fascism in Germany* (New York: Monthly Review Press 1989), espec. pp. 194–209.

[9] James and Suzanne Pool, *Who Financed Hitler,* p. 8.

[10] See Oberman, *The Roots of Anti-Semitism;* Caute, *Great Fear;* Daraul, *A History of Secret Societies.*

[11] Gardner, *Safe for Democracy,* pp. 197–8.

[12] Alexander Cockburn, "Beat the Devil," *The Nation,* 6 March 1989, p. 294. Lately whenever the subject comes up I notice words such as "had their lives damaged" by Stalinism. This is an entirely different thing. If "damaged lives" are the criterion then that damage must be compared with the damage other countries inflict on minorities within their own societies. An interesting appraisal of Stalinist terror is made by Soviet dissident Roy Medvedev, "Parallels Inappropriate," *New Times,* July 1989, pp. 46–7.

[13] Milton Mayer fled ahead of the Jewish Holocaust and returned to Germany after the war to find out how a population had been guided to commit mass murder. The ten Germans he became acquainted with and interviewed over a period of two years informed him they thought they were free. They were not being persecuted; it was those communists and Jews who were a threat. Mayer concluded it was all done with a cold

war identical to the one being waged in the U.S. ever since World War II. Mayer thus titled his book, *They Thought They Were Free.*

## 4. The Cold War

[1] Sidney Lens, *Permanent War* (New York: Schocken Books, 1987), p. 22.

[2] *NBC News,* 16 February 1987, discussed the twelve thousand troops from Washington and Michigan that went into the Soviet Union through Vladivostok. D. F. Fleming, *The Cold War,* p. 26, mentions the fifty-five hundred from Montana who landed at Archangel and Murmansk; D. F. Fleming, *The Cold War,* p. 1038.

[3] Kennedy, *The Rise and Fall of the Great Powers* (New York: Random House, 1987), p. 321.

[4] Vilnis Sipols, *The Road to Great Victory* (Moscow, USSR: Progress Publishers, 1985), pp. 109, 132, 179–80.

[5] Kennedy, *Rise and Fall,* p. 352, quoting J. Erickson, *The Road to Berlin* (London: 1983), p. 447.

[6] Jeffrey Jukes, *Stalingrad at the Turning Point* (New York: Ballantine Books, 1968), p. 154; the figure of eight hundred thousand Soviets killed was cited on *National Geographic TV,* 23 August 1987.

[7] Fleming, *Cold War,* p. 157.

[8] Fleming, *Cold War,* p. 252.

[9] Kennedy, *Rise and Fall,* pp. 357–58; last quote is from Greider, *The New Yorker,* 16 November 1987, p. 100 (Kennedy says 50 percent increase in yearly production but his statement of over 15 percent increase per year indicates Greider is correct). Oleg Rzheshevsky, *World War II: Myths and the Realities* (Moscow, USSR: Progress Publishers, 1984), p. 175.

[10] McNeill, *Pursuit of Power,* p. 366; Peter Pringle and William Arkin, *S.I.O.P.: The Secret U.S. Plan for Nuclear War* (New York: W. W. Norton & Company, 1983), pp. 52–3; Fleming, *Cold War,* p. 522, makes it clear that many scientists were warning that it would only be a short time till the Soviets had the bomb.

[11] Michio Kaku and Daniel Axelrod, *To Win a Nuclear War* (Boston: South End Press, 1987), p. x.

[12] For sincere scholars it is instructive to read Seldes, *Even the Gods,* p. 12. Before World War II the Pentagon was preparing contingency plans called Operation Musk-Ox to invade the Soviet Union via the Arctic Circle. Such a plan could only be considered harebrained to the extreme, except when considered in conjunction with other plans of other powers. These scholars should combine this knowledge with the books of Polyani, *The Great Transformation;* Caute, *The Great Fear;* Poole, *Who Financed Hitler;* Sanders, *Peddlers of Crisis;* Jim Garrison, *On the Trail of the Assassins* (New York: Sheridan Square Press, 1988); Christopher Simpson, *Blowback* (New York: Weidenfield & Nicolson, 1988); John Prados, *Presidents' Secret Wars* (New York: William Morrow and Company, 1986; I. F. Stone, *The Hidden History of the Korean War* (Boston: Little, Brown and Company, 1952); Allan A. Ryan, Jr., *Quiet Neighbors* (New York: Harcourt Brace Jovanovich, Publishers, 1984); John Loftus, *The Belarus Secret* (New York: Alfred A. Knopf, 1982); Thomas Bodenheimer and Robert Gould, *Roll Back* (Boston: South End Press, 1989).

[13] Pringle and Arkin, *S.I.O.P.,* p. 63; see also D. F. Fleming, *Cold War,* espec. p. 627.

[14] Kaku and Axelrod, *To Win,* pp. x–xi; see also Fleming, *Cold War,* espec. pp. 321, 391–415.

[15] McNeill, *Pursuit of Power,* p. 366.

[16] E. P. Thompson and Dan Smith, *Protest and Survive,* paperback (New York: Monthly Review Press, 1981), p. viii; Fred Kaplan, *The Wizards of Armageddon* (New York: Simon and Schuster, 1983), p. 99.

[17] Thompson and Smith, *Protest,* pp. viii, 123–7.

[18] David Wallechinsky and Irving Wallace, "Military Scrapbook," *The People's Almanac* (New York: Doubleday, 1975), p. 653.

[19] Jerry W. Sanders, *Peddlers of Crisis,* paperback (Boston: South End Press, 1983). Estimates have been made that there are at least fifty well-financed right-wing groups in Washington, D.C. See also Prados, *Presidents' Secret Wars,* and Stone, *The Hidden History of the Korean War.*

[20] Kaplan, pp. 275–77; Niel Sheehan, Hedrick Smith, E. W. Kenworthy, and Fox Butterfield, *The Pentagon Papers* (New York: Bantam Books, 1971).

[21] Thompson and Smith, *Protest,* p. viii.

[22] Thompson and Smith, *Protest,* p. 123.

[23] Robert C. Aldridge, *First Strike* (Boston: South End Press, 1983), p. 371.

[24] Thompson and Smith, *Protest,* p. 127.

[25] Thompson and Smith, *Protest,* p. viii.

[26] Kaku and Axelrod, *To Win,* pp. 209–10; the warhead totals were quoted in the 25 September 1988 presidential debate between Michael Dukakis and George Bush. The Soviets have developed solid-fueled intermediate-range missiles and are working to catch up on solid-fueled intercontinental missiles.

[27] Charles L. Mee, Jr., *The Marshall Plan* (New York: Simon and Schuster, 1948), p. 57. That the Soviets did not plan an aggressive foreign policy had already been proven by the earlier elimination of Trotsky and his supporters, who were advocating exporting Marxist revolution.

[28] Fleming, *Cold War,* pp. 49, 428, 788.

[29] John Lukacs, *A History of the Cold War,* paperback (Garden City, NY: Anchor Books, 1962), p. 105.

[30] Fleming, *Cold War,* pp. 49, 428, 788; test suspension, p. 913. In 1987 the Soviets canceled a suspension of over one year that we had ignored.

[31] Ye. Potyarkin and S. Kortunov, editors, *The USSR Proposes Disarmament: (1920–1980s)* (Moscow, USSR: Progress Publishers, 1986), espec. pp. 145–78.

[32] Dr. Mack explained this at the Institute for Media Analysis seminar 11–13 November 1988. This gives a little insight into why the American people are unaware of these peace overtures.

[33] Henry Trewhitt, Jeff Trimble, Robin Knight, and Robert Kaylor, "A Different Call to Arms," *U.S. News and World Report,* 13 March 1989, p. 25.

[34] *World Monitor,* 6 June 1989.

[35] These were a group of superhawks whose primary role has been directing U.S. policy towards imperialism. Kaku and Axelrod, *To Win,* p. 39; Richard J. Barnet, *The Alliance* (New York: Simon and Schuster, 1983), p. 130. The history of this right-wing think tank was written by Lawrence H. Shoup and William Minter, *Imperial Brain Trust* (New York: Monthly Review Press, 1977). Fleming credits Dulles with being one of the primary architects of the Cold War; see also Bodenheimer and Gould, *Roll Back;* Prados, *Presidents' Secret Wars;* Stone, *The Hidden History of the Korean War;* and Garrison, *On the Trail of the Assassins.*

[36] Barnet, *Alliance,* p. 130.

[37] Kaku and Axelrod, *To Win,* p. 105; for further information on Dulles's contributions to Cold War hysteria read Fleming, *Cold War,* pp. 791, 931–2, 943, 969–70, 983–4, 987–8, and Louis L. Gerson, *John Foster Dulles* (New York: Cooper Square Publishers, Inc., 1967).

[38] Fleming, *Cold War,* p. 488.

[39] Due to the activities of such as the Committee on the Present Danger, Americans widely believed that the Soviets were undertaking an enormous military buildup even when CIA studies showed that Soviet arms expenditures had not increased. Konrad Edge, "CIA Figures on Soviet Spending Undercut Reagan's Claims," *The Guardian,* 13 March 1985, p. 3; John B. Judis, "CIA: No Big Soviet Arms Boost in 70s," *In These Times,* 7–13 December 1983, p. 3; Sivard, *World Military and Social Expenditures,* p. 9.

[40] John Loftus, *The Belarus Secret;* Christopher Simpson, *Blowback,* espec. p. 55; Allen A. Ryan, Jr., *Quiet Neighbors.*

[41] Richard D. Mahoney, *JFK: Ordeal in Africa* (New York: Oxford University Press, 1983). For one very persuasive view that supports this analysis of a minority right wing in charge of American policy and why Kennedy was killed read Garrison, *On the Trail of the Assassins.*

[42] Good sources on the subject are *Media Monopoly* by Ben Bagdikian; *Even the Gods Can't Change History* by George Seldes; *Manufacturing Consent: The Political Economy of the Mass Media* by Edward S. Herman and Noam Chomsky; and Stone, *The Hidden History of the Korean War.*

## 5. Those Peddlers of Crisis: The Arms Manufacturers

[1] Fleming, *Cold War,* p. 854–5.

[2] Anthony Sampson, *Arms Bazaar,* paperback (New York: Bantam Books, 1978), p. 90.

[3] Sampson, *Bazaar,* p. 189.

[4] Sampson, *Bazaar,* chapters 1-4. For an account of the creative accounting that is now standard practice in weapons procurement, see Seymour Melman, *The Permanent War Economy,* second edition, revised and updated (New York: Simon and Shuster, 1985), chap. 2.

[5] Sampson, *Bazaar,* pp. 70–71.

[6] Sampson, *Bazaar,* 76.

[7] Sampson, *Bazaar,* p. 103; Melman, *War Economy,* p. 158.

[8] Mumford, *Technics and Civilization,* p. 165.

[9] Sampson, *Bazaar,* chap. 10.

[10] Sampson, *Bazaar,* p. 147.

[11] Sampson, *Bazaar,* p. 147.

[12] Sampson, *Bazaar,* chap. 13.

[13] Sampson, *Bazaar,* p. 250.

[14] Sampson, *Bazaar,* p. 109.

[15] Sampson, *Bazaar,* pp. 125–6, 146.

[16] Philip S. Foner, *Labor and World War I,* paperback (New York: International Publishers, 1987), pp. 8–9.

[17] Sanders, *Peddlers of Crisis,* p. 212; Sampson, pp. 72–7, 103, 109, 126; Aldridge, *First Strike,* p. 271.

[18] Lee Smith, "The Real Cost of Disarmament," *Fortune,* 22 December 1986, p. 130.

[19] Mumford, *Technics and Civilization,* pp. 85–9; Kennedy, *Rise and Fall,* p. 6.

[20] Carl Cohen, editor, *Communism, Fascism, Democracy* (New York: Random House, 1962), pp. 12–15.

[21] Cohen, 13–14; Lens, *Permanent War,* p. 16, obtained from Stephen E. Ambrose and James Alden Barber, Jr., *The Military and American Society,* pp. 4, 10–11; military expenditures, Sivard, *World Military and Social Expenditures,* p. 6.

[22] "Weapons Spending at $900 Billion Worldwide During Year of Peace," AP, *The Missoulian,* 24 November 1986, p. 7 col. 1, obtained from Sivard.

[23] Melman, *Profits,* p. 88. Melman's calculations are secure as from 1980 to 1987 military costs have been rising faster than the rest of the economy.

[24] Parenti, *Democracy,* fourth edition, pp. 106–7.

[25] Mumford, *Technics and Civilization,* pp. 93–94.

[26] Lens, *Permanent War,* pp. 20–21; see also William Appleman Williams, *Tragedy,* pp. 208, 235.

[27] Lens, *Permanent War,* p. 28; Gardner, *Safe for Democracy,* covers this effort well in chapters 6–8, and backs up Lens's assertion. The West did offer the Eastern bloc Marshall Plan credits but only on the condition they open their borders. This would have destroyed the fledgling Soviet industry and could not be accepted.

[28] Sampson, *Bazaar,* pp. 246–47.

[29] Baron and Sweezy, *Monopoly Capital,* p. 153.

[30] Fred Hiatt and Rick Atkinson, "Defense Spending Saps Engineering Talent of Nation," *The Missoulian,* 12 December 1985, p. 27, col. 5; Thompson and Smith, *Protest,* p. 119.

[31] Others have concluded the total labor force directly and indirectly employed by the military is 11 percent. Parenti, *Democracy,* fourth edition, p. 94.

## 6. The Economy of the Soviet Union

[1] Kennedy, *Rise and Fall,* p. 322.
[2] Vladimir Gurevich, "Pricing Problems," *Soviet Life,* October 1988, p. 24.

## 7. An Offer the Soviets Cannot Refuse

[1] General Secretary Mikhail Gorbachev's speech, *New Times* 45, November 1987, p. 14.
[2] Noam Chomsky, *The Culture of Terrorism,* paperback (Boston: South End Press, 1988) p. 195.
[3] Stansfield Turner, *Secrecy and Democracy* (Boston: Houghton Milton Company, 1985), p. 92.
[4] Melman, *Profits,* p. 151.
[5] Melman, *Profits,* p. 88. Melman's calculations are still applicable, as from 1980 to 1987 military costs have been rising faster than the rest of the economy.
[6] Rolf H. Wild, *Management by Compulsion* (Boston: Houghton Mifflin Company, 1978), pp. 75–6.
[7] Kennedy, *Rise and Fall,* p. 360; *ABC News* and *NBC News,* 4 June 1987.
[8] Castro, *World,* p. 211.
[9] *Nova,* PBS, 10 May 1988.
[10] *Webster's New Universal Unabridged Dictionary,* second edition (New York: Simon and Schuster, 1972).
[11] Fleming, *Cold War,* p. 478; this partially contradicts my earlier statement that the Marshall Plan was designed to contain communism. Fleming explains that, though it started with idealism, it was converted into an instrument to contain communism.
[12] Lens, *Permanent War,* p. 27.
[13] Ho Chi Minh sent nine letters to the U.S. government asking for support to throw out the French.
[14] Greider, *Temple,* pp. 173–74.

# Book Three

## Introduction

[1] Kaku and Axelrod, *To Win,* p. 231.
[2] Holly Sklar, editor, *Trilateralism,* paperback (Boston: south End Press, 1980); twenty-five authors do a very credible job of explaining what Trilateralism is.
[3] Kaku and Axelrod, *To Win,* p. 231.
[4] Jerry Sanders, *Peddlers of Crisis,* tells the story very well.
[5] Fleming, *Cold War,* p. 1066.
[6] Phil Grant, *The Wonderful Wealth Machine* (New York: Devon-Adair Company, 1953), p. 24.
[7] George Seldes, *Never Tire of Protesting* (New York: Lyle Stuart Inc., 1968), pp. 111–13. Seldes names the members of that committee; John Kennoth Gailbraith recognizes this same problem in various places throughout his book *Economics in Perspective,* paperback (Boston: Houghton Mifflin Company, 1987), espec. pp. 217, 219, 240, 284.
[8] William Greider, "Annals of Finance," *The New Yorker,* 16 November 1987, pp. 72, 78 (this was a serialization of Greider's book *Secrets of the Temple*); see also Greider, *Temple,* chapter 8, espec. pp. 243, 263, 271, 282, 294.
[9] Greider, "Annals of Finance," *The New Yorker,* 16 November 1987, p. 72; see also Lawrence Goodwyn, *The Populist Moment* (New York: Oxford University Press, 1978). The progressives at the turn of the century built on these Populist ideas. A few such as women's suffrage and direct election of senators were also instituted. However, as true

rights are economic, no real rights accrued to the majority of the people until the New Deal under President Franklin D. Roosevelt.

[10] Greider, *Temple,* pp. 372, 456, 516, 552.

[11] Thurow, *Inequality,* p. 14; "Worker's State," *The Nation,* 19 September 1988, p. 187–8.

## 1. Monopolization of Land

[1] Michael Parenti, *Power and the Powerless,* paperback (New York: St. Martin's Press 1978), pp. 184–5, quoting Jean Jacques Rousseau, "A Discourse on the Origins of Inequality," in *The Social Contract and Discourses* (New York: Dutton, 1950), pp. 234–5.

[2] Grant, *Wealth Machine,* p. 283; Ralph V. D. Magoffin and Frederic Duncan, *Ancient and Medieval History* (New York: Silver Burdett and Company, 1934) p. 383.

[3] Grant, *Wealth Machine,* p. 283; Magoffin and Duncan, *Ancient and Medieval History,* pp. 185, 190–94.

[4] Susan George, *Other Half,* p. 249; W. R. Halliday, *The Growth of the City State* (Chicago: Argonaut, Inc., Publishers, 1967), p. 186.

[5] Thurow, *Inequality,* p. 14; "Worker's State," *The Nation,* 19 September 1988, p. 187–8.

[6] "States' Right, Hawaii's Land Reform Upheld," *Time,* 11 June 1984, p. 27; "The High Court: This Property Is Condemned," *Newsweek,* 11 June 1984, p. 69.

[7] Petr Kropotkin, *Mutual Aid,* paperback (Boston: Porter Sargent Publishers Inc., undated), p. 225.

[8] Kropotkin, *Mutual Aid,* p. 225.

[9] Kropotkin, *Mutual Aid,* p. 226.

[10] Kropotkin, *Mutual Aid,* p. 234–5.

[11] Kropotkin, *Mutual Aid,* p. 226.

[12] Lewis Mumford, *The City in History,* paperback (New York: Harcourt Brace Jovanovich, Publishers, 1961), p. 264.

[13] Beard, *Economic Interpretation,* p 28; Howard Zinn, *A People's History of the United States,* paperback (New York: Harper Colophon Books, 1980), p. 48.

[14] Zinn, *People's History,* p. 48.

[15] Aptheker, *Colonial Era,* pp. 37–8.

[16] Zinn, *People's History,* p. 83; Herbert Aptheker, *The American Revolution,* paperback (New York: International Publishers, 1985), p. 264; quoted in Beard, *Economic Interpretation,* p 23.

[17] Beard, *Economic Interpretation,* quoting C. H. Ambler, pp. 23, 27–8.

[18] Hufton, *Privilege and Protest,* 113.

[19] Herbert Aptheker, *Early Years of the Republic,* paperback (New York: International Publishers, 1976),p. 125.

[20] Wessel and Hartman, *Trading the Future,* p. 14.

[21] Quoted in Lyon, *Day Coach,* p. 6. See also Edward Winslow Martin, *History of the Grange Movement* (New York: Burt Franklin, 1967, originally published in 1873); Joe E. Feagin, *Urban Real Estate Game,* paperback (Engelewood Cliffs, NJ, Prentice-Hall, Inc., 1983), pp. 57–8; speech by U.S. Representative Byron Dorgan, North Dakota, the statistics researched out by his staff and quoted in *the North Dakota REC.,* May 1984.

[22] Lyon, *Day Coach,* p. 6.

[23] John Kenneth Gailbraith, *Economics in Perspective,* paperback (Boston: Houghton Mifflin Company, 1987), chap. 5, espec. p. 55, 168.

[24] William Spencer, *Social Statics* (1850 unabridged edition); Nadudere, *Political Economy,* p. 44; Grant, *Wealth Machine,* pp. 416, 434–8; Hufton, p. 113.

[25] Grant, *Wealth Machine,* pp. 389–95.

[26] *60 Minutes,* CBS, 25 October 1987.

[27] At its peak (1986–87) this represented almost half of all net farm income. *Statistical Abstract of the U.S.* 1987, p. 616, figure 23.1, shows the average farm income for 1980 as about $33 billion per year. The $26-billion agricultural supports for 1987 are much larger than for most years.

[28] Gore Vidal, "The National Security State: How To Take Back Our Country," *The Nation*, 4 June 1988, p. 782.

[29] Grant, *Wealth Machine*, p. 331.

[30] Gailbraith, *Economics in Perspective*, p. 267.

[31] Bert Caldwell, "Help for Farmers, Hurt for Lenders?" and Judy Tynan, "Farm Credit System's Transfers Face Trial," *The Spokesman-Review*, 31 December 1986, pp. A9 and A12.

[32] "Tomorrow," *U.S. News and World Report*, 6 April 1987, p. 27.

## 2. Monopolizing Society's Tools

[1] Adam Smith, *Wealth of Nations*, Modern Library edition (New York: Random House, Inc., 1965), p. 64.

[2] *Public Power Directory and Statistics for 1983* (Washington, D.C.: American Public Power Association, 1983); Kilmer, "Public Power Costs Less," pp. 28–31; the late Senator of Montana Lee Metcalf and his executive secretary Vic Reinemer presented an in-depth study of this phenomenon in their book *Overcharge.*

[3] Martin, *Grange Movement*, pp. 62, 70.

[4] Mathew Josephson, *Robber Barons*, paperback (New York: Harcourt Brace Jovanovich, Publishers, 1962), p. 92; Feagin, *Urban Real Estate Game*, pp. 57–8; Lyon, *Day Coach*, p. 6; see also Martin, *Grange Movement.*

[5] Wilfred Owen, *Strategy for Mobility* (Westport, CT: Greenwood Press, 1978), p. 23.

[6] Lyon, *Day Coach*, p. 6; Feagin, *Urban Real Estate Game*, pp. 57–8; Foner, *Colonial Times*, p. 62.

[7] All of what I am describing on appropriation of capital and fictitious capital is well described by Martin, *Grange Movement;* Josephson, *Robber Barons;* and Lyon, *Day Coach.*

[8] Josephson, *Money Lords*, pp. 38–48.

[9] Josephson, *Money Lords*, pp. 38–48, 52–3, quoting *Time* magazine.

[10] Josephson, *Money Lords*, p. 52.

[11] Josephson *Money Lords*, pp. 96–8, 132.

[12] Thorstein Veblen, *Essays in Our Changing Order* (New York: The Viking Press, 1934), p. 33.

[13] Mumford, *Pentagon of Power*, pp. 134, 139; Stuart Chase, *Men and Machines* (New York: The Macmillan Company, 1929), chapters 3–4.

[14] Chase, *Men and Machines*, pp. 42–43.

[15] *Nova*, PBS, 2 September 1986.

[16] Chase, *Economy of Abundance*, chapter 8.

[17] Grant, *Wealth Machine*, pp. 301–6.

[18] Nadudere, *Political Economy*, p. 255.

[19] Karl Marx, *Capital*, paperback (New York: International Publishers, 1967), vol. 1, p. 375, footnote no. 2.

[20] Nadudere, *Political Economy*, p. 38, quoting Leo Huberman, *Man's Worldly Goods*, p. 128–9.

[21] Mumford, *Technics and Civilization*, pp. 227–8, 438.

[22] Chase, *Economy of Abundance*, p. 166.

[23] Grant, *Wealth Machine*, pp. 301–6.

[24] Polyani, *Transformation*, p. 277, quoted from Pirenne, *Medieval Cities*, p. 211.

[25] Marx, *Capital* vol. 1, pp. 372–4, 428, 435, 562.

[26] Barnet, *Lean Years*, p. 260.

[27] Zinn, *A People's History*, p. 277.

[28] Josephson, *Robber Barons*, pp. 258.

[29] Lacey, *Ford*, pp. 118–40.

[30] Lacey, *Ford*, pp. 105–6.

[31] Wohl, *Medical–Industrial Complex*, pp. 69–71; Illich, *Medical Nemesis*, p. 245.

[32] Nadudere, *Political Economy*, p. 251, quoted in part from *The International Patent System*, 1951, p. 29.

[33] Stephen Budiansky, "An Act of Vision for the Third World," *U.S. News and World Report,* 2 November 1987, p. 14.

[34] "Firm Claims Breakthrough in High-Definition Television," AP, *The Spokesman-Review,* 13 July 1989, p. A9, col. 5–6.

[35] Lyon, *Day Coach,* p. 17.

[36] Veblen, *Engineers and the Price System* (New York: B. W. Huebsch, Inc., 1921), p. 107.

[37] "Adam Smith" (George J. W. Goodman), *Supermoney* (New York: Random House, 1972), pp. 21–2.

[38] "Smith" (Goodman), *Supermoney,* pp. 221–2.

[39] Thurow, *Inequality,* p. 14; "Worker's State," *The Nation,* 19 September 1988, p. 187–8.

[40] Thurow, *Generating,* p. 149.

[41] Thurow, *Generating,* p. 154.

[42] Chase, *Economy,* p. 165.

[43] Lester Thurow, *Dangerous Currents* (New York: Random House, 1983), p. 233.

[44] Wild, *Management by Compulsion,* pp. 92, 94–5.

[45] Wachtel, "Funny Money," p. 788.

[46] 1987 presidential hopeful Representative Richard A. Gephardt of Missouri, in a speech to the Securities Industry Institute of the Wharton School of Business; Haynes Johnson, " 'Teflon' 80s Bear Striking Resemblance to 'Giddy' 20s," *The Missoulian,* 25 March 1987, reprinted from *The Washington Post,*

[47] Paul Richter, "Commodity Marts Face Fraud Fallout," *Los Angeles Times,* quoted in *The Missoulian,* 4 July 1989, p. A2, col. 1–5.

[48] Anthony Banco, "Playing With Fire," *Business Week,* 16 September 1987, p. 78.

[49] Charles Mackay, *Extraordinary Delusions and Madness of Crowds,* second edition (New York: Farrar, Straus and Giroux, 1932), vol. 1, pp. 90–97.

[50] Mackay, *Delusions,* pp. 1–45; John Train, *Famous Financial Fiascoes* (New York: Clarkson N. Potter, Inc., Publishers, 1985) pp. 33–41, 108–9.

[51] Mackay, *Delusions,* pp. 46–88; Train, *Fiascoes,* pp. 88–95; Charles P. Kindleberger, *Manias, Panics, and Crashes,* paperback (New York: Basic Books, Inc., Publishers, 1978), pp. 220–21.

[52] Wachtel, *Money Mandarins,* pp. 153–54; see also Malkin, *National Debt,* chap. 7.

[53] Parenti, *Democracy,* fourth edition, p. 26; see also Perlo, *Super Profits and Crisis,* pp. 164–96.

[54] "More Billions for Mike," *Newsweek,* 17 April 1989, p. 6.

[55] Felix Rohatyn, "The Blight on Wall Street," *The New York Review,* 12 March 1987, pp. 21–2; see also Malkin, espec. pp. 75, 77.

[56] Wachtel, *Money Mandarins,* p. 155; see also Malkin, chap. 7.

[57] ABC News commentator Richard Threlkeld, *ABC News,* 19 June 1986; see also Perlo, *Super Profits and Crisis,* pp. 164–96; and Malkin, chap. 7.

[58] Greider, *Secrets,* p. 81; see also Malkin, chap. 7.

[59] Leo Cawley, "The End of the Rich Man's Boom," *The Nation,* 5 December 1987, p. 676; see also Malkin, chap. 7.

[60] Cawley, p. 676; see also Malkin, chap. 7.

[61] Royhatyn, pp. 21–2; see also Malkin, *National Debt,* pp. 86–88.

[62] Melman, *Profits,* pp. 12, 249, 261.

[63] Center For Popular Economics, *Economic Report to the ~~President~~ People* (Boston: South End Press, 1986), pp. 174–75.

[64] "The Raiding Game," *Dollars and Sense,* March 1987, p. 13.

[65] Wachtel, "Funny Money," p. 785.

[66] Wachtel, *Money Mandarins,* p. 190–93.

[67] Wachtel, *Money Mandarins,* pp. 190–91.

[68] Wachtel, *Money Mandarins,* 191.

[69] Wachtel, *Money Mandarins,* p. 155, quoted from "Deconglomerating Business," *Business Week,* 24 August 1981, p. 126; further outlined in *Money Mandarins,* pp. 170–75.

[70] Moffitt, "Shocks, Deadlocks," p. 566, 568.

[71] Moffitt, Shocks, Deadlocks," p. 566.

[72] *Economic Report to the ~~President~~ People,* p. 174.

[73] Seymour Melman covers this very well: *Profits without Production* and *The Permanent War Economy,* updated and revised.

[74] *CNN News,* 14 January 1985.

[75] Richard L. Stern, "The Inside Story," *Forbes,* 12 March 1987, p. 62

[76] Ted Gest and Patricia M. Scherschel, "Stealing $200 Billion the Respectable Way," *U.S. News and World Report,* 20 May 1987, p. 83.

[77] Parenti, *Democracy,* fourth edition, p. 140; $200 billion is only 5 percent of the GNP. Parenti, however, includes all white collar crime in his statistics, while *U.S. News and World Report* only considers insider trading.

[78] Greider, *Secrets,* p. 705.

[79] Rohatyn, p. 21.

[80] Barnet, *Lean Years,* p. 120.

[81] Timothy Green, *The New World of Gold* (Ontario: John Wiley and Sons, 1981), p. 137.

[82] Michael Moffitt, *The World's Money,* paperback (New York: Simon and Schuster, 1983), p. 186; a comprehensive story has been put together by Stephen Fay in *Beyond Greed.*

[83] Lappé and Collins, *Food First,* p. 212.

[84] Baron and Sweezy, *Monopoly Capital,* p. 49; quoted from T. K. Quinn, *Giant Business: Threat to Democracy* (New York: 1953), p. 117.

[85] Melman, *Profits without Production,* pp. 19, 21.

[86] Melman, *Profits without Production,* pp. 267–68.

[87] Bluestone and Harrison, *Deindustrialization,* p. 4; Bruce Schmiechen, Lawrence Daressa, and Larry Adelman, "Waking From the American Dream," *The Nation,* 3 March 1984.

[88] Seymour Melman, lecture at the University of Missoula, 25 February 1988; quoted from a conference held with the university economists.

[89] Michael Goldhaber, *Reinventing Technology,* paperback (New York: Routledge & Kegan Paul, 1986), p. 185.

[90] This very sensible approach was, in part, suggested by Goldhaber, *Reinventing Technology,* pp. 98, 184–87, 189, 198.

[91] Goldhaber, *Reinventing Technology,* p. 197.

[92] Chase, *Tragedy,* p. 204–5.

[93] Chase, *Tragedy,* p. 204–5.

[94] William H. Davidow, *Marketing High Technology: An Insider's View* (New York: The Free Press, 1986), pp. 13–14, 17, 19, 21.

[95] Davidow, *Marketing High Technology,* pp. 102–3.

[96] John Paul Newport, Jr., "A Supercomputer on a Single Chip," *Fortune,* 29 September 1986, p. 128.

[97] Personal communication with Montana Microsystems of Kalispell, Montana, August 1988.

[98] John Hillkirk, "Users' Aim 1 Language in all Computers," *USA Today,* 7 June 1988, p. B1.

[99] Josephson, *Money Lords,* p. 173.

[100] "Adam Smith" (George J. W. Goodman), *Nightly Business Report,* 17 June 1987; Josephson, *Money Lords,* p. 173.

## 3. Money, Money Capital, and Banking

[1] Greider, *Secrets,* p. 335.

[2] Gailbraith, *Money,* pp. 62–70.

[3] Gailbraith, *Money,* pp. 167–78; Greider, "Annals of Finance," *The New Yorker,* 16 November 1987, p. 81; Greider, *Secrets,* p. 228, 282.

[4] Foner, *From Colonial Times,* p. 67.

[5] Cohen, *Communism, Fascism,* pp. 13–14; Kennedy, *Rise and Fall,* p. 53.

[6] Gailbraith, *Money,* pp. 18–19.

[7] Kennedy, *Rise and Fall,* p. 53.

[8] S. P. Breckinridge, *Legal Tender* (New York: Greenwood Press, 1969), chap. 7; Gailbraith, *Money,* pp. 72–75.

[9] Sampson, *Money Lenders,* pp. 92, 220; Moffitt, *World's Money,* pp. 26–8.

[10] Marcia Stigum, *Money Markets* (Homewood, IL: Dow Jones-Irwin, 1978), p. 18.

[11] Greider, *Secrets,* pp. 61–62.

[12] Chase, *Economy of Abundance,* p. 156.

[13] Stigum, *Money Markets,* pp. 29,96.

[14] Stigum, *Money Markets,* pp. 95–6.

[15] Greider, *Secrets,* p. 156.

[16] Moffitt, *World's Money,* pp. 49–50, 57; L. J. Davis, *Bad Money* (New York: St. Martin's Press, 1982), pp. 115, 124–5, 128–9; Stigum, *Money Markets,* pp. 63–6, 85–6, 100–112, 181, 403; Paul DeRosa and Gary H. Stern, *In the Name of Money* (New York: McGraw-Hill Book Company, 1981), p. 2; Sampson, *Money Lenders,* p. 278.

[17] Davis, *Bad Money,* p. 115.

[18] Stigum, *Money Markets,* pp. 1, 7.

[19] Martin D. Weiss, *The Great Money Panic* (Westport, CT: Arlington House Publishers, 1981), p. 45.

[20] Monroe W. Karmin, "Risky Moments in the Money Markets," *U.S. News and World Report,* 2 March 1987, pp. 44–5.

[21] Stigum, *Money Markets,* p. 7.

[22] Wachtel, "Funny Money," p. 786; liquidity statistics obtained from Greider, "Annals of Finance," *The New Yorker,* 9 November 1987, p. 79.

[23] Wachtel, *Funny Money,* p. 786.

[24] Wachtel, *Money Mandarins,* pp. 16, 91; Moffitt, *World's Money,* pp. 65–66.

[25] Stigum, *Money Markets,* pp. 100–105; Greider, *Secrets,* p. 142.

[26] Sampson, *Money Lenders,* pp. 304–16.

[27] Sampson, *Money Lenders,* pp. 240–43; Moffitt, *World's Money,* p. 201; Wachtel, *Money Mandarins,* pp. 92, 93.

[28] Wachtel, *Politics* p. 31.

[29] Wachtel, "Funny Money," p. 788.

[30] Josephson, *Robber Barons,* p. vii (1934 edition); Davis, *Bad Money,* p. 68.

[31] Davis, *Bad Money,* p. 68.

[32] Moffitt, *World's Money,* p. 211.

[33] Moffitt, *World's Money,* pp. 209–10.

[34] Moffitt, *World's Money,* pp. 209–10.

[35] Wachtel, *Money Mandarins,* pp. 190–93.

[36] Wachtel, *Money Mandarins,* pp. 190–93.

[37] Moffitt, *World's Money,* p. 185–7.

[38] Moffitt, *World's Money,* p. 187; Greider, *Secrets,* pp. 144–5, 190.

[39] Moffitt, *World's Money,* p. 163.

[40] Wachtel, *Money Mandarins,* p. 220, and Wachtel, *International Money,* p. 25.

[41] Moffitt, *World's Money,* p. 136; Eva Pomice, "The Forex Wheel of Fortune," *U.S. News and World Report,* 10 October 1988, pp. 4–3.

[42] Stigum, *Money Markets,* pp. 166–73; Rich Thomas, "Uncle Sam The Cosigner," *Newsweek,* 8 June 1987, pp. 50, 52.

[43] Wachtel, *Money Mandarins,* p. 37; where most financial analysts say that the Fed has not accepted being lender of last resort to other central banks, William Greider says they have played this role for selected nations. Greider, *Secrets,* p. 486.

[44] Jane Bryant Quinn, "Is 'Junk' Still Worth Buying?," *Newsweek,* 13 April 1987, p. 55; Thomas, "Uncle Sam the Cosigner," pp. 51, 52; 1988 figures and quote from Dennis

Cauchon, "Savings-Loan Bailout May Hit Taxpayers," *USA Today,* 8–10 July 1988, p. 1, col. 5; Kevin Kelly, "Who'll Save the Savings and Loans?," *In These Times,* 9–15 November 1988, p. 3, col. 1–4.
45 *NBC News,* 14 June 1989.
46 Quinn, "Is 'Junk'," p. 55; Thomas, "Uncle Sam the Cosigner," pp. 51, 52; 1988 figures and quote from Cauchon, p. 1, col. 5; Kelly, p. 3, col. 1–4; Greider, *Secrets,* p.508.
47 *CBS News,* 6 June 1988.
48 "Adam Smith" (George J. W. Goodman), *Supermoney,* pp. 31–50, espec. p. 43.
49 Wachtel, *Money Mandarins,* p. 17; Greider, *Secrets,* p. 628.
50 Karmin, "Risky Moments," p. 44.
51 This figure is low.
52 *CBS News,* 20 January 1986.
53 Malkin, *National Debt,* p. 41.
54 Malkin, *National Debt,* p. 24.
55 Malkin, *National Debt,* pp. 25–6, 37, 39–41, 57, 59.
56 Greider, *Secrets,* pp. 657–8, 663–4, 708.
57 Greider, *Secrets,* pp. 663–4, 706–8.
58 Foner, *From Colonial Times,* pp. 144–49. Where both the monopolists and the governments are currently trying to keep the financial boat afloat, it was not always that way. In 1834, when the U.S. government was trying to rein in the speculations of the banking monopoly, Nicholas Biddle, the president of The Bank of The United States, created a depression by violently shrinking the money supply.
59 Greider, *Secrets,* pp. 663–4, 706–8, 697, 680–82.
60 Robert S. Mcintyre, "The Populist Tax Act of 1989," *The Nation,* 2 April 1988, pp. 445, 462.
61 Wachtel, "Funny Money," p. 784, 786.
62 Barnet, *Lean Years,* p. 280. The communications industries of these countries were originally publicly owned but their monopolization by corporations has begun. Herbert I. Schiller, *Information and the Crisis Economy,* paperback (New York: Oxford University Press, 1986), p. 114.
63 Greider, "Annals of Finance," *The New Yorker,* 16 November 1987, pp. 72, 78.
64 Greider, "Annals of Finance," *The New Yorker,* 16 November 1987, pp. 72, 78.
65 Greider, *Secrets,* p. 630. The savings and loan statement was made by a financial analyst on an evening network newscast in February 1989.
66 Darrell Delamaide, *Debt Shock,* updated edition, paperback (New York: Anchor Press/Doubleday, 1985), pp. 239–40.
67 George Tucker, *The Theory of Money and Banks Investigated* (New York: Greenwood Press, 1968), p. 219, 255.
68 Moffitt, *World's Money,* p. 197; John H. Makin, *The Global Debt Crisis* (New York: Basic Books, 1984), p. 162.
69 Gailbraith, *Economics in Perspective,* p. 279.
70 Stigum, *Money Markets,* pp. 434–5.
71 Michael Rogers, "Smart Cards: Pocket Power," *Newsweek,* 31 July 1989.

## 3. Monopolizing the Communications Industry

1 Joseph C. Goulden, *Monopoly,* revised and updated, paperback (New York: Pocket Books, 1970), p. 96.
2 "TV Direct From Satellite to Your Home—It Could Be Soon," *U.S. News and World Report,* 26 June 1967, p. 68.
3 Mark Green, *The Other Government,* revised, paperback (New York: W. W. Norton & Company, Inc., 1978), p. 222.
4 Bernard D. Nossiter, "The F.C.C.'s Big Giveaway Show," *The Nation,* 26 October 1985, p. 403; *MacNeil/Lehrer News Hour,* PBS, 21 March 1987; Alvin P. Sanoff with Clemens P. Work, Manuel Schiffres, Kenneth Walsh, Linda K. Lanier, Ronald A. Taylor, and Robert J. Morse, "Who Will Control TV," *U.S. News and World Report,* 13

May 1985, p. 60; the 40- to 60-percent profits were reported on *CBS News,* 25 March 1985.

[5] John Stromnes, "Rural Montana Gets Taste of Public TV," *The Missoulian,* 8 October 1987, p. 9, col. 1–2. Strommes' source is Dan Tone from University of Nevada at Reno.

[6] Sanoff et al., "Who Will Control TV," p. 60.

[7] Goulden, *Monopoly,* p. 110.

[8] Goulden, *Monopoly,* p. 104.

[9] "Firm Claims Breakthrough in High-Definition Television," AP, *The Spokesman-Review,* 13 July 1989, p. A9, col. 5–6.

[10] William D. Marbach and William J. Cook, "The Revolution in Digitech," *Newsweek,* 19 March 1985, p. 49.

[11] Conversation with local director for Mountain Bell.

[12] Goulden, *Monopoly,* p. 96.

[13] Parenti, *Democracy for the Few,* second edition only, p. 79, referenced from Steve Babson and Nancy Brigham, "Why Do We Spend So Much Money," *Liberation,* October 1973, p. 19.

[14] Gregory C. Staple, "The Assault on Intelsat," *The Nation,* 22 December 1984, p. 665.

[15] Stuart Gannes, "The Phone Fight's Frenzied Finale," *Fortune,* 14 April 1986, p. 53.

[16] Gannes, "Frenzied Finale," p. 53.

[17] Hillkirk, "Users' Aim 1 Language," sec. B, p. 1, col. 2.

[18] Chase, *Tragedy of Waste,* p. 222, quoting Thorstein Veblen.

[19] Veblen, *Engineers and the Price System,* p. 110.

[20] William J. Cook, "Reach Out and Touch Someone," *U.S. News and World Report,* 10 October 1988, p. 49–50.

[21] Ivan Ladanov and Vladimar Pronnikov, "Craftsmen and Electronics," *New Times* 47, November 1988, pp. 24–5.

[22] Bagdikian, *Media Monopoly,* updated and expanded, 1987, p. 148.

[23] Bagdikian, *Media Monopoly,* updated and expanded, 1987, pp. 138–40, 148, 229.

[24] Harry F. Waters and Janet Huck, "The Future of Television," *Newsweek,* 17 October 1988, pp. 84–93.

[25] Anne Windishar, "Expert: 20% of Gifted Kids Drop Out," *Spokane Chronicle,* 7 January 1988, p. B7. col. 2–5.

[26] *CNN News,* 24 May 1988.

[27] During a telethon requesting donations, Salt Lake City's PBS station said $1 million per year rented all their tapes.

[28] *Broadcasting and Cablecasting Yearbook;* Stromnes, "Rural Montana," p. 9, col. 1.

[29] David Armstrong, *Trumpet to Arms,* paperback (Boston: South End Press, 1981), p. 340.

[30] Schiller, *Information and the Crisis Economy,* pp. 109, 122.

## 5. Conclusion

[1] Greider, *Secrets* pp. 499, 525–6.

# Bibliography

*ABC News,* 13 May 1985; 19 July 1985; 19 June 1986; 27 June 1986; 28 October 1986; 30 December 1986; 31 March 1987; 4 June 1987.

*Adam Smith's Money,* PBS, 6 July 1986.

Addison, Charles G. *The Knights Templar.* London: Longman, Brown, Green, and Longmans, 1842.

Aldridge, Robert C. *First Strike.* Boston: South End Press, 1983.

American Heart Association booklet. *1987 Heart Facts.*

Anderson, Scott, and Jon Lee. *Inside the League.* New York: Dodd, Mead & Company, 1986.

Annual report of the Department of Health and Human Services. "American Life Today: Longer and Healthier." AP, *The Missoulian,* 23 March 1985.

Aptheker, Herbert. *The American Revolution.* New York: International Publishers, 1985.

Aptheker, Herbert. *The Colonial Era.* Second edition. New York: International Publishers, 1979.

Aptheker, Herbert. *Early Years of the Republic.* New York: International Publishers, 1976.

Armstrong, David. *Trumpet to Arms.* Boston: South End Press, 1981.

Aronowitz, Stanley. "The Myth of Full Employment." *The Nation,* 8 March 1986.

Auerbach, Jerold S. *Justice Without Law.* New York: Oxford University Press, 1983.

"Autos: Engine of the Future?" *Newsweek,* 11 November 1974.

Babson, Steve, and Nancy Brigham. "Why Do We Spend So Much Money." *Liberation,* October 1973.

Bagdikian, Ben. *Media Monopoly.* Boston: Beacon Press, 1983.

Bagdikian, Ben. *Media Monopoly.* Updated and expanded. Boston: Beacon Press, 1987.

Baker, Craig, and Amy Dru Stanley. "Incarceration Inc.: The Downside of Private Prisons." *The Nation,* 15 June 1985.

Banco, Anthony. "Playing With Fire." *Business Week,* 16 September 1987.

Bandler, Richard, and John Grinder. *Frogs Into Princes.* Moab, UT: Real People Press, 1979.

Baron, Paul A., and Paul M. Sweezy. *Monopoly Capital.* London: Monthly Review Press, 1968.

Barnet, Richard. *The Lean Years.* New York: Simon and Schuster, 1980.

Barnet, Richard J. *The Alliance.* New York: Simon and Schuster, 1983.

Beard, Charles A. *An Economic Interpretation of the Constitution.* New York: Macmillan Publishing Co., Inc., 1913, 1935, 1941.

Becker, Craig. "The Downside of Private Prisons." *The Nation,* 15 June 1985.

Beeching, Jack. *The Chinese Opium Wars.* New York: Harcourt Brace Jovanovich, Publishers, 1975.

Bellant, Russ. Policy Research Associates, Cambridge, MA.

Bemis, Samuel Flagg. *A Diplomatic History of the United States.* New York: Henry Holt and Company, 1936.

Bennet, Jon. *The Hunger Machine.* Cambridge, England: Polity Press.

Bergin, Edward J. *How to Survive In Your Toxic Environment.* New York: Avon Books, 1984.

Bluestone, Barry. "Deindustrialization and Unemployment in America." *New Perspectives on Unemployment.* Edited by Barbara A. P. Jones. New Brunswick, NJ: Transaction Books, 1984.

Bluestone, Barry. *The Deindustrialization of America.* New York: Basic Books, Inc., 1982.

Bodenheimer, Thomas, and Robert Gould. *Roll Back.* Boston: South End Press, 1989.

Bogomolov, Paval. "Tackling the Problems of Growth." *New Times,* 21 September 1987.

Boorstein, Edward. *What's Ahead? . . . The U.S. Economy.* New York: International Publishers, 1984.

Borsodi, Ralph. *The Distribution Age.* New York: D. Appleton & Co., 1929.

Braithwaite, John. *Corporate Crime in the Pharmaceutical Industry.* London: Routledge & Kegan Paul, 1984.

Breckinridge, S. P. *Legal Tender.* New York: Greenwood Press, 1969.

Bronson, Gail. "Name Rank and Serial Number." *Forbes,* 20 April 1987,

Budiansky, Stephen. "An Act of Vision for the Third World." *U.S. News and World Report,* 2 November 1987.

"Buffalo Battalion—South Africa's Black Mercenaries." *Covert Action Information Bulletin* 13, July–August 1981.

Burns, James. *The Knights Templar.* London: Payne and Foss, 1840.

Caldwell, Bert. "Help for Farmers, Hurt for Lenders?." *The Spokesman-Review,* 31 December 1986.

Cantor, Daniel, and Juliet Schor. *Tunnel Vision.* Boston: South End Press, 1987.

Carson, Rachel. *Silent Spring.* New York: Fawcett Crest, 1962.

Carsten, F. L. *Britain and the Weimar Republic.* New York: Schocken Books, 1984.

Castro, Fidel. *Nothing Can Stop the Course of History.* New York: Pathfinder Press, 1986.

Castro, Fidel. *The World Economic and Social Crisis.* Havana, Cuba: Council of State. 1983.

Cauchon, Dennis. "Savings-Loan Bailout May Hit Taxpayers." *USA Today,* 8–10 July 1988.

Caute, David. *The Great Fear.* New York: Simon and Schuster, 1979.

Cawley, Leo. "The End of the Rich Man's Boom." *The Nation,* 5 December 1987.

*CBS News,* 12 February 1984; 25 Mar 1985; 20 January 1986; 19 June 1986; 20 June 1986; 9 March 1987; 13 October 1987.

"China Maneuvering Around Quotas to Market Textiles to United States." *The Spokesman-Review,* 10 January 1989.

Chinweiezu. "Debt Trap Peonage." *Monthly Review,* November 1985.

Chomsky, Noam. *The Culture of Terrorism.* Boston: South End Press, 1988.

Center For Popular Economics. *Economic Report to the ~~President~~ People.* Boston: South End Press, 1986.

"Change." *Railway Age,* November 1984.

Chase, Stuart. *The Economy of Abundance.* New York: The Macmillan Company, 1934.

Chase, Stuart. *Men and Machines.* New York: The Macmillan Company, 1929.

Chase, Stuart. *The Tragedy of Waste.* New York: The Macmillan Company, 1925.

Chase, Stuart. *The Economy of Abundance.* New York: Macmillan and Company, 1934.

Choucri, Nazli, and Robert C. North. *Nations in Conflict.* San Francisco: W. H. Freeman and Company, 1974.

Clark, Matt. "Still Too Many Caesareans?" *Newsweek,* 31 December 1984.

Clifford, Harlan C. "Exploiting a Link Between Farm Debt and Soil Erosion to Aid U.S. Farmers." *Christian Science Monitor,* 5 July, 5 August, 5 September 1984.

Clifford, Harlan C. "My turn." *Newsweek,* 4 June 1984.

Cloward, Richard A., and Frances Fox Piven. *New Class War,* New York: Pantheon Books, 1982.

*CNN News.* 14 January 1985; 28 October 1985, Senate hearing to outlaw the dumping of patients; 22 January 1986.

Cockburn, Alexander. "Beat the Devil." *The Nation,* 6 March 1989, p. 294.

Cohen, Carl, editor. *Communism, Fascism, Democracy.* New York: Random House, 1962.

Cook, William J. "Reach Out and Touch Everyone." *U.S. News and World Report,* 10 October 1988.

Council on International and Public Affairs. "In Short." *In These Times,* 10–16 February 1988.

*Covert Action Bulletin* 19, Spring–Summer 1983.

Cowley, Leo. "The End of the Rich Man's Boom." *The Nation,* 5 December 1987.

Crompton, Kim. "Self Insurance Lets the County Save $1 Million." *The Spokesman-Review,* 19 March 1989.

Dacey, Norman F. *How to Avoid Probate.* Updated. New York: Crown Publishers, Inc., 1980.

Danaher, Kevin; Frances Moore Lappé; and Rachel Schurman. *Betraying the National Interest.* New York: Grove Press, 1987.

Daraul, Arkon. *A History of Secret Societies.* Secaucus, NJ: Citadel Press, 1961.

Darnton, Nina. "Committed Youth." *Newsweek.* 31 July 1989.

Davidow, William H. *Marketing High Technology.* New York: The Free Press, 1986.

Davis, L. J. *Bad Money.* New York: St. Martin's Press, 1982.

DeCormis, Anna. "Cooking the Books on Joblessness." *The Guardian,* 20 August 1986.

De Ligney, Roland. "Voluntary Euthanasia Estimated at 5,000 Annually in the Netherlands." AP, *The Missoulian,* 8 April 1987.

Delamaide, Darrell. *Debt Shock.* Updated. New York. Anchor Press/Doubleday, 1985.

Dempsey, Paul Stephen. "Fear of Flying Frequently." *Newsweek,* 5 October 1987.

Department of Health and Suman services. "American Life Today: Longer and Healthier." AP, *The Spokesman-Review,* 23 March 1985.

DeRosa, Paul. *In the Name of Money.* New York: McGraw-Hill Book Company, 1981.

"Disappearing Railroad Blues." *The Progressive,* August 1984.

Dobbowski, Michael, and Isodor Wallimann. *Radical Perspectives on the Rise of Fascism in Germany.* New York: Monthly Review Press, 1989.

Dorgan, Bryan. Representative for the state of North Dakota. *North Dakota REC Magazine,* May 1984.

Downey, Janice. "Proposed Bill Would Alter Traditional Role of Court in Divorces." *The Missoulian,* 28 February 1987.

Downs, Peter. "Your Money." *The Progressive,* January 1987.

Doyal, Lesley. *The Political Economy of Health.* Boston: South End Press, 1981.

Dumaine, Brian. "Turbulence Hits the Air Carriers." *Fortune,* 21 July 1986.

Dunne, Jim, and January P. Norbye. "Honda's New CVCC Car Engine Meets '75 Emissions Standards Now." *Popular Science,* April 1973.

Dunne, Jim. "Stratified Charge: Is This the Way Detroit Will Go." *Popular Science,* July 1975.

Easterbrook, Gregg. "The Revolution in Medicine." *Newsweek,* 6 December 1987.

Easterbrook, Gregg. "Cleaning Up." *Newsweek,* 24 July 1989.

*The Economic Report to the President 1980.*

Edge, Konrad. "CIA Figures on Soviet Spending Undercut Reagan's Claims." *Guardian,* 13 March 1985.

Edge, Konrad. "Free Enterprise Behind Bars." *Guardian,* 9 October 1985.

Ehrenreich, Barbara, and John Ehrenreich. *The American Health Empire.* New York: Vintage Books, 1971.

Ehrenreich, John, editor. *Cultural Crisis of Modern Medicine.* New York: Monthly Review Press, 1978.

Epstein, Samuel, M.D. *The Politics of Cancer.* San Francisco: Sierra Club Books, 1978.

"Euthanasia Estimated at 5,000 Annually in the Netherlands." AP, *The Missoulian,* 8 April 1987.

"The Far Shores of America's Bulging Prisons." *U.S. News and World Report,* 14 November 1988.

Farhang, Mansour. *U.S. Imperialism.* Boston: South End Press, 1981.

Faux, Jeff. "The Austerity Trap and the Growth Alternative." *World Policy Journal* 5:3, Summer 1988.

Fay, Stephen. *Beyond Greed.* New York: Viking Press, 1982.

Feagin, Joe E. *The Urban Real-estate Game.* Engelewood Cliffs, NJ: Prentice-Hall, Inc., 1983.

"Firm Claims Breakthrough in High-Defiintion Television", AP, *The Spokesman-Review,* 13 July 1989.

Fisher, Fritz. *Germany's Aims in the First World War.* New York: W. W. Norton & Company, 1967.

Fleming, D. F. *The Cold War and its Origins.* Two volumes. New York: Doubleday & Company, 1961.

Foner, Philip S. *Labor and World War I.* Paperback. New York: International Publishers, 1987.

Foner, Philip S. *Abraham Lincoln: Selections from his writings.* New York: International Publishers, 1944.

Foner, Philip S. *From Colonial Times to the Founding of the American Federation of Labor.* New York: International Publishers, 1947.

Foner, Philip S. *From the Founding of the A.F. of L. to the Emergence of American Imperialism.* Second edition. New York: International Publishers, 1975.

"Four of 10 Hospital Stays are Unneeded." AP, *The Missoulian,* 13 November 1986.

Friedman, Milton, and Rose Friedman. *Free to Choose.* New York: Avon Books, 1981.

Gailbraith, John Kenneth. *Money.* New York: Bantam Books, 1976.

Gailbraith, John Kenneth. *Economics in Perspective.* Boston: Houghton Mifflin Company, 1987.

Gamble, Andrew. *Britain in Decline.* Boston: Beacon Press, 1981.

Gannes, Stuart. "The Phone Fight's Frenzied Finale." *Fortune,* 14 April 1986.

Gardner, Lloyd C. *Safe for Democracy.* New York: Oxford University Press, 1984.

Garfinkel, Judi M. "Doctors Push Plan for Comprehensive Care." *Guardian,* 8 February 1989.

Garrison, Jim. *On the Trail of the Assassins.* New York: Sheridan Square Press, 1988.

Gelb, Alan H. *Cooperation at Work: the Mondragon Experience.* London: Heinemann Educational Books, 1983.

George, Susan. *Ill Fares the Land.* Washington, D.C.: Institute for Policy Studies, 1984.

George, Susan. *How the Other Half Dies.* Montclair, NJ: Allen Osmun and Co., 1977.

Gerson, Louis L. *John Foster Dulles.* New York: Cooper Square Publishing, Inc., 1967.

Gest, Ted, and Patricia M. Scherschel. "Stealing $200 Billion 'The Respectable Way.'" *U.S. News and World Report,* 20 May 1985.

Gibbs, Lois Marie. *Love Canal: My Story.* New York: Grove Press, 1982.

Gilson, Lawrence. *Money and Secrecy.* Paperback. New York: Praeger Publishers, 1972.

Goldhaber, Michael. *Reinventing Technology.* Paperback. New York: Routledge & Kegan Paul, 1986.

Goodman, Amy. "The Case Against Depo-Provera." *Multinational Monitor,* February/March 1985.

Goodman, David. "Political Spy Trial in Pretoria." *In These Times,* 19–25 September 1984.

Goodman, Robert. *The Last Entrepreneurs.* Boston: South End Press, 1982.

Goodspeed, D. J. *The German Wars.* New York: Bonanza Books, 1985.

Goodwyn, Lawrence. *The Populist Moment.* New York: Oxford University Press, 1978.

Gorbachev, Mikhail. *New Times* 45, November 1987.

Gorz, André. *Ecology as Politics.* Boston: South End Press, 1980.

Gould, Robert, and Thomas Bodenheimer. *Roll Back.* Boston: South End Press. 1989.

Goulden, Joseph C. *Monopoly.* Revised and updated, New York: Pocket Books, 1970.

Grandon, Roland E. *How to Survive In Your Toxic Environment.* New York: Avon Books, 1984.

Grant, Phil. *The Wonderful Wealth Machine.* New York: Devon-Adair Company, 1953.

Green, Gil. *Cuba . . . The Continuing Revolution.* New York: International Publishers, 1983.

Green, Larry. "Subsidies: Half of '87 Farm Income to Come from Government." *Los Angeles Times,* reprinted in *The Missoulian,* 25 October 1987.

Green, Mark. *The Other Government.* Revised. New York: W. W. Norton & Company, Inc., 1978.

Green, Timothy. *The New World of Gold.* Ontario, Canada: John Wiley and Sons, 1981.

Greenberg, Michael. *British Trade and the Opening of China 1800–1842.* New York: Monthly Review Press, reprint of 1951 edition.

Greider, William. *The Education of David Stockman and Other Americans.* Revised and updated. New York: New American Library, 1986.

Greider, William. "Annals of Finance." *The New Yorker,* 9 November 1987; 16 November 1987; 23 November 1987.

Greider, William. *Secrets of the Temple.* New York: Simon and Schuster, 1987.

Greider, William. "The Money Question." *World Policy Journal,* Fall 1988.

Gross, Jane. "Desperate AIDS Patients Seeking Cure or Comfort." *New York Times,* reprinted in *The Spokesman-Review,* 15 May 1987.

Gross, Bertram. "Rethinking Full Employment." *The Nation,* 17 January 1987.

Gross, Bertram. *Friendly Fascism.* Boston: South End Press, 1980.

Gurevich, Vladimar. "Pricing Problems." *Soviet Life,* October 1988.

"Half of Children Avoid Tooth Decay." AP, *The Spokesman- Review,* 22 June 1988.

Halliday, W. R. *The Growth of the City State.* Chicago: Argonaut, Inc., Publishers, 1967.

Hammer, Joshua. "AIDS, Blood and Money." *Newsweek,* 23 January 1989.

Harrington, Michael. *The New American Poverty.* New York: Penguin Books, 1984.

Harrison, Bennett. *The Deindustrialization of America.* New York: Basic Books, Inc., 1982.

Hartman, Betsy, and James Boyce. *Needless Hunger.* Revised. San Francisco: Institute for Food and Policy Development, 1982.

Healy, Kathleen. "Name, Rank and Computer Log-on." *Business Week,* 20 April 1987.

Hebert, Richard. "Rosemary Freed." *Americans for Legal Reform* 5:2, 1985.

Heckscher, Eli F. *Mercantilism.* Volume 2. New York: The Macmillan Company, 1962.

Herman, Edward S., and Noam Chomsky. *Manufacturing Consent: The Political Economy of the Mass Media.* New York: Pantheon Books, 1988.

Hiatt, Fred, and Rick Atkinson. "Defense Spending Saps Engineering Talent of Nation." *The Missoulian,* 12 December 1985.

"High Court: This Property Condemned." *Newsweek,* 11 June 1984.

Hightower, Jim. *Eat Your Heart Out.* New York: Vintage Books, 1976.

Hillkirk, John. "Users' Aim: 1 Language in All Computers." *USA Today,* 7 June 1988.

Himmelstein, David U., M.D., and Steffie Woolhandler, M.D., M.P.H. "Sounding Board: Cost Without Benefit: Administrative Waste in U.S. Health Care." *New England Journal of Medicine,* 13 February 1986.

Hinckle, Warren, and William Turner. *The Fish is Red: The Story of the Secret War Against Castro.* Cambridge: Harper and Row, 1981.

Hope, Marjorie, and James Young. "Even Doctors Are Prescribing a Real National Health Scheme." *In These Times,* 8–14 February 1989.

Hufton, Olwen. *Europe: Privilege and Protest.* Ithaca, NY: Cornell University Press, 1980.

"Hunger as a Weapon. *Food First Action Alert.* Institute for Food and Development Policy, undated.

Hunt, Charles W. "AIDS and Capitalist Medicine." *Monthly Review,* January 1988.

Icantalupo, Tom. "Average Car in 1995 Could Cost $13,800." *Newsday,* reprinted in *The Missoulian,* 12 March 1987.

Illich, Ivan. *Medical Nemesis.* Bantam edition. New York: Bantam Books, 1979.

Immarigeon, Russ. "Prison Bailout." *Dollars and Sense,* July/August 1987.

Insurance Institute for Highway Safety report. "Highway Death Rate Cut in Half." Reprinted in *The Missoulian,* 13 September 1986.

Isikoff, Michael. "Lawyers Gain From Defective-Product Suits." *Washington Post,* reprinted in *The Missoulian,* 1 September 1985.

Jacobson, Michael, and Phillip Kasinitz. "Burning the Bronx for Profit." *The Nation,* 15 November 1986.

Jenkins, John A. "Corporations Find 'Minitrials' Nice Way to Kiss and Make Up." *Americans for Legal Reform* 5:1, 1984.

Jezer, Marty. *The Dark Ages*. Boston: South End Press, 1982.

Johnson, Haynes. "Teflon 80s Bear Striking Resemblence to 'Giddy' 20s." *The Missoulian*, 25 March 1987.

Josephson, Mathew. *Robber Barons*. Paperback. New York: Harcourt Brace Jovanovich, Publishers, 1934, 1962.

Josephson, Mathew. *Money Lords*. New York: Waybright and Talley, 1972.

Judis, John B. "CIA: No Big Soviet Arms Boost in 70s." *In These Times*, 7–13 December 1983.

Jukes, Jeffrey. *Stalingrad at the Turning Point*. New York: Ballantine Books, 1968.

Kaku, Michio, and Daniel Axelrod. *To Win a Nuclear War*. Boston: South End Press, 1987.

Kaplan, Fred. *The Wizards of Armageddon*. New York: Simon and Schuster, 1983.

Karmin, Martin W. "Risky Moments in the Money Markets." *U.S. News and World Report*, 2 March 1987.

Kelly, Kevin. "Who'll Save the Savings and Loans?" *In These Times*, 9–15 November 1988.

Kendall, Don. "Meat-eaters Consuming Less Fat." AP, *The Missoulian*, 4 February 1987.

Kendall, Don. "U.S Farmers Look to the Third World." AP, *The Spokesman-Review*, 5 January 1988.

Kennedy, Paul. *The Rise and Fall of the Great Powers*. New York: Random House, 1987.

Kenton, Walter S., Jr. *How Life Insurance Companies Rob You*. New York: Random House, 1982.

Kessler, Ronald. *The Life Insurance Game*. New York: Holt, Rinehart and Winston, 1985.

Khanin, Grigory. "When Will the Ruble be Made Convertible." *New Times* 30, 25–31 July 1989.

"Kidneys Worth $13,000." AP, *The Spokesman-Review*, 4 November 1985.

Kilmer, Jeanie. "Public Power Costs Less." *Public Power Magazine*, May–June 1985.

Kindleberger, Charles P. *Manias, Panics, and Crashes*. New York: Basic Books, Inc., Publishers, 1978.

Kireyev, Alexei. "Cost Accounting for Disarmament Economics." *In These Times*, 24–30 January 1989.

Klein, Karen E. "Party of the First Part Favors Plain Talk." *Los Angeles Daily News*, quoted in *The Spokesman-Review*, 6 February 1988.

Kwitny, Jonathan. *The Crimes of Patriots*. New York: W. W. Norton & Company, 1987.

Kwitny, Jonathan. *Vicious Circles: The Mafia in the Market Place*, New York: W. W. Norton & Company, 1979.

Kyle, Cynthia, and Mort Hartman. "Health Wealth and Competition." *U.S. News and World Report*, 10 November 1985.

Lacey, Robert. *Ford*. New York: Ballantine Books, 1986.

Ladanov, Ivan, and Vladimar Pronnikov. "Craftsmen and Electronics." *New Times* 47, November 1988.

Lappé, Frances Moore; Joseph Collins; and David Kinley. *Aid as an Obstacle—Twenty Questions About Our Foreign Aid and the Hungry*. San Francisco: Institute for Food and Development Policy, 1980.

Lappé, Frances Moore. *Diet for a Small Planet*. Revised. New York: Ballantine Books, 1978.

Lappé, Frances Moore; Rachel Schurman; and Kevin Danaher. *Betraying the National Interest*. New York: Grove Press, 1987.

Lappé, Frances Moore, and Joseph Collins. *Food First: Beyond the Myth of Scarcity.* Revised and updated. New York: Ballantine Books, 1979.

Lappé, Marc. *Germs That Won't Die.* Garden City: Anchor Press/Doubleday, 1982.

Lash, Jonathan; Katherine Gillman; and David Sheridan. *A Season of Spoils.* New York: Pantheon Books, 1984.

Lee, Dwight E. *Europe's Crucial Years.* Hanover, NH: Clark University Press, 1974.

Lee, Katherine J. "Justice Has Broken Down." *Americans For Legal Reform* 4:2, 1985.

Lefebvre, Georges. *The Coming of The French Revolution.* Translated by R. R. Palmer. Princeton, NJ: Princeton University Press, 1967.

Lens, Sidney. *Permanent War.* New York: Schocken Books, 1987.

Levine, Jonathan B. "Will a Takeover Derail Burlington Northern's Makeover." *Business Week,* 3 August 1987.

Levine, Murray. *Love Canal.* New York: Grove Press, 1982.

Lewis, Hunter, and Donald Allison. *The Real Cold War.* New York: Coward, McCann and Geoghegan, 1982.

Lincoln, W. Bruce. *In War's Dark Shadow.* New York: The Dial Press, 1983.

Linden, Eugene. "Frederick W. Smith of Federal Express: He Didn't Get There Overnight." *Inc.,* April 1984.

Livovich, Gregg. "Self–insurance Plans May Be Delayed for at Least One Month." *Star Tribune* (Casper, WY), 5 August 1985.

"Logic of Stagnation." *Monthly Review,* October 1986.

Loftus, John. *The Belarus Secret.* New York: Alfred A. Knopf, 1982.

Longgood, William. *The Poisons in Your Food.* New York: Simon and Schuster, 1969.

"Low Cholesterol Beef Produced on State Ranches." AP, *The Missoulian,* 15 October 1986.

Lukacs, John. *A History of the Cold War.* Paperback. Revised edition. New York: Anchor Books, 1962.

Luther, Jim. "Shafting the Poor." AP, *The Missoulian,* 15 January 1987.

Lyon, Peter. *To Hell in a Day Coach.* New York: J. B. Lippincott Company, 1968.

Mack, John. "The Enemy System." *The Lancet,* 13 August 1988.

Mackay, Charles. *Extraordinary Delusions and Madness of Crowds.* Second edition, volume 1. New York: Farrar Straus and Giroux, 1932.

Magdoff, Harry, and Paul M. Sweezy. *Stagnation and the Financial Explosion.* New York: Monthly Review Press, 1987.

Magoffin, Ralph V. D., and Frederick Duncan. *Ancient and Medieval History.* New York: Silver, Burdett and Company, 1934.

Mahoney, Richard D. *JFK: Ordeal in Afrika.* New York: Oxford University Press, 1983.

Makin, John H. *The Global Debt Crisis.* New York: Basic Books, 1984.

Malkin, Lawrence. *The National Debt.* New York: Henry Holt and Company, Inc., 1988.

Marbach, William D., and William J. Cook. "The Revolution in Digitech." *Newsweek,* 19 March 1985.

Marbach, William D.; William J. Cook; David L. Gonzalez; and Daniel Shapiro. "Punishment Outside Prisons." *Newsweek,* 9 June 1986.

Martin, Edward Winslow. *History of the Grange Movement.* New York: Burt Franklin, 1967 (originally published in 1873).

Marx, Karl. *Capital.* Edited by Frederick Douglas. New York: International Publishers, 1967.

Mayer, Milton. *They Thought They Were Free.* Chicago, University of Chicago Press, 1955.

McKafee, Kathy. "Caribbean Paradise for Sale." *Dollars and Cents,* October 1987.

Mcintyre, Robert S. "The Populist Tax Act of 1989," *The Nation,* 2 April 1988.

*The MacNeil/Lehrer Show,* PBS, 21 March 1987; 16 February 1989.

McNeill, William H. *The Pursuit of Power.* Chicago: University of Chicago Press 1982.

Mead, Walter Russell. "After Hegemony." *New Perspective Quarterly,* 1987.

Mead, Walter Russell. *Mortal Splendor.* Boston: Houghton Mifflin Company, 1987.

Mead, Walter Russell. "American Economic Policy in the Antemillenial Era." *World Policy Journal,* Summer 1989.

Mee, Charles L., Jr. *The Marshall Plan.* New York: Simon and Schuster, 1984.

Melman, Seymour. *The Permanent War Economy.* Revised and updated. New York: Simon and Schuster, 1985.

Melman, Seymour. *Profits Without Production.* New York: Alfred A. Knopf, 1983.

Metcalf, Lee, and Vic Reinemer. *Overcharge.* New York: David McKay Company, Inc., 1967.

Methuin, Eugene H. "How Uncle Sam Robs the Poor." *Readers Digest,* March 1985.

Michener, James. *Hawaii.* New York: Fawcett Crest, 1959.

Milko, George. "It's Hassle Free Down Under." *Americans for Legal Reform* 6:3, 1986.

"Million Mile Bug." *The Missoulian,* 15 July 1987.

Mirow, Kurt Rudolph, and Harry Maurer. *Webs of Power.* Boston: Houghton Mifflin Company, 1982.

Mitford, Jessica. *The American Way of Death.* New York: Fawcett Crest, 1978.

Mitford, Jessica. *Kind and Unusual Punishment.* New York: Vintage Books.

Moffitt, Michael. "Shocks, Deadlocks, and Scorched Earth: Reaganomics and the Decline of U.S. Hegemony." *World Policy Journal,* Fall 1987.

Moffitt, Michael. *The World's Money.* New York: Simon and Schuster, 1983.

Mocken, Richard, editor. Book one. *Introduction to Aristotle.* New York: Random House, Inc., 1947.

"More Billions for Mike." *Newsweek,* 17 April 1987.

Morley, Morris, and James Petras. *The United States and Chile.* New York: Monthly Review Press, 1975.

Morgan, Dan. *Merchants of Grain.* New York: Penguin Books, 1980.

Morris, David. *Self-Reliant Cities.* San Francisco: Sierra Club Books, 1982.

Morris, Richard B. *Basic Documents in American History.* Princeton, NJ: D. Van Nostrand, Inc., 1956.

Mostowy, Thomas. "Just Open Your Doors." *Americans for Legal Reform* 5:2, 1985.

Mumford, Lewis. *The City in History.* New York: Harcourt Brace Jovanovich, 1961.

Mumford, Lewis. *Pentagon of Power.* New York and London: Harcourt Brace Jovanovich, 1964 and 1970.

Mumford, Lewis. *Technics and Civilization.* New York and London: Harcourt Brace Jovanovich, 1963.

Mumford, Lewis. *Technics and Human Development.* New York: Harcourt Brace Jovanovich, 1967.

Murray, Charles. *Losing Ground.* New York: Basic Books, 1984.

Nader, Ralph. Speech given at the University of Missoula. *KPAX News,* 29 January 1987.

Nadudere, Dan. *The Political Economy of Imperialism.* London: Zed Press Ltd., 1977.

*National Geographic* TV program, 23 August 1987.

National Highway Traffic Safety Administration. *Spokane Chronicle,* 17 December 1987.

*The National Labor Tribune,* 15 May 1875.

"Nation's Health Bill Expected to Triple." *Washington Post,* reprinted in *The Missoulian,* 9 June 1987.

Naueckas, Jim. "Land Trusts Offer American Land Reform." *In These Times,* 3–16 August 1988.

Navarro, Vicente. "What Is Socialist Medicine." *Monthly Review,* July–August 1986.

*NBC News,* 16 February 1987; 4 June 1987; 10 August 1987; 5 October 1987; 16 December 1987; 30 December 1987.

Newport, John Paul, Jr. "A Supercomputer on a Single Chip." *Fortune,* 29 September 1986.

*Nightly Business Report,* PBS, 21 January 1986; 3 November 1986; 10 February 1988.

Norbye, Jan P., and Jim Dunne. "Honda's New CVCC Car Engine Meets '75 Emissions Standards Now." *Popular Science,* April 1973.

Nordheimer, January. "Rosemary's Baby Has Nation's Lawyers Worried." *New York Times,* reprinted in *The Spokesman-Review,* 13 August 1984.

Nossiter, Bernard D. "The F.C.C.'s Big Giveaway Show." *The Nation,* 26 October 1985.

*Nova,* PBS, 18 February 1985; 2 September 1986.

"Oasis." *Social Security Reference,* December 1983.

Oberman, Heiko A. *The Roots of Anti-Semitism.* Philadelphia: Fortress Press, 1984.

O'Connell, Jeffrey. *The Lawsuit Lottery.* New York: The Free Press/Macmillan Publishing Co., Inc., 1979.

Olson, McKinley. *Unacceptable Risks.* New York: Bantam Books.

Oglesby, Carl. *Project Nazi File.* Unpublished. Cambridge, MA.

Owen, Wilfred. *Strategy for Mobility.* Westport, CT: Greenwood Press, 1978.

"Pacemakers Often Useless." AP, *The Spokesman-Review,* 30 May 1985.

Parenti, Michael. *Democracy for the Few.* Fourth edition. New York: St. Martin's Press, 1983.

Parenti, Michael. *Democracy for the Few.* Second edition.

Parenti, Michael. *Inventing Reality.* New York: St. Martin's Press, 1986.

Parenti, Michael. *Power and the Powerless.* New York: St. Martin's Press, 1978.

Parker, Richard. "Assessing Perestroika." *World Policy Journal,* Spring 1989.

Paul, Stephen Dempsey. "Fear of Flying Frequently." *Newsweek,* 5 October 1987.

Pauly, David; Judith Evans; and Rich Thomas. "The Dirty Little Debt Secret." *Newsweek,* 17 April 1989.

Perlo, Victor. *Super Profits and Crisis.* New York: International Publishers, 1988.

Petras, James, and Morley Morris. *The United States and Chile.* New York: Monthly Review Press, 1975.

Piven, Frances Fox, and Richard A. Cloward. *New Class War.* New York: Pantheon Books, 1982.

Plowboy Interview. *The Mother Earth News,* March/April 1982.

Polyani, Karl. *The Great Transformation.* Boston: Beacon Press, 1957.

Pomice, Eva. "The Forex Wheel of Fortune." *U.S. News and World Report,* 10 October 1988.

Pool, James, and Suzanne Pool. *Who Financed Hitler.* New York: The Dial Press, 1978.

Popkova, Olga. "Not By Money Alone." *New Times* 50:87.

Potyarkin, Ye., and S. Kortunov, editors. *The USSR Proposes Disarmament:* (1920–1980's). Moscow, USSR: Progress Publishers, 1986.

Powell, Bill; Carolyn Friday; and Peter McKillop. "The Man of Steel." *Newsweek,* 20 October 1986.

Press, Aric. "The Blessings of liberty." *Newsweek*, 25 May 1987.

Pringle, Peter, and William Arkin. *S.I.O.P.: The Secret U.S. Plan for Nuclear War.* New York: Norton & Company, 1983.

*Public Power Directory and Statistics for 1983.* Washington, D.C.: American Public Power Association, 1983.

Quinn, T. K. *Giant Business: A Threat to Democracy.* New York: 1953.

Quinn, Jane Bryant. "Is 'Junk' Still Worth Buying?" *Newsweek*, 13 April 1987.

Quinn, Jane Bryant. "The War for Your Savings." *Newsweek*, 26 September 1988.

Quinn, Jane Bryant. "A Warning to Donors." *Newsweek*, 19 December 1988.

"Raiding Game." *Dollars and Sense*, March 1987.

Raeburn, Paul. "Too Many Children Being Hospitalized for Psychiatric Problems." *The Missoulian* 2 October 19,87.

*Raphael, Sally Jesse, Show.* 30 May 1988.

Reece, Ray. *The Sun Betrayed.* Boston: South End Press, 1979.

Reutter, Mark. "Workman's Compensation Doesn't Work or Compensate." *Business and Society,* Fall 1980.

Rich, Bruce. "Conservation Woes at the World Bank." *The Nation,* 23 January 1989.

Richter, Paul. "Commodity Marts Face Fraud Fallout." *The Missoulian,* 4 July 1989.

Rodell, Fred. *Woe Unto You Lawyers.* Littleton, CO: Fred B. Rothman & Co., 1987.

Robinson, Donald. "The Great Pacemaker Scandal." *Readers Digest,* October 1983.

Rolf, H. Wild. *Management by Compulsion.* Boston: Houghton Mifflin Company, 1978.

Rohatyn, Felix. "The Blight on Wall Street." *The New York Review,* 12 March 1987.

Rogers, Michael. "Smart Cards: Pocket Power." *Newsweek*, 31 July 1989.

Rubin, James H. "Chief Justice Says Legal system 'Painful, Inefficient'." AP, *The Missoulian,* 13 February 1984.

Russell, Bertrand. *The Prospects of Industrial Civilization.* Second edition. London: George Allen and Unwin Ltd., 1959.

Ryan, Allan A., Jr. *Quiet Neighbors.* New York: Harcourt Brace Jovanovich, Publishers, 1984.

Rzheshevsky, Oleg. *World War II: Myths and Realities.* Moscow, USSR: Progress Publishers, 1984.

Sale, Kirkpatrick. *Human Scale.* First Peregree printing. New York: G. P. Putnam and Sons, 1982.

"Same Drug, Higher Price." *Time,* 1 December 1986.

Sampson, Anthony. *The Seven Sisters.* New York: The Viking Press, 1975.

Sampson, Anthony. *Money Lenders.* New York: Penguin Books, 1983.

Sampson, Anthony. *Arms Bazaar.* New York: Bantam Books, 1978.

Samuelson, Robert H. "The Missing $500 Billion." *Newsweek*, 27 January 1986.

Sanders, Jerry W. *Peddlers of Crisis.* Boston: South End Press, 1983.

Sanders, Jerry W. "America in the Pacific Century." *World Policy Journal,* Winter 1988–89.

Sanoff, Alvin P.; Robert J. Morse; Linda K. Lanier; Ronald A. Taylor; Clemens P. Work; Kenneth Walsh; and Manuel Schiffers. "Who Will Control TV." *U.S. News and World Report,* 13 May 1985.

Schachter, Oscar, and Robert Hellawell. *Competition in International Business.* New York: Columbia University Press, 1981.

Schaeffer, K. H., and Elliot Sclar. *Access for All.* Morningside edition. New York: Columbia University Press, 1980.

Schapiro, Mark. *Circle of Poison.* San Francisco: Institute for Food and Development Policy.

Schell, Jonathan. *The Abolition.* New York: Alfred A. Knopf.

Schell, Jonathan. *The Fate of the Earth.* New York: Alfred A. Knopf, 1982.

Schiller, Herbert I. *Information and the Crisis Economy.* Boston: Oxford University Press, 1986.

Schiller, Herbert I. *Mind Managers.* Boston: Beacon Press, 1973.

Schiller, Herbert I. *Communications and Cultural Domination.* White Plains, NY: M. E. Sharp, Inc., 1976.

Schlesinger, Stephen, and Stephen Kinzer. *Bitter Fruit.* New York: Anchor Press/Doubleday, 1984.

Schlosstein, Steven. *Trade War.* New York: Congdon and Weed, 1984.

Schmiechen, Bruce; Larry Adelman; and Lawrence Daressa. "Waking From the American Dream." *The Nation,* 3 March 1984.

Seldes, George. *Even the Gods Can't Change History.* Secaucus, NJ: Lyle Stuart, Inc., 1976.

Seldes, George. *In Fact.* New York: Lyle Stuart, Inc., 1968.

Seldes, George. *Never Tire of Protesting.* New York: Lyle Stewert, Inc., 1968.

Seldes, George. *Witness to a Century.* New York: Ballantine Books, 1987.

Seneker, Harold. "The World's Billionaires." *Forbes,* 5 October 1987.

Serrin, William. "Playing Down Unemployment." *The Nation,* 23 January 1989.

"Seventy Years Have Passed." *Soviet Life,* January 1988.

Shapriro, Walter; Richard Sandza; Peter McKillop; Mark Miller; and Elisa Williams. "The Naked Cities." *Newsweek,* 26 August 1985.

Shoup, Lawrence J., and William Minter. *Imperial Brain Trust.* New York: Monthly Review Press, 1977.

Sheehan, Niel; Hedrick Smith; Fox Butterfield; and E. W. Kenworthy. *The Pentagon Papers.* New York: Bantam Books, 1971.

Sheely, Tom. "The United States vs. the World: How We Score in Health." *Prevention,* May 1986.

Sheridan, David. *A Season of Spoils.* New York: Pantheon Books.

Shirley, Steve. "Lawyers' High Fees Push Work-Comp Bills to the Edge." *The Missoulian,* 13 October 1986.

Shorrock, Tim. "Disappearing Act for the Economic Miracle." *Guardian,* 11 December 1985.

Shulin, Deng. "Leprosy on the Way Out." *China Reconstructs,* May 1986.

Siegal, Loren. "Law Enforcement and Civil Liberties: We Can Have Both." *Civil Liberties,* February 1983.

Signor, Catherine A. "A Glut of Guns: Arms Race Threatens U.S." *The Missoulian,* 26 February 1988.

Simpson, Christopher. *Blowback.* New York: Weidenfeld & Nicolson, 1988.

Sipols, Vilnis. *The Road to Great Victory.* Moscow, USSR: Progress Publishers, 1985.

Sivard, Ruth Leger. *World Military and Social Expenditures.* Washington, D.C.: World Priorities, 1986 and 1987–88.

*60 Minutes,* CBS, 6 June 1984; 17 March 1985; 15 July 1985; 28 July 1985; 5 January 1986; 23 March 1986; 2 July 1986; 20 July 1986; 10 November 1986; 25 October 1987; 20 April 1987; 27 March 1988; 2 May 1988; 7 May 1989.

Sklar, Holly, editor. *Trilateralism.* Boston: South End Press, 1980.

Smith, Adam. *Wealth of Nations.* Modern Library ed. New York: Random House, Inc., 1965.

"Smith, Adam" (George J. W. Goodman). *Supermoney.* New York: Random House, 1972.

"Smith, Adam" (George J. W. Goodman). *Nightly Business Report,* 17 June 1987.

Smith, Lee. "The Real Cost of Disarmament." *Fortune,* 22 December 1986.

"Snags in Working Part Time." *US News and World Report,* 28 July 1986.

Soboul, Albert. *Understanding the French Revolution.* New York: International Publishers, 1988.

Staple, Gregory C. "The Assault on Intelsat." *The Nation,* 22 December 1984.

"States' Right: Hawaii's Land Reform Upheld." *Time,* 11 June 1984.

*Statistical Abstract of the United States.* Published by U.S. government. 1983; 1984; 1985; 1986; 1987.

Stern, Gary H. *In the Name of Money.* New York: McGraw-Hill Book Company, 1981.

Stern, Richard L. "The Inside Story." *Forbes,* 12 March 1987.

"The Sting in the Pits." *Newsweek,* 30 January 1989.

Stokes, Naomi Miller. *The Castrated Woman.* New York: Franklin Watts, 1967.

Strom, Tamara. Dentistry in the 80's: A Changing Mix of Services. *JADA* 116, May 1988.

Stubbing, Richard A. *The Defense Game.* New York: Harper and Row, Publishers.

Stigum, Marcia. *Money Markets.* Homewood, IL: Dow Jones-Irwin, 1978.

Stockwell, John. *In Search of Enemies.* New York: W. W. Norton & Company, 1978.

Stromnes, John. "Denman's First Law: Be Your Own Attorney." *The Missoulian,* 24 April 1984.

Stromnes, John. "Rural Montana Gets Taste of Public TV." *The Missoulian,* 8 October 1987.

Sullivan, Patricia. "House Sales in Missoula Show Spark." *The Missoulian,* 3 November 1985.

"'Teflon' 80s Bear Striking Resemblance to 'Giddy' 20s." *The Washington Post,* reprinted in *The Missoulian,* 25 March 1987.

Tell, Lawrence J., and Paul Angiolillo. "From Jury Selection to Verdict—In Hours." *Business Week,* 7 September 1987.

Thomas, Rich. "Uncle Sam The Cosigner." *Newsweek,* 8 June 1987.

Thompson, E. P., and Dan Smith. *Protest and Survive.* New York: Monthly Review Press, 1981.

Thurow, Lester. *Generating Inequality.* New York: Basic Books, Inc., 1975.

Thurow, Lester. *Dangerous Currents.* New York: Random House, 1983.

Tobias, Andrew. *The Invisible Bankers.* New York: The Linden Press/Simon and Schuster, 1982.

*Today Show,* NBC, 25 March 1988.

"Tomorrow." *U.S. News and World Report.* 23 September 1985; 6 April 1987; 22 June 1987; 29 June 1987.

Train, John. *Famous Financial Fiascoes.* New York: Clarkson N. Potter, Inc., Publishers, 1985.

Trewhitt, Henry; Robin Knight; Robert Kaylor; and Jeff Trimble. "A Different Call to Arms." *U.S. News and World Report.* 13 March 1989.

Tucker, George. *The Theory of Money and Banks Investigated.* New York: Greenwood Press, 1968.

Tuchman, Barbara. *The March of Folly.* New York: Alfred A. Knopf, 1984.

Turner, Stansfield. *Secrecy and Democracy.* Boston: Houghton Mifflin Company, 1985.

"TV Direct From Satellite to Your Home—It Could Be Soon." *U.S. News and World Report,* 26 June 1967.

*20/20,* ABC, 11 December 1986.

Tynan, Judy. "Farm Credit System's Transfers Face Trial." *The Spokesman-Review,* 31 December 1986.

Unger, Michael. "Drugs for the Mentally Ill Can Ravage Body." *Washington Post,* reprinted in *The Missoulian,* 17 July 1985.

"Unnecessary Operations Reported." *New York Daily News,* reprinted in *The Spokesman-Review,* 15 March 1985.

Uribe, Armando. *The Black Book of American Intervention in Chile.* Translated by Jonathan Casart. Boston: Beacon Press, 1975.

*USSR in Figures 1985.* Moscow, USSR: Finansy i Statiska Publishers, 1986.

Van Tyne, Claude Halstead. *The Loyalists in the American Revolution.* New York: Burt Franklin, 1970.

Veblen, Thorstein. *Essays in Our Changing Order.* New York: The Viking Press, 1934.

Veblen, Thorstein. *The Vested Interests.* New York: B. W. Huebsch Inc., 1919.

Veblen, Thorstein. *Engineers and the Price System.* New York: B. W. Huebsch, Inc., 1921.

*Vital Statistics of the U.S., 1981.* Volume two. Published by U.S. government.

Wachtel, Howard M. "The Global Funny Money Game." *The Nation,* 26 December 1987.

Wachtel, Howard M. *Money Mandarins.* New York: Pantheon Books, 1986.

Wachtel, Howard M. *The Politics of International Money.* Amsterdam: Transnational Institute, 1987.

Wallechinsky, David, and Irving Wallace. *The People's Almanac.* New York: Doubleday, 1975.

Wasserman, Harvey; Norman Solomon; Robert Alvarez; and Eleanor Walters. *Killing Our Own.* New York: Dell Publishing Company, 1983.

Waters, Harry F., and Janet Huck. "The Future of Television." *Newsweek,* 17 October 1988.

"Weapons Spending at $900 Billion Worldwide During Year of Peace." AP, *The Missoulian,* 24 November 1986.

*Webster's New Universal Unabridged Dictionary.* Second edition. New York: Simon and Schuster, 1972.

*Week in Review,* PBS, 15 December 1983.

Weiss, Martin D. *The Great Money Panic.* Westport, CT: Arlington House Publishers, 1981.

Weissman, Steve. *The Trojan Horse.* Revised edition. Palo Alto: Ramparts Press, 1975.

Welch, William M. "Insurance Bills Rock Officials." AP, *The Missoulian,* 19 August 1985.

Wessel, James, and Mort Hartman. *Trading the Future.* San Francisco: Institute for Food and Policy Development, 1983.

*Western Livestock Marketing Information Project.* Obtained from Montana State University, Bozeman, MT.

Wild, Rolf H. *Management by Compulsion.* Boston: Houghton Mifflin Company, 1978.

Wilhelm, Kathy. "Chinese Real Estate, Peasants May Be Permitted to Buy and Sell Land Rights." AP, *The Missoulian,* 27 October 1987.

Williams, William Appleman. *The Tragedy of American Diplomacy.* New York: W. W. Norton & Company, 1988.

Williams, Eric. *From Columbus to Castro.* New York: Vintage Books, 1984.

Windishar, Anne. "Expert: 20% of Gifted Kids Drop Out." *Spokane Chronicle,* 7 January 1988.

Winter, Bernard, M.D. "Health Care: The Problem Is Profits." *Progressive,* October 1977.

Wohl, Stanley, M.D. *The Medical-Industrial Complex.* New York: Harmony Books, 1984.

Woodruff, Steve. "Grazing Fee Status Stalled." *The Missoulian,* 1 January 1985.

"Workers' State," editorial in *The Nation,* 19 September 1988.

*World Monitor,* 6 June 1989.

Xinzhong, Quin. "How China Eliminated Venereal Disease." *China Reconstructs,* June 1985.

Zeagler, Jean. *Switzerland Exposed.* New York: Allison & Busby, 1981.

Zinn, Howard. *A People's History of the United States,* New York: Harper Colophon Books, 1980.

Zimmermann, Bill. "$60 Million War in California." *The Nation,* 7 November 1988.

# Index